A History of Postwar Africa

Books by the same author

THE DILEMMA OF SOUTH AFRICA

NEW FROM AFRICA

EVERYMAN'S AFRICA

AFRICA TODAY AND TOMORROW

JOHN HATCH

A History of Postwar Africa

FREDERICK A. PRAEGER, *Publishers*
New York • Washington

BOOKS THAT MATTER

Published in the United States of America in 1965 by
Frederick A. Praeger, Inc., Publishers
111 Fourth Avenue, New York 3, N.Y.

© 1965 by John Hatch

Library of Congress Catalog Card Number: 65-18078

Printed in the United States of America

To Neville Hind
who first encouraged me
to study history

Contents

Maps

Preface

The African political revolution has been the most dramatic international phenomenon since the war. Within a few years more than thirty new nations were born. The continent was transformed from a European imperialist preserve into a mosaic of African states. Some two hundred million Africans found themselves ruled by their own people for the first time in living memory.

It is the story of this revolution that I have tried to tell. The revolution was basically political, and therefore I have deliberately confined myself to its political aspects. But political changes are significant only in so far as they affect people. Wherever possible, therefore, I have related political events to their impact on the peoples of the various countries involved.

The revolution was also more anti-colonial than 'nationalist'. The boundaries of Africa were drawn by Europeans and have never enclosed communities with the common history normally essential to national consciousness. But African 'nationalists' accepted them rather than confuse their movements by trying to define new national units. They used the most powerful weapon at hand and this was a common antagonism to alien rule. But, although I agree with Lord Hailey in regarding this as an 'Africanist' rather than a 'nationalist' revolution, I have kept to the term 'nationalist' as the one most commonly understood.

I have confined myself broadly to the period from the end of the war to the achievement of independence in each country, for the revolution I have attempted to describe was essentially a revolution aiming at independence. But as history neither begins nor ends, there is some over-lapping. The stories of those territories not yet independent nor yet under African governments, like Southern Rhodesia, Angola, Mozambique and South Africa, have been told up to the early sixties. Their dénouement will come later, certainly influenced by the revolution in the rest of the continent.

There are obvious dangers in writing contemporary history. No doubt different perspectives will be accorded these changes by historians looking back with greater knowledge of their consequences. Nevertheless, I believe there to be equal advantages in describing events in which one has participated or which have been personally observed. It is particularly valuable to have known the personalities involved and have had some insight into their motives, fears and hopes.

It is an ambitious task to attempt to relate the history of a continent. I have inevitably had to make many choices, to select and to discard. In doing so, my criterion has been to emphasise what I believe to have had most significance over continental African affairs and to discard most of what is of solely local interest. The story is of the African revolution, and its effect on all Africa's peoples.

I feel especial gratitude to Mrs Gillian Hollings for her invaluable assistance in research and typing, and to my wife for more forms of help than can be listed here. Responsibility for the text is, of course, mine alone.

1

Europe Seizes Africa

The African revolution was essentially a revolt against European rule. In the mid-twentieth century virtually the entire African continent was divided between European imperial powers. They had drawn the frontiers and decided who should be recognised as suzerain over each area. No one suggested that the African inhabitants should be consulted before becoming subjects of France, Belgium, Britain, Spain, Portugal or the Boers. A variety of impulses, collectively known as imperialism, had led nineteenth-century Europe to deploy its superior powers in order to add African lands to its overseas empires. And so for three-quarters of a century almost all Africans were compelled to obey rulers whom they regarded as aliens.

Yet it was commercial imperialism which brought the African peoples into the modern world. For two centuries contact between Europeans and Africans had hinged on the slave trade. Vast fortunes were made by the slave traders, whilst millions of Africans were removed from their homes and transported across the Atlantic. But this gave Europeans no more than a superficial knowledge of the continent, for most of the actual process of capturing, collecting and selling the slaves was conducted by Africans and Arabs. The European slave traders confined themselves mainly to buying and carrying to the New World, simply maintaining forts on the African coasts to protect their trade. Thus their acquaintance with Africa was almost entirely confined to a few coastal slave centres. The only important exception was at the Cape, where the Dutch settlement of 1652 had spread gradually inland.

The emotional inheritance of the slave trade has survived into the twentieth century, remaining to plague relations between Africans and Europeans generations after slavery itself was abolished. The sense of subservience, or its aggressive repudiation, on the African side, and the masterful superiority, or atonement for the sense of

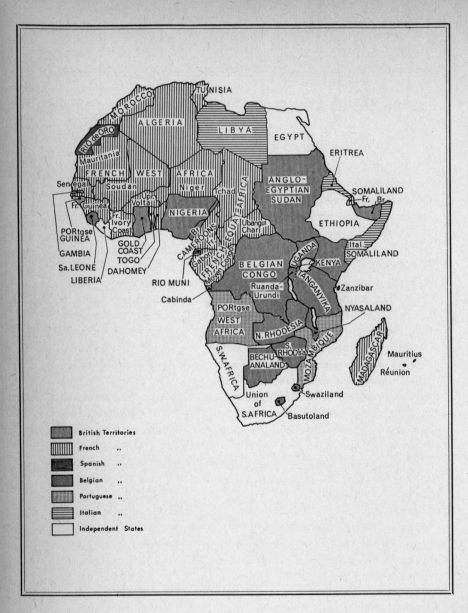

British Territories
French   ,,
Spanish   ,,
Belgian   ,,
Portuguese   ,,
Italian   ,,
Independent   States

1945

guilt, on the European, have been major handicaps to an acceptance of common humanity between the races. Yet it was not the slave trade which brought Africa into the orbit of that international society built mainly by Europeans.

There were, of course, many factors involved in the complex imperialist spirit which took Europeans into the heart of the African continent. To many it seemed a duty to take Christianity to the heathen, civilisation to the barbarians. Geographical exploration was combined with evangelism and commerce in the journeys of Livingstone, Speke and Burton which caught popular imagination. Moreover, many missionaries showed courage and devotion in taking not only their dogma but the first rudiments of literacy, medicine and agricultural techniques to remote communities. This was also an age of bombastic nationalism in Europe. Imperial estates were regarded as proof of national prestige, an attitude constantly stimulated by politicians, press, schools, youth organisations, clergy and military leaders.

Yet beneath this ideological surface there always ran the economic river. It was estimated that there were a million paupers in Britain in the early eighteen-seventies. Unemployment was rapidly increasing. New markets had to be found, new materials to feed the machines. Only half the population could be fed from home produce. Food supplies from overseas must be secured and safeguarded from potential enemy interference. The nation's inhabitants were multiplying at an increasing rate. New lands must be obtained in which they could settle. As all the major European states faced similar problems at the same time, fierce rivalry and competition provoked a chain reaction of imperialist adventures.

Nor did it appear paradoxical to link commercial and Christian expansion. This was, indeed, Livingstone's own prescription for African advance. So whilst the churches established their missions, British, French, Belgian and German commercial adventurers roamed Africa, their pockets stuffed with treaty forms to which they persuaded local potentates to affix their marks, signing away land and mineral rights which did not belong to them for the price of baubles, liquor and arms. And the companies which then formed to exploit these rights expected their governments to defend them from foreigners, to provide forces to expand their commercial empires and to supply capital to build the infrastructure of imperial economic life. Economic needs and economic ambitions were basic to Europe's imperialist occupation of Africa.

Europe entered the African heartland with sustained purpose only when capital and commerce began to seek their needs within the continent. As soon as Germany, France, the United States, and, to a lesser extent, Belgium, had caught up with Britain's industrial lead, the drive to control African territory started. The Americans confined their interest to their own continent, the Pacific and Asia, but to the European rivals Africa lay ready to hand, able to supply their several needs. As increasing industrialisation took place, so surplus capital accumulated, seeking new outlets for profitable investment. As tariffs and trade barriers grew higher, so governments were increasingly brought into commercial affairs. In an age which saw business depersonalised through the growth of limited liability companies, the exploration potential of African wealth beckoned the speculator. It was the European companies which first took Europe seriously to Africa and brought back African wealth to Europe. They were followed, and sometimes accompanied by soldiers. National prestige became involved. Conditions favourable to trade had to be established and governments took some responsibility for providing them. Resisting other European rivals and suppressing African hostility to European interference soon became matters of state. Economic penetration of Africa quickly became a national and then an international issue. Before long the European states involved resolved to decide all African affairs through agreement between themselves in Europe. The partition of Africa divided virtually the whole of the continent between European imperial powers, a settlement which inevitably brought African peoples into the orbit of international society.

Incidentally, the occupation of Africa, together with the simultaneous expansion of commerce to other parts of the world, postponed Europe's crisis of surplus capital and manufactures. It gave Europeans a temporary economic security, allowing a wholesale increase in living standards, the growth of democratic representation, and a degree of tolerance based on the sense of security produced by economic elbow room. The reckoning of capitalist over-production forecast by Marx and analysed by Keynes, as well as the necessity for state economic planning were postponed by half a century.

The main period of partition, the last twenty years of the nine-teenth century, began with some Europeans already in partial con-trol of certain areas in the continent. The French, deprived by the Napoleonic Wars of their former empire, had seized Algeria in 1830. Its coastal strip had valuable economic advantages, it was a pirate base menacing Mediterranean trade, whilst control of its deserts, bitterly contested by the Berbers, was essential to security on the coast. Both Britain and France exercised some influence in Egypt, for long the strategic key to Asia, and even more vital after the opening of the Suez Canal in 1869. The French had also extended their old trading highway in Senegal into the hinterland, which produced useful export crops and left her poised to strike into western Sudan. British coastal colonies had been established in Gambia, Sierra Leone and Lagos, with the Portuguese similarly placed in Guinea, and the French in Gabon. Portugal had retained her coastal control of Angola and Mozambique, Britain considered Zanzibar her preserve, whilst France had influence in Madagascar. Both the Italians and the French had established themselves in the Horn across the Red Sea from the British in Aden. There were the British colonies in the Cape, Natal and Basutoland, Afrikaner re-publics in Transvaal and Orange Free State, and a shadowy suze-rainty of the Turks over Egypt, Libya and Tunis. The rest of the continent belonged to Africans. Twenty years later the whole of Africa had been colonised, except for Ethiopia, Morocco and Liberia.

King Leopold of Belgium took the first initiative. He founded his African International Association in 1876 and proceeded to open up the Congo area. His train of militarised trading stations, together with Stanley's work in his employ in building a transport system, enabled Leopold to persuade the European powers to recognise his personal commercial empire. Whereupon the French quickly sent de Brazza to seek concessions in the lower Congo region. The Portuguese joined in, backed by Britain, who hoped to keep the river free from interference for shipping. Meanwhile the British were active again in Egypt. Together with the French they had controlled the prodigal Khedive's finances since 1876. A national uprising in 1882 was to have been met by a joint Anglo-French expedition, but the overthrow of the French government left Britain to occupy Egypt alone, though with the consent of the Ottoman Sultan and

the Germans who formed the majority of Egypt's creditors. Together with Disraeli's purchase of Suez Canal shares in 1875 and the
administration of Cyprus, this left Britain with comfortable security
over her Indian sea lane. The year before, in 1881, France had occupied Tunis, despite the Italian presence there; Italy now found con-
solation in the Sudanese port of Massowah.

By now it had become alarmingly obvious to European statesmen
that real dangers of international conflict attended their efforts to
take control of Africa. They therefore accepted Bismark's suggestion
to hold an international conference in Berlin. This opened in
December 1884 and was immediately marked by a general recognition of Leopold's 'Congo Free State', which Germany, France and
the United States had already recognised. The French position on the
north bank of the Congo was also accepted, whilst it was agreed to
allow the Portuguese up to the south bank.

Although the conference had been called principally on the issue
of the Congo basin, its influence on African colonisation went much
wider. Its most ambitious effort was the attempt to establish a
principle by which imperialist claims could be tested and recognised.
Britain first introduced the phrase 'effective occupation', demanding
that it should imply sufficient strength to enforce conditions in which
trade could be practised and rights protected. The proposal was
rejected, except for coastal claims, but the second British phrase,
'sphere of influence', designating an area for future claim, was
accepted.

The Germans had been busy during the conference sittings.
Immediately after its dispersal they published a collection of treaties
secured by their East Africa Company laying claim to territories
signed away by a number of chiefs. Their action convinced the other
Europeans that occupation, however tentative, was now to be the
test of legitimacy. The conclusion of the conference marked the
opening of the flood-gates to an intensive, uninhibited seizure of
African territories.

It took Germany only a few months over the period of the conference preparations and sittings to lay claim to her African empire.
In 1884, before the East African concessions won by Karl Peters were
announced, Togoland, the Cameroons and South-west Africa had
been taken over. For a time it looked as though the Germans had
ambitions to control an east–west belt right across the continent, for

their agents entered the lands neighbouring Natal and tentatively began to negotiate with the Transvaalers, who had gained independence from Britain in 1881. But this trick was trumped by the British, who, determined to keep open access to Central Africa from the Cape, annexed southern Bechuanaland and negotiated a protectorate with the chiefs over the rest of the territory.

It was not only the Germans who had ambitions to link their African territories into a contiguous bloc. The Portuguese hoped to join Angola and Mozambique, whilst the French were pushing their way eastwards from their west African bases. The British line or expansion took the contrary direction, north and south, dramatised by Cecil Rhodes' Cape to Cairo dream. If any one of the powers had achieved its aim, the advantages in controlling rail, road and telegraph communications would have provided powerful bargaining strength for the future. In the event, Britain was most successful, both in frustrating her rivals and achieving her aims. The direction of her development conveniently prevented any east–west barrier being built across the continent.

Thus Rhodes' British South Africa Company, chartered in 1889, moved into Bechuanaland, the territory now known as Southern Rhodesia, and Northern Rhodesia, meeting the Belgians in the Congo. Meanwhile the German threat in South Africa was resolutely met by British annexation of native territories between the Cape and Natal and most of Zululand. The Portuguese were thwarted in their ambitions in Nyasaland by the proclamation of a British protectorate followed by an ultimatum to the Portuguese government. At the same time, the British East Africa Company had negotiated a treaty with the Kabaka of Buganda and in 1890 the British government agreed east African frontiers with Germany, declaring a protectorate over the company's territories, including Zanzibar and Pemba, which were surrendered by the Germans. French claims to Madagascar were recognised as part of the same agreements, whilst frontier arrangements with the Italians in Somaliland and the Portuguese in Central Africa were also approved.

By now the Congo Free State had come completely under the sway of King Leopold and his financiers, the French were well established on the upper Niger, and the British on the Nigerian oil rivers. As the French pushed on to Lake Chad and Timbuktu, pressing towards British West Africa, Britain began to re-organise her four west African territories. Gambia was separated from Sierra Leone, and the Gold Coast from Lagos. Control of hinterlands was recognised as essential to restrict French and German expansion. Ashanti and the Northern Territories were added to the Gold Coast, protectorates extended behind the Sierra Leone colony, whilst the Royal Niger Company manœuvred with the French in the Niger valley. It was not until 1898–9 that settled West African boundaries were agreed between France and Britain, whereupon the Niger Company surrendered its charter which was replaced by protectorates in Northern and Southern Nigeria.

In the nineties the French began to advance from Gabon to meet their compatriots moving from the west towards Lake Chad. When they turned eastwards, however, they soon encountered the British southward expansion through the Sudan. Kitchener was destroying Dervish armies, and building a railway; and eventually he took Khartoum. For a moment it seemed that the converging British and French might meet in conflict on the Nile, with the probability of an open war between the two nations. The French, however, greatly outnumbered, decided that withdrawal was politic. An Anglo-Egyptian condominium completed the conquest of the Sudan. It was this incident that finally shattered the French dream of creating an African empire stretching between west and east Africa and the Mediterranean.

European conquest of the African continent was not achieved without resistance. Most Africans, living in their tribal villages and kraals, were ignorant of the revolutionary changes in the control of their regions. The new traders and missionaries might bring hitherto unknown goods and ideas into their societies, but did not at first interfere to any appreciable extent with traditional ways of life. It was not until the need for labour in the mines, on farms, and in public works prompted the introduction of new taxation methods, or missionaries tried to change pagan customs to fit European conceptions, that African society began to be seriously affected by its new masters. European settlement, involving seizure of land, was generally to come later, except in the south, where it had spread since the eighteenth century.

Nevertheless, where direct contact was made by European conquerors on African society, resistance often occurred. The Ashanti

Wars, fighting with Moslem Emirs in Nigeria, the long struggles in the Sudan, Islamic resistance led by Samori against the French, opposition to the Germans in the east, the Matabele and Mashona risings, are only a selection of many bloody struggles provoked by European conquest.

In one instance African resistance was successful. When the Italians tried to take Abyssinia they suffered complete defeat by Menelik's French-armed troops at Adowa in 1896, and had to retire discomfited to their coastal colonies.

The most severe military resistance to European encroachment came, of course, in South Africa. Here the circumstances were different, for the war was fought between European and European. Cecil Rhodes, using a combination of commercial enterprise and political intrigue, determined that Paul Kruger's old-fashioned Afrikaners in the Transvaal and the Orange Free State should not frustrate his dream of leading militant British imperialism through the continent. He was supported by the British government when it came to war. Neither side was concerned with the wishes or welfare of the African inhabitants, but Britain was very much concerned with the effects on her European imperialist rivals. Kruger, however, failed to secure the support he expected from European states. Indeed, Britain had already eliminated Germany as a dangerous factor in the South African situation by signing a secret agreement whereby she would guarantee loans to the Portuguese and arrange to divide Portugal's African colonies in the case of Portuguese bankruptcy. So the Boer republics were eventually conquered and added to British Africa.

In 1911 France took control of Morocco, for the price of allowing a small share to Spain, giving Germany part of the French Congo to add to the Cameroons, and recognising the British position in Egypt. In the same year Italy consoled herself for her failure in Ethiopia by conquering Libya, still nominally part of the Ottoman Empire. Thus, before the first world war opened, the entire African continent had been brought under European control with the two exceptions of Ethiopia, which kept its ancient independence until Mussolini's conquest in 1935, and Liberia, economically in pawn to the Americans, but politically sovereign.

From the conclusions of the partition era until the end of the second world war Africa passed largely off the international stage.

Apart from the Italian conquest of Ethiopia, the only territorial changes were the division of the German colonies between France, Britain, Belgium and South Africa as mandates under the League of Nations. The Union of South Africa also gained sovereignty under the Statute of Westminster in 1931, becoming, like Canada, Australia and New Zealand, a sovereign state linked to Britain only through voluntary association in the Commonwealth. Egypt was declared a British protectorate for the purposes of the first war, and although officially declared independent in 1922 and signing a treaty of alliance with the British Government in 1936, remained virtually dependent on British military demands.

From the time that the continental boundaries were finally drawn and rival imperialisms ceased to manœuvre with each other, the affairs of Africans themselves came to depend heavily on the men on the spot. Governments had early taken over administrative responsibility from the companies. Even Leopold's brutal personal empire was handed over to the Belgian government. At first only a handful of officials with paltry resources controlled these vast territories. They were charged with the tasks of keeping order and attempting to build economic self-sufficiency, for the metropolitan governments had little desire to continue paying subsidies. The varying characteristics of government imposed depended largely on local problems and the personalities of the administrators. These were the factors that determined the effects of alien government on the inhabitants.

In all the new colonies the demand for labour affected the able-bodied, and often people not so able. Public works of all kinds, roads, railways, public buildings, were built and maintained by various forms of compulsory labour. In many cases, through the influence of companies with governments, labour for commercial concerns was provided by the same means. Inevitably, the effect of such recruitment spread widely through African society. Similarly, recruitment for military and police forces had its impact, though these recruits normally enjoyed far better living standards than labourers. On the other hand, recruiting police and soldiers involved local politics. Chiefs, their councillors, and their followers had to decide whether it was better to co-operate with the conqueror, resist him, or try negative non-co-operation. The decisions varied and were frequently not accepted by some members of the community.

Thus bitterness was often provoked between African and African, sometimes aggravated and exploited on the principle 'divide and rule'.

So long as self-sufficiency remained the ark of governments, administrators had to find revenue where they could. Some encouraged mining or trading companies, others invited settlers to build farms or plantations, in places the Africans themselves were enjoined to produce cash crops. It was where the mining companies found minerals that the demand on labour had its widest impact on African social life; it was where Europeans settled that land became the most important issue. In Southern Rhodesia and Kenya, European possession of land directly affected a large number of Africans, though only a small percentage of the total population. But European farming, together with the tighter administration, indirectly affected African life much more widely. It confined to a limited area tribes accustomed to a nomadic existence, either as pastoralists or as agriculturalists used to periodic movement in the search for virgin land. At a time when population growth was exerting one pressure, a contrary pressure from limited food resources often reduced living standards.

In the early stages of African colonisation, imperial governments, still unaccustomed to ideas of social or economic responsibility for their people at home, adopted an even more casually *laisser-faire* attitude to government in the colonies. Provided reasonable order was kept and few demands made on the Treasury, the administrator in charge was left to his own devices. Education was almost entirely a matter for the missions, economic development was left to companies and private individuals, and medicine and hygiene, although improved for government officials, hardly touched the colonial subjects. Most Africans remained under continued African rule, with many of the chiefs and elders responsible to the new government. Where the chieftain system did not exist it was often invented by the government as the simplest method of control.

Although there were some exceptions, the general outlook of colonial administrators was conservative and paternalistic. Many of them felt a subconscious nostalgia for the rural, village life of feudal Britain, France and Germany, now fast disappearing from their homelands. Colonial officials and settlers alike created an ideal of the African 'noble savage', with heavy overtones of the simple respectful peasant on whose subservience they could no longer feed their egos at home. They therefore based much of their authority on sustaining the power of conservative chiefs, whilst feeling profound suspicion that the effects of education, mining or commerce on the rural virtues of ignorant, 'unspoiled' Africans would lead to insubordination. In many respects this attitude, although sometimes protecting their 'wards' from more brutal types of exploitation, put the brake on economic development. By perpetuating tribal society, the insecurities of its breakdown were postponed; but so was the training of its members for participation in modern life.

It was during the later stages of this colonisation period that colour prejudice became a serious factor in the character of colonial social life. The growth of prejudice in South Africa is usually taken to date from 1717, the year in which the decision was taken to rely on slave labour instead of encouraging immigration of European workers. No such single date stands out in the history of modern colonial Africa; but the new feature generally associated with the growth of colour prejudice was the arrival of white wives in the tropics. It would require much deeper psychological research than can be attempted here to make any confident analysis on the root causes of this tragic social phenomenon. Certainly it has always had close connections with sexual attitudes and its worst outbursts of hysteria have been related to matters of sex. It has shown itself in wider and more profound forms in those countries administered and settled by the Protestant British, Germans, Dutch and Huguenots than where Catholic French, Portuguese or Belgians were in control. It has emanated from Christian Europe, not from African or Arab Mohammedanism. When all this has been said, the most important fact in understanding modern life in Africa is the realisation that colour prejudice, based on the belief in white superiority and a fundamental division between white and coloured, became the most active social factor in colonial Africa. The emotions which it stirred profoundly affected the personalities of rulers and ruled, vitally influencing both their relations and the subsequent character of African society.

The most disastrous effects of the first considerable contact of Europeans with African societies arose from an almost complete lack of understanding. Even though there were in those days no experienced sociologists, anthropologists, political scientists or economists to study African society, there seems to have been a singular lack of imagination and humility amongst the Europeans who did visit Africa. Of course, they came out of a period of European self-assured dogmatism, in which the new wonders of science, technology and fire-power had induced a conviction that European values were divinely inspired absolutes, the yard-stick against which all other mores were to be measured. Such a society hardly encouraged a spirit of inquiry or understanding.

So it was the brutality of African tribal life which impressed Europeans, and because the beliefs, customs and practices of Africans sharply differed from those of Europe, they were assumed without question to be inferior. The communal security of tribal life based on the extended family; the intricate inter-locking structure of politics; the artistic value of handicrafts and the profound knowledge of nature; above all, the intensely spiritual quality of African society, were all ignored in the general judgement of 'brutish pagan life'. It was widely assumed that Africans were naturally lazy and unambitious, lacking in initiative and a sense of responsibility. Few seem to have imagined the debilitating effects caused by centuries of endemic infection, the social ravages of the slave trade, or the habitual attitudes induced by a life of subsistence. In fact many African societies at this time closely resembled those of Europe in the Middle Ages, a stage from which many peoples in Central and Eastern Europe had even then barely emerged. They were superstitious, because they had no rational means of explaining natural phenomena; they were brutal to enemies and often to the victims of their traditional practices, for they had never encountered humanitarian influences; they thought little of plans or expectations for the future, for they had made no contact with the scientific age which gave humanity control over the forces of nature. But they also had a wider sense of social responsibility, often better human relations, and less predatory outlooks than the Europeans who derided them.

Inevitably, the new, personal, insecure relations between unimaginative men and women with the power of Europe behind them, and peoples untouched by modern knowledge, were dominated by misunderstanding. Attitudes of colour superiority, dominance and subservience were to affect more profoundly than was then realised the future associations of African and European.

Nevertheless, it was this imperialism of modern Europe, set in motion by its dynamic economy and supported by its physical strength, which brought Africa for the first time into the scientific, industrialised society of the twentieth-century world.

2

The Eve of Revolution

The two world wars profoundly affected millions of Africans. In the first war, fighting was widespread in and around the German colonies; extensive campaigns were mounted in South-west Africa, Togoland, the Cameroons and East Africa, whilst there was a revolt in South Africa and Britain declared a protectorate in Egypt. The opposition to European rule was not yet sufficiently sophisticated to tempt Africans into taking advantage of the embarrassment of the imperialists and rebelling whilst they were occupied in warfare. Indeed, most Africans proved surprisingly loyal to whichever European power ruled them, serving alike in the forces of Germany, Britain, France and Belgium.

The first world war was to prove the war-time value of Africa to Europe, a lesson already learnt by the second. The strategic value of the routes to and from the Middle East was soon apparent, whilst Africa's materials and manpower became of significant importance to the combatants. Apart from her casualties and some minor destruction, Africa lost little from the first war. Indeed, many of her communications were improved for war purposes, the output of some of her products was increased, whilst a number of her citizens considerably widened their horizons.

At the end of the war, Britain, France, Belgium and South Africa took over the German colonies under the new League of Nations' mandate system. Despite all the hypocrisy talked and written on the subject of war aims, in 1917 Lloyd George had privately told Colonel House, President Wilson's special envoy, that possession of the German colonies was one of the allied objectives. Britain found herself the possessor of a larger empire than at any time in her history.

Once the war was over manpower losses and the need to restore her national prestige strengthened the psychological appeal of French imperial expansion, whilst African raw materials and foods could help her national reconstruction.

It was less the change in imperial masters than two new international conceptions which interested the handful of African intellectuals and those progressives in the metropolitan countries concerned with colonial issues. Lenin and Woodrow Wilson, in their different ways, both introduced the term 'self-determination' into international parlance. Although the allied victors, both in their separate imperial policies and in their League of Nations policies, paid only lip service to the principle, never admitting that it applied to their own colonial possessions, the concept exerted profound influence on international philosophy. After all, allied propaganda had been trying to persuade the world that the war was being fought to establish the right of small nations to govern themselves. Not for the last time, propaganda phrases were to be turned against those who used them.

African society was not yet sufficiently organised in 1919 and the years following to take more than superficial advantage of the chink in the imperialist armour which had been exposed. But the concept of the right of self-determination changed the character of international relations. It directly refuted imperialist assumptions. Though it might only be a hostage for the future in the tongues and pens of a few African nationalists, ultimately the right of Belgians to freedom from German rule implied the same right for Africans to free themselves from British, French, Belgian and Portuguese imperialism.

The second product of the European war which interested Africans was the new mandate idea of the League of Nations. Article XXII of the Covenant declared that 'the well-being and development' of peoples 'not yet able to stand by themselves under the strenuous conditions of the modern world . . . form a sacred trust of civilisation'. The concept was elaborated by Lord Lugard in his 'Dual Mandate in British Tropical Africa' and by the French Colonial Minister, Albert Sarraut. Both asserted that imperial powers bore a responsibility to develop their colonies for the benefit of the subject peoples and the wider civilised world. It was in accord with these sentiments that the Devonshire declaration in 1923 laid down that 'Primarily, Kenya is African territory', where African interests must be considered paramount whenever they might be in conflict with those of other inhabitants. The same conception of imperial responsibility to subject peoples was to lead Britain to pass her first Colonial Development Act in 1929 and extend its scope and finances in the Development and Welfare Act of 1940.

For the first time the well-being of colonial peoples became officially recognised as a responsibility of imperial governments. Slowly and meagrely governments introduced medical, educational, social and economic facilities for the direct benefit of their subjects. The cynic would say that this was the consequence of new ideas of enlightened self-interest. Certainly capital continued to find its way to the richest sources of profit; by the beginning of the second war, for instance, two-thirds of all European investment in Africa was concentrated in the mining countries of the south and centre. It is also true that during the inter-war years Europe began to develop those potentials in minerals, raw materials and foodstuffs she had vaguely visualised during the period of partition. Profits and supplies flowed to the European imperial powers more readily than previously. It was necessary to improve the health and capabilities of labour to serve these needs. Nevertheless, whatever the motives, the entrance of government into social and economic activity made possible the growth of that African public consciousness which was to make radical change possible.

This new economic development inevitably brought with it urban growth, an aggregation of workers and a stimulation of social consciousness. New towns grew up and others multiplied their populations. Dakar, for example, grew from 32,440 in 1921 to 132,000 by 1946; Leopoldville from 26,622 in 1935 to 110,280 in 1945. Repeated attempts were made to form trade unions, often repressed by colonial governments, but providing modern social experience for those who made the attempt. A wholesale variety of religious movements sprang up, expressing a social frustration which was to find eventual outlet in political activity. Newspapers made their appearance for the first time on any considerable scale, whilst various intellectual and quasi-political associations began to develop.

Above all, the spread of education presaged the appearance of an intelligentsia which would be capable of influencing the semi-literate masses. As Macaulay had foreseen in India a century earlier, education was the progenitor of self-government. Once Englishmen, Frenchmen and Belgians began to teach, they had to use the language and ideas current in their own democracies. It might be that the emphasis was on teaching crafts, husbandry, medicine, as was the case in British Africa; or on French culture, as in the territories of France; or even merely on artisan industrial training, as in the Belgian Congo. No matter; once an education system of the most rudimentary or irrelevant character was started, it gathered its own momentum. The missionaries might teach the Bible, but their pupils used their knowledge of words to read about the ideas of the French Revolution or the Covenant of the League of Nations. It might seem harmless, and to some useless, to teach the classical languages; but they were used to cull the lessons of Plato. Once the chains of ignorance were struck, the steps of the prisoners released from ignorance could not be controlled. Before the second war had come Africans from Senegal, the Ivory Coast, Algeria, the Cameroons, and Gabon were to be found in Paris; their compatriots from the Gold Coast, Nigeria, Kenya, or Uganda were in London and New York. They were few in numbers, and the Belgians, Portuguese and Rhodesians were still holding back the tide, whilst poor countries like Tanganyika and Nyasaland had not yet found the paths to higher education. But these were the pioneers of what was soon to be a throng of colonial students in Europe and North America, and they took back to Africa an interpretation of world society drawn from personal experience. Many returned with a message of revolutionary import.

Although African affairs were no longer matters of constant international attention, the years between the wars saw little diminution in the argument over the imperialist principle. Its grounds had changed a little, for the dispute now centred, not on whether European powers should adopt imperial expansionist policies, but what they ought to do with the colonies already acquired. Much of the discussion was conducted over the case of India, obviously the most noteworthy example, but it was reflected in Africa, for African issues increasingly demanded the attention of the protagonists.

At first sight it would seem that the immediate post-first war period should have represented spectacular success for the imperialists. Although the German empire had gone, France, Britain and Belgium were at the zenith of imperial success. Not only had they acquired vast new territories, but their trade figures would have

brightened the eyes of imperialist supporters in the previous generation. When, at the turn of the century, Joseph Chamberlain was
vigorously leading the imperialist lobby, he had to contend with the
awkward fact that British trade with foreign nations was valued at
£711 million whereas that with the empire stood no higher than
£237 million. Now, to take the year 1923 as an example, British
exports to foreigners amounted to £300 million; and the empire
figure was only £15 million less.

Certainly the mystique of empire was preserved amongst the
masses during the inter-war period, serving to assuage some of the
fears lingering in the wake of the European war, which had drastically shaken the self-assurance of European society. School children
still learned their geography and history from maps on which the
colours of France and Britain remained predominant; conventional
society still spoke of 'The Empire' in the same reverent terms used
for monarchy and deity; the global military power of British and
French imperialism seemed to remain the major feature of international life.

But there were differences for those who cared to look. It was
apparent soon after Versailles that a basic change had occurred in the
balance of naval power. From 1922 onwards it was clear that the
British naval position was only maintained on American sufferance
The final triumph of Irish nationalism, resulting in the separation of
Eire, betrayed a new British weakness and was to serve as an encouraging example to Egypt and India. The Statute of Westminster,
though acclaimed as a British triumph in bringing her older, white-
governed colonies to maturity, was nevertheless a blow to pure
imperialism, with ominous hints that the time would come when the
dominions might look elsewhere for military protection and economic association. Then again, the diarchy which grew up as various
forms of local colonial governments were created alongside the
imperial government seemed to many a reluctant retreat from true
principles of imperial governance.

The fact was that imperialists became confused and defensive
during the inter-war years. The moral and intellectual climate
turned sharply against them, particularly over Indian affairs, where
they were continually out-manœuvred by Gandhi. Too often they
looked like thick-headed, slow-witted 'Colonel Blimps', clinging to
meaningless anachronistic phrases as alternatives to facing current

realities. They were caught in a hopeless net of their own weaving by the dictators; for whilst the rise of Japan, Germany and Italy directly menaced the French and British empires, to oppose the Japanese in Manchuria, Mussolini in Ethiopia or Hitler in Europe seemed to imperil the very social order on which imperialism was built. The dictators were only following the well-worn paths trodden by earlier imperialisms, basing their policies on the doctrine 'might is right'. So they were allowed and even encouraged to amass their strength and offered apologias by the very same British and French leaders whose imperial treasures they coveted.

At the same time, the radical and socialist groups, although constantly attacking the assumptions of imperialism, also suffered from their own confusions. They had criticised the Versailles Treaty and constantly preached that the victorious allies had been unjust to vanquished Germany. They sympathised with the 'have' and 'have not' theory as an explanation of German revival and consequently appeared at times to be accepting the propaganda used by Hitler in claiming the return of Germany's former African colonies. There were those, too, who maintained the nineteenth-century radical tradition by arguing that reform should start at home before colonial grievances were considered. Moreover, both the continuity in over-seas' policy accepted within the British party system and a form of class consciousness prevented the British Labour Party from pledging itself to end imperialism immediately it gained power. As late as 1935 Wedgwood was indignantly denying that Labour would simply hand India over to the Indians, for, he declared, that would mean surrendering the Indian masses to their princes and capitalists. The confusion caused by mixing the trusteeship principle, which was inherent in the better forms of imperialist belief, with anti-imperialism, runs right through Labour debating in this period. It usually led to a demand for reform in the colonies, to which many imperialists subscribed, accompanied by the type of reservation used by Mac-Donald when he warned that the problems of imperialism would have to be met by a Labour government according to the situation it inherited. French socialists, accepting the traditional assimilationist doctrine of their country, were even more clearly in favour of reform without committal to colonial self-determination.

On the other hand, socialists had adopted the role of keeper of the national conscience from before the first war. MacDonald himself had accepted the creed of John Stuart Mill that no people had the right to govern another. The liberal tradition of Britain was completely opposed to the doctrine of subjection and it seemed self-evident that the growth in democracy at home was incompatible with a continuation of imperialism. It took some time before this logic worked itself out, for democracy was open also to the sentimental appeal of jingoism.

Nevertheless, the rise of the British Labour Party, comprising radical socialist groups as well as the conservative factions within the broad Labour movement, provided a potential, and at times a practical, spearhead of attack on imperialist doctrine. It had to reconcile the paradox of supporting nationalism in the colonies whilst condemning nationalist ambitions in international affairs. It flirted with the catalyst offered by Norman Angell, who saw international control of colonial territories as the ideal alternative to imperialism. It walked the precipice to which it was enticed by cynical Communists, concerned only to use imperialist embarrassments in the interest of Soviet foreign policy, and for a time accepted Russian anti-imperialism at its face value. It survived the disillusion resulting from the apparent failure of two Labour governments to reverse imperialist policies and apply the principle of self-determination to the colonies. By the start of the second world war it was confused and divided on the imperialist issue, but it had retained sufficient faith in its first principles to remain the one organ of British political life capable of co-operating with the infant forces of anti-imperialism stirring in the colonies themselves. That this was true of British socialism in contrast to the French and Belgian movements was to become significant to post-war Africans.

It was war again which gave the imperialist idea perhaps its final stimulating injection. For war provided a release from the necessity to argue, to justify, to reason. War brought an end to semi-despised intellectual exercises, identified an undisputed enemy, and demanded that all thought and effort be concentrated on an issue no more complicated than his defeat. Moreover, although the war was being fought for a variety of reasons, its conduct quickly came under the strong influence of the imperialists, led by their arch-priest, Winston Churchill, who had fought such a lonely struggle on its behalf during the inter-war years. To Churchill there returned all the ebullient romance of British imperial power. The 'Empire', patriotism, allegiance to the Crown, represented a way of life in which the emotions could discount the intellect. It was this call which Churchill made to the British people in their 'finest hour'. And Churchill firmly believed that the Pax Britannica of the imperial nineteenth century could be re-established, and would be the only guarantee of international peace. He therefore often fought his war for imperial ends, in Burma, the Pacific and the Middle East, much to the suspicious impatience of Stalin and Roosevelt.

Of course, this was only a last romantic tilt of the Union Jack. It bore no relation to reality, as many of Churchill's political and military colleagues frequently tried to show him. The empire in the East in fact crumpled before one of the non-European 'lesser breeds without the law'. The Pacific was an American lake and even Australasia would henceforth have to look to the United States for security. Russia quickly assumed German pretensions to European hegemony, and could never be expected to leave the Middle East to unchallenged western imperialist control.

Moreover, the Indians, in particular, had again taken advantage of the inconsistencies in the British war argument to expose its hypocrisy. If this were a war against dictatorship, authoritarianism, and racial doctrines, they asked, if it were a war for freedom, democracy, and self-determination, what were the British doing in Egypt, Africa or the rest of their far-flung empire? The barb went home, for although Churchill was never vulnerable to such logic, he had Labour colleagues in his war-time government uncomfortably aware that they themselves had used the same arguments only a short time previously. The sight of white men using all the horrors of scientific brutality on each other for a principle they denied to their non-white subjects made a profound psychological impact on colonial subjects throughout the European empires. It was immensely heightened on those thousands who again served their imperial masters in war theatres all over the world. It was brought directly home to Africans who saw two French governments, those of Vichy and De Gaulle, contending for their support, or listened to the South African-Rhodesian fevered debates on the danger of arming black men. The mystiques of European power and morality waned; the war to restore imperial glory in fact destroyed the myths on which imperialism depended.

The end of the war in 1945 thus saw a new watershed in European-African relations. Probably more Africans than ever before in the history of the continent, with the exception of the slave trade days, had been abroad, encountered new attitudes, absorbed fresh ideas and returned home unwilling to accept previous conditions. Many rough European and American forces had been seen in Africa for the first time, shattering the assumption that all white men were superior 'gentlemen'. The resources of the continent had been shown to be a vital element in the European war efforts, and it was likely that they would play an even more important part in world reconstruction. Above all, the awe in which Europeans and European life had hitherto been held was drastically shaken; in future Africans were going to demand some of the modern amenities they had seen enjoyed by Europeans and would not be prepared to accept the opinions of their white masters as to which were good for them.

Yet all these factors would have been unlikely to provoke a successful revolution in post-war Africa if there had not been strong external influences at work. Most of the same factors had been present after the first war, but little effect had been seen in the African continent. Moreover, there could be no doubt that the enormous increase in weapon power and techniques developed during the second war left the imperial states far stronger in relation to their colonial territories than ever before. Colonial revolution could not expect to succeed by force of arms in such circumstances.

The most important new factor in 1945 was the change in accepted principles of international behaviour. Now the vague principles of self-determination enunciated by Wilson and Lenin after the first war had been reinforced by specific declarations from the victorious great powers. The Atlantic Charter, for instance, proclaimed 'the right of all peoples to choose the form of government under which they live'. Churchill might deny that the Charter applied to colonial subjects, but the anti-colonial traditions of America and the Soviet Union suggested that they would see that it did. The world which emerged from the 1939–45 war saw much more clearly than its 1918 predecessor the dangers arising from the principle that 'might is right' and its corollary that the powerful may legitimately govern the weak. As imperialism had derived its justification from these assumptions it was thereby weakened by the new international atmosphere. It might seem hypocritical that the two great post-war powers should simultaneously use their newly-felt strength to pursue their own national interests and condemn older European colonialism. But the fact that they were prepared to do so, that the new United Nations was better able to commit itself against imperial rule than the League had ever been, and that international responsibility for under-developed peoples was seriously recognised for the first time, was more important to the anti-colonialists than political consistency.

By the end of the war, too, many of the progressive groups within the imperial nations had begun to resolve their pre-war dilemmas. The Nazis and Fascists had been imperialists – in Europe, Africa and Asia. Western democracy found that it had its own Achilles' heel when it tried to oppose their philosophy whilst still maintaining its imperial rule over millions of colonial subjects. The same handicap remained when it attempted to condemn Soviet imperialism after the war. So, although in most European progressive movements the attitude of paternalistic trusteeship remained, whilst many labour leaders continued to insist that the interests of their own workers should be given priority, the influence of anti-imperialism emerged stronger than ever before. It was from the groups in European parties who were beginning to accept the need to destroy rather than reform empires that the colonial nationalists secured new support.

In France many colonial leaders had been accustomed to play some part in French political and trade union life. In Britain the association between progressive forces and Indian leaders gained spectacular success in the 1947 Indian settlement. Whilst African leaders were trying to capitalise on their war-time assistance to the Free French by participating in the drafting of the new constitution in Paris, their counterparts were organising the famous 1945 Pan-African Congress in Manchester. French Africans gained strength from association with socialists and communists. British Africans, Kenyatta, Nkrumah, Peter Abrahams, Wallace Johnson, were co-operating not only with the powerful West Indian anti-imperialist lobby, Padmore, James, Milliard and Makonnen, but also with the left-wing of the Labour Party, the Independent Labour Party and the Fabian Colonial Bureau.

Yet it would be unrealistic to suggest that the new post-war strength of the anti-imperialist movement was drawn simply from intellectual and political sources. The fact was that, despite the new powers developed during the war, the European empires had begun to display signs of fallibility. In Asia the Japanese had challenged and defeated European might. France had been conquered, its African subjects witnessing fratricidal strife amongst French administrators divided between Vichy and De Gaulle. Life in the Congo had been maintained despite the occupation of Belgium. Britain emerged having finally lost her world paramountcy, clearly less powerful than America and Russia.

Above all, the European imperial powers had exhausted most of their treasure during the war. They needed to develop new wealth in their colonies, but this would only be possible in peace. Despite their tremendous military power, they could not afford to maintain expensive colonial garrisons nor face the danger of extensive colonial wars. Their people now demanded peace, social security and prosperity. Thus economic, social and political factors all combined to prepare suitable ground for an assault on continued European domination of Africa. It remained to be seen whether, when and how this opportunity would be taken.

The situations in the various African territories in 1945 were strongly conditioned by the different forms of European rule practised over the past fifty years. The European imperial powers had not governed their colonies on identical lines and the differences in their approach were to affect the post-war development of their African subjects. Spain and Portugal had long lost their massive American empires, and neither country had kept pace with the modern trends of the other European imperial powers. In their attitude to their African subjects they tended to fall equally behind modern methods. Spain governed few Africans, but the Portuguese retained control over the large possessions, Angola and Mozambique, and the smaller western enclave, Portuguese Guinea. Colonial rule was laid down by an Act of 1930, at a time when Salazar was Minister of Colonies. It unified all colonial administration in the hands of the state, fixed national control over the economies and emphasised the need to maintain Portuguese sovereignty. In these territories life tended to be quiet, in the absence of a rigorous colour bar, but few opportunities existed for the African to gain education or training. The Portuguese boasted that they accepted educated

Africans, known as assimilados, into European society, but this had more value as propaganda than reality. Five years after the end of the war less than 35,000 Africans out of a total of ten million in the two main territories had been granted this status.

The Portuguese were actually practising a form of racial separation in which the African masses were dragooned by often brutal methods into providing labour for the state and white settlers, and were virtually deprived of all civil rights.

Belgium also provided a few opportunities for educated Africans to be recognised as part of European society. But again, in practice, social and economic segregation was the general rule. The Belgian colonial outlook was strongly influenced by the attitudes dominant at home. Belgians were industrious, commercially-minded and Catholic. They believed in applying the same outlook in the Congo and in Ruanda-Urundi, the former German territory. They candidly expressed a belief in their civilising mission, bringing their African subjects under the dual disciplines of the mining companies and the Catholic Church. Thus they spread education widely but thinly, concentrating on primary schools and artisan training, with the priesthood as the only opening for higher learning. Politics were excluded for black and white alike, authority stemming solely from Brussels.

It was, however, the colonial policies of France and Britain that were to influence African affairs most profoundly. The principle from which French policy took its main inspiration was laid down during the Revolution, drawn from the declaration 'all men, without distinction of colour, domiciled in the French colonies are French citizens and enjoy all the rights assured by the Constitution'. The principle has been applied in practice no more frequently than most other political principles. Yet it has always been linked to a French assumption that the highest prize to be offered any people is acceptance within French civilisation. Thus the ultimate aim of French colonial policy, however much its practice might fall short, was to integrate colonial subjects into a greater France, extending to them the benefits of French society. So, despite the traditional French ideal of democratic liberty, France took much longer to offer representative political institutions to her imperial territories than did the British. She preferred the idea that one day they would all be represented in Paris. And when local representation was offered it was always weighted against the indigenous peoples and frequently manipulated to serve imperial purposes.

Before and after the second war, the French set their faces against African nationalism, sometimes justifying this attitude by arguing that nationalism was anachronistic in the twentieth-century world and proposing that it should be bypassed in Africa in the cause of the higher international ideal. At the Brazzaville Conference of 1944, attended incidentally only by French officials, the objectives of French policy were laid down in these terms: 'the aims of the work of civilisation accomplished by France in its colonies exclude all idea of autonomy, all possibility of evolution outside the French bloc of the Empire; the eventual establishment, even in the distant future, of self-governance is to be dismissed'. The extent to which the French had influenced African leaders by these ideas was to be seen as recently as 1957, when Félix Houphouet-Boigny, leader of the Ivory Coast and at the time a member of the French Cabinet, rejected Nkrumah's policy of African independence, posing the alternative of interdependence between nations.

From 1848 onwards France had, indeed, declared the theoretical right of her colonial subjects to elect deputies to the National Assembly. Senegal had sent deputies and even enjoyed self-government in its municipalities. Yet these rights were never extended to the rest of French West or Equatorial Africa. There, the limitation of French citizenship to a tiny minority, the imposition of forced labour and the penal system known as *indigénat* which deprived Africans of many civil rights and gave French administrators authoritarian powers, clamped on the mass of French Africans an authoritarian system, living their lives virtually dependent on the local French administrator or their French employers. Whilst a handful of colonial evolués found their way to Paris, to be largely absorbed in French ideas and even to take high places in French social and political life, the African masses in the French empire lived rather like French peasants in the pre-Revolutionary era.

Yet, if there was much that was hypocritical in the pretensions of French colonial policy, it could at least point to the presence of African faces in parliament. This would have been unthinkable to Westminster. The British, though no doubt equally convinced of the superiority of their civilisation, always considered it their own exclusive prerogative. It is true that the work of administrators, settlers and missionaries took many British forms and ideas to the colonies. Their object, however, was to teach other people how to live in their own societies rather than to invite them into British civilisation, which, in any case, was considered quite out of their reach. Nevertheless, as early as the end of the eighteenth century, there were black men in the Sierra Leone legislature, whilst in 1888 the first African was nominated to the Gold Coast Legislative Council. The fact is that, where there were no white settlers to complicate the issue, either rudimentary forms of representative institutions were established in the British dependencies or existing forms of African government were maintained and supported. This policy frequently allowed some freedom of expression in speech, press and association, albeit ultimately imperially controlled. In addition, haphazard, though sometimes considerable, educational facilities had developed, usually through missionary activities. Thus, by the start of the second world war, opportunities had slowly arisen for some British African leaders to lay the early foundations of nationalism. The way had also been unintentionally prepared for modern political activists to challenge the power of the indigenous conservative traditionalists who were being sustained by the policy of indirect rule.

Whilst this situation was developing mainly in West Africa, where few Europeans had settled, in the settler countries of east and central Africa the perspective was very different. Despite the protection promised to African interests in the Devonshire declaration of 1923, British policy, particularly in Kenya and the Rhodesias, seemed to be subconsciously drawn from the precedents of the older white dominions. Legislatures of various kinds were slowly growing in power, but the nominees and representatives within them were drawn almost exclusively from white inhabitants. As early as 1923 when only 35,000 Europeans lived beside one and a half million Africans in Southern Rhodesia, Britain had granted almost complete internal self-government to that colony on a basis of white rule. It appeared as though there were dangers that the policy of 1909–10 in South Africa might be repeated.

During the inter-war years British imperial rule seemed to have suffered the same confusions in Africa as in the rest of the empire. Policy was based neither on evolutionary democratic representation leading to independent sovereignty with continued association in the

Commonwealth, the policy followed by the older dominions; nor on the conception of a greater imperial state, such as was conceived by some Frenchmen; nor on permanent direct imperial rule.

To British politicians and to most Africans it seemed in 1945 that British colonial rule would continue undisturbed for at least the rest of the twentieth century. Yet institutions had been created, opportunities provided and ideas proffered which were to give leadership in settling the imperial issue to British Africans. Few realised what kind of seeds had been sown.

When the war ended in 1945, the whole of Southern Africa was dominated by white settlers and colonial administrators. The Union was independent under a government representing the white community of just over two million, plus a few Africans and Cape Coloureds. The mass of the eight million non-Europeans were subjected to the will of their white masters. South-west Africa was still mandated to the Union, its only representative institutions being similarly dominated by its white population. In the three High Commission Territories, Swaziland, Basutoland and Bechuanaland, Britain retained authority, though continually pressed by South African governments to surrender it. Resident Commissioners in each governed the territories with the help of Advisory Councils. The High Commissioner to South Africa acted also as their overlord. Southern Rhodesia was virtually self-governing in its domestic affairs, though still a British colony. Its parliament was elected on a roll which, although nominally non-racial, was almost entirely composed of white inhabitants, who were virtually the only citizens able to satisfy the franchise requirements. Northern Rhodesia and Nyasaland remained British protectorates, both having witnessed the appearance of Legislative Councils, but each controlled by colonial officials in partnership with white representatives. The Belgian Congo was still administered from Brussels, and although its Governor-General had a Council to advise him, he nominated all its members. Ruanda-Urundi remained a Belgian mandate from the time of Versailles. The two Portuguese territories on the east and west of the continent, Mozambique and Angola, were also administered from Europe without any form of local representative institutions.

French Equatorial Africans had attracted some sympathies through their loyalty during the war to the Free French Government of De Gaulle. The constituent states (Gabon, Middle Congo, Ubangui-Chari and Tchad) had been promised economic and political development, though whatever form this was to take excluded secession from France. Similarly, in the French West African states (Senegal, Mauritania, Guinea, the Ivory Coast, Soudan, Dahomey and Niger) the link with France remained unchallenged. Whilst Senegal had a long history of internal political activity, this was largely in association with French politics, and in the other territories political interest was only just beginning to stir. Togoland and the French Cameroons remained as mandated territories governed from Paris.

British West Africa was much more politically conscious than its French neighbours. Two African members had sat in the Gold Coast Executive since 1942, while ten Africans, four of them elected, had been in the Nigerian Legislative Council since 1922. In both Sierra Leone and Gambia Executive and Legislative Councils existed and included Africans amongst their members. African political activity, expressed through an electoral system, was at a higher state in British West Africa than in any other area of the continent.

Liberia retained its role as the only independent state of West Africa, although largely controlled by American finance. It had its own President, Senate and Legislative Chamber, with elections on a restricted franchise and a constitution modelled on that of the United States.

On the other side of the continent Legislative and Executive Councils had also been established in Uganda, Tanganyika, Kenya and Zanzibar. These were still controlled by colonial officials and included numbers of European settlers, but in Kenya an African sat in the Legislative Council for the first time in 1944. The Sudan was still an Anglo-Egyptian condominium, administered by a Governor-General and Council, whilst the Somalilands had been recovered by the allies from the Italians during the war and were now administered by military governments.

Egypt and Ethiopia were both independent states, although the former had been virtually occupied and controlled as a British military base throughout the war. The king, dependent on British power, nominated most of the members of his Senate, though elections were sometimes held to a lower chamber. Ethiopia was recaptured from the Italians in 1941 and the Emperor restored, the government reverting to his control with nominated chambers. Eritrea had also been taken from the Italians and in 1945 was still administered by Britain, though its future was to be decided by the United Nations. France and Britain had established military rule in the provinces of Libya, also conquered from the Germans and Italians.

The three Maghreb countries, Algeria, Morocco and Tunisia, remained under French rule. Algeria was considered to be an integral part of France under a Governor-General assisted by Consultative and Superior Councils; three Senators and ten deputies represented the eight million inhabitants in Paris. Morocco and Tunisia were both French protectorates, the former under the Sultan, Mohammed V, and the latter under its Bey.

Thus, with the exception of South Africa, Liberia, Egypt and Ethiopia, in their several ways nominally independent, the whole of the African continent in 1945 was a European imperial preserve. Its forms of government varied widely, its customs were multifarious, its masters came from different European nations. Europe and Europeans had dominated the life of the continent for over fifty years and few supposed that the post-war years would see much change. Yet, with hindsight, it is now possible to detect the presence of incipient influences, educational, political, economic and social, which together revealed a small storm cloud in the clear skies of imperial rule. The history of the African revolution during the succeeding fifteen years is the story of how this tiny cloud became a thunderstorm, which was to wash away the roots of European imperialism, if not entirely out of the continent, at least into its precarious southernmost tip, still fearfully awaiting the final deluge.

3

The West African Volcano

The revolt against the established imperial order which swept western Africa after the war was first planned in Europe. At the Paris Constituent Assembly in late 1945, and in the Manchester Pan-African Congress, meeting almost simultaneously, campaign plans were hammered out that were to transform west Africa. In Paris the representatives of French West Africa concentrated on seeking equal status for their people with white Frenchmen; in Manchester Africans from British territories quoted the Atlantic Charter and the Four Freedoms as their text for the campaign against imperial rule.

It was not coincidence which took French and British Africans to the metropolitan countries. Léopold Senghor, M. Lamine Guèye, Fily Dabo Sissoko, Yacine Diallo and Félix Houphouet-Boigny knew Paris as well as they knew Dakar, Abidjan or Bamako. Kwame Nkrumah and Nnamdi Azikiwe were accustomed to the life and talk of London as well as that of Accra or Lagos.

From the early days of imperialism in Africa, in the nineteenth century, there had been nationalist politicians and political movements. The Aborigines' Rights Protection Society was founded in 1897, originally to protest over land issues. Professor W. E. B. Du Bois, the American Negro, had been organising pan-African conferences since 1900, and that of 1945 was the sixth in this succession. The 1920 National Congress of British West Africa, under the inspiration of J. E. Casely-Hayford, a Gold Coast Lawyer, aimed at some form of unity between the four British West African colonies, an objective visualised in even more radical terms by the West African Youth League of the following decade. In French West Africa political activity was usually promoted by metropolitan parties, of which the Senegalese section of the French Socialist Party, the SFIO, was most prominent.

The pre-1939 period was essentially one of bourgeois, intellectual cosmopolitanism. African political activists thought in broad, ideal-istic terms, aspired to recognition within international intellectual society but had only tenuous contact with the social and economic life of their own people. They were mainly second generation pro-fessional classes. Their fathers had used their training in law and letters to make occasional protests against the actions of the imperial government on such matters as land and civil rights. The second generation, lawyers, doctors, teachers, journalists, looked for greater chances of inclusion within the imperial system. In British territories they demanded increased representation in councils, better oppor-tunities in government service, and increased educational facilities. In French Africa the intelligentsia aimed to break down the barriers between themselves and French society, concentrating particularly on that discrimination in the legal code known as *indigénat* and the restricted opportunities to qualify for citizenship.

It was in the 1930s that the first signs of modern militant political activity appeared. Student groups in London, Paris and America, youth movements in west Africa itself, the appearance of a radical popular press associated with such names as Azikiwe and Wallace Johnson, combined to stimulate militant programmes and a higher degree of organisation. Self-government was talked about, yet, although the international depression was gravely affecting the economic life of West Africans, little thought was spared for the masses. The grievances of the cocoa farmers in the Gold Coast during 1937–8 were never recognised as political ammunition and they were left to turn to the chiefs for support. The pre-war intelli-gentsia were still too self-conscious of their new social status to feel any affinity with illiterate masses. They sought personal acceptance, even if it were merely acceptance as critics within the system.

It was inevitable that the war should affect the political climate for it made a drastic impact on the social and economic structures from which sprang political activities. It produced the beginnings of a new proletariat drawn from ex-servicemen and new town dwellers. It accelerated pre-war developments, stimulating a fresh generation of politicians to extend their political theories beyond the limited aims of their predecessors. It was the use made of social and economic factors by the politicians and the new political objectives which emerged that produced the transformation in west African society.

These political policies owed much to European influence. Parisian intellectuals still accepted the axiom that French society offered the highest attainments of civilisation. Thus Africans from the French territories aimed at becoming full French citizens and directed their political activities towards that end. British Africans, in contrast, encountered both the exclusiveness of British society and the separatist colonial ideas of British radicals, strongly affected by their associations with Indian nationalism and the particularly British interpretation of Marxism as socialism within separate nation states. They identified the colonial status as their enemy and aimed at self-rule.

It has been widely assumed that the independence objective of British Africans was more radical than the assimilationist ambitions of the French. This is not necessarily so. Obviously in socially backward territories such as Niger, Mauritania or Soudan continued domination of political life by Moslem chiefs with French support retarded social or economic development. Yet these conditions were not dissimilar to those in Northern Nigeria or the Northern Territories of the Gold Coast. Where, as in Senegal and the Ivory Coast, the situation was comparable to that in the southern regions of Nigeria or the Gold Coast, where the drive for African independence was strongest, the assimilationist policy was deliberately espoused by African political leaders. They argued that the era of genuine national sovereignty was past, that international influence could only be achieved by larger groupings, and that once they achieved equality with Frenchmen, Africans could play a leading part in a supra-national state based on federal, confederal or integrated foundations. There was one similarity between this vision and that of the British imperial idealists who had formerly advocated an imperial union. Both of them depended on an acceptance of equality between metropolitan and colonial citizens. Both foundered on this same rock.

Thus the African leaders assembled in 1945 in Paris and in Manchester followed their own separate and different stars. The French sought guarantees in the new French constitution which could lead to equality for African citizens within the Fourth Republic. The British made their plans for carrying the principle of self-government to the mass of their people. This divergence perpetuated the almost total absence of contact and knowledge between the two sets of African leaders in pre-war times; it resulted in sharply dividing immediate post-war west African history between the separate experience of French and British Africans.

The impact of war had been felt more directly in French than British Africa. Certain features affected both; several hundred thousand servicemen, shortages of imports, high prices, inflation, demand for products, increased urbanisation, unemployment. Here was the basis of a socio-economic revolution at least in urban society, for it affected rural areas less. But in addition to these common consequences of war, French Africans had been torn by the division within France itself.

From the time of the fall of France in 1940 until the invasions of North Africa in 1942, most of West Africa was subject to Vichy rule. Inevitably authoritarianism increased, with more extensive compulsory labour, forced cultivation and widespread use of *indigénat*.

Some support was shown by certain Africans for the Free French cause and a number of chiefs and their followers left French Africa, making their way to British territories. With the weakening of Vichy during the North African campaigns and the removal of the danger that Dakar would become a Nazi base, De Gaulle's influence increased. Yet economic dislocation, harsh treatment of Africans, and divided loyalties damaged relations with France. Certainly there could be no return to the pre-war mixture of patronage and bureau - cratic authority.

This fact was recognised early by De Gaulle's government. In January 1944 a conference of Free French politicians and colonial officials met in Brazzaville. On citizenship, legal rights and compulsory labour, its proposals were timid. On one vital issue it was adamant; there could be no question of autonomy for African states. Yet it proclaimed the right of Africans to participate in drawing up the post-war constitution of the French Republic and to be elected to French parliaments. In adhering to the federal principle in future French institutions it foreshadowed the Union Française, which was to represent both metropolitan and overseas Frenchmen.

Thus, when the French African delegates met in Paris to form a constituent assembly with their French colleagues, their participation in future French institutions had already been accepted. Up to this time only Senegal had been allowed to elect members to the French parliament. The first African deputy appeared in the chamber in 1914. In future this right would be extended to the rest of French African territories. Contrast with the British outlook could hardly have been sharper. The idea that a score of black faces might appear on the benches in Westminster would have outraged British public opinion. And in these contrasting attitudes lies the secret of the profoundly different feelings held by French Africans for France compared with those felt by British Africans for Britain.

The debate on the overseas territories came late on the agenda of the constituent assembly. When it was held in March 1946, the African leaders concentrated on their basic claim for equal French citizenship. They emphasised the need to abolish forced labour, to lower taxes, to reform the system of land tenure, and to raise the living standards of the African masses. For a time the progressive mood of post-war France prevailed and the assembly drew up a constitution which would have given the French territories considerable control over their own affairs, with a semi-federal relationship to Paris. This constitution was rejected by the French electorate. Thereon the French colonial business lobby went into action to minimise concessions granted to the colonies. The traditional policies of centralisation and assimilation were re-affirmed, the emphasis moved from self-government to participation in French institutions, and the trends towards a federal relationship were reversed.

Nevertheless, the October 1946 constitution represented a major advance towards representative government in French Africa. In the past, government had been organised in a hierarchical pyramid with its apex in Paris, authority devolving down from the French Minister of Colonies and Parliament, through the Governor-General in Dakar to the territorial Governors and their officials. Councils were purely advisory, except in Senegal, where the only institution resembling a democratic body was situated. Under the new constitution, not only were colonial Africans to be represented in the French parliamentary institutions, the Chamber, the Senate and the French Union Assembly, but they were to have their own territorial and regional assemblies. Whilst the French Parliament remained legislatively supreme, considerable powers, including control over local budgets, devolved on the new assemblies. It is true that the territorial governors and commandants of the cercles, or smaller administrative units, retained strong administrative and executive powers. Yet the significance of the constitution lay in its opportunities rather than its details. African deputies would be drawn into political society in Paris. Elections in the territories would compel political organisation. Relaxation in the penal code offered new opportunities to criticise the administration. The application of the Monnet Plan for economic development, with its implications of industrial expansion, agricultural growth, and an increase in medical and educational provision, made it clear that a door had been opened to profound political, social and economic changes.

Argument in Africa centred at first around the method of electing the new representatives. The 1944 Brazzaville conference had recommended that whenever possible universal suffrage should be introduced. The 1946 constitution provided for only a limited franchise which allowed an electorate of only just over a million in a total population of sixteen million. Yet African opinion was even more concerned about the electoral college system. Except in Senegal, electors were divided into French citizens and non-citizens. Most of the former were white Frenchmen; all the latter were black. Each electorate voted in a separate college to elect its own representatives to the territorial assemblies, or General Councils. The numbers of members elected varied, with the second college of non-citizens always having a majority. But the first colleges of whites and African évolués were given much higher proportional representation than their number warranted.

This system of election was further complicated by the adaptations used for elections to the other assemblies. The Grand Council, composed of five representatives from each territory, meeting in Dakar and given vaguely federal powers over the whole region, was elected by the members of each territorial General Council. Members of the French Union Assembly were elected in the same way. But deputies to the National Assembly in Paris were elected by French citizens only, whilst the deputies and the General Council together formed a separate electoral college to elect senators.

It was this system of electoral colleges, dividing French white residents and Africans who had acquired citizenship on the one hand, from the African masses on the other, which was most bitterly attacked by African politicians. The 1946 constitution allowed

French West Africa only thirteen seats out of 622 in the National Assembly, and although this number was later raised to twenty, it obviously made a mockery of any pretensions to equality between metropolitan and overseas Frenchmen. Yet such was the French orientation of African political life that its leaders had their eyes fixed on increasing their proportion of representation in the Assembly in Paris to build a Union Française in which black and white would be equal members of a greater France. At this stage French Africans did not identify France with 'white' as British Africans thought of Britain. Yet in the new local political scenes French African leaders were as strongly critical of the greater weight accorded to the votes of white residents as were their cousins in the British colonies.

Meanwhile, in the same 1945–6 period, British West Africa was also experiencing political stirrings. Representation in local legislative and advisory councils had a far longer history here than in the neighbouring French territories. The first direct elections of African members had occurred in 1923 in Nigeria when Lagos and Calabar elected their members to the Legislative Council. In the same year the Colony area of Sierra Leone had also elected members to its Council, and the Gold Coast followed suit two years later with elected representatives from its three municipalities. During the war Africans had also been invited into the Executive Councils, or governments, of the territories.

Although never torn by war divisions as French Africa had been, by the end of the war similar economic and social upheavals were being felt in British West Africa. High prices, the return of ex-servicemen, scarce imports, rapidly growing towns with consequent social dislocation, a boom in exports and an impact from international liberal ideas, all combined to disturb the British conception of political evolution. Moreover, the social tensions within African society, particularly in the Gold Coast and Nigeria, were generally more powerful than in the French colonies.

There was a curious dichotomy in both French and British policy towards the social stratification of African society. In certain respects the French had given their African évolués a privileged position during the inter-war period. This attitude followed naturally from the mystique of the French civilising mission. If the highest attainment for an African was to be accepted as a French citizen, then French African citizens must be treated differently from those who had not qualified for citizenship. They should not be expected to pay the same taxes, be called on for military service or subject to compulsory labour. They should be invited into cultured society and introduced into some of the professions. Meanwhile, French administrators were generally ignoring the traditional chiefs and reducing the lesser ones to the status of minor functionaries. So, whilst the educated élite in French Africa enjoyed a much higher social status than their brothers under British rule, conflict between traditional and modern politicians hardly arose. Traditionalists were inevitably strengthened under Vichy, and even the 1944 Brazzaville conference proposed to retain traditional institutions in local government, much to the annoyance of the young urban intelligentsia. The French mind was split on this issue. Its intellectual tradition was affronted by the superstitious, hierarchical, irrational systems of local African rule. It welcomed the appearance of black Frenchmen who had adopted the French cultural heritage. Yet it was frightened when these black gentlemen began to talk politics. Then it turned nostalgically towards the safe 'noble savage' idea of the African, at least until African leaders should have been absorbed into the French party system.

On the other hand, the British were deeply influenced by Lord Lugard's theory of indirect rule. The chiefs could be recognised as black squires, so much more respectful than the urban riff-raff or clerks, lawyers, teachers, journalists. So, particularly in the northern areas of Nigeria and the Gold Coast, and in the Sierra Leone Protectorate, chiefs were given imperial support and administrative power. Preservation of the social order thus became associated with continuing colonial rule. Yet an imperial policy which embraced expanding education, economic development and introducing elections, was simultaneously undermining the power of traditionalists.

When political ideas began to circulate amongst the educated, therefore, revolt took social as well as political forms. It was directed not only against the impositions of the imperial government, but also against the social system maintained by the chiefs in Northern Nigeria, the Northern Territories of the Gold Coast and Ashanti. By contrast, few educated Creoles in Sierra Leone were attracted to social rebellion, preferring to retain their own social status by insulating themselves from the 'natives' in the Protectorate. So when political reform appeared, it made little social impact, being super-imposed on Creole bourgeois traditions in the Colony and the maintenance of chiefly status in the Protectorate.

It was the significance of social revolt which was vaguely recognised at the Manchester Pan-African conference of 1945. In Britain the organisers, Kwame Nkrumah and George Padmore, were assisted and influenced by radical socialists, particularly from the Independent Labour Party. George Padmore himself had experience in the international communist movement. He had broken from it, but retained some of its socio-economic perspectives. The young coloured South African, Peter Abrahams, and Jomo Kenyatta from Kenya, who also took a prominent part in the conference, were both influenced by Marxist analytical methods without accepting the sycophancy demanded by membership of the Communist Party. With this outlook, nationalism was not enough. A transformation in society, together with some form of association between the new nations after independence had been won from the imperial powers, were the dominant themes.

This radical approach fitted the post-war situations in Nigeria and the Gold Coast. Already, ten years earlier, Nnamdi Azikiwe had returned from his studies in America to demonstrate the power of a popular press amongst the restive young educated urbanites of Accra and Lagos. Now, at least two generations of intelligentsia had returned from education abroad, many thousands of African soldiers had seen conditions in other countries, some experience had been gained in district and municipal councils, African traders wanted to make money in commerce and finance, a professional middle class had established itself. In southern Nigeria and the colony area of the Gold Coast the atmosphere was heavy with expectation of radical change. Imperial power and traditional authority were the twin bulwarks of the status quo; once the lightning of revolt flashed, it was bound to strike against them both.

Late in 1944 Governor Alan Burns started off the first rumbles by announcing that a new constitution was to be provided for the Gold Coast. In March 1945 a new constitution was published in Nigeria. The Burns constitution in the Gold Coast and the Richards constitution in Nigeria angered the intellectuals in both countries and for the same reason. In the Gold Coast twenty-five out of thirty and in

Nigeria forty-one out of forty-five members in the new Legislative Councils were to be either nominated by the colonial government or indirectly elected through institutions largely controlled by chiefs. In Nigeria, for example, members of the regional assemblies were to be nominated by the local native authorities or to be chiefs; it was proposed to use these assemblies as the electoral colleges, to elect the Legislative Council. In the Gold Coast, of the eighteen elected members of the Legislative Council nine were to be chosen by the Joint Provincial Council in the Colony and four by the Ashanti Confederacy Council, both controlled by the chiefs. The Northern Territories were not to be represented at all in the Council.

Thus both constitutions reflected the outlook and maintained the power of traditional African rulers. When the British Colonial Office later defended the Burns constitution against the allegation that it was 'outmoded' it unconsciously exposed its ignorance of the social forces now gaining influence in West Africa. It justified itself by pointing out that press, public and Legislative Councils had approved the constitution, that Africans had been members of the Executive since 1942, and that there was an unofficial majority in the Legislative Council. It thus revealed its view that so long as black men were consulted and black faces appeared on the benches liberal progress was being made. It did not occur to the Colonial Office to differentiate between Africans. The fact that it was assumed that traditional chiefs could represent the mood of their people, whilst popular politicians were written off as self-seeking agitators, shows how blind were the British colonial administrators to the social movements of this time.

West African political society in this period was divided into three sectors. Between the traditionalists and the radicals there was an older, professional group, some related to chiefly families, all established and comparatively affluent. This group was more apparent in the Gold Coast than in Nigeria, for in Nigeria social ideas were more closely linked to the tribal structure, which in its turn was reflected in the regional divisions. Yet, in a sense, the Yorubas of the Western Region reflected this middle-class approach, combining chiefs with a modern outlook and the professional classes of the towns; whilst the Ibos of the East, without chiefs, assumed a more radical standpoint.

In the Gold Coast this triple social division had a direct bearing on the political scene. The traditionalists had helped the imperial authorities to draw up the Burns constitution and were satisfied with the under-pinning of their authority which it provided. The professional middle-class group had already begun their attack on colonial rule in the thirties and now sought greater power than they were being offered. They were particularly impatient with the continued presence of an official majority in the Executive, for their main objective was to take over control of the government. The radicals, mostly less educated and less affluent, representing largely the new urban discontents, concentrated their attack on the undemocratic nature of the legislature, demanding universal suffrage and direct elections.

Thus, these latter two groups were both, for their different reasons, unsatisfied by the Burns constitution. For a short time they formed an alliance. When J. B. Danquah, the leader of the bourgeois group, brought the politically conscious members of the Council together to form the United Gold Coast Convention in 1947, he was at first supported by all those opposed to the constitution. But the stated objective of his Convention, 'to ensure that by all legitimate and constitutional means the direction and control of government should pass into the hands of the people and their chiefs', showed how limited was the change it sought. The lawyers, businessmen and aspiring politicians wanted to wrest the offices of government from the hands of the colonial officials. Their aim was to replace white ministers by black, not to change African society as it had developed under colonial rule.

At first the Nigerians seemed to be imbued with the more radical spirit of opposition. An outburst of protest against the 1945 constitution in the press and at public meetings was followed by a general strike, which, although primarily a revolt against low wages and high living costs, was quickly used in political agitation. Azikiwe formed his National Council for Nigeria and the Cameroons, an association of various protest organisations, which immediately fixed the flag of universal suffrage to its masthead. The main object of attack was the colonial government, for Azikiwe's strength lay in the towns and in Iboland. As chieftainship was unimportant or non-existent in Ibo society, whilst the very size of Nigeria kept the northern home of traditionalism distant from the immediate scene of struggle, social conflict did not play as prominent a role as in the

Gold Coast. Yet Azikiwe had a flair for mass appeal and when he organised an NCNC delegation to protest to the Colonial Secretary in London he became a national hero, at least throughout the southern half of Nigeria. His party, too, tried to organise on a national basis and at this time could fairly claim to represent the aspiration of Nigeria's modernists.

It would be an exaggeration to portray the situation in Nigeria and the Gold Coast at this time as a social revolution parallel to such examples as the French or Russian. There was considerable discontent, mainly in the new urban societies and amongst the wealthier farmers, but there was never the depth of desperation which drove the French or Russian masses to revolt. The impact of European imperial rule had been three-fold. It weakened traditional tribal rule by undermining the static nature of society; it created a new bourgeoisie of lawyers, doctors, teachers, farmers, traders; and it produced an urban petit bourgeoisie-cum-proletariat, composed of skilled workers, teachers, clerks, small merchants, journalists. These were becoming the politically conscious classes during the war. They lived beside the great mass of peasantry and the genuine urban proletariat of poorly paid, ill-fed, badly housed workers and hangers-on.

All classes had reasons for discontent in the immediate post-war years. Traditional rulers felt they were in danger of losing their authority; farmers were getting high prices for their produce but found themselves unable to buy because of the shortage of imports; the professionals felt the frustrations of discrimination as expatriates with no higher qualifications maintained their privileges; all the lower classes suffered from rising living costs arising out of inflation and from the slow provision of social improvements due to war-time shortages.

Meanwhile an increasing number of literates had acquired the means to express protest. This was voiced not only against colonial rulers but by the younger generation against traditional authorities, by workers against African exploiting employers. Protest against colonial rule came originally from the professional bourgeoisie supported by wealthy businessmen. But as most of the shops and stores were owned by Europeans or Asians, whilst the colonial government was held responsible for housing and social amenities, social and economic discontent soon led to anti-alien feelings spreading to all classes except the traditional rulers. It was stimulated by press, students, social organisations and by the rumours of events in India and other parts of Africa.

The picture was indistinct, but it certainly revealed a scene ripe for revolt. Perhaps the greatest single common factor was the crack in the aura of respect which had previously surrounded Europeans. One highly educated man in West Africa once told me of his astonishment on first seeing a white man riding a motor cycle during the war. The appearance of rough, often wild, white sailors and soldiers on African soil, together with the experience of African servicemen amongst Europeans in other countries, finally destroyed the stereotype of powerful white dignity previously portrayed by imperial administrators. It began to dawn on Africans that Europeans were men like themselves; from that moment the maintenance of imperial rule was doomed.

Some kind of change was bound to come. What form it would take depended on the outcome of two conflicts. Nationalists would certainly wage war against imperial rule. But within the nationalist camp there was another struggle between two groups for control of the nationalist movement itself. The members of these groups were usually representative of different sections in the nation, almost corresponding to the rival classes of Europe. The victors would use nationalist successes to rectify their own grievances and create the kind of society sought by their own supporters.

Turning back to French West Africa, we can see the same kind of economic factors producing similar, though not entirely identical, social and political results. Apart from sharp increases in the demand for coffee and timber, the economic effects of the war perhaps hit French Africans harder than British. The banana export trade had almost disappeared, whilst that of cocoa was halved. On the other hand, the demand for the import of capital goods greatly increased and supplies were often difficult to obtain. Education, as in the British territories, continued to develop, just about doubling the number of pupils between 1937–8 and 1948–9. Yet the total number of children at school in French West Africa remained far below that in the Gold Coast alone, with a population only about a quarter of its size.

In general, the impact of European education and economic

activity remained weaker in French West Africa than in neighbouring Nigeria and the Gold Coast. Moreover, it was much less
evenly spread. Although it was mainly in the southern areas of the
British territories that the full effects were felt, they were sufficiently
dynamic to spread progressively in the years following the war to an
only slightly lesser extent amongst the northern peoples. Yet in
French West Africa more than half the 231,666 African wage
earners were to be found in two territories; the Ivory Coast and
Senegal, as late as 1947. The huge semi-arid areas of Soudan, Niger
and Mauritania, with small, scattered populations, had scarcely any
wage workers at all. In these countries Mohammedanism had a
strong grip, though sectarianism amongst the Moslems was common.
Traditional conflict centred on hostility between 'white' nomads and
the sedentary Negroes, between the Moorish Arab and Berber conquerors, notorious as slavers, and the Negro peoples settled as subsistence producers. In all three countries the effects of the end of the
war were less far-reaching than in the more urbanised and heavily
populated territories, and chiefly authority was rarely challenged.
Nevertheless, in the Soudan, despite its deserts and scattered rural
communities, the main town, Bamako, trebled its population in the
six years following the war. This caused an increase in trade unions
and various semi-political associations which inevitably began to
challenge the authority of the chiefs. The growth of town life also
began to precipitate a social struggle along similar lines to that
appearing in the coastal towns. In the Soudan towns it was a cultivated, stable Moslem bourgeoisie which was challenged by the new
urban workers partially organised in unions.

Dahomey was a poor, over-populated territory and although its
people were comparatively well-educated and noted for their intelligence, many of them had to seek employment in Nigeria,
Togoland or the Ivory Coast. The traditions of the well-organised
kingdom of Abomey, together with the village confederations ruled
by chiefs, preserved a social structure unlikely to disintegrate easily
under post-war stresses. Here was the same division between backward north and progressive south as in Nigeria and the Gold Coast,
whilst the Catholic missions, although providing considerable
educational opportunities, threw their influence against the rise of
radical politics.

Upper Volta had been dismembered in 1932 as an administrative unit and was not re-constituted until 1947. Its territory was divided between its three neighbours, Soudan, Ivory Coast and Niger. The powerful Mossi people, led by their hereditary Moro Naba, were naturally concerned first with restoring their national pride by re-gaining national status.

The presence of bauxite, iron ore and diamonds in Guinea, together with the fact that many European planters were to be found there, presaged a social struggle. The bauxite workings were heavily mechanised, employing few African workers, which led to a suspicion that much of the money spent in the country was con-cerned only to finance European interests. The Peulh, or Fulani, chiefs in Upper Guinea had already lost much of their power, al-though supported by the French administration, and had become little more than paid officials of the colonial government. It was clear that here was a situation simmering near boiling point, but the forces of revolt were not yet sufficiently organised to make an im-mediate challenge.

It is thus in the two most developed countries of French West Africa, Senegal and Ivory Coast, that we must seek the major initiative in the post-war socio-political struggle. Senegal, through her long contacts with France, produced the most sophisticated of all French Africans. Lamine Guèye, the Moslem, and Léopold Senghor, the Catholic, both had honoured places in the French Socialist Party, living with a background of French culture. Senghor, indeed, was a poet and scholar notable in Parisian intellectual circles. Their country was poor, but had the immense asset of the port of Dakar, a city which also served as the administrative capital of all French West Africa. Educational opportunities were higher and the trade union movement was better organised than elsewhere. Because Senegal alone was allowed a single college system of elec-tions, the presence of the large white community did not unduly disturb the political situation. Indeed, the ground was well cleared for undisturbed conflict between traditional and modern authority. The chiefs still retained power in the rural areas, looking very sus-piciously at the urban évolués with their French habits and asso-ciations.

By comparison with Senegal, the Ivory Coast was wealthy. It boasted good agricultural land, diamonds, forest timber and ex-ported such quantities of coffee and cocoa as to attain a favourable balance of trade, even in dollars. Its port, Abidjan, was second only to Dakar, whilst its European planters, although sometimes described in propaganda as parasitical exploiters, made a considerable contribution to national wealth and were often elected to African-controlled councils. The chiefs formed an association as early as the time of the 1945 municipal elections in Abidjan, but they were quickly forestalled by Félix Houphouet-Boigny, who attracted the support of small African farmers and trade unionists. Much of the post-war history of Ivory Coast surrounds the personality and policies of this medical doctor, descended himself from a chief's family. It had already become clear by 1945 that he would be acting in a situation sensitive to both racial tensions and social conflicts. The economic potential was bound to provoke both social and political dissensions.

Despite this uneven progress of political consciousness in the eight constituent territories of French West Africa, common feelings between them were still strong. The federal form of administration which had existed since 1904 had brought their leading personalities into much closer contact than was the case in the British territories. When they attended the Paris constituent assembly in 1945-6, therefore, their outlook was regional as well as national. Their common feelings were greatly strengthened by the French rejection of the first constitution and the gathering strength of reaction which followed.

Thus, whilst the British African leaders had to confine themselves at this time to the somewhat vague, long-term aspirations of Pan-Africanism in Manchester, less than a year later the French Africans were taking practical measures to co-ordinate their political attack. Five of them, Houphouet-Boigny, Yacine Diallo from Guinea, F. D. Sissoko from Soudan, G. d'Arboussier of Ivory Coast, together with a representative from French Equatorial Africa, Félix Tchicaya, signed a manifesto calling for a common front in the struggle for political and social democracy in Africa. The declaration led directly to the summoning of a congress held in Bamako in October 1946 and attended by several hundred representatives of French Africa.

It was from the Bamako conference that the Rassemblement Démocratique Africain emerged, an organisation which was to become the most powerful political force in French Africa. From the start it aimed at equality for Africans within the French Union, rejecting the policy of attaining autonomous states separate from France. It concentrated its attacks on the double college system of elections, the denial of universal franchise, and all other forms of discrimination between white and black Frenchmen. It represented French West and Equatorial Africa and the trust territories of Togoland and Cameroons, creating a federal structure through which parties in each territory were affiliated to the centre.

But the RDA failed from the start to attract all political organisations to its banner. The Socialists and most of the trade unions which supported them refused to enter this united front. Senghor, Lamine Guèye and Diallo did not attend the Bamako congress, and Sissoko left the RDA soon after it had been held. Socialist policy differed from that of the RDA and the socialist leaders had been members of the French SFIO since before the war. They had suffered under Vichy and many of them had joined the resistance movement. They had built their movement on the trade unions, strongest in Senegal and Soudan, and suspected the motives of RDA leaders, some of whom were from traditionalist families. Before long, too, the Communist leanings of the RDA provoked similar antagonisms to those between the Socialist and Communist parties in France.

So Ivory Coast became the nerve centre of the RDA, with Houphouet-Boigny as leader and the Eurafrican former French official, Gabriel d'Arboussier, as secretary-general. Senegal remained the heart of socialist organisation. The two movements shared the west African seats in the 1946 National Assembly, winning six each, with the thirteenth taken by a third small group.

For two years after its formation the RDA made great strides. It established itself with considerable influence in all the territories except for Senegal and Mauritania. Even in the Niger deserts an affiliate was formed, whilst after the restoration of Upper Volta united opposition from the Mossi people and the French administration could not prevent the growth of an affiliated party. In Dahomey the southern leader, Souron Apithy, remained with the RDA until 1948, whilst, in Soudan, Mamadou Konaté carried the RDA flag against socialist Sissoko. Guinea saw the appearance of Sékou Touré, a trade union organiser, who developed his affiliated party on extreme radical lines. He was aided by reaction against a European right-wing party which took the opportunity of the double college system to secure the election of some of its members to the French Parliament and territorial council.

The sudden rise in influence of the RDA was greatly assisted by the situation in Ivory Coast. Here Houphouet was at first much helped by the sympathy of Governor Latrille, who supported the policy of the RDA and of the Communists. The African bourgeoisie was also behind Houphouet, particularly in his attacks on French planters and commercial interests. From the Ivory Coast stronghold the RDA leaders were able to build strong links with each of their federal affiliates.

Yet from the start the RDA sowed the seeds of its own destruction. In its formative years it attracted the radicals in most territories and was opposed by the traditional chiefs. Yet the fact that it was so closely woven into the political fabric of France prevented it even thinking out either a strategy or tactics relevant to African conditions. Its original policy of forming a united front for progress within a wider French Union reflected the outlook of the French Communist Party, then in the French Government and hoping for reinforcement from the African territories. When the French CP left the government in 1947, the RDA slavishly followed the new line of violent attacks against reactionary imperialism.

This rigid party line was imposed on the RDA by its secretary-general, d'Arboussier, himself a member of the French CP, and Raymond Barbé, the emissary of the party itself. They consistently led the party to oppose the chiefs, even where, as in Niger, they had virtually no one to replace them. After the withdrawal of the CP from the government, the policy laid down was that the RDA must become a mass movement, organise a united front of all progressive parties and pursue the class struggle. It is particularly significant that the Communists at this time were opposed to nationalism or separation from France. They feared that a nationalist movement would fall into the hands of the African urban bourgeoisie and thus pass out of their control.

But there was another, deeper reason for French Communist hostility towards African nationalism. Consciously or sub-consciously the CP line was dictated by the interests of European communism stemming from the needs of the Soviet Union. This is the real explanation of the failure of communism in Africa. There were undoubtedly many communists, white and black, who felt genuine sympathy for the Africans. But the party line paid no attention to the circumstances or needs of the local people. They were no more than pawns of communist strategy on the wider international board.

Thus the social struggle in French West Africa became overlaid with sloganised tactics irrelevant to the actual situations. A class struggle was waged in words against chiefs and bourgeoisie before there was any proletariat to supersede them. The peasant masses were neglected because they did not fit into the communist blue print. The campaign to transform a medieval society into a modern one was ignored in slavish adherence to a party line drawn in Europe. Behind these tactics lay the fact that French communism needed African reinforcements just as the French state needed more soldiers; so French Africa must remain part of the French Union.

Curiously, the Socialists failed for the same basic reason as the Communists. They tried to become too faithful adherents of the French socialist cause. The SFIO was doctrinally a Marxist party and rigid Marxism is irrelevant to African conditions. Thus, although for a time Lamine Guèye built on the reputation he gained as the author of the 1946 law conferring equal citizenship on the inhabitants of the overseas territories, and was to win equal conditions for African officials in 1950, the pragmatists soon began to leave the movement. In 1948 Senghor broke with Guèye and the SFIO to form his own party in Senegal and a loose parliamentary group known as Indé-pendants d'Outre Mer. Senghor saw that the French political outlook and the form of French organisations did not meet African condi-tions. He thus set out to draw into his party tribal and traditional associations, whilst widening the appeal of his trade unions to include peasants and small farmers. He based his socialist economic policy on the development of co-operatives. And he took the lead in pro-claiming the importance of a genuine African culture in contrast to the general acceptance of assimilation into French civilisation.

Meanwhile Communist domination was threatening to destroy the RDA. Outside the Ivory Coast reaction against the party line was widespread, resignations multiplied and popular support evapo-rated. French administrators took active measures against the party, as, for instance, when many of its members were gaoled during the 1948 Upper Volta elections.

The real showdown was to come in Ivory Coast itself. Governor Latrille had been replaced by an anti-RDA administration which began to take repressive measures against members of the party. Some members of the RDA had themselves begun to use intimidation against their opponents. There were resignations from the party and new parties were formed. Houphouet saw the danger and broke with d'Arboussier but not before violence had broken out during 1949. The tension continued and from early in 1950 strikes and boycotts of European goods spread rapidly. Troops were sent from Senegal, arrests were made, and twenty-one members of the RDA given sentences of imprisonment.

In the elections of the same year the RDA lost half its seats in the Senate. Houphouet was finally convinced. He broke with the Communists, and reversed his policy, turning to collaboration with the French Government, the administration in the Ivory Coast, and the local Europeans. His prestige inevitably suffered for a time, but he had rid himself of the communist shackles which were destroying his influence in Africa. After abortive negotiations with Indépendants d'Outre Mer, Houphouet took his RDA into association with M. Pléven's party and supported his government in Paris. The CP was left with few remnants. Some trade union leaders, students, study groups, remained loyal to it. But its inability to understand African conditions or to use its imagination in Africa, had killed it as a major influence. Its failure to utilise the Ivory Coast disturbances of 1949 and 1950 – for it had no organised group capable of doing so and no battlecries meaningful to the African masses – exposed it as incapable of seizing opportunities to practise its own theories.

The only country in which French communism retained any important influence was the Cameroons. Unlike the British, France had administered her two trust territories, Togoland and the Cameroons, as separate from her colonies. Whereas Britain linked the administration in her parts of Togoland and Cameroons to Ghana and Nigeria, the French regarded them as individual territories, not even part of their West African Federation. Both had shared in the 1946 constitutional advances of the French Union, sending members to the French parliamentary institutions and electing their own territorial assemblies. Interference in the elections by the French administration kept the strong Ewe unity movement out of power in Togoland, ensuring that parties favourable to close association with France were elected. But as a trust territory there was always the opportunity of petitioning at the United Nations,

an opportunity which Sylvanus Olympio, leader of the Ewe movement, used to maximum political effect.

In the Cameroons, however, the RDA affiliate, led by Um
Nyobe, became the strongest political force. It was one of the more
extreme branches of the RDA and Nyobe knew how to appeal to
tribal and religious elements as well as taking a modern political
approach. He found most of his support in the south, particularly in
the two main towns, Douala and Yaounde. And he had no intention
of following Houphouet and the moderates when they broke with
the Communists. He and his party remained affiliated to the French
CP, a decision which was to affect the future of many people in the
Cameroons within a short time.

French West Africa now had to look more to its own resources,
determine its own policies, and detach itself from the embrace of
French politics. The first five years after the war had forced the
pace of political organisation to meet the new electoral system,
whilst raising social and economic issues previously hidden. These
problems were specifically African; they would need African
solutions.

Whilst French West Africans were tentatively trying out their
political wings, gathering a strength they were still doubtful how to
apply, African leaders in British territories were acting more decisively. Here the political issue was not clouded by thoughts of
integration into an alien society. From 1945 the attack was deliberately directed along nationalist lines, with independent statehood as
the clear objective. To the extent that traditional authorities and the
colonial administration, either separately or in collaboration, obstructed this aim, they would be declared enemies.

Agitation in British Africa was always concentrated on constitu-
tion-making. This rose to fever pitch in the years immediately after
the war. Not only had the Burns constitution raised a furore in
Ghana and the Richards in Nigeria, but even the smaller territories,
Sierra Leone and Gambia, were affected. As a matter of fact, the
spirit of liberalism emanating from the war even lightly brushed the
face of Liberia, for long an embarrassment to African nationalists
and the example quoted by white racialists when warning of the
horrors attendant on African self-rule. President Tubman, elected
in 1943, was at this time extending the vote, though retaining his

strict control over its use, reforming the legal system, and trying to bring the hinterland peoples into public life. A strike of workers on the Firestone rubber plantations in 1947, though illegal, proved that in even this backward country some of the population were sensing the mood of revolt.

In Sierra Leone progress towards more representative government was hindered by the antagonism between Creole society around Freetown and the tribal Africans of the interior. The Governor, Sir Hubert Stevenson, met with Creole opposition when he proposed to introduce a constitution which would more nearly reflect the much larger numbers of people living in the Protectorate. By 1948 there were more unofficials than officials in the Legislative Council, but those from the hinterland were nominated. Under the new constitution, which came into operation in 1951, seven members were to be elected in the Colony by direct elections on property and literacy qualifications, and fourteen were to be indirectly elected from the Protectorate. The Executive was to be equally balanced between officials and unofficials. Sierra Leone had not yet envisaged a social struggle. It was left to the battle between the self-conscious, privileged bourgeoisie of closed Creole society, and the traditionalists of the interior, anxious to participate in the modern form of politics whilst retaining its own hierarchical social structure.

There were certain similarities with this situation in the Gambia, that geographically ridiculous territory carved out of Senegal, fourteen miles wide along 300 miles of river. The Protectorate was again ruled by chiefs, whilst the colony area on the coast knew something of modern life in the town of Bathurst. Political tensions were not so high here, and a new constitution in 1947 produced the first elected members to the Legislative Council from Bathurst, together with a number of nominated unofficial members. These unofficial members, including the elected members, were also to serve in the Executive. But the real issue in the Gambia was clearly to be whether it should join Senegal, particularly when the failure of the British egg scheme and of an ilmenite mine exposed its economic weakness. At this time the Protectorate chiefs feared that incorporation would undermine their traditional authority, whilst public opinion in the Colony was opposed to surrendering control over its own affairs.

It was, of course, in Nigeria and the Gold Coast that the decisive events occurred which were to determine the future of West Africa. After Nigeria's immediate post-war agitation against the Richards constitution, the country had to slow down its pace for a time. The size of its population, over thirty million, the divisive effect of tribalism, the comparative paucity of its évolués and the lack of communication between its centres, all combined to prevent revolt taking a national form.

Yet the effects of the early agitation against traditional authority and colonial rule were not negligible. As in the Ivory Coast, a change in administration altered the political climate, although here in a reverse direction. When Sir John Macpherson succeeded Sir Arthur Richards as Governor, a new breath of progress swept in. The Colonial Office insisted that the Richards constitution must be given a chance of proving itself, but Macpherson announced that he would consult all representative Nigerians regarding its ultimate revision. From 1949 onwards, regional, provincial and village conferences were held throughout the country to discuss the next stage in constitutional progress. In 1950 a national conference was called to consider recommendations from the local discussions. It had become clear that policy would now evolve through increasingly representative government until self-government and independence were attained. Chief Awolowo, the Yoruba leader and a former cocoa farmer, showed his appreciation of this situation by returning from his London legal studies in 1951 to found the Action Group in Western Nigeria.

Macpherson's reforms inevitably retarded the growth of radicalism. Nationalists were now brought into consultation by the government, whilst new opportunities were opened to the educated in the civil service, local government and the professions. Azikiwe used his membership of the Legislative Council and his newspapers to continue his attacks on traditionalist power and the colonial system. But he had now realised that the forces ranged against him were so deeply entrenched that he would have to concentrate first on his own Ibo region in the East. He therefore based his main attack on a demand for a federal system which would enable him to circumvent the established traditionalists who had proved too strong for frontal assault. Meanwhile, all Nigeria looked to constitutional reform providing the next springboard for advance.

It was in the Gold Coast that the double revolution against

traditionalism and colonialism had its best opportunity. Here was a country small enough for a single-minded political party to envisage mass organisation, wealthy enough to have evolved a considerable bourgeoisie, and with a sufficiently advanced economy to have produced enough modernists to challenge the power of traditional authorities. It needed only the right men with clear political vision to take advantage of a situation in which revolution could be mounted with a strength capable both of expelling colonial rulers and overthrowing traditional authority.

The revolutionary period opened on December 16, 1947, when Kwame Nkrumah arrived home from Britain. He had been invited to return and become Secretary of Danquah's United Gold Coast Convention. His education in America and Britain, in addition to his contacts with socialist political groups, had given him a grounding in political strategy which was to prove the decisive influence in Gold Coast history. Until his arrival political agitation had been largely confined to efforts by the professional and commercial bourgeoisie to get rid of colonial rule and replace it by their own. Nkrumah was to lead a political revolution based on profound social change.

The new Secretary immediately threw himself into an organising drive to recruit members and form branches of the party amongst the masses. This attitude soon began to make some of the respectable, well-established leaders uneasy. Nkrumah's central political tactic was to use every grievance to point the political moral and seize political advantage. Thus a month's boycott was organised against the high prices charged by European and Syrian traders during the period of post-war shortages. Campaigns were waged over the swollen shoot trouble amongst the cocoa farmers. The ex-servicemen organised protest demonstrations against their treatment on returning home. It was a combination of the boycott and the ex-servicemen's demonstration which in 1948 led to riots in Accra followed by looting, shootings and deaths. The protests spread to other towns and in the end twenty-nine people had lost their lives whilst 237 suffered injuries. Inevitably the Governor, Sir Gerald Creasy, blamed the UGCC, the only serious party, for these disorders whose scale shocked both West Africa and Britain. Its leaders were described as 'communists' and 'agitators', although such terms were in fact a ludicrous parody of the actual nature of almost all those respectable gentlemen. Six of them, including both Danquah and Nkrumah, were arrested and banished to the Northern Territories, though they did not stay there for long.

In order to investigate these violent disorders the British Government appointed a Commission of Enquiry under the chairmanship of Mr Aiken Watson, a barrister. The commission quickly discovered that there was more beneath the unrest than wanton agitation. It found the constitution to be 'outmoded' even before it came into operation and recommended that a new one should be drafted by Africans themselves. The Watson Commission thus independently justified Nkrumah's first tenet. Government must become more representative of the people. A British commission could hardly be expected to recognise his second conviction, that radical change was needed in the social composition of government. When the Governor came to appoint the members of the Coussey Committee, an all-African body under an African judge, he chose conservative members of the UGCC like Grant and Danquah, ignoring Nkrumah.

By now relations between the conservative and radical wings of the party were becoming strained. A Committee of Youth Organisations provided the medium for radical pressure and was sufficiently powerful inside the party to repulse the attempt to dismiss Nkrumah from the secretaryship. The CYO, dissatisfied with cautious, bourgeois leadership, then decided to hold a special conference at Tarkwa in June 1949, and it was here that the Convention Peoples' Party was founded. A few weeks later it gained a mouthpiece from the establishment of the Accra *Evening News*.

The conservative leadership was now in an impossible dilemma. It recognised that the CPP was liable to seduce the young active members away from the UGCC, but dare not submit to democratic control in the knowledge that it would be voted out of office. After abortive attempts at arbitration and mediation, the UGCC went its own way as a bourgeois reformist party, whilst the CPP, backed by the trade unions, set out to organise the masses, particularly the young, semi-literate urban workers, to provide the driving force of national and social revolution. It hoped too that its appeal would extend to Ashanti and the Northern Territories as well as to the coastal Colony, for it laid stress from the start on the need for unity throughout the country. In this effort, especially, it was bound to come up against the traditional authorities, natural allies of the colonial régime so long as it maintained its power and of the bourgeoisie as soon as imperialism weakened.

The CPP was soon presented with a focus for its activities. In October 1949 the Coussey Committee reported, recommending a new Legislative Assembly of eighty-four members, only five of whom would be directly elected. The rest were to be elected through electoral colleges and Chieftainship Councils, with minor representation for business interests. In the Executive it was proposed that there should be an absolute African majority, but expected that this would be drawn from a variety of groups in the Assembly. The Colonial Secretary in London specifically objected to the proposal for a Leader of the House, who would be almost a Prime Minister, considering that it was too early to expect a party system to emerge. He also vetoed the proposal for a Senate on the grounds that it would isolate too many able men. The Colonial Office was still thinking in terms of rule mainly by chiefs and the professional class.

Nkrumah immediately condemned the Coussey proposals. He described them as 'bogus and fraudulent'. Supported by the TUC, the party held a massive Representative Assembly in November, 1949, attended by a multitude of small organisations from all over the country. The Coussey report was rejected; in its place a demand was made for immediate self-government, Dominion status within the Commonwealth, and a Constituent Assembly to draw up a new constitution. In particular, the attack was focused on the undemocratic nature of indirect elections and the continued presence of three colonial officials in the Executive. Here was the first, pragmatic platform on which the CPP would canvass national support. It attacked both enemies simultaneously. Traditional authority was shown to be holding on to its power through the electoral college system of elections in defiance of democratic demands. The imperial government was held to be offering a superficially representative system whilst retaining the realities of power through its Governor and officials.

Naturally the Chiefs refused to support this party programme, and the new Governor, Sir Charles Arden-Clarke, rejected the demands. The party then prepared to apply the Gandhian method of non-violent resistance, which Nkrumah had christened 'Positive Action'. The government began to prosecute editors of the CPP journals for sedition, but the party pressed on with its preparations to begin open defiance, reinforced by a general strike at midnight on January 8, 1950. So the Governor moved decisively, declared a State of Emergency, muzzled the press and imprisoned most of the CPP leaders, including Nkrumah himself.

The State of Emergency could not last indefinitely. It was lifted in March and immediately those party officials still out of gaol, led by Komla Gbedemah, who had completed his sentence, renewed their organisational methods. It is a remarkable testimony to Nkrumah's hold over the party and to the loyalty of his lieutenants that no attempt was made to supplant him during his imprisonment. Nkrumah still directed the campaign from inside prison and his directives were faithfully carried out.

By now the CPP had gained the enthusiastic support of almost all the urban areas and was making progress in the countryside. It gained all seven seats in the Accra Town Council in April, won by-elections in the Cape Coast, and proceeded to take all the seats in the Kumasi elections in November.

The UGCC and the chiefs with whom they had now made common cause then made one last attempt to salvage their leadership. In December 1950, at a conference in Kumasi, they appealed for a national front to submit candidates for the general election due to be held under the Coussey Constitution early in 1951. The plea was rejected by the young radicals. The CPP prepared to fight the elections as a disciplined party. To its own delighted surprise in the elections of February 8, 1951, its candidates won thirty-four of the thirty-eight seats in the Colony and Ashanti elected either directly or through the electoral colleges. Though thirty-seven other members were elected through the Chieftainship Councils or from the Northern Territories, they could clearly not compete in cohesion with the solid bloc of CPP members. Despite all the fears about the undemocratic constitution, it had produced the basis of a party government. And that party was radical, anti-traditionalist, anti-colonial, based on mass support. Ghana had taken the first decisive step into the modern world of representative government, national sovereignty and individual socio-economic rights.

This achievement in Ghana provides a watershed in African history. From this moment a new horizon could be envisaged. No longer was African destiny seen in terms of preserving traditional forms under different supervision. The significance of the Ghana achievement was that it offered the prospect to Africans of entering the technical, scientific, individualistic world already created in Europe, North America and some parts of Asia. Whilst efforts would be made to preserve those features of traditional African life regarded as valuable, this would only be possible if they could be integrated into modernistic progress. Above all, the legitimacy of government was boldly declared to depend on the will of the people, a direct challenge to traditional authority and imperial rule alike. The traditionalist mask of Africa was cracked; henceforth the Ghana example would provide an inspiration to Africans unwilling to accept the old forms of society in every corner of the continent.

4

The Southern Oligarchies

In post-war Africa militant black nationalism on the west coast was counter-balanced by powerful white autocracies in the south. In South and South-west Africa, in Portuguese Angola and Mozambique, and to some extent in Southern Rhodesia, Bechuanaland, Basutoland and Swaziland, the white ruling class looked askance at the anti-colonial revolutions in the north, sternly resolving to prevent any such challenge to their own authority.

The motives prompting this southern resistance to developments in the rest of the continent varied. The only genuine white nationalism in southern Africa was that of the Afrikaner community in South Africa. Some of the white inhabitants in the three British High Commission Territories hankered after association with it. The Portuguese who settled in Angola and Mozambique remained attached to Portugal, trusting in the permanency of the Portuguese colonial empire. In Southern Rhodesia, and to an only slightly lesser degree in Northern Rhodesia, the white hope was to remain British but also to create their own nation. This ambition was for many years maintained also by English-speaking South Africans. So, apart from the Afrikaners, the justification for white domination was based on expediency rather than on ideology.

But it was Afrikaner nationalism which formed the heart of this white resistance, pumping out strength to the outer links through arteries of Afrikaner immigrants and never fearing to proclaim its philosophy of white supremacy as an inspiration to weaker brethren.

The Afrikaner community was a peculiar amalgam of Dutch, French and German elements. Its varied national units were linked first by a common puritanism, Calvinist and Lutheran, then by remoteness from their European derivation, finally by deliberate severance of all ties with the rest of the world. During the formative years of the Afrikaner nation, the eighteenth and nineteenth centuries, its citizens were several months distant from Europe. Those who joined them from European countries were usually the victims of religious persecution. Consequently, the progress of European intellectual life either passed them by or was deliberately rejected. They became an introverted community, developing a strong persecution mania, compensating for their isolation by a constant self-assurance of their unique rectitude.

All these traits were strengthened by the circumstances in which the community found itself. Established as a tiny refreshment station for Dutch ships calling at the Cape in the mid-seventeenth century, the settlement gradually spread outwards until it marched with the lands inhabited by African tribes which had been simultaneously moving south-westwards. They thus quickly visualised themselves as a tiny Christian community defending the sanctity of the Word against rapacious pagan hordes.

To this hostile experience with Africans was added relations with coloured peoples within the community itself. The first Dutch settlers met only a few Hottentots and Bushmen in the Cape. Some of these were early absorbed into the settlement. They were joined by slaves from the East Indies brought by returning Dutch ships. From 1717 onwards it became the declared policy of the Dutch East India Company to develop the settlement on a basis of white masters and slave workers. Christianity, wealth and masterhood became identified on the white side of the colour line; paganism, poverty and slavery on the black.

Having developed this tight frontier community on strict caste lines, the Afrikaners found their social dogma assailed by the arrival of the British early in the nineteenth century. Affronted by the new ideas imported from Europe and unwilling to consider any alternative beliefs to their own revealed truths, they characteristically fled from the contact with stronger intellects. They found new homes in the Orange Free State and the Transvaal where they could transplant the roots of their traditional creed remote from the danger of further interference.

But the effects of continuous warfare with African tribes and the accident of gold discoveries soon destroyed the isolation. Again they were pursued and infiltrated by Britishers. This time they could not flee. The realities of modern life had begun to catch up with them.

Culminating in the Boer War, the blood spilt in conflicts with Britain deepened Afrikaner conviction of their messianic purpose. They eagerly accepted the evangelical opportunity offered by union with British-oriented Cape Colony and Natal in 1910, seizing the chance to expand Afrikaner nationalism over the whole of South Africa. Britishers within all four provinces were tolerated only in so far as they accepted the tenets of Afrikanerdom. Those from within the Afrikaner community who tried to build a united white nation were constantly harried and derided as traitors. Those who toyed with the liberal ideas growing in the outside world were virtually excommunicated.

In the mind of the true Afrikaner there was constantly fixed a picture of the past ideal society drawn from the stories of the Voortrekkers. A patriarchal family clan gathered around the head of the house as he read from a leather-covered family Bible at eventide; no smoke to be seen on the horizon, ensuring solitude from the nearest neighbour; native farm workers out of sight in the mud shanties neither civilised nor Christian; the black hordes far away in their reserves, but still threatening God's people, and so to be chastened from time to time; Coloureds banished from mind, Indians about to be sent back to India; towns still rural burghs, dominated by the kerk; Britishers packing their bags, leaving God's own land and the creatures therein to be ordered by His Chosen People.

All this was, of course, a fantasy. Nevertheless, it is important to recognise the fantasy ideal within many Afrikaner minds to understand events in South Africa.

In fact, South African life had radically changed during the twentieth century. Afrikaner farms still existed on the high veld, but more and more of their children now took the reverse trek, from farms to the new towns. A gradual industrial revolution was adding secondary industries to the gold and diamond mining which had first disturbed Afrikaner peace. Modern cities, Johannesburg, Cape Town, Port Elizabeth, Durban, had replaced the sleepy old burghs. They were developing large industrial conurbations, increasingly dependent on African and Coloured labour. Nor did industry regiment its labour in the mining tradition. Thus the new industrial non-European masses, whose numbers were now overtaking those of urban Europeans, had begun to live individual and family lives in townships adjacent to the cities. They were becoming permanent urban inhabitants in contrast to the migratory labour which served the mines for fixed periods under semi-military conditions and then returned to the reserves. It was the new industrial life, added to the mineral wealth, which created the modern Southern African economy. It incidentally subsidised low-efficiency farming and thus made it possible to retain a measure of traditional Afrikaner life without compelling agricultural revolution.

The South African industrial revolution followed the traditional course in its basic elements, but the special social characteristics of the country diverted its tide into particular channels. Thus, there was the normal flow of people from the rural into the urban areas and a growth of skilled, semi-skilled and unskilled classes. Class conflicts were provoked and industrial organisations established amongst employers and workers. Similarly, urban slums mushroomed with the inevitable consequences of disease, social difficulties and discontent.

Yet, because of the colour caste structure of South African life, the effects of the industrial revolution were more contrived and less haphazard than elsewhere. The employers and the skilled workers were virtually all drawn from the white community. The unskilled were almost entirely black. For a time the semi-skilled was the most mixed class, European, Coloured and African. But political action soon intervened to prevent whites, whatever their capabilities, having to be content with semi-skilled or unskilled employment. Where competition threatened the 'poor white' was cushioned against his misfortune or inability at the price of down-grading competitive non-whites or up-grading inefficient whites. Similarly, poverty and poor social conditions were artificially confined to the non-Europeans. There were, of course, certain exceptions to this general rule. A handful of successful Indian traders became very wealthy, a small class of professionals managed to break through the disabilities in each racial group, whilst the Coloureds were given a privileged position compared with Africans in the Cape. But these exceptions only threw into greater relief the general colour line operating throughout the country.

The result of this political guidance of the industrial revolution was a unique distortion of the classical pattern of social progress. Thus, white employers and white workers fought each other over wages and conditions of work. But there was little co-operation in the social struggle between white and coloured workers. Instead, the non-whites found the European artisans to be their most bitter opponents when they sought advance, for they were seen to be their first competitors whenever promotion was contemplated. Sometimes the employers exploited this division within labour; at others, they tried to overcome the artificial barrier to the training and promotion of non-whites, recognising the unprofitable waste and inefficiency of the system. Yet political considerations always took precedence over economic needs.

Meanwhile the industrial revolution was never accompanied, as in most other countries, by a parallel revolution in agriculture. The small proportion of land reserved for African occupation became increasingly eroded and remained under the most primitive forms of cultivation; white farming continued its inefficient way, cushioned by subsidies provided from industrial earnings. For any substantial change in rural life could only be effected by shaking Afrikaner farmers out of their anachronistic outlook and investing large capital in a modernisation of the reserves. Both these measures would have severely undermined the social conventions of South African white society.

So, at the outbreak of the war, South African society was more complicated in its social divisions than perhaps any other society in the world. There were two distinct employer classes, the urban financiers, industrialists and mine-owners, and the rural farmers, with little in common. The white artisans formed a working class when faced by employers, but were usually employers of African servants themselves and the most intransigent opponents of non-white labour advance. They really formed a labour aristocracy. There were four distinct middle classes, white, Coloured, Indian and African, with virtually no links, although some slight contact between the professional elements. And finally, a huge mass of African miners, industrial workers, servants, farm labourers and subsistence tribal peasants formed the proletariat, with additions of smaller Coloured and Indian communities. But this class was also fragmented, lacking any cohesive purpose theoretically, emotionally, or practically.

Events during the thirties had made possible a greater degree of collaboration between Afrikaner and British sections of the ruling class than at any time since just after the Union. The international financial crisis had forced a coalition government between Hertzog, leader of the Afrikaner Nationalists, and Smuts, whose party represented the British community, finance, business, and the broader-minded section of Afrikaners. As the price of following the Smuts line on economics, Hertzog had extracted his rival's support for removing Africans from the Cape electoral roll, for taking new powers to expel as many as possible from the towns, and for making a new land settlement offering larger reserves.

The outbreak of war shattered the coalition and with it the Afrikaner-British alliance. For, whilst Smuts was determined that South Africa should join Britain and France, Hertzog declared for neutrality. Smuts secured a small majority, becoming Prime Minister, whilst Hertzog joined Malan in a reunited Nationalist opposition. The truce between the two Nationalists did not last long. Before his death in 1942 Hertzog and Havenga had broken with Malan to form the Afrikaner Party. By the end of the war Malan and Havenga were uneasily co-operating against Smuts.

The impact of the war years aggravated every major South African problem. The activities against the war effort of secret and semi-secret Afrikaner Nationalist organisations, such as the Ossewa-brandwag, the Broederbond, the Grey-shirts, and the Reddingsdaadbond, together with Nazi propaganda published by Dr Verwoerd in *Die Transvaaler*, deepened the cleavage between British South Africans and the Nationalist section of Afrikaners. The Pegging Act of 1943, designed to prevent any extension of Indian trading opportunities in the Transvaal or land purchase in Natal, antagonised the quarter of a million Indian inhabitants. The establishment in the same year of a Coloured Advisory Department inflamed political opinion amongst the million or so Cape Coloureds, frightened that this was a first instalment of legislative segregation for their community.

Yet, more profoundly significant even than this aggravation of antagonisms, was the effect of the war on national economy. At first sight it might be seen to have prospered as a result of war stimulation. The national external debt had been entirely repatriated, gold production ensured the security of imports, and both heavy and secondary industries had been expanded to meet war needs. Yet, on the other hand, this very expansion demanded new skilled workers which the colour bar denied; inflation hit the poorer sections, particularly the Africans, desperately hard; there was a chronic shortage of houses and other social amenities; transport had been starved of supplies; and agriculture still stagnated, remaining incapable of supplying the food needs of the population. South Africa was a poor country, despite the high standard of white living. The eight million Africans lived on an average of £10 a year; the million Coloureds on £25; even the £125 of the two and a half million whites only brought the national average up to about £36.

Above all, the major effect of the war had been to stimulate the flow from the country to town. During the ten years between 1936 and 1946 the population of Johannesburg had grown from 519,384 to 727,943, of Cape Town from 344,223 to 454,052, of Germiston from 79,440 to 128,971, of Pretoria from 128,621 to 236,367. And the Africans were moving into the towns in larger proportions than Europeans. During the same period the increase in the urban African population was 57·16 per cent compared with the European figure of 31·51. Nearly two million Africans were now living in towns and their numbers were increasing by over five per cent each year. Moreover, there had been a considerable increase in the Africans now living in European rural areas, leaving less than forty per cent of the African population in the reserves. As many of these were periodically absent on the mines, a great deal of the work on African farms was now left to women, children and old men. It had become clear that the reserves could only support a small fraction of the African community and then on no more than a meagre subsistence standard.

In short, the effect of the war had been to speed the pre-war process of forcing a large section of the African population into the European economy. Mines, industry and farms needed ever more African labour. Many Africans could only keep themselves alive by working outside their reserves. Large numbers of them were now detribalised, permanent town dwellers. Hard economic facts were making nonsense of the traditional South African ideology that European and African life should be kept separate.

It was this sharp dichotomy between economics and ideology which faced post-war South Africa with her deepest dilemma. Nor had she the machinery likely to discover reconciliation through discussion or compromise. The white community had a form of parliamentary democracy which allowed them to elect their representatives to the Assembly and Senate. There was considerable weighting of constituencies in favour of the rural, mainly Afrikaner, population. A number of prominent Nationalists had also been strongly critical of the democratic system during the war, declaring it to be alien to Afrikaner principles. Nevertheless, the parliamentary form was well rooted and provided the white community with an adequate forum in which to settle their differences by debate.

But if the whites were governed according to parliamentary norms, the rest of the population was subject to autocratic rule. At the time of Union each province retained its own method of non-European representation, which left those Africans and Coloureds who could qualify on the Cape voters' roll, but offered no direct representation to non-Europeans in Natal, Transvaal or the Orange Free State. In 1936 the Africans had been removed from the Cape roll and given three separate white members as compensation. Four white senators were indirectly elected by Africans from all over the country. Indians had neither parliamentary votes nor representation. So at the end of the war the 8 million Africans were represented by three of the 153 members of the Assembly and four of the forty-four senators, and all members of both houses were white. Even the Coloureds who remained on the electoral roll in the Cape were allowed only male franchise and had to fulfil qualifications to claim it.

The non-Europeans of South Africa had become colonial subjects of their white rulers. The main difference between the South African situation and colonial rule was that the South African government represented the white population of the country itself, instead of the comparatively detached electorate of an imperial power. Moreover, South African governments had few or none of the contacts with their colonial subjects which had been established in most colonies. The white and non-white communities resembled two hostile camps rather than sections of the same nation. As compensation for the removal of Africans from the Cape electoral roll in 1936, a Native Representative Council had been established, but it never had more than advisory powers, was representative of very little, and eventually adjourned itself *sine die* because of the government's lack of consultation. There were also non-European political organisations, the African National Congress, formed in

1912, the All-African Convention, a young body created to fight
the 1936 bills, the African Peoples' Organisation, which represented
the Coloureds, and the Indian Congresses. But by the time the war
broke out there was practically no communication between any
of them and the government. South African problems were destined
to be met by rival, hostile sections of the population with virtually
no common language.

These were the elements of the South African dilemma; but how
did the people involved feel about them?

The Afrikaners were in a peculiar difficulty which affected the
minority emancipated from isolated puritanism as well as the
traditional dogmatists. Partly because they were originally largely
composed of fugitives, and partly because of their isolation, almost
all ties with the countries of their origin had been severed. They had
become a separate, distinctive national community. There was no
other home to which they could return if threatened. Yet they
numbered less than two million in a country where nearly ten
million other peoples lived. Integration with these others, black,
brown or white, would have sunk their national identity, whilst
generations of conditioning caused them to reject with revulsion
any thought of even considering thus broadening their national
community. The choice seemed to them to be either mastery or
extinction. Many of them, whilst terrified of the black hordes they
had been taught to believe were awaiting the opportunity to ravish
them, nevertheless had a kindly affection for their own African or
Coloured servants. The few more intelligent Afrikaners, especially
in Stellenbosch University, recognised both the profound colour
prejudice of their fellows and the justice of African claims. They
met the dilemma by proposing complete separation of the races,
with full governmental powers for both communities. They faced
up to the need implied in this solution to provide land and capital
from white resources if the black states were to have any chance of
becoming viable, and openly told their fellow whites that they
would have to learn to do without black labour.

But overshadowing the kindliness, godliness and national pride of
the Afrikaners lay an overwhelming sense of fear. The community
felt beleaguered by millions of Africans in its own country and the
countless further millions in the rest of the continent. It was to this
underlying sense of terror that most of its religious and political

leaders appealed. The need for racial mastery, 'baaskap', was a demagogic cry which drowned nobler feelings and could be substituted for facing the harsh problems of social realism.

The English-speaking or British section of the European population were frankly less interested in politics than in profit. They lived in the country mainly because it provided them with a more comfortable and wealthy life than they could find in Britain. There were large profits to be made in mining, industry and commerce, whilst in the professions real incomes were higher, competition less and social comforts more plentiful. Although they were not normally ideological racialists like the Afrikaners, they found it benefited them materially to maintain colour bars with the same rigidity. They took a similar kind of attitude as the white settlers of Southern Rhodesia and Kenya, justifying their colour prejudices on the grounds of African backwardness, the maintenance of white standards of life, or the defence of western civilization. In Natal, where they came into contact with wealthy, educated Indians as well as the African and Asian masses, a special type of colour reaction developed. It had little ideological content, but was as fanatical in its determination to use political power to suppress social competition from the Indian community as anything in Afrikaner nationalism.

Yet the British South Africans found that, although the profits and comfort continued, social peace continually diminished. Life in cities like Johannesburg and Durban, where large numbers of Britishers were concentrated, was ever more disturbed by the violent reactions within a society based on racial discrimination. Locks on doors, bars on windows, burglar alarms were constantly being reinforced. Firearms became accepted domestic necessities and housewives took target practice in the gardens. Moreover, while legislation was always racially discriminatory, the Britishers learnt by experience that restrictions on liberty tend to cross all barriers. The executive powers taken by governments to suppress non-European opposition to white domination inevitably began to restrict the personal freedom of whites as well as non-whites. Many Britishers shut their eyes and increased the number of their bridge parties, but they found that they had to shut their eyes with increasing frequency. And always the British South African felt that if conditions became intolerable he had a second home awaiting him in Britain.

Yet, despite the feverishness of European life, there were always men and women within both the Afrikaner and British communities who fought against the tide of public opinion. Liberal-minded Europeans were more numerous in South Africa than anywhere else in the continent. They varied from those who sympathised with communists or Marxist doctrine, to democratic socialists, liberals and conservative industrialists with unquiet consciences. They were to be found in all walks of life, but especially in the professions. Their iconoclastic life tended to be uneasy, and many of them felt it necessary to leave the country, either for the sake of their own peace of mind or for that of their families. The plight of the Afrikaner liberal was particularly harsh, for not only was he victimised more severely than his British counterpart, but he had no other home country in which to find asylum. Yet it was William Schreiner who led the opposition to the discriminatory implications of the act of Union in 1909, and he has had liberal successors within the Afrikaner community ever since.

In the Indian community the gulf between the two social extremes was wider than anywhere else in South African society. A handful were very rich, living lives of luxury, although subject to racial restrictions. The masses lived in the same degraded conditions as Africans, in urban slums or farm shanties. A considerable middle class included both professionals and traders. Jealousy between Indian and African was common, for the Indian traders were often suspected of exorbitant prices, many Africans were in debt to Indian money-lenders and there was some sexual hostility between the two communities. This tension became particularly marked soon after the war, especially in the Durban area, and was aggravated by Afrikaner nationalist propaganda amongst Africans against the Indians.

Probably politically conscious Indians, mainly within the professional group, felt discrimination more keenly than any other race. Not only was their pride in their ancient civilisation affronted when comparatively uncultured whites treated them as lower grade citizens, but they lived under the constant threat of expulsion from the country in which most of them had been born and reared. For the Afrikaners and many Britishers considered that they had no right to remain in South Africa and devised various schemes for their repatriation to India. Alone amongst the racial groups of the country they were denied the right of any kind of participation in the election to parliament. Many wealthy Indians were content to buy their comfort at the price of occasional insults. The masses thought more about employment, wages and houses than about politics. But the educated, sensitive Indian felt a deep humiliation which grew into bitter resentment.

In some ways the Cape Coloured community was in the most tragic situation. Its members varied in appearance from the near-African to those who could pass for white. They were the product of sexual mixing over three centuries, living proof that by no means all South African whites were averse to cohabitation with non-whites. Often brothers and sisters were of such varied hues that they had to go to different schools and keep separate company. For a long time the white community had somewhat shamefacedly accepted the Coloureds as poor relations, never to be treated as equals, but an unfortunate off-shoot entitled to limited rights. Their best-known leader, Dr Abdullah Abdurahman, was often consulted by Smuts and reciprocated by persuading those of his people who had the vote to cast it for Smuts' party.

Yet the Coloured community had no horizon, no future hopes. Some of them had attained social respectability as skilled artisans, a number were professionals serving their own community, the majority remained unskilled slum dwellers. All were rejected by white and black alike. Whoever eventually won the racial battle, the Coloureds were doomed to ostracism. This hopelessness drowned the younger generation increasingly into an introspective factionalism and during the war fragmentation of their political efforts increased. Some sought to maintain tenuous links with the European world, others tried to stake out a separate Coloured identity, yet others attempted to associate with Africans in a common non-European front. Many of the younger Coloureds saw their only chance of future happiness in emigration.

Finally, can we attempt to comprehend the feelings of Africans? Whatever degree of homogeneity existed amongst other racial groups, there was certainly none among Africans. Indeed, it was probably meaningless to conceive of Africans as a community unless one recognised common colour, racial origins or social disabilities as social characteristics. Africans were tribal pastoralists or cultivators, doctors, teachers, mine workers, farm labourers, servants, labourers in the public services, chiefs, lawyers, odd job men, gangsters or unemployed. They lived in kraals in the reserves, shanties on the outskirts of towns, respectable houses in locations, or shacks beside farms. They spoke many different languages, their tribal customs varied considerably, they belonged to a wide variety of religions. Even their political status varied in different parts of the country.

There could thus be no such thing as an African public opinion. The African National Congress had tried since 1912 to organise and canalise African ambitions for a better, more dignified, freer life, but its impact was still largely confined to the small group of politically-conscious Africans in the towns. The tribal peoples in the reserves spent most of their efforts in trying to scrape a living out of their meagre lands, ignorant of modern methods of agriculture. Many of the young men spent much of their time away in the mine compounds. Here they sometimes learnt something of the power of labour, but generally they were kept under strict control, segregated from their urbanised brothers. Most of the farm labourers were inured to white command and had grown up in an atmosphere of subservience to the white master. In the towns there was frequent unrest, stemming from poverty and aggravated by discrimination, but organisation hardly existed and outlets were found in crime and violence within the African communities themselves as well as being directed against the whites. The highest proportion of the politically-conscious were to be found, as usual, amongst the professionals, partly because of their education, partly because they felt indignities more personally, and partly because they had greater leisure. So the urge to revolt varied widely in its form.

As an industrialised country, South Africa provided many of its Africans with higher material standards than in the rest of the continent; but the combination of pass laws, prohibitions on trade union organisation, legal and civil disabilities, police persecution, together with endemic poverty in the reserves and squalor in the towns, created a huge potential of mass discontent. Once the personalities had emerged capable of fertilising it into conscious protest all the elements of revolution would exist. A few Africans were determined to realise this potential; the white leaders were as resolved to destroy it.

The whole socio-economic structure of South Africa was so

confused that class allegiances had a variety of cross currents. One section of the community, the rural Afrikaners, had never emerged from the feudal stage. The industrial revolution which followed the discovery of diamonds and gold took place alongside this feudalism but industrialism hardly challenged and never destroyed the traditional rural mores. So industrial and financial capitalism divided the country with agricultural feudalism, the political reins remaining largely in the hands of the rural community. Mining thrived on the cheap labour vouchsafed by African serfdom, for the mines, unlike industry, could profit from limitless unskilled labour. The two successive stages of social evolution, elsewhere deadly enemies, here uneasily joined hands.

The consequence of this strange alliance was to divide those who could have been expected to join the battle against the new industrial masters. The racial concepts of Afrikaner feudalism had infected those of the industrial proletariat who bore white skins, many of whom came from Afrikaner families. Thus, although there were conflicts on the industrial stage between mine-owners and miners, between industrial capitalists and their workers, they took place within the white social sector. The mass black proletariat were deliberately excluded. When they found their working life intolerable, as in the 1946 mining strike, they could expect no help from their white fellow workers. White labour stood by while Smuts and his capitalist-supported government sent in their troops to drive African miners down the mines, or forced them to the surface when they adopted stay-down tactics. Just as feudalism had extracted a truce from its traditional capitalist enemy and hence not only survived but flourished, so capitalism itself rested secure on the division amongst its labour opponents.

The antagonism of white to black labour had also infected politics. The South African Labour Party represented the interests of white workers. It might fulminate against the evils of capitalism, but it had joined with the Nationalists in 1924 to form a racialist government. It was to expose the same trait when it gained control of Johannesburg City Council in 1947; it then clinched its reputation with non-Europeans by using the police to throw the African workers out of the shanty town they had built themselves when they found themselves without a chance of finding houses.

It would be false to assume that the non-European masses had yet begun to organise themselves on anything like a socialist basis. The leaders of the African National Congress had a distinctly bourgeois outlook. They had not yet recognised even equality as an objective, limiting themselves to such essentially bourgeois aims as the right to own property, to trade, to possess land, and to share in political life.

Thus the post-war situation in South Africa did not include the seeds of its own solutions. Problems which were essentially social and economic could not be examined by political dialectic, for society was not basically divided according to economic interest. It was divided by colour. The conflicts within that society were destined to be fought between hostile racial camps, obscuring the real social and economic issues which faced the inhabitants.

This preoccupation with race as an alternative to facing genuine national issues had become a characteristic of Smuts' government. Instead of resolutely tackling the very real problems of housing and health in Natal and the Transvaal, his government had passed the 'Pegging Act' of 1943 which prohibited for three years any extension of Indian trading in the Transvaal or land purchase in Natal. The establishment of a Coloured Advisory Department in the same year warned the Cape Coloureds that they too must expect to be segregated. The following year Smuts revealed his attitude to the growing problem of urbanisation, and, incidentally, foreshadowed Nationalist legislation, by declaring that the townward flood of Africans must be checked, their unemployed sent back to the reserves, and anyone who taught them subversive doctrines dealt with severely.

So the pattern was already set before the end of the war. The period which followed the war, which ought to have been spent in reconstruction and a determined attack on social evils, saw only a continuation of the government's racial attitude. In 1946, when the 'Pegging Act' was due to expire, Smuts introduced his Asiatic Land Tenure and Indian Representation Bill. This measure seriously restricted the right of Indians in Natal to buy European property, whilst offering them and Transvaal Indians one nominated and one elected senator, together with three white members of the Assembly, all elected by a separate communal roll. In addition, Natal Indians were offered the right to elect two members of their own race to the Provincial Council.

The terms of this bill were fiercely attacked by Malan's Nationalists and by the extreme pro-British imperialist, but very racialist, Dominion Party which drew most of its strength from Natal. On the other hand, it was accepted as only a first instalment of Indian rights by Smuts' liberal lieutenant, Hofmeyr. But it was utterly condemned by the Indians' own organisation, the Natal and Transvaal Indian Congresses. Dr Yusuf Dadoo, the Transvaal leader, described it as a 'spurious offer of a sham franchise'; and a 'diabolical attempt to strangulate Indians economically and degrade them socially'. The 'spurious offer' was not accepted and the bill was never implemented.

In the same year Africans also publicly rejected the policy of Smuts' government. When they were removed from the common electoral roll in 1936 the Africans of the Cape had been offered a Native Representative Council as part compensation. This body was elective, but as it was confined to advisory functions it had been condemned by African militants. Smuts used its existence as evidence that the Europeans were educating Africans in self-government. It was therefore a severe blow to his public image when the moderate members of this council, angered by the treatment of African strikers in the mines in 1946, affronted by continual discriminatory legislation, and convinced that they were never to be allowed genuine powers, decided to adjourn *sine die*.

About this time South African policies also began to become international issues. Smuts had been one of the main authors of the United Nations Charter, but the organisation was not a year old when he found himself arraigned before it on account of his illiberal policies. His attitude towards the Indians was bitterly attacked by Nehru's sister, Mrs Pandit, followed by an Indian economic boycott. Smuts was also roundly condemned for his refusal to bring the mandated territory of South-west Africa under a trusteeship agreement with the United Nations. He had, indeed, already promised the Europeans in South-west Africa that they should have representation in the Union parliament, and he hoped to secure complete incorporation of the territory in South Africa. He claimed that a referendum showed that the majority of the Africans supported incorporation, though few took the conduct of the referendum seriously.

But when this policy was attacked at the UN Smuts would do no more than promise to report to the Trusteeship Council on his administration of the territory. As South-west Africa had originally been mandated to the Union by the League of Nations, its administration, status, and the welfare of its people were clearly matters of international responsibility. Yet already it was clear that the 50,000 Europeans within the territory, and both major South African parties, intended to incorporate it within the Union, keeping the African inhabitants under South Africa's racial policy. Smuts' stand at the UN brought him unusual popularity amongst his own Europeans and Malan even urged him to take South Africa out of the organisation.

In 1948 the parliament elected at the height of the war in 1943 ended its term and the parties prepared for a general election. There had been increasing signs from by-elections that Smuts' United Party was losing support. Many Afrikaners had been infuriated by the suspicion that Smuts was undermining the foundations of the Afrikaner nation by such measures as outlawing the xenophobic Broederbond to public servants, offering Indians votes, and providing more money for African education. Many white artisans suspected that the United Party would not defend them adequately against non-European competition because its capitalist supporters needed labour. They considered it represented the wealthy rather than the poorer whites. The Cape Coloureds, whose votes had some importance in a number of seats, had been antagonised by the new segregation measures.

These were all electoral considerations. From the deeper perspective of South Africa's future the charge against Smuts' government was that it had never faced up to the real problems which were threatening to undermine society. The Fagan Commission which Smuts appointed as an alternative to government action to deal with dangers repeatedly exposed, revealed the extent of social confusion created by lack of urban housing, deteriorating health, complicated pass laws, failure either to provide for or to control the rapid African influx into town life, the wasteful nature of migratory labour.

Smuts was a victim of the society in which he lived. He was infrequently willing and never able to control the social forces within his society. Equipped with a mind and experience which revealed to him the South African dichotomy between racial prejudice and economic need, he nevertheless allowed himself to escape from the dilemma into aristocratic racialist feelings in place of meeting unpleasant realities. So he accepted the price demanded from his fellow Afrikaners to secure the support needed to give him power, whilst falling into the temptation of playing an international role as an alternative to meeting his domestic responsibilities. As a result, racialism was stronger at the end of his period in office than it had been at the beginning, and he himself had played an active part in laying the legislative and administrative foundations on which Nationalists could build their apartheid society.

Yet, despite the electoral weakening and the failure of statesmanship, no one expected Smuts to lose the 1948 election. His United Party had an electoral pact with John Christie's Labour Party, and although it had lost the allegiance of the more racialist Labour followers and of the Dominion Party, these groups had little strength amongst the electorate.

The opposition also formed an electoral pact, Malan's National Party and Havenga's Afrikaner Party making common ground on the need to preserve white civilisation under the rallying cry of the new Afrikaner word 'apartheid'.

The election itself was fought in a welter of racial emotions, no one meeting the real national issues. The Nationalists attacked the 'liberalism' of the United Party, concentrating on the personality of J. H. Hofmeyr, Smuts' lieutenant, who would have liked to have the power to put rational social measures into practice, but who had to content himself largely with frequent threats to resign from the government. The United Party defended itself against the attack by trying to convince the electorate that it could defend white civilisation better than the Nationalists.

To everyone's surprise the Nationalist-Afrikaner coalition gained the day with a majority of five. Although, through the weighting of rural seats and high United Party victories in the fewer urban constituencies, Smuts and his supporters polled over 100,000 more votes than their opponents, the Nationalists gained twenty-five and the Afrikaner Party seven seats from the government. The United Party found itself virtually unrepresented in Afrikaans-speaking constituencies.

For the purpose of the election the new mystique of 'apartheid' had come to mean little other than a more strident version of traditional Afrikaner 'baaskap', or white masterdom. It was to take on a deeper intellectual and political significance. In his report published in 1948, Mr Justice Fagan analysed opinion in South Africa in these terms: 'On the one wing are the advocates of a policy that may be called that of total segregation. The goal at which they aim is an absolute territorial division between European and Native; ultimately there would be in South Africa a territory in which no Native, and another in which no European would be regarded as a permanent inhabitant . . . On the other wing we may place those who consider that there should be no racial discrimination in the law and in administration. The third view, which one may place between the two already mentioned, is that European and Native communities, spread over the country as is the case today, will continue to exist permanently side by side, and they must therefore be recognised as permanent, but that there are differences between them which legislation must take into account and which make a measure of separation in matters of administration necessary and advisable.'

The last view was held by the United Party; the second by a handful of white liberals, socialists and communists, and by the non-European leaders; the first was the one now identified by the term 'apartheid'.

Intellectually, the theory of apartheid, which simply means 'separateness', was produced by a group in the university town of Stellenbosch. They formed an organisation known as the South Africa Bureau of Racial Affairs, a rival to the liberal Race Relations Institute of Johannesburg. Several future ministers were amongst its foundation members, but its chief brain was Professor Eiselen, who was to become Permanent Secretary to the Native Affairs Department. Professor Eiselen laid down the classic intellectual definition of the theory of apartheid in these words. He first defined 'race' as: 'A large natural group of people which by virtue of certain permanent, because hereditary, characteristics, common to all its members, clearly distinguishes itself from other groups sharing a different set of hereditary characteristics.'

He then proceeded to define the meaning of apartheid. 'By separation I mean this separating of the heterogeneous groups, from the population of this country, into separate socio-economic units, inhabiting separate parts of the country, each enjoying in its own area full citizen rights, the greatest of which is the opportunity of developing such capabilities as its individual members may possess to their optimum capacity.'

The Professor then posed what he saw as the choice for South African Europeans.

'. . . the alternatives are EITHER to remain in partnership with the Natives, to hold them in subjection for a shorter or longer period and eventually to admit to a status of inimical and uneasy equality, when they are sufficiently organised to force your hand, OR to accustom yourself gradually to manage without their labour, to educate them for self-sufficiency and to add to their land, and to add liberally after they had demonstrated their ability to farm gainfully and at the same time to preserve and increase the fertility of the land.'

However academic this theory may have appeared in the face of South African economic realities, it did bluntly warn white South Africans that racial separation implied dispensing with African labour and giving up land to them. This, of course, was not the kind of apartheid which had attracted votes for the Nationalists. The white voters wanted the best of both worlds, African labour in mines, factories, and kitchens, but the removal of Africans from their sight. The new Prime Minister, Dr Nathaniel Malan, soon had to calm the fears of his farming supporters that they might lose their labour, by declaring that his government had no intention of introducing total apartheid, but was fully committed to maintaining European power over the whole country. The assurance was repeated by other ministers, including a later successor, Dr Verwoerd.

Nevertheless, even if total apartheid, or the policy which came to be known as 'Bantustan' was not to be immediately applied, something decisive had occurred in South African life. The election posters had hardly begun to peel from their hoardings before people of all races saw the changes. Segregation notices appeared for the first time in the Cape on trains and in post offices. African artisans found that they could no longer obtain training lest they compete with European labour. Coloureds began to lose their jobs in the public services so that poorer whites could be employed. Unemployed African workers found that they could no longer draw benefit. Indians were offered larger bribes to return to India, whilst the former offer of a limited franchise was withdrawn. African housing schemes were abandoned, the police suddenly became rougher, and those Afrikaners accused of treason during the war were brought back into public life.

The new government had three main objectives. First, it was determined to make contact between white and non-white as difficult and infrequent as possible. Secondly, it aimed to entrench the dominance of the Afrikaner community over the Britishers. Thirdly, it intended to use the full powers of legislation and administration to destroy every form of opposition to its apartheid policy, from black, brown or white. As Eric Louw, Minister of Economic Affairs, told American reporters, control of South Africa was to be kept in the hands of 'representatives of European culture', lest it should fall under the control of 'a black proletariat with strong Communist backing'. For, in the words of J. H. Strijdom, Minister of Lands, opposition to apartheid was as treasonable as refusing to defend one's country.

In a spate of legislation during the 1949 and 1950 sessions long steps were taken towards all three objectives. An act making marriage illegal between European and non-European affected few people directly, though those few suffered intensely, but closed the door to further integration. It was followed by an amendment to a 1927 Immorality Act, extending the prohibition of African sexual intercourse with Europeans to all non-Europeans. It resulted in a reign of spying by a special police branch on personal relations between men and women throughout the country and a series of prosecutions in which whites and non-whites found themselves in the dock for completely private actions.

The government then decided that if segregation was to be effective, every inhabitant of the country must be racially classified. After all, the existence of over a million Coloureds bore testimony to the fact that ministers could not trust the white community to observe segregation in sex. Moreover, it had been shown by research that a large number of white families, many within the Afrikaner community, had coloured blood in their veins. So a Population Registration Act provided for the registration of the whole population, who would subsequently be compelled to carry identity cards indicating to which racial group they belonged. This was clearly to impose special hardships on the Cape Coloureds, who often included within the same family children who could pass as whites and others with strong African characteristics.

Personal privacy and dignity were again to be sacrificed on the altar of racial dogma.

The apogee of this separation process was reached in the Group Areas Act, designed to give the government powers to designate which racial groups should live, trade or conduct business in specified areas. By using these powers the minister could declare any area designated for the exclusive occupation of a particular race. He could send inspectors and police to examine dwellings or business premises, without prior notice and at any time, subsequently evicting the occupants and forcing them to sell for any price they could obtain. In practice, this was likely to hit Indian traders financially, African and Indian homes socially, and leave the Coloureds defenceless in certain Cape areas. It gave the government absolute powers to determine where every inhabitant should live or work.

It was in the 1949 Citizenship Act that the Nationalists took powers to ensure the dominance of Afrikaners over British. On the morrow of the election they had announced the end of indiscriminate immigration, declaring that in future they would exercise more discrimination in selecting prospective immigrants. Now, they increased from two to five years the qualifying period for newcomers to gain franchise rights, even then leaving the minister discretion in each case as to whether they should be granted. As most immigrants came from Britain, this measure was deliberately designed to restrict the political influence of Britishers, keeping them off the electoral roll at least until after the next election, thus reinforcing the voting advantage which always lay with the heavily weighted Afrikaner rural constituencies.

It was, however, in taking powers to destroy opposition to apartheid that the Malan government revealed its authoritarian character most clearly. The 1950 Suppression of Communism Act may have been passed by a parliamentary system; it nevertheless exposed as thorough an anti-democratic spirit as any Communist or Fascist state.

In their election manifesto the Nationalists had declared, 'Churches and societies which undermine the policy of apartheid and propagate doctrines foreign to the nation will be checked.' The implication was that citizens of South Africa would be allowed political rights as long as they supported apartheid; otherwise, the right to express their opinions would be abolished. Now the government was to prove that this was no mere electoral propaganda designed to appeal to the Afrikaner backwoodsmen; it was to be put into law and rigorously applied.

Communist ideas were, of course, a threat to South African racial society. Conventional communism is concerned with social classes, not with races. Its object is to destroy the rule of the class which draws its power from wealth. In South Africa, the supporters of communism were naturally in sympathy with more blacks than whites, but because they were poor, not because they were black. Indeed, the communists strongly criticised the main African organisation, the African National Congress. They condemned its 'liberalism' and its 'bourgeois' objectives. They attacked the reformist policies of the African nationalists and their liberal-minded European sympathisers, insisting that only militant action for uncompromising demands could ever secure advance.

After the Nationalist electoral victory in 1948, government policy continually justified the communist claim. Those middle-class Africans who had been working for gradual progress were discredited by events. In both the African and Indian Congresses more militant leaders came to the fore, some of them with communist sympathies.

Yet communism in South Africa would not have been recognised as communism anywhere else in the world. Its sole appeal to Africans, Indians and Coloureds was that it made an unreserved demand for complete racial equality and had a number of courageous followers who were prepared to suffer for this cause. It was Nationalist policies which drove many natural opponents of communism amongst the non-Europeans into close co-operation with the communists in the struggle for racial equality.

But the Suppression of Communism Act was not really concerned with communism as such. Within its definition of communism was included any 'encouragement of feelings of hostility between European and non-European races', which might result in radical changes within the Union. In terms of the Act anyone could be classed as a communist by the Governor-General if accused of advocating the achievement of any objective of this type of 'communism' – and the onus lay on the accused to prove his innocence.

In fact, the Act gave the government power to close down any organisation which it disliked and to drive any opponent out of public life. The year after it was passed an amendment gave it retrospective power, so the effect of the voluntary dissolution of the Communist Party was circumvented and the meagre limitations remaining on government absolutism further reduced.

This body of legislation, allied to new restrictive regulations and the use of discriminatory powers in administration, consolidated the 1948 electoral victory of the Nationalists, gave them powers to bully all their opponents, and began building the superstructure of a caste system of society on foundations laid formerly. Many now openly declared their intention to introduce a republican form of government more in line with the old authoritarian ideas of the Voortrekkers and the Afrikaner republics than the parliamentary system inherited from the British. They were equally determined to abolish the three seats representing Cape Africans in parliament and to remove the Cape Coloureds from the electoral roll. But as Havenga believed that these aims could not be achieved without much greater support in the country, and as they still depended on his small Afrikaner Party for their majority, they were forced to wait impatiently for these further aims.

The Nationalists took one more step towards unrestricted power when in 1950, in defiance of the views of the United Nations, they virtually incorporated South-west Africa into the Union. For the first time the European adult population of 26,000 was given the opportunity to elect six members to the Union Assembly. The Nationalists gambled on the electorate, with its considerable German element, supporting them and allocated double the number of seats proportionate to the population. The gamble paid off, for the Nationalists won all six seats, thus considerably reducing their dependence on Havenga and his party.

In addition to the South-west African mandate another international issue concerned the Malan government. Ever since the Union in 1910, successive South African governments had been urging Britain to surrender her role as protector of the High Commission Territories, Basutoland, Swaziland and Bechuanaland. The Nationalists not only considered British retention of control over these territories as an affront to national pride, but feared that British policy within them might endanger their own apartheid. Basutoland was a complete island within South African territory, Swaziland almost so, and Bechuanaland had a common frontier of several hundred miles. They had all been grossly neglected by British governments and many of their peoples sought work on South African farms or in the mines. But the kind of apartheid now being practised by the Nationalists did not operate there. Malan and his colleagues believed that the time had come for Britain to fulfil the half-promise she had given at the time of Union and hand them over.

The issue came to a head over the Seretse Khama case. The young Bamangwato chief-presumptive married an English girl in London. South African whites were appalled, for to have an African chief living with his white wife close to their border would be an open challenge, not only to apartheid, but to the basic premises of South African life. There was some opposition within the Bamangwato tribe itself, led by the regent, Seretse's uncle, Tshekedi. This was seized on by the British government to exile Seretse and banish Tshekedi from the Bamangwato lands. It seemed that Malan had won his point, but the incident raised South African fears for the future and provoked renewed demands that the territories should be handed over to South African rule. The demands were vigorously contested by the African populations, who formed the vast majority of the inhabitants in each of the territories. Although politically dormant, the threat of South African rule began to arouse their consciousness. It first took the form of claiming the right to be included within the ambit of British colonial policy, with its economic aid and gradually shared political responsibilities.

Meanwhile, South Africa under Nationalist leadership was rapidly becoming the core of white nationalism throughout the southern half of the continent. There were many white inhabitants in the Rhodesias, the High Commission Territories and Kenya who had begun to look on her policies as specially fitted to maintain white rule, although the high proportion of Britishers in these communities was suspicious of the Afrikaner anti-British attitude.

There were no such reservations in the Portuguese colonies of Mozambique and Angola, although the Portuguese did not accept the tenets of apartheid. Indeed, it was despite their differences that the South Africans and Portuguese colonists respected and sympathised with each other. In Mozambique and Angola the scarcity of white women had led to an acceptance of miscegenation. This was, of course, completely contrary to South African first principles.

Nor did the South Africans support the assimilado theory, by which a small African élite was allowed to enter white society, although they noted with approval the severely limited manner in which the Portuguese operated it and their reluctance to allow Africans facilities for higher education. Above all, the South Africans admired the Portuguese insistence on completely centralised government which debarred their African population from participation in politics. Vigorous colonial rule, accompanied by policies based on a characteristic Portuguese Catholic belief in the social responsibility of labour, provided the South African mines with a plentiful supply of cheap workers for their mines. It was therefore natural that their common authoritarian outlook, their mutual military and economic interests should appear to both South Africans and Portuguese of greater importance than the details which divided them.

In 1950 Smuts died. His chief lieutenant and only intellectual equal, Hofmeyr, had died soon after the 1948 election. These two irreplaceable losses to the Opposition completed the powerful hand now held by the Nationalists. Henceforth it was clear that nationally organised opposition to apartheid within the white community would be bereft of that intellectual leadership capable of presenting a serious challenge. The United Party passed into opportunist hands, accepting all the principles of apartheid, whilst conducting its opposition functions only so far as was consistent with electoral expediency.

Thus the rise to power of the Nationalists and their successful efforts of consolidation ensured that the problems of South Africa would be met by stronger traditional methods rather than any innovation. For another era the industrial revolution was to be prevented from overthrowing rural feudalism; the potential markets offered to industry by a population of 13 million were to be severely restricted by limiting increases in purchasing power amongst the 10 million non-Europeans; racial ideology was to take precedence over economic opportunities. The mass proletariat, Africans, Indians and Coloureds, was to be kept to the status of serfdom, whilst as many as possible of those who had become workers in industrial society were to be compulsorily returned to their tribal, subsistence society. The whole force of governmental power was to be ruthlessly employed to prevent any development of modern political thought, organisation or action amongst the non-European masses, even if this were to drive militants to forget their racial differences and form a common non-European front. The Nationalists had shown that they were determined to gamble the whole future of the country on their ability to reverse the natural social and economic evolution of South African society.

5

Where Imperialisms Meet

It was in the central belt of the continent that the greatest variety of European imperialisms met each other. The four territories comprising French Equatorial Africa had common frontiers with the Belgian Congo to its north and west; the Congo marched with British East and Central Africa; to the east and west of the area lay the Portuguese colonies, to the north Italian Libya, to the south the Union of South Africa. Central Africa itself had been ruled since the nineteenth century by the three major imperial powers, Britain, France and Belgium.

Apart from these varieties of European rule, the area itself displayed widely differing features. Most of it was grossly underpopulated, partly because the slave trade had prevailed in most of its regions, partly through a climate which brought widespread disease and high mortality. Yet two of its areas, Ruanda-Urundi and Nyasaland, had such a high population density that, in combination with scarce resources, it forced a large proportion of the population to seek work abroad. Again, while a large part of the area consisted of forest, scrub or desert, in certain districts, Katanga, the Copper Belt, Gabon, Salisbury and Bulawayo, there developed considerable concentrations of mining and industry. So although most of the central African peoples still lived a rural, tribal, clan or village life, growing numbers of them had either some experience of urban life or had actually settled in towns.

The war had as profound an effect on the peoples of central Africa as anywhere in the continent. In its early years experience varied. The British territories, Nyasaland and the two Rhodesias, were automatically at war from the moment of the British declaration until the armistice nearly six years later. But in 1940 Belgium and France were overrun by the Nazis. The future role of the Congo and French Equatorial Africa had thus to be decided by the balance of forces within those territories themselves.

There was little difficulty in retaining Congo adherence to Britain for there was no desire on the part of the triumvirate of ruling influences, the church, the companies, and government officials, to help those who had invaded their homeland. Nor did there appear to be any inclination amongst the Africans to take advantage of Belgian weakness to revolt.

But it was a different matter in' the French territories. Opinion amongst government officials was divided between obeying the orders from Vichy and joining with those Frenchmen who continued to support the British effort. Moreover, these territories were the most neglected of French possessions, and the African peoples were oppressed and exploited, sometimes with considerable brutality. Yet when the choice had to be made it was not only French civilians and army officers who overthrew those high officials favouring Vichy; the maltreated Africans surprised everyone by volunteering for De Gaulle's forces and contributing towards war collections. Only Gabon of the four territories remained under Vichy control for more than a few weeks, and it changed its allegiance after a six weeks' siege of Libreville.

So, by November 1940, the whole of central Africa was engaged in whole-hearted support of the British war against the Nazis and Fascists. Many Africans served overseas, thus breaking through their isolation from the outside world and learning something of other men's ways. As elsewhere in Africa this experience was to have a most profound effect on African psychology, particularly in their relations with the Europeans in their own territories.

Yet the war had a much deeper effect on life in central Africa than its impact on race relations. The area became an important supply centre for the allied war effort, stimulating the production of copper, gold, rubber, cotton and other supplies desperately needed for the war effort. Towards the end of the war far-seeing business men in the Congo even began to produce uranium.

The effects of these new demands was the same as in other parts of the continent, but multiplied by the special value of the goods produced in this area. There was the same rush to the towns – Leopoldville increasing its population from 40,000 in 1939 to 100,000 in 1945. Capital investment and exports increased enormously; in the Congo investment rose from 1,000 million francs annually before the war to 11,000 million by 1948, exports from 2,250 million to 10,000 million during the same period. Northern Rhodesia had increased her exports ninefold over the pre-war figures by 1953 and her government revenue twentyfold. Both the Congo and the French territories, cut off from their normal supplies from Belgium and France, began to establish their own industries to supply their own people. Intensified agricultural cultivation, particularly of rubber and cotton, reduced the wretchedness of rural Africans to still lower depths, but in the towns new workers' associations and trade unions began to protect urban Africans for the first time. This led directly to stimulated social and political awareness, marked in the Congo by strikes and rioting in 1941 and 1944.

It might appear that here were all the elements of industrial revolution followed by social revolt. At least it could be expected that these radical changes in the life of Central Africans would provoke strong anti-imperialist agitation. After all, if the French and Belgian governments had been proved incapable of defending their homelands, how could they resist efforts to end their rule in the middle of Africa?

Yet, in the event, industrial advance moved at an evolutionary rather than revolutionary pace; social unrest was minimal; no revolt against imperial rule occurred, even when it seemed certain that Britain, France and Belgium would be conquered by the Nazis.

The reasons why events did not follow hypothetical expectation must be sought in the effects of imperial policies. France, Belgium and Britain based their imperial governance on different principles. The French hoped that sometime in the distant future they would have transformed their African subjects into black Frenchmen. The Belgians sought to train their Africans in the virtues of Roman Catholicism and artisan skills, with a vague implication that in the very long run they might share in running their own country. The British equivocated between their principle of paramountcy for indigenous interests and the need for settler self-government learnt at the Boston Tea Party.

Yet if the three imperial policies differed in long-term objectives, there was much in common between their practical administration. Above all, each of them was dominated by large overseas companies. The copper companies in Northern Rhodesia and Katanga, the

British South Africa Company in Southern Rhodesia, and the concessionary companies in the French territories so powerfully controlled economic life as virtually to run their own administrations. And in these peasant lands the wages offered by the companies, though infinitesimal in comparison to those paid in Europe or to their own white workers, provided an escape from a life on subsistence level. Moreover, in Katanga and the Copper Belt, the companies had begun to provide welfare services unobtainable elsewhere in their territories, whilst their housing schemes, in contrast to South African mining practice, were beginning to make provision for settled family life.

This infant welfare capitalism had the effect of cushioning the new proletariat against more extreme distress common to early industrial life. It consequently arrested that social and political agitation which usually arises in young industrial communities. In the rural areas, illiteracy, lack of social organisation and the hold of traditional rulers combined to prevent any serious expression of discontent.

It is significant that in the French territories, where conditions seemed most likely to provoke revolt, a deliberate policy to avoid it was followed. Félix Eboué disapproved of the traditional French assimilation policy because he believed that the few educated Africans accepted into French society were being dangerously detached from the masses. He foresaw this leading to movements of discontent. At the same time, he considered that the effect of the companies was to destroy tribal traditions in the rural areas by attracting young people away from their villages to the towns and plantations. He therefore tried to reverse these processes by seeking out traditional chiefs and elders, giving them new authority and encouraging them to defend local society. Meanwhile, he insisted that where labour was needed it should be recruited on a permanent basis and provided with decent urban amenities. Again, welfare acted as a buffer against potential agitation, with Eboué actually exploiting war needs to introduce an economic and social new deal for African workers.

The industrial, social and political scenes in all these territories were complicated by the presence of European settlers. In the Rhodesias, Nyasaland, and the Congo basin, Europeans originally arrived in search of land and minerals. They found both. Indeed, in Southern Rhodesia they claimed half the country as their own.

Scattered amongst the farms and plantation appeared mines – gold, copper, coal, tin, cobalt were all found. Mines attracted skilled labourers from Europe, the land brought wealthy farmers. The presence of these European communities led to the erection of a variety of colour bars in the three regions, each restraining African development in skill, responsibility and status, whilst ultimately provoking angry reactions. The war period came too early for African resentment to challenge European control, but the outcome of the war was to create the circumstances for that challenge, while enormously accelerating the processes which were to lead to a confrontation of the rival forces.

This post-war socio-economic background was broadly common to all three imperial areas. The political approaches of the British, French and Belgians differed sufficiently, however, to warrant examining each separately.

British governments never seemed quite sure whether the Devonshire declaration on the paramountcy of indigenous interests applied to their central African territories. Nor could they ever make up their minds as to whether the best interests of Africans were to be judged by the imperial trustee, the Europeans living in the countries, or by the Africans themselves. In any case, the Devonshire declaration came too late to affect Southern Rhodesia, for it was issued in the same year, 1923, in which the whites of that country were offered internal self-government.

Because Southern Rhodesia had originally been conquered by white invaders from South Africa, the white residents were considered to possess special rights over the country and its inhabitants. The fact that a number of Cecil Rhodes' emissaries were able to persuade the Matabele king, Lobengula, to cede them rights which were not in his gift, whilst the British South Africa Company was later able to suppress the protests of his followers, was taken to invest European settlers with the right to treat the country as their own. Possession by conquest is often recognised by international law. So the descendants of Lobengula and his followers were left with the choice of submitting to the rule of the white settlers, fighting them until they in turn could claim conquest, or relying on the long, sophisticated, speculative process of persuading their masters to cede powers to them.

By 1923 the Company had decided to relinquish its administrative rights and sell them to the British government. Southern Rhodesia became a colony, but its electorate, almost entirely white, was given the choice of internal self-government or linking up with South Africa. By about four to three the 15,000 electors decided that their country should become self-governing with Britain retaining only minor reserved powers.

So by the end of the war Southern Rhodesian whites had exercised virtually unlimited power over the structure and development of their country for over twenty years. Britain had retained the power of veto over legislation discriminating against non-Europeans, but this had not prevented Southern Rhodesian governments allocating half the land to Europeans and only one-third to Africans, or separating the races and keeping governmental powers in European hands. In these circumstances it would have been only academic to ask whether the Devonshire declaration applied to Southern Rhodesia.

Northern Rhodesia and Nyasaland were not colonies but protectorates. They had both come under the British crown at the request of their chiefs. When the charter of the British South Africa Company expired in 1924 the administration was taken over by the British government, but there was no doubt that its primary responsibility as the protecting power was to act as trustee for the interests of the African inhabitants. Yet because franchise rights were restricted to British 'subjects', whilst the Africans were British 'protected' persons, it was virtually only European inhabitants who were allowed to vote. One European member was nominated to the LegislativeCouncil in order to represent African interests, but the European population was allowed to elect half the members of the Council. Whatever concern she might have for her protectorate responsibility, Britain had not forgotten her experience with the American colonies. Those of her people who emigrated to British territories, protectorates or colonies must increasingly be given the right to govern their own affairs. But, of course, Africans were far more numerous than the Red Indians had been.

Nyasaland was also a protectorate, but it had such a tiny European population that instead of holding elections, its members on the Legislative Council were selected by public bodies, and government officials retained majority control.

One major difference between British policy in her protectorates and Southern Rhodesian policy should be noted. In contrast to Southern Rhodesian practice, by far the largest share of land in the protectorates was reserved for African use. Africans also valued the absence of the pass system and other discriminatory regulations in the northern territories, although in fact certain customary social practices in Northern Rhodesia were more discriminatory than in the self-governing colony.

The years immediately after the war saw boom conditions develop in most of central Africa. Thousands of Europeans, especially from Britain, decided that life in the privileged social environment of Africa offered more than in war-torn Europe. Southern Rhodesia was particularly attractive, for tobacco growing and agriculture were prosperous, gold output was rising and secondary industries had developed during the war. The rush was so great that before long an acute shortage of accommodation developed and an Aliens Act was passed to provide for the limitation and selection of immigrants.

This sudden increase in the number of white Rhodesians considerably aggravated the racial issue. The Prime Minister, Sir Godfrey Huggins, was always equivocal on the race question, but he had certain liberal ideas. He not only compelled the municipalities to clean up their African locations, but bluntly told those Europeans who had begun to follow South African ideas that the white community could not live without African labour. Some of the newcomers added to the small ranks of those whites who took responsibility for social welfare amongst the Africans, but the large majority exhibited their new-found social superiority by demanding that Africans should be kept in servile status and preferably relegated to their reserves. There was little of the rabid racial fanaticism seen amongst the Nationalist Afrikaners in the Union, but the effect had similarities. The Prime Minister and his few colleagues with any sense of liberalism found little support for measures designed to aid Africans. The basic dilemma of white Rhodesians with liberal feeling was already apparent; the majority of white inhabitants were anti-liberal, and the white inhabitants had a virtual monopoly of votes.

On the other hand, Sir Godfrey Huggins was by no means a fully committed liberal. Whilst he believed in Africans living in decent conditions and being helped to make economic and social progress, he also believed in keeping them in their place. And for the fore-seeable future that place was separate from Europeans and under European tutelage. So, like Smuts, Huggins passed his Urban Areas Act, debarring Africans from living in the town areas occupied by Europeans, confining them to the locations. As in South Africa, this policy showed a Canute-like attitude to the mass African urbanisa-tion which took place as a result of the rapid increase in labour demand.

The Prime Minister was fond of preaching a gospel of 'parallel development' for the two races. To many Africans, however, and particularly to the few politically conscious, this was merely camou-flage for a policy designed to keep power in the hands of the 100,000 or so Europeans, enabling them to continue their rule over nearly 2 million Africans. They pointed to the unfair distribution of land, the refusal to legalise African trade unions, the barriers to positions of responsibility, the disparity in educational opportunity, as evi-dence that 'parallel' development in fact implied unequal treatment.

Indeed, if any Africans doubted the intention of the whites to maintain their power, the doubts were laid by the government's political policies in the first six years after the war. It had been the boast of Huggins that Southern Rhodesia had retained the old Cape system of franchise. Voting rights paid no heed to colour. Anyone with an income of £100 a year or property valued at £150 and with ability to pass a simple literacy test in English could qualify for the vote. In practice, out of an electorate of about 50,000 only about 450 Africans were on the voters' roll. Many more might have qualified, although literacy in English excluded those who spoke only native languages and some others were frightened that to qualify might render them liable to income tax. In effect, though, these qualifications were designed to maintain white control over parliament. Moreover, no non-European had ever sat in the Southern Rhodesian house.

However, in the late forties, the Southern Rhodesian Labour Party, the more liberal wing of the Labour movement, began to admit Africans to membership and organise their enrolment on the electoral register. This was enough to frighten Huggins and his colleagues that 'civilisation' might not be a sufficiently stiff test to preserve white power over the franchise. At first they intended to separate European and African voters, as had been done in South Africa. But this might have provoked the Labour Government in Britain to use its constitutional veto for the first time. So they changed their policy and raised the income qualifications to £240 and the property qualification to £500. Thus was Southern Rhodesia made safe for a 'civilisation' measured by wealth. It included white barmen but debarred black teachers or clergymen.

It was in Northern Rhodesia that the dichotomy in British policy was most apparent. The 60,000 or so Europeans had continually pressed for a reduction in Colonial Office control, together with greater powers to rule the country of their adoption. Amongst them were not only farmers, but a hard core of tough copper miners who had staked out their privileged position at a time when skilled miners were in short supply, conditions in the Copper Belt unattractive to Europeans, and there was little prospect of training Africans to do skilled work. Their basic wage, at around £100 a month, was twenty times that of African miners, and they were quite determined that it should stay that way. When, in 1945, Roy Welensky, the Polish-Jewish-Afrikaner ex-boxer, ex-engine driver from Southern Rhodesia, took over the leadership of European politics, pressure against the Colonial Office became rapidly heavier.

Yet the Africans had also shown that they would not stand by and see their country follow the example of Southern Rhodesia or South Africa. In 1940 fifteen thousand African miners had gone on strike at Nkana and Mufilira. Police and troops killed seventeen and wounded sixty-five, but the Africans had tasted mass action and demonstrated powers of organisation. Another African strike in 1945 on the railways convinced even Welensky that African workers should be given the right of organising their own trade unions.

The British government tried to appease both communities simultaneously, although always giving the greater concessions to the more clamant Europeans. Thus, in 1945, official control of the Legislative Council disappeared when the number of unofficial members was increased to thirteen out of a total of twenty-two. Eight of the thirteen were elected, almost entirely by Europeans, the other five nominated, three to represent African interests. This was a long step on the way to securing a representative Legislative Council which would bring legislation under the control of local Europeans. As four elected members had been members of the

Executive Council since before the war, it seemed that Northern Rhodesia was following the traditional colonial pattern of developing a system in which government was ultimately controlled by an elected parliament. If voting rights were to continue to be a virtual monopoly of Europeans, the Southern Rhodesian pattern would be repeated, with the eventual prospect of sovereignty being gained on the South African model.

When the British government (since 1945 a Labour Government, with Arthur Creech Jones, the well-known Fabian colonial theorist, as Colonial Secretary from 1946) allowed the elected members of the Executive to administer government departments and then ordered the Governor to follow the unanimous advice of these members, the self-government picture was almost completed. All that was now required was the replacement of the five remaining officials in the Executive by further elected members, the use of the term 'ministers' and a withdrawal by the Governor, who would keep a few reserved powers.

But other changes were taking place likely to raise barriers to this evolution. In 1948 two Africans were permitted to enter the legislature, elected by the African Representative Council, a body partly nominated and partly chosen by local provincial councils. Later the number of Africans was to be doubled. Moreover, by this time considerable progress had been made in the development of African trade unions and producer co-operatives. The despatch of an experienced Scottish trade unionist, W. M. Comrie, and an authority on peasant co-operatives, W. K. H. Campbell, to Northern Rhodesia by the British government brought rapid results. In particular, the development of the African Mineworkers Union, led by Lawrence Katilungu, with Comrie's help, provided the country with an organised labour movement scarcely ever previously equalled within Africa.

As there was no urban areas legislation comparable to that of Southern Rhodesia or South Africa, Africans here were able to settle in the towns. Indeed, it was the policy of the copper companies, in contrast to the practice on the Witwatersrand, to encourage permanent family life in the mining townships. So that, although social segregation and discrimination continued, Africans were becoming increasingly organised as social groups, encouraged rather than hindered by the government.

It was natural to find this development soon reflected in politics. In 1948 Godwin Lewanika used his leadership of the Federation of African Welfare Societies to found the Northern Rhodesian African National Congress. He did not survive long as its leader, being quickly replaced by Harry Nkumbula, just returned from the London School of Economics. The African barriers were being raised against white control. British policy, by encouraging both communities in the belief that the future lay with them, was inevitably stimulating a clash between the two races.

Although also a protectorate, and governed by the same British colonial policy, Nyasaland was a vastly different country from Northern Rhodesia. It is true that outside the Copper Belt most of the latter territory was inhabited by subsistent peasants, similar to the vast majority of Nyasas. But apart from the fact that there was no Copper Belt, or anything resembling it, in Nyasaland, the country was comparatively densely populated, whereas the rural areas of Northern Rhodesia were very sparsely inhabited. The absence of mining and industry left Nyasaland without either industrial colour bars or trade unions, though the country was so poor that a large number of its able-bodied men were regularly abroad, working in South Africa, Mozambique, or the Rhodesias. Here they learnt the lessons of industrial communities, just as the 30,000 Nyasa soldiers who had served in the war had gained experience of other peoples, their ideas and customs.

Nevertheless, there was little sign that rebellious ideas had been taken back to Nyasaland immediately after the war. Ever since the formation of the African National Congress in South Africa in 1912, Nyasas had maintained contact with it and tried to build some similar form of political organisation in their own country. In 1944 they managed to establish an African National Congress, but its early demands, like those of the Northern Rhodesian Congress, were purely reformist. They simply asked for social and economic progress for Africans and opposed discrimination.

The fact is that even in the context of widespread African social conservatism, Nyasaland was a feudal backwater. The handful of Europeans were either missionaries, or administrators, traders or tea planters. The Scottish missionaries had been there since the nineteenth century, were generally liked, and provided most of the education and social welfare. The colonial servants also usually maintained friendly, if paternalistic, relations with the Africans, whilst there was probably more suspicion felt towards Asian than European traders. Conditions on the plantations varied between welfare feudalism and irresponsible feudalism, but there was little organised opposition to the plantation system itself. Nor were there any serious political ambitions amongst the Europeans. They were content to elect their members of the legislature through public bodies instead of by direct elections. The same method was accepted by the Asian community for their single member, so that when Africans were offered election by the African Protectorate Council (similar to the Representative Council in Northern Rhodesia) there was no sense of inferior treatment. Indeed, the Africans were content for the moment to leave government in the hands of the Colonial Office and its officials whilst they thought out how their almost entirely agricultural country could develop its own modern economy and provide them with a base on which to build a national political structure.

Dr Hastings Banda, who had left Nyasaland at the age of thirteen to walk to South Africa in search of education, was the guiding spirit behind political strategy. He had eventually qualified in medicine in both America and Britain and established himself in a London practice. He kept constant contact with the politically-minded Nyasas and advised them on the formation of the Congress. For the time being he realised that Colonial Office tutelage could provide the best guarantee that power would not be handed over to the Europeans so that Africans might be given time to work out their own destiny.

But this atmosphere of calm in Nyasaland, the hesitant progress in Northern Rhodesia, and the political vacuum in Southern Rhodesia were superficial. Beneath the surface a volcano was already rumbling.

It had begun as a whisper in 1915. This was the year in which the first moves were made to create a single state from combining the two Rhodesias. Opposition had come first from whites in Southern Rhodesia, who feared that amalgamation with the north would implicate them in a colonial policy likely to provide Africans with opportunities to acquire technical skills. Many of them preferred to envisage association with South Africa which, they believed, would offer them a better opportunity to safeguard their privileges.

In 1923, however, a referendum showed that a small majority of the white community preferred to govern their own affairs rather than join the south. They still believed that this would free them from interference by the dangerously liberal policies being pursued by Britain in the north.

But in the late twenties discovery of the extent of Northern Rhodesia's copper deposits and increased demand for the mineral produced a tremendous expansion in northern revenues. The southerners now began to recognise the value of association with the north. Pressure for some form of association was brought to bear on the British government, which responded by appointing a Royal Commission. This Hilton-Young Commission of 1927–9 and the similar Bledisloe Commission of 1938–9, appointed to meet the same kind of pressures, both reported against amalgamation, pointing out the contrast between the territories in their policies towards Africans. It was clear from both reports, however, that advantages could be gained from some form of closer economic association. So in 1945 a Central African Council was set up in Salisbury, composed of the three territorial governors and members of the legislatures. It was a purely consultative body, but had its own secretariat and administered a variety of common services.

Yet, although the Council did useful work, it could not satisfy the increasing demands from Europeans in both Rhodesias for release from British authority and for control over their own affairs.

So the campaign for links between the two Rhodesias gained momentum and now some of the Europeans in Nyasaland were brought in. Motives varied. Some saw European association between the three territories as the only method of stemming the rising tide of African strength and preserving European control. The growth of African trade unions, political parties and participation in legislation lent point to this argument. Even Europeans in Northern Rhodesia felt that this danger was more serious than the suspicion that Southern Rhodesians only wanted to share in their copper wealth. On the other hand, there were Rhodesians who saw closer association as the only alternative to the spread of apartheid from South Africa. Fear of South African policies greatly increased from 1948 when the Nationalists gained office in the Union. Although there were many Afrikaners in both Rhodesias and some continuing hopes of joining South Africa, feeling for the British connection was much stronger. Many believed that only by building a strong British state in Central Africa could Afrikaner imperialism against Britishers be halted at the Limpopo.

The two main proponents of linking the Rhodesias, Sir Godfrey Huggins and Roy Welensky, recognised the hard political facts of the situation. Although the British Labour government had considerably increased Welensky's power, both men realised that there was little chance of it ever surrendering its ultimate control to them. Meanwhile they saw the same British government encouraging African trade unions, producer co-operatives and political representation. They recognised that the logic of African progress would be an ultimate challenge to white supremacy.

So Huggins, as the tactician, switched his attack from amalgamation to federation. In February 1949 he arranged a conference at Victoria Falls under the chairmanship of his friend, Sir Miles Thomas. It was attended by Huggins, his Finance Minister, and Welensky, who represented European legislative members in Northern Rhodesia and Nyasaland. No Africans were invited. The conference agreed to substitute a federal scheme for the amalgamation plan previously discussed, and accepted that in a federal parliament Africans would have to be represented, preferably in an upper house. A committee of experts was appointed to draft a detailed plan.

News of this conference raised apprehensions amongst politically-conscious Africans and rumours began to circulate amongst the masses. The Barotse of Northern Rhodesia asked Huggins whether he was prepared to substitute the comparative liberal racial policy of the northern protectorates for his own separate development plans. The British Colonial Secretary, though re-affirming Britain's refusal to transfer her responsibilities for Africans and ignoring Welensky's Legislative Council motion supporting federation, nevertheless promised to consider any federal scheme submitted to him. As he chose this moment to give Northern Rhodesian European members of the Executive power to determine policy, whilst at the same time advising the supporters of federation to persevere with the Central African Council, it was clear that the dichotomy in British policy still existed.

It thus became apparent, five years after the end of the war, that

British Central Africa was destined to be a battlefield for the opposing forces of white and black political ambitions. Those Europeans
who had settled in the Rhodesias and Nyasaland had become
accustomed to the idea that public policy in their countries was
their prerogative. They considered it reasonable to assume that
ultimately complete control of government would be handed to
them. After more than twenty years' governmental experience in
Southern Rhodesia they believed that the time had come for this to
happen. Since the war they had been joined by thousands of Britishers and a lesser number of Afrikaners, varying the social mixture
of the community, but scarcely increasing its liberal tendencies.
Most of the new immigrants were seeking a more comfortable life
than that offered by post-war Europe, added a brashness to the
privileged status already assumed by the pre-war upper-class
Rhodesians, and contributed their own element of inverted snobbery.

As in South Africa, a two-tier class structure developed. Many of
the new immigrants were working-class whites, as were the established copper miners in the north. They fought the conventional
class battle with the employers, particularly with the copper companies. But far below them in the social and economic scale was the
mass proletariat composed of African workers. There was virtually
no co-operation between the two working communities. Indeed, it
was usually the white workers who formed the most intransigent
barrier to black advance, their racial snobbery reinforced by fear of
economic competition. And, again as in South Africa, the more
intelligent industrial concerns recognised that labour efficiency
demanded an abolition of the colour bar, but could do little about the
determined resistance of white labour.

These complicated consequences of an industrial revolution within
a racial caste society had only just begun to appear in Rhodesia
during the first years following the war. Most Africans still lived in
their peasant, subsistence communities, but even they began to feel
the effects of the developing storm. As racial politics were super-
imposed on the social complexities, colour was given priority over
class or economic interest. A South African situation in miniature
seemed in prospect.

To see the difference in ordinary African life caused by divergent
imperial policies one had only to watch the Northern Rhodesian-
Congo frontier crossed by the railway. Locomotives were driven

to the Congo side of the border with Africans on the footplate. At the frontier they were replaced by white drivers and firemen. Yet whilst Congo Africans were allowed to drive trains, none of them would be found in Belgian universities. Africans in Northern Rhodesia were not trusted on the footplate, but some of them were studying in London, Manchester and Edinburgh.

In meeting the problems arising in Central Africa from the stimulation of economic activity and the social disturbance caused by the war, the Belgians and French had already an established philosophy from which to work. Unlike the British, who had little more than the alternatives of a rather vague Fabian liberalism and traditional conservative imperialism, neither of which met the realities in postwar Africa, the Belgians and French had fairly clear objectives. If, in hindsight, criticism is to be levelled against imperial policies in central Africa, it would be that the British were confused about their aims and had never thought out consistent policies, whilst the Belgians and French had set themselves unobtainable objectives and followed inflexible policies even when they had proved themselves unreal.

Belgian policy in the Congo has often been described as 'paternal'. It is true that Belgian colonial policy assumed that Africans had only reached an infant stage of development and needed to be brought up to adulthood by gradual evolution. Yet there were wider social implications in Belgian rule. The Belgians are an essentially middle-class nation in their social outlook. So when they found themselves in charge of the huge Congo and realised that it was a very wealthy territory, they set out to develop it as a part of their Belgian economy and taught its inhabitants the virtues of thrift, industry and Christianity which prevailed in Belgium itself. In sharp contrast, when the Belgian administrators accepted the mandate for Ruanda-Urundi, formerly part of German East Africa, at the end of the first world war, they found it poor and over-populated. It offended their commercial instincts and many Belgians considered it a mistake to have accepted the burden of subsidising it from Belgian and Congo resources.

The implication of this policy in the Congo was that the colonial power should first build sound foundations for a modern society before attempting to create the superstructure of European societies.

Thus wider provision for education was made than in any other part of the continent, but it was almost entirely confined to literacy and techniques. Welfare services in the form of housing and medicine were of a high grade, but Africans themselves were only trained in the lower skills needed to service them. Politics were almost entirely forbidden for black and white alike, although a start had been made on the experience of advisory local government. The huge copper combines provided the revenue for this social policy and maintained their own welfare schemes, but they did little to bring Africans into the higher ranks of their administration and frowned heavily on any ideas of trade unionism.

It was entirely characteristic of Belgian policy that immigrants from Europe had to pay a substantial deposit for themselves and their families before being allowed into the Congo. The Belgian authorities did not want white workers competing with unskilled African labour and, above all, they were anxious that Europeans in the Congo should project middle-class values by example and precept.

So, under the triple guidance of State, Church and Companies, the foundations were laid of a modern society undisturbed by the distracting influences of politics and philosophy already appearing in other parts of the continent. There was consistency and some reason in the theory. It may, indeed, be a better policy to give wide elementary education before skimming off the minority to secondary schools and universities. It can be argued that in a country with 100,000 European inhabitants living amongst 13 million Africans, it will avoid any danger of racialism distorting the political scene if politics are barred to all until Africans have sufficient education and experience to take control without provoking conflict with the whites. One important element in this evolution may well be the provision of social services.

What eventually destroyed Belgian policy was not its oppressive nature but the fact that it proceeded too slowly in view of the pace of African advance elsewhere. It is true that the policy itself was no more perfectly put into practice than policies have been in other countries. There was such a gap between Europeans and African living standards as to make envy inevitable. Much of the policy favoured the interests of the immigrant community, to an extent which roused suspicions that it was dictated by the settlers. There

was a considerable degree of social segregation and little social contact between the races. Government was often arbitrary and at times
harsh.

Nevertheless, some of the aims were achieved. Primary education
was widespread, Africans did more semi-skilled work than in most
parts of industrial Africa, health and housing were comparatively
good in the towns, and an African bourgeoisie developed in trade,
if not in the professions.

So the social revolution which seemed imminent for a moment
during the war was staved off. The war had brought isolation from
Brussels which was quickly exploited by both white and black
workers alike to develop organisations previously prohibited. White
workers secured legality for their trade unions in 1942 and two years
later gained recognition of their right to strike. In 1942 also, the
African workers went on strike for higher wages, a strike which was
followed by violence and bloodshed. But the companies, particularly the Union Minière, immediately learnt the lesson. Confrontation between the Belgian employers and the new African proletariat was avoided by increased wages and fringe benefits, such as
free hospitals, education, insurance, housing, pensions and food.
Trade unions were allowed, although controlled by the companies
and without genuine bargaining power. Welfare capitalism was
intelligent enough to recognise that it risked losing its copper eggs
unless it nurtured those needed to lay them. Even so, an army
revolt at Luluabourg in 1944, followed by strikes and riots at
Matadi in 1945, showed that the Congolese were not entirely
insulated from those effects of the war which were shaking other
African societies.

As soon as the war was over the Belgian government learnt something of the same lesson and resumed its administration along the
lines of company policy. Reforms were minor compared with what
was happening in some parts of Africa, but the Belgians still believed
that material progress held more prospect for contentment than
radical political progress. They therefore kept the political reins in
their own hands, convinced that their slow, evolutionary policy
would eventually create a modern, integrated state in which Africans
would have the experience, education and wealth to take over
government, together with those Europeans who had integrated
themselves into Congo society.

So the restored Belgian government reconstituted its Colonial Council under its Minister of the Colonies, with the King nominating eight members and the two Houses of Parliament three each. In the Congo itself the Governor-General continued to legislate by decree, assisted by a nominated council. Each of the six provinces also had its governor and council.

Yet, in accord with the faint stirrings of new attitudes in postwar Congo, the government began to bring in one or two Africans to its advisory conciliar system. Africans were already associated with local government through the preservation of traditional tribal organisation in the rural areas, and in the urban local government system known as 'centres extra-coutumiers', which were in charge of Belgian-appointed chiefs, assisted by local councils. In 1947 Africans were appointed in place of Europeans to represent native interests in the government and provincial councils, but they were chosen from amongst the traditionalists and appointed by the government.

These slight reforms were a gesture, but they did not satisfy the small politically-conscious section of the African community which had emerged after the war. Here was an Achilles' heel in the Belgian policy. Its concentration exclusively on primary education, the power given to the church, the barriers to higher education, overseas visits and genuine trade unions, had all been designed to prevent the growth of an intelligentsia separate from the masses. Yet Belgian policy itself led inevitably to the creation of a minor élite. The encouragement given to Christian conversion, to the growth of a middle class, to westernisation, naturally resulted in a small number of Africans absorbing such progress quicker than others. This advanced group then found that social theory and practice were different. Like settlers elsewhere, the Belgian white community showed no desire to open their doors to black évolués. And their reluctance was supported by legal discrimination, by wage contrasts, by a wide gap in living standards, by an administration based on the assumption that all Africans were ignorant, poor, unhygienic and irresponsible.

So, from about 1948 onwards, the évolués began to press for what they termed the 'statut unique', or equal salaries and conditions for all workers in the administration. In addition, the first overt signs of political demands began to be made.

One stimulation to political awakening in the Congo came from neighbouring Ruanda-Urundi. Belgian policy there closely resembled that in the Congo, with links between the administrations and economies, and the League of Nations mandate had become a trust agreement under the United Nations. The Belgians allowed traditionalist Watutsi rulers to continue their domination not only over their own people, but also over the more numerous Bahutu. But the United Nations now had powers of investigation. So pilot elections for advisers to the Belgian administration were held in Usumbura as early as 1949. The Congo évolués naturally asked why if elections could be held in backward Ruanda-Urundi they should not also be held in the Congo.

Some minor moves were made to appease the Congo élite. In 1948 a 'carte de mérite civique' was introduced, giving évolués a certificate to prove that they were of good behaviour, though few precise privileges. The following year a commission was set up to look into the whole question of the évolués and to investigate the system of 'immatriculation' which, from 1892, legally allowed an African to register as civilised and enjoy the same status as a European. In 1948, too, racial discrimination in schools began to be undermined by opening European schools to Africans and Coloureds, followed in 1950 by the abandonment of all discrimination in schools, though African children were examined as to their backgrounds before admission.

Yet, despite these faint shadows of battles to come, the Congolese élite remained few and weak. Africans in the Congo were deliberately isolated from contacts with developments in the rest of the continent and offered higher material standards than in most African and Asian countries. Belgian evolutionary policy, administered by a combination of state, church and capitalism, had hardly been challenged and could expect to pursue its leisurely way for many years to come.

Until the outbreak of the second world war there were strong similarities between the position of the French Equatorial African territories and the Belgian Congo. In both, concessionary companies had acquired a major influence. The administration of the French colonies was centred on Paris through the person of the Governor-General, as the Belgians based their colonial government in Brussels.

In both areas rural backwardness, allied to tribalism and isolation from the outside world, prevented any significant protest against colonial rule.

The impact of the war caused the two regions to diverge quite sharply. The unexpected loyalty of French territories to De Gaulle, the leadership of Eboué and the acceleration of French policy brought political developments within the French area unknown to the Congo. The pattern for the future was laid down at the 1944 Brazzaville Conference, itself largely due to the initiative of Eboué. Loyalty to the French had changed the relationship between France and her central African subjects. From being regarded as primitive savages, unwelcome burdens on the metropolitan country, ungrateful for membership of the French Empire, they had been transformed into loyal French heroes. They should therefore be accorded the reward of greater recognition as minor citizens within French civilisation, allowed to participate in framing the post-war French constitution, and given parliamentary representation in the Union which was to succeed the Empire.

So, as in French West Africa, the central African colonies sent delegates to the Constituent Assembly which opened in Paris in November 1945 charged to draft a new French constitution. This constitution would apply not only to metropolitan France, but also to her overseas territories. The French conception of her colonial subjects as members of a greater France was to be given practical expression.

Of course, again as in the case of West Africa, theory and practice showed sharp contrasts. The constitution finally approved in 1946 gave central Africa six seats out of the 622 in the National Assembly, and of these six two were virtually reserved for Europeans through the operation of the double college system of elections. The total electorate of the four colonies was only 110,029 out of a population estimated at 4,406,000, for only certain categories of adults were allowed the franchise.

Nevertheless, even this limited form of representation brought radical changes to public life. Perhaps more important than representation in the Assembly, Senate and Union Assembly, was the creation of local assemblies, one in each territory, and a Grand Council for the Federation. This stimulated local political activity and, although the main concern of these assemblies was financial, whilst the local administrators and Paris remained firmly in control, some form of political organisation became inevitable.

Before the war there had been much less political activity in French central Africa than in the west. The area was sparsely populated, very poor, and extremely backward. A few mutual aid associations had existed, together with a variety of religious sects, but always within the context of a continuing tribal society. Gabon was the only one of the four territories where parties had appeared, this being the only territory with any considerable wealth, but even there they were short-lived.

Even after the war, despite the economic stimulation, the urbanisation, and the miseries suffered under forced intensive cultivation of cotton and rubber collection, there was little early sign of political awakening. This torpor was soon apparent when elections were held to the 1945 Constituent Assembly in Paris. Although, through the double college electoral system, the Africans, voting through the second college, had roughly double the representation of the Europeans, in fact, they only elected one African, Jean-Félix Tchicaya from Moyen-Congo, to the Assembly. There was still a widespread feeling that Europeans knew best about politics and were the right people to elect for dealing with such matters.

To some extent, this feudalist outlook explains the lesser attention paid to central Africa than to the west by French political parties. The influence of De Gaulle persisted after the war had ended and his Rassemblement du Peuple Français made the first impact in all the territories except Gabon. It was usually supported by the administrators, whose influence was very powerful in the early days of the new constitution, and attracted adherence from both Europeans and Africans. It kept its prestige longest in Tchad, but even in Ubangui-Chari it was always dominated by the administration and the Europeans, whilst it rapidly lost African support in Moyen-Congo.

The French Socialists, the Section Française de l'Internationale Ouvrière, established a branch at Brazzaville in Moyen-Congo, and attracted the support of Jacques Opangault and the M'Bochi tribe which he led. Later, too, Ahmed Koulamallah, a Moslem merchant, formed a socialist branch in Tchad. But the socialists never captured the trade union movement and only made progress when they virtually adopted tribalism.

The story of French communist efforts in central Africa is

characteristic. They formed study groups as early as February 1946, and tried to establish trade unions affiliated to their Confédération Générale du Travail. Then they backed the RDA as in west Africa. But as soon as they tried active intervention, through the person of Raymond Barbé again, they revealed their failure to understand a local situation. They attacked the colonial government, the traditional chiefs, De Gaulle and the local Resistance leaders. This immediately resuscitated war-time loyalties and alienated Africans and Europeans alike.

Thus none of the metropolitan parties which had developed such strong influences amongst French Africans in the west had any lasting success in central Africa. On the other hand, despite continued suspicions about associating with west Africa, the new politicians in Equatorial Africa gave considerable support to the RDA. In Tchad Gabriel Lisette, a Negro from the French Antilles who had studied in Paris, worked in the French administration, been active with the Free French and was married to a Frenchwoman, formed his Parti Progressiste Tchadien as the local affiliate of the RDA. He quickly secured the support of the African évolués, particularly from the Sara tribe. In Moyen-Congo, Tchicaya, who was one of the original signatories of the RDA manifesto, built an affiliated party named Parti Progressiste Congolais around the Vili tribe. The Union Oubanguienne in Ubangui-Chari, although a branch of the RDA, was largely the personal party of Antoine Darlan, a mulatto whose communist connections and aggressive personality tended to alienate potential supporters.

In Gabon the RDA did not take root until much later. Jean Aubame dominated Gabon politics, and he faithfully followed Léopold Senghor. He had the backing of the important Fang tribe, although his party, Union Démocratique et Social Gabonaise, was to be challenged by Léon Mba, another Fang, and his Bloc Démocratique Gabonaise.

The truth is that the economic and social conditions in all four French Equatorial African colonies were so miserable at the end of the war that political development here never rivalled that of French West Africa. Not only did many Africans believe that Europeans should continue in control of politics, but they still looked to the traditionalist chiefs as the natural repositories of local power. So the RPF flourished amongst Europeans and many urbanised

Africans, whilst most of the early African parties were dominated by tribal chiefs and elders. Radical movements had little appeal and were opposed by all the powers of the administration. Even in Gabon, with its mineral wealth and widespread education, modern political activity hardly appeared in the first five years after the war, partly due to the decline in the population of the dominant Fang tribe. In Ubangui-Chari, Moyen-Congo and Tchad, it was even less apparent.

Nevertheless, the new representative institutions created a forcing house for political activity, and the appearance of the RDA was a small sign that it was African parties which already held the key to the future.

Although each of the four countries suffered from a lack of capable leaders, whilst the few who emerged, like Lisette, Tchicaya and Aubame, preferred Parisian politics to the struggle at home, parties were being formed for the first time and Africans were voting. French Africans in these countries might not seem likely to set Africa alight, but they had already acquired the machinery with which to participate to some degree in the African political revolution.

6

The Eastern Patchwork

East Africa is a patchwork of contrasts. Its seaboard is hot, humid, steaming, yet within a few miles there rises the snow-crested crater of Kilimanjaro, nearly four miles high. Its people vary from nomadic herdsmen to sophisticated men of the world, at home in London, New York, Moscow or Peking. Its economic life includes not only subsistence standards but the wealth of cotton, coffee, diamonds, the modern city life of Nairobi beside bare existence in peasant mud huts. Its lands range from desert and swamp to some of the most fertile acres in the world. Its countries have displayed most varieties of constitutional status; the oldest sovereign state in Africa, protectorates, a semi-protectorate, semi-colony, United Nations trust territories, a French Overseas Territory, and an ex-Italian colony which became first a trust territory and then a sovereign state. If we included the islands of Madagascar, Mauritius and the Seychelles we should have still wider variations, but as they have had little effect on life in the African continent, we shall make only passing reference to them.

It is arbitrary to place the frontiers of East Africa around Tanganyika, Zanzibar, Kenya, Uganda, Somalia, Ethiopia, Eritrea and French Somaliland. It is also convenient. They do not have a common history, but they have common features separating them from the northern states of Arab Africa or from the central bloc described in the previous chapter.

Although most of this area has been governed by the British, within the British Empire, the European population has for long been cosmopolitan. Tanganyika, which was German East Africa until the end of the first world war, has not only retained many Germans, but also has a large Greek community. Poles, Italians, and Scandinavians are to be seen in Nairobi, whilst South Africans are prominent amongst the Kenyan farmers. Dutchmen grow sugar in

Ethiopia, where Swedes are also working, while many Italians still live in their former colonies, Somaliland and Eritrea.

Yet, more important than the cosmopolitan nature of the European community, was the change in its character effected during the war. This was particularly noticeable in Kenya. Nairobi suffered during the war from being a non-combatant military centre, with all the snobbery, false gentility and moral deterioration attendant on that function. Many of the brigadiers and colonels making up the war-time pseudo-gentry escaped from post-war British socialism to become settlers or businessmen in a country where they could maintain their social status. They were accompanied by lower ranks of ex-servicemen, who became traders, technicians, or farm managers, whilst their wives and daughters served in shops or worked in offices. Thus, the post-war years brought an increase in the number of white inhabitants, a dilution in the generally upper-class character of the pre-war community, and strong reinforcement to those elements mainly concerned to use Africans as cheap labour with a permanently inferior social status. Nairobi itself became the centre of a 'smart set', with its own fringe imitators. Those who had gone to Kenya to make their homes, who had worked hard to create farmlands out of wilderness, were for a time overwhelmed by the antics of the newcomers. It was this curiously mottled community which tended to dominate the white image in East Africa.

In the other territories the white communities were much less strident, although sections of them took their lead from Nairobi. The problem of land alienation never became of major importance outside Kenya, and although there was some measure of racial discrimination in both Uganda and Tanganyika, it did not take on as offensive a character as that in Kenya. There was never much doubt that Uganda would become a state wholly ruled by Africans, nor that Tanganyika, under the protection of the United Nations Trusteeship Council, would become self-governing with Africans in the dominant role. There were many Italians in Eritrea, but they had little political ambition after the defeat of Italy, often performed quite humble occupations, and, in any case, were under British military rule. Indeed, it seemed, as in the rest of Africa, that the fewer Europeans living in a territory, the less racial tension existed, whereas it was where considerable white communities had settled that race relations were most embittered.

The Europeans, however, were not the only immigrant community. They were, in fact, greatly outnumbered by the Indians, or Asians, as they came to be known after the partition of India and Pakistan. The history of contact between Asians and the coast of east Africa went back long before European exploration of this area. Not only had Arabs traded down the coastline from very early times, leaving considerable settlements in Zanzibar and the Mombasa area, but Indians themselves had certainly crossed the Indian Ocean before Vasco da Gama and had returned home with African slaves.

The building of the railway from the coast to Uganda in the 1890s attracted a large number of Indian labourers into the interior. By the time of the second war they dominated much of the trade and commerce of the three British east African territories. They were firmly established in Nairobi, Dar-es-Salaam and Kampala, but they also took their wares into the heart of the bush, providing goods in remote African villages unobtainable from any other source. Inevitably, they became suspect of exploiting their monopoly by charging extortionate prices. In some ways they resembled the Jews of medieval Europe, indispensable as money-lenders and traders, but hated for the power this gave them over those who made use of their services.

The Europeans detested the Indian community for the competition some of its members offered them in wealth and education. When, in 1923, Indians were given political representation in Kenya there was almost violent rebellion from the whites. After the war, particularly when India and Pakistan had achieved independence, dark hints were frequently heard among Europeans that India had imperialist ambitions in east Africa and was using resident Asians as her fifth column. In fact, Pandit Nehru and the Aga Khan (whose Ismaili sect played an important part in east Africa) made a special point of urging their followers to regard themselves as east Africans.

Africans, as well as Europeans, disliked the Asians. Although most politically-conscious Africans valued the support given them by Asian leaders, the masses were suspicious. They had two main complaints. First, they accused Asians of acting as a barrier to African progress by monopolising small business and occupying most of the lower professional and semi-skilled posts. Secondly, they accused the Asians of living within a closed culture. Because of the dominant impact of European society, the Africans had broadly developed with a European cultural outlook. They might be barred from the inner sanctums of European society, but it was to them that they aspired, for their education, institutions and cultural development had all been modelled on European lines. They therefore resented an Oriental society, normally excluding them from participation, transplanted into their midst. They particularly criticised the Asian clan outlook in economic life, where many firms and businesses exclusively employed members of a particular Asian family group, escaping any regulation of hours, wages or conditions.

This African-Asian tension was apparent in Kenya, Uganda and Tanganyika, continually souring relations within the movements designed to attack European privileges and British imperial rule. Nevertheless, it did not prevent outstanding Asians from taking leading roles in social welfare, educational advance, and the drive for political emancipation.

The circumstances of ordinary life in east Africa hardly made for a revolutionary situation by the end of the war. The vast majority of Africans were living in bare subsistence, with little to stimulate ambition. Illiterate masses living in endemic poverty do not themselves raise revolt. They need leaders to fire them with discontent; only then does their penury become the fuel of revolution. And the leaders are usually found among the intelligentsia, among people who read books, see the ways of others and seek to find the means of emulating them. There were few educated Africans in east Africa at the time the war ended, and virtually no industrial or mining centres where discussion and social organisation could focus. There was Makerere College in Uganda, the only institution of higher education in the whole area; but its numbers were few and east Africans had not yet been given the opportunities to study in London, Paris or America, where most ideas of revolt were born. To the typical farm worker, nomad, or tribal peasant, racked by generations of tropical diseases, weakened by lack of the right foods, ignorant of events in the next village, more ignorant of the rest of the continent, the white farmer and the imperial administrator seemed as permanent a part of life as sun and land. Physical and mental energies were all devoted to scraping up the means of existence, leaving no surplus for thoughts of emulating the white man's entirely different way of life or removing the District Officer and replacing him with a black man.

Yet, whilst this was the general picture, there were some contrary influences stirring, even in the most primitive areas. East Africans had not only been affected by war-time influences, they had actually seen warfare in their own lands. The British had defeated the Italians in Eritrea, Somaliland and Ethiopia, with many east Africans serving in their forces. The Italian conquest of Ethiopia in 1935 had aroused African emotions and the restoration of Emperor Haile Selassie was considered a defeat for European imperialism. It was actually witnessed by many east Africans, who could not fail to recognise the contrast between the restoration of sovereignty to an African-governed state and the European imperial rule to which they returned in their own countries.

Ethiopia might be a primitive, undeveloped land, subject to a feudal ruling class with the Emperor acting as virtual dictator. It might have practically no recognisable roads outside Addis Ababa, very few schools, and remain dependent on foreign advisers for its administration. But its people were ruled once more by their own African rulers, as they always had been except for the period of Italian occupation between 1936 and 1941. This was a pregnant thought for those Africans from other countries who were witnessing African self-government for the first time.

Racialism also had a profound influence. It might be that the vast majority of the African population at this time accepted imperial government as inevitable. Yet there was one grievance which smouldered deep below the surface of east African society. This was the issue of land. It affected Kenya most directly, but it was felt to only a lesser extent throughout east Africa. No matter how the European farmers argued that when they took the land in the early years of the century it had been unoccupied, Africans had such mystical feelings towards land that this argument could never dowse the fires of resentment. They counter-argued that the land was only temporarily uninhabited, due to cattle pest and human disease, and that, in any case, this was the land of their fathers which could never be severed from tribal ownership. The fact that Europeans had seized 16,000 square miles, about a quarter of the entire arable land of Kenya, for the exclusive ownership of about 4,000 white farmers, leaving five and a half million Africans to content themselves with the rest, opened a running sore of racialism throughout east Africa. That the British colonial government had confirmed this white ownership by legislation and even prevented Africans from being employed as farm managers in the white highlands, only identified the British with this racial policy.

Although only a few Africans were directly deprived, and most of them were not Kikuyu, as often assumed, the effects of colonial rule and the settler establishment progressively increased the sense of resentment. Health measures and veterinary science brought about a steady increase in human and cattle populations. African tribes in this area had been accustomed to travelling about before the arrival of Europeans, exhausting one area before leaving it to recover and moving to another. Colonial government kept the tribes static at a time when they were multiplying without appreciably changing their methods of agriculture. So increasing numbers had to exist on land which became rapidly eroded without the previous opportunities for moving to new areas. Meanwhile, they looked with anger at the areas reserved for the handful of whites, some of them not even cultivated.

Racialism is a negative emotion. It does not promote the search for a new society, but only for a different set of faces. It provokes envy and colour obsession, often masking genuine social evils. And in societies such as those of Kenya and some of the other areas in east Africa, the practice of racial superiority inevitably breeds counter-racialism, which becomes widely infectious. This form of resentment is dangerous ammunition for political reformers to handle, but it can create the mass discontent which no politician can afford to ignore. Kenya had been warned of the danger by observant writers from the nineteen-twenties. And events in Kenya profoundly coloured the outlook in the whole of east Africa.

One particular example of this Kenyan influence was seen immediately after the war. Just before the war ended it was decided by the British government to create institutions which would maintain the co-operation between the three east African territories developed during the war. An inter-territorial assembly was to be established to provide for political consultation and after the war proposals for its composition were published in a government White Paper (Cmd. 191). These provided for equal representation on the unofficial side between Europeans, Asians and Africans. Despite the fact that, proportionate to their numbers, the Africans were grossly under-represented, their leaders accepted this arrangement as an improvement on the past and a hope for the future. But the Kenya Europeans raised a loud outcry, accusing the British government of betraying the white man's interest. The British Colonial Office, although under a Labour Secretary of State, heeded the European protest and the advice of Governor Sir Phillip Mitchell. It issued another White Paper (Cmd. 210) eighteen months later, in 1947, introducing a more complicated system of election and selection to the assembly from the three territories, the effect of which was to give the Europeans a larger number of seats than any of the other races. Inevitably, this caused intense resentment amongst non-Europeans throughout east Africa.

It was this kind of discriminatory policy which continually stimulated a racial approach to politics, aggravating the resentment felt towards the European land holdings.

To the observant there were also features of the east African economy likely to cause trouble unless remedied in the years immediately after the war. Urbanisation was not as great an immediate problem to east Africa as it was in the other parts of the continent, for few large towns existed and the region was largely agricultural. Yet the problem had appeared and, linked to the growing land difficulty, it bore the seeds of future discontent.

The number of factory workers in Kenya rose to nearly 10,000 during the war, concentrated mainly in Nairobi, but also seen in Mombasa. A Trades Dispute Tribunal was set up in 1942 and trade unions legalised in the following year. A number of strikes broke out amongst railway workers at this time and it was clear by the end of the war that urban African workers had become a significant factor in the Kenya social economy. By this time about 70,000 Africans were living in the environs of Nairobi alone.

This situation inevitably presaged the rise of the usual kind of urban organisations, together with industrial and political agitation. But the problem went deeper. Africans were considered by employers to be essentially rural dwellers. They were therefore paid as single men, sojourning only temporarily in towns. Not only were their urban locations built as bachelor quarters, inevitably becoming squalid slums as people poured into them from overcrowded reserves, but their entire social security rested on the assumption that they all had stakes on the land. It was expected that the African worker would maintain his family from his plot in the reserve, which would also provide him with security in sickness and old age. The system was socially degenerating and economically retarding. It concentrated a large number of men and few women in the townships, leaving much of the agricultural work to be done by women, old men and children. At the same time, it prevented the development of a stable urban family population, with the skills, training and experience which could only come from permanent urban employment. Kenya's African workers were neither peasant farmers nor industrial workers, but an inefficient mixture of the two. The consequent brake on progress in skill, production and wages was bound to bring trouble. Few Europeans living in east Africa were concerned with deep-rooted seeds of trouble. They were more interested in making a white man's paradise. To achieve this they had tried to adopt the policy followed by their cousins in the Rhodesias and South Africa. They believed that if they could establish some form of link between the three British territories and get rid of Colonial Office rule then they would be able to escape from the logic of the racial proportions and maintain white rule indefinitely. The Achilles' heel of this imitation South African ambition was that their numbers were too few. In South Africa whites formed twenty per cent of the total population; in east Africa there were more than 250 Africans for every white man, and even in Kenya Europeans could muster less than one per cent of the population. The settlers did not recognise this as an insuperable obstacle, and, in spite of its rejection by the Ormsby-Gore Commission in 1927, continued to pursue the goal of federation or some other form of close association to ensure white supremacy. Shortly after the end of the war, a secret meeting was held with leaders from the Rhodesias to discuss the possibility of a wider association under white control. Such moves kept the politically-conscious Africans in a state of continual nervous suspicion, for the whole of British east and central Africa always had the South African lesson in the forefront of its mind. The establishment of the East African High Commission in 1948, although only concerned with common services between the three territories, was widely suspected by Africans for this very reason.

So that although there was no immediate threat of revolt against the established order in east Africa soon after the war, the roots of conflict, particularly in Kenya, were already growing.

In its own areas, the British government believed that slow evolution in representative institutions would meet any foreseeable demands. The Africans were to be gradually introduced into local and national government, at first selected by the administration, as it was not thought possible for the illiterate masses to operate an electoral system. Yet British policy revealed two large flaws. The final objective had not been thought out and therefore could not be held out to the people; the pace of representative advance was much too slow to meet the tempo of post-war political awakening and was too often retarded by obstruction from the white settlers. Thus, each step in African advance appeared to have been forced from a reluctant imperial government which seemed to hold a scarcely-veiled preference for leaving Europeans in control.

Nevertheless, at the end of the war the British initiated a sudden acceleration in African representation, as they were doing in other African colonies. This was partly due to the advent of a Labour government in Britain, strongly influenced in its colonial policy by Fabian thinkers who had devoted a great deal of consideration to the post-war situation in British colonies. But it was also due to the effects of the war on the political climate, for several of these reforms were actually prepared by a Conservative Colonial Secretary, Oliver Stanley, before the war ended.

In Tanganyika a further influence was working towards a greater African representation. As a mandated territory, its administration was supervised by the Permanent Mandates Commission. After the war, when the mandatory status ended with the death of the League, it became a United Nations Trust Territory. A delegation from the Trusteeship Council visited Tanganyika every three years, examining its administration, hearing opinions from its inhabitants and making reports, including recommendations. Both these international bodies pressed Britain to increase African representation. The Mandates Commission had tried to persuade the British government to include Africans on the Legislative Council which was established in 1926, but Sir Donald Cameron, the Governor, consistently argued that there were no representative Africans capable of taking part in the Council debates. Actually, Cameron's ideal was parallel development for the races, eventually with two councils representing Africans and non-Africans. So, until 1945, the

Legislative Council was composed of officials and a number of European and Indian members selected by the Governor.

In 1945, however, the new post-war attitude of the British Colonial Office was demonstrated by the appointment of two Africans to the Council. Both were chiefs, always favourites with colonial administrations, but, in fact, there was virtually no évolué class from which representatives could have been chosen.

The next step was for Africans to gain entrance to the Executive Council which, although only advisory to the Governor, played the part of an embryo government. This was not achieved until 1951, when another chief, albeit an educated young man, became the first African member. In the meantime, the European residents of the territory had been making political headway. In 1948, their representatives on the Executive became 'Members' with departments, a status less than that of minister, but one intended to ease them gradually into ministerial office.

By this time visiting missions from the Trusteeship Council were pressing more heavily than ever for greater African representation. The 1948 mission, for example, criticised the slow political progress being made by Africans and called for increased educational facilities to enable more Africans to enter the political and administrative fields. Britain pointed out in reply that a ten year plan, initiated in 1947, would provide over £5 million for African education, but insisted that the development of democratic institutions amongst Africans must be gradual. It was this same mission which recommended that Africans be given seats on the Executive, but the British still maintained that suitably qualified Africans could not be found.

There was, however, some sign that Britain was concerned to promote constitutional progress. Another two Africans were nominated to the Legislative Council and, in 1949, all the unofficial members of the Council were appointed as a Committee on Constitutional Development. Their task was to make recommendations for future constitutional developments in the territory. It was this committee which recommended that an African should be appointed to the Executive. It further proposed a re-organisation of the Legislative Council, so that, whilst retaining an official majority, it would have an increased number of unofficial members, with equal representation for Europeans, Asians and Africans.

Slow progress towards something like a representative system could be seen during the first few years after the war. There was no serious African movement to spur advance, for there were few educated Africans and most of those were scattered through the huge, sparsely populated country. On the other hand, there was no real political drive from the Europeans either. They were a mixture of nationalities, not more than 20,000 in all, including administrators, and they knew that even if they could persuade the British government, the United Nations would never allow them to rule an independent Tanganyika. They pressed for the maintenance of their majority representation at all constitutional discussions and half-heartedly flirted with closer east African association, but actually there was little political fire in their breasts.

Politics in Tanganyika reflected the stagnant state of the economy. Only about thirty-four per cent of the land is cultivable, white farmers were allowed only a minute portion of it and African land rights were jealously guarded. Sisal and the Williamson diamond mine provided the only important wealth and neither required social concentrations of African labour. There was therefore no such urban stimulation of political thought as occurred in some other parts of Africa. The Chagga tribe in the north began to develop their coffee growing co-operatives, but they were far away from Dar-es-Salaam on the slopes of Kilimanjaro. The British government's attempt to grow vast quantities of groundnuts, started in 1948, had foundered by 1950 due to the lack of preparation and investigation, even though the project was for a time under the auspices of Unilever's United Africa Company.

So Tanganyika generally slumbered, with occasional brief periods of semi-wakefulness when prodded by a United Nations mission, the progressive ideas of a governor like Sir Edward Twining, or activities across the Kenyan border. The social atmosphere was characterised by a grumbling tolerance between the races, accompanied by a degree of reluctant good-humour and even affection. The country awaited ideas, ambition, leadership; the man who was to supply them was still quietly studying history amid the grey stones of Edinburgh.

An atmosphere of tolerant race relations was to be found also in Uganda, but in very different circumstances. Here, by African standards, the country was rich. Its cotton and coffee ensured ready exports, and as, through a combination of tsetse flies and deliberate policy, Europeans were not allowed to settle, much of the wealth accrued to Africans. So the real struggle in Uganda was between the common people and their African feudal rulers.

The first brush in this conflict had come before the end of the war, at the beginning of 1945. Despite the absence of white settlement, there was always a lurking suspicion in the minds of Uganda's Africans that European control might appear from somewhere. It was proposed that some privately-owned land be compulsorily acquired, with compensation, for public use, including the provision of a site for Makerere University College. Agitation against this proposal was reinforced by strikers demanding higher wages in Kampala to meet the war-time rise in the cost of living. Protests were concentrated in Buganda, the richest province of the protectorate where, arising out of the policy of indirect rule prevailing from the time of the original agreements with the chiefs, a separate monarchy, government and parliament existed. The young Kabaka, Mutesa II, was prepared to co-operate with the colonial government of the protectorate on this land issue. Public opposition forced him to change his Prime Minister, or Katikiro. The new appointee was quickly pronounced insane by the British and deported. His successor, again anxious to co-operate with the colonial administration, was assassinated. Further deportations followed, particularly of rebellious chiefs, before the measure was finally approved.

This sudden flare-up of popular expression had one immediate consequence. The Kabaka's parliament, known as the Lukiko, had been packed with traditional representatives and dominated by his court. Now the Kabaka agreed that 36 of its 89 members should be elected, although through the indirect system of electoral colleges.

This issue also led to the appearance of the first genuine political party in Uganda, the Bataka. The name of the party referred to ancient burial rights of the peasants, but the party based its programme on economic and social reform, and attacked the considerable land holdings of the Christian missions. It was not long before the colonial government took powers to restrict the freedom of the press and limit the holding of open air meetings. Meanwhile, a second form of political association appeared in the shape of the African Farmers' Union. The two organisations worked closely together, both fighting the domination of traditional chiefs and demanding an increase in the elected membership of the Lukiko from 36 to 60. In 1949 they organised a mass demonstration and a three-day strike in support of their claims. This led to more police action, arrests and trials. Eventually, both movements were banned by the colonial government, the leader of the Bataka, Kumu Mulumba, remaining in London, and Ignatius Musazi, the Farmers' Union president, being placed under house arrest.

It seemed that the colonial authorities, who controlled the government of the protectorate, though not of Buganda, were using their power to maintain traditional authority. In Buganda the Kabaka held a mystical sway over his subjects and his court dominated all governing functions. In the other three kingdoms, Toro, Ankole and Bunyoro, the power of the rulers was only slightly less. Yet, when a younger educated group began to rebel against this autocratic rule and closed ruling class, they found that they had to face not only their traditional rulers, but the colonial power too.

Yet this was not the whole story. The Governor, Sir John Hall, made it publicly clear in 1947 that Uganda was to be developed as a primarily African state, that it was not to have a unitary form, and that special arrangements would have to be made for the kingdom. In 1945 the protectorate's Legislative Council saw the appearance of African members for the first time beside Indians and Europeans. These Africans were appointed by the traditional authorities – including the Kabaka – and were all chiefs. But the door had been opened. The number of African members was increased in 1949 and again in 1950, giving Uganda its distinctive version of racial 'parity' – equal numbers between African and non-African. Thus in the Council eight Africans sat beside four Europeans and four Asians. (In Tanganyika 'parity' was interpreted as equal numbers from each race; in Kenya, equality between European and non-European.)

The colonial government still kept control over the legislature by balancing the sixteen unofficial members with sixteen officials, with the Governor as its chairman. Unofficial members were also still nominated by the Governor, but he consulted various bodies before doing so. In 1950, also, the first non-European, an Asian, the Hon. A. M. Maini, Mayor of Kampala, was appointed to the Executive. He was not only the first non-European, but also the first unofficial member, for no European representative had yet been invited to join.

Thus, although the inheritance of indirect rule continued to influence British administrators in supporting the traditional authorities, they were at the same time building representative institutions which could become instruments of democracy. Whether or not they were used for this purpose would largely depend on the outcome of the struggle between the new progressive forces and the traditionalists. Riots in 1945 and 1949 had been directed against the feudalism of the Kabaka's court and its attendant landlords, not against the colonial power. Indeed, the Lukiko, still dominated by traditionalists, demonstrated its opposition to the progress of democracy by refusing to appoint Baganda members to the Legislative Council in 1950, though the Kabaka later did so himself. The nationalist movement in Uganda thus had to battle first against traditionalist power, whilst the colonial government, with its policy of constitutional evolution, had to deal with the complications of semi-autonomous feudal kingdoms.

Over all this complicated political scene hung an atmosphere of commercialism. In Uganda the price of cotton, suspected Asian overcharging in their bush stores, Asian control of the cotton ginneries, commerce and banking, were all more important issues than self-government or independence. Uganda was essentially a bourgeois, commercial society – for Africans as well as for Europeans or Asians. Indeed, much more for Africans than for Europeans, who were more concerned about school or college ties. The Africans established their own Chamber of Commerce, owned many shops, built co-operatives, and produced their own wealthy class. In this curious mixture of African feudal monarchy, commercial prosperity, and snobbery, combined with a colonial government traditionally supporting the feudal authorities, it is little wonder that no clear political drive emerged in the period following the war.

Although these events in Tanganyika and Uganda were interesting, had begun to change the outlook of the 14 million people living in the two territories, and would have a profound influence on the whole of east Africa in the future, it was Kenya which was the principal storm centre in the region. There seems little reason to doubt that the reason for this was the effect of white settlement. Uganda was a much richer country and had in Buganda a social structure of a higher standard than anything Kenya had known.

Tanganyika was a much larger country and also had white settlers. Yet, from the nineteen-twenties until the mid-fifties, British and world interest in east African events was almost entirely concentrated on Kenya.

The fact that a large proportion of the European farmers were British, and that many other Britishers went out to banks, commerce, administration and skilled technical work, only partly accounted for the interest in Kenyan affairs. For, by the end of the war, there were still less than 30,000 Europeans in the country, and a proportion of these were from other European countries or from South Africa. The numbers quickly increased after the war, but they never grew so large as to warrant the importance given to this community. It was the public relations of the Europeans rather than their numbers which commanded attention. A section of the settlers, supported after the war by the newcomers in Nairobi, used every opportunity to publicise their complaints and found ready support in the British press and parliament. The intemperate outbursts of this group may have given them some release from fears and conflicts, whilst providing British newspapers with extravagant copy, but they were also heard and read by many Africans. They inevitably provoked African reactions.

To unravel the tangled skeins of emotion, politics, economics and social anthropology which made Kenya the most fascinating, yet the most tragic, drama of British Africa in the years immediately following the war we must simplify, with the danger of over-simplifying. This country, parts of which are amongst the most fertile in the world, was inhabited by something over 5 million people. Population figures were always approximate in Africa, for few reputable censuses had been conducted. (The older the figures the more wildly inaccurate they proved.) Of these, at the end of the war, just over 20,000 were Europeans, 120,000 Asians, the majority Indians, but also including 24,000 Arabs and a small number of Goans. The rest, 97 per cent, were Africans, some of whom lived in traditional tribal communities, others as labourers or squatters on European farms, still others in the semi-detribalised surroundings of town life. The impact of European settlement and government had been far greater than their numbers would suggest. They had not simply built splendid farms and homes in the Highlands, but, through increasing missionary work, economic activities and administration, they had directly affected the life of Africans within their own communities.

It is a mistake to believe, as many Kenyan whites and others assumed, that African society before the coming of the white man was chaotic and brutal. Most of it was primitive but highly organised. Some practices seem cruel and undoubtedly caused pain and suffering; no society has yet found the way to prevent its customs causing suffering to some of its members. The supernatural played a big part, particularly in ancestor worship, but again, this has been common to many societies outside Africa. There were many inter-tribal wars, but the deaths involved never remotely reached the slaughter caused by European wars.

It was natural and inevitable that missionaries should try to abolish practices which they found cruel or immoral. They attacked the use of women to carry heavy loads and the practice of female circumcision. By any humane standards both practices in the life of, for instance, the Kikuyu tribe, are cruel. Actions which produce unnecessary pain are by definition cruel, and it does not lessen the cruelty to argue that they are part of traditional social observance. Yet much of the humanising argument of the missionaries was lost. They were neither anthropologists nor psychologists and therefore could not understand the meanings of what they encountered. Consequently, they condemned it blindly, often provoking an adverse reaction to their teachings rather than securing conversion. Moreover, they could only offer another form of supernatural belief for tribal superstitions, whilst acceptance of the individualism inherent in Christianity seemed to many Africans to undermine the communal strength of tribalism. Thus, whilst Christian missions brought the elements of an educational system, introduced some modern health measures, and in places modified cruelty, their effect on African society was often profoundly disruptive.

This was one of the effects of European on African society. And it was this impact which was eroding relations between the races in Kenya. The two societies were living too close to avoid both contact and constant evidence of its effects. Kikuyu and Luo found themselves herded in ever-increasing numbers on too little and unfertile soil; their neighbours were white farmers with land to spare on large farms. The missions condemned witchcraft, ancestor worship and the traditional customs of the tribes, whilst these ancient beliefs proved helpless against the white man's powers. So the younger generation rebelled against the old disciplines and the authority of the elders crumbled. Yet the new faiths and principles taught by the missionaries were manifestly not practised by the white men themselves. African life was contemptuously derided, yet when Africans acquired European education they found themselves still excluded from the closed, privileged circle, and often treated with more aggressive contempt than even their illiterate brethren.

So the Africans saw their own society being destroyed without anything more attractive or superior being offered in its place. To some extent this feeling was experienced by most Kenyan Africans, but it was particularly severe among the Kikuyu. They lived next to the White Highlands, Nairobi with its inaccessible riches and pleasures was on their threshold, and more of them had attained European skills, with the subsequent rejection.

Moreover, it was mainly the Kikuyu who heard and read the claims of the vociferous settler element against the colonial government. It was they who most frequently listened to this group proclaiming the backwardness of the African, the inferiority of his intellect, the baseness of his instincts. They were able to hear the white politicians condemning the colonial government for its refusal to hand over power, read the intemperate letters in the local press, and witness the pressure put on governors and their officials. It was the Kikuyu who saw at first hand the arrogant conviction of certain white leaders that Kenya belonged to the white community and would soon be ruled by it.

So the Kikuyu opened their defensive counter-attack soon after the first war. The Kikuyu Central Association was formed in 1922 under the leadership of Harry Thuku, later to become a strong opponent of militancy. Jomo Kenyatta was secretary-general of the KCA, which concentrated on such grievances as the White Highlands, was strongly Africanist, and at times used almost anti-white propaganda. The Kikuyu were striking back at the white men who derided them and undermined their social foundations. Thus it was that the KCA, despite its comparatively sophisticated propaganda, fought against the missionary campaign to abolish female circumcision. Nor is it surprising that it was the Kikuyu who started their own school system, partly because of a shortage of schools for Africans, but also in order to combat the teaching of the missionary schools on such subjects as polygamy and circumcision. To provide teachers for this Kikuyu Independent Schools Association, Peter (Mbiyu) Koinange, bearing an honoured name in Kikuyu society, founded a teachers' training college at Githunguri, the college at which Kenyatta was to become principal.

The KCA was proscribed during the war, but the return of east African soldiers from 1945 onwards hastened the breakdown of tribal authority and speeded the growth of political consciousness. These soldiers had been away from tribal society for too long to slip back into easy acceptance of its customs. In other countries they had imbibed new ideas of human relations and sensed something of the revolt against an established authority such as imperial rule.

So when a group of politically-conscious Africans formed a new party in 1944 they soon had ample reserves of discontent on which to call. In the same year the first African had been appointed to the Legislative Council. He was Eliud Mathu, who was selected from a list proposed by the local native councils. Mathu, together with a group of prominent leaders, including Apolo Ohanga, James Jeremiah and J. J. Chemallan, decided that in order to work constitutionally for a redress of African grievances, a political party should be formed. They called their new party the Kenya African Union, significantly using the national instead of the tribal title. The party stood for African self-government, with safeguarded minority rights, reform of the Legislative Council to include more African members, opposition to the unequal racial representation in the East African Central Assembly, more land and education for Africans, and better social conditions, including an end to the 'kipande' system of labour contract.

This programme was reformist. The strategy was to use existing institutions and gradually increase African participation in them. It demanded no changes which could not be supported by liberal opinion in Britain. It suggested no revolutionary action. Its revolutionary implications derived only from European objectives, for the reforms proposed by KAU were inconsistent with a white-controlled Kenya.

This white-black struggle dominated Kenyan public life. If the Colonial Office was unaware of the gathering storm it was because its officials ignored the warnings of students of Kenya such as Norman Leys, Margery Perham and Negley Farson – to name but three of several. Yet the Colonial Office apparently could not make up its mind whether the Europeans or the Africans should be supported. It adopted the characteristic British role of trying to appease both, despite the fact that their objectives were mutually incompatible.

So although the first African was brought into the Legislative Council in 1944, the following year the 'Membership' system, a quasi-ministerial device, was introduced into the Executive and the first European settler, Major Cavendish-Bentinck, became responsible for agriculture. In 1947 a second African, Apolo Ohanga, was taken into the legislature, but in 1948 the unofficial members of the Legislative Council, dominated by Europeans, were given a majority over the officials. In the same year African representation was increased to four, with the addition of Jeremiah and Chemallan, but they were still appointed, whilst eleven Europeans, five Asians and one Arab were all elected. (Another Arab was appointed, making eleven Europeans and eleven non-Europeans.) In 1950 a second European resident, E. A. Vasey, was appointed to the Executive, and in 1952 the first African, Mathu, joined the same body.

The governor, Sir Phillip Mitchell, and the Colonial Office were fumbling their way through concessions to contending pressures towards a system which they termed multi-racial. This was to include members of all the races on both legislative and executive bodies. But the system observed neither principle nor consistency. The Europeans aimed at a government freed from Colonial Office authority and controlled by themselves; the Africans demanded democratic representation which would give them dominant power through their superior numbers. Both the claims of 'civilised government' and 'democratic government' could lay some claim to principle. But to try and make government dependent on the power balance of the various races at any one time was mere expediency.

Meanwhile, tensions in the colony continued to rise as a result of these concessions and counter-concessions. The Africans feared that the colonial government, on which they relied to hold the Europeans at bay until they had mobilised their own strength, was abdicating and conceding power to the Europeans. The settlers saw the introduction of Africans into representative bodies as dangerously encouraging the pretensions of a few agitators appealing to uncivilised masses.

In 1947 there were riots outside Nairobi over the refusal of a bacon company to dismiss a clerk who had refused to contribute to a political fund. The following year there were further riots in the Kikuyu reserve against a government agricultural improvement scheme. The growth of trade unions and the support of some Asians made possible a general strike in 1949.

To this welter of tension returned the one African capable of combining an appeal to traditional Africanism with the modern leadership demanded by the new generation of Africans. Jomo (Burning Spear) Kenyatta, with his black beard, huge red ring and elephant head stick, returned to Kenya from London in 1946. He had been left an orphan soon after birth at the end of the last century and brought up by Scottish missionaries. His magnetic personality soon gave him the leadership of the Kikuyu Central Association whilst his pen was employed by a number of Kikuyu-language newspapers. From 1929 to 1946 he had lived in Europe, studying anthropology at the London School of Economics under Professor Malinowski, and at Moscow University, writing a book on Kikuyu customs, *Facing Mount Kenya*. During and immediately after the war he became one of the London group which organised the Manchester pan-African conference, and which included Kwame Nkrumah, George Padmore, Peter Abrahams and Burghardt DuBois. He became acquainted with the work of the Fabian Colonial Bureau, the Independent Labour Party, and similar idealist socialist organisations. He returned to Kenya influenced by these ideas, immediately became president of the Kenya African Union, leader of the Independent Schools Association and principal of the training college. He was entirely dedicated to fighting the colour bar and all forms of discrimination against Africans. He was worshipped by many Kikuyu and had an hypnotic authority over the younger generation in the reserve and in Nairobi. His followers were drawn also, though in smaller numbers, from other tribes, for he was accepted as the leader of Kenyan nationalism.

The future was conditioned by whether Kenyatta would be given the opportunity to lead his people along constitutional paths to their democratic objectives, whether attempts were made to barricade such paths by political obstruction, and, if so, whether he would draw on tribal mystiques or modern political means to remove them.

We need not trouble much about Zanzibar at this stage, for, although it forms part of east Africa, it was not until later that it emerged significantly into the African pattern. Its mixture of Arab landowners, Asian traders and African workers continued to grow and sell their cloves after the war almost undisturbed by African politics. The Arab dhows sailed into the harbour before the monsoons as they had done for centuries, though by now they were bartering dates, rugs and camels instead of slaves, as they had when Zanzibar was the largest slave market in the world. The Sultan continued his traditional rule, though his ten-mile strip on the mainland had been leased to Britain. He was 'advised' by the British Resident. The British connection brought its effects in 1948 when the first two Africans were appointed to the Legislative Council, joining three Arabs, two Asians and one European, with officials still in the majority. The Executive remained entirely composed of official members. Political agitation had not yet touched this romantic medieval survival, though some inhabitants complained of excessive British influence in their protectorate.

Of more importance, though again not yet directly involved in African affairs, was Madagascar, the fourth largest island in the world. The Malgaches had been affected by the war, for after the adherence of its administration to Vichy on the fall of France, Madagascar was occupied by Britain to prevent its seizure by the Japanese. After the war this island was treated in the same way as other French colonies and elected four deputies to the French Chamber by the double college system. Madagascar also had its own internal assemblies, as in the French African colonies.

But the Malgaches were not Africans. They were a mixture of Polynesian, Malay and African descent, living alongside a considerable European population. Their culture and language was both distinctive and advanced. So the French attempts at assimilation had a strong core of local patriotism to meet from an advanced people numbering nearly 5 million.

Nationalism developed early to contend with French policy. Three of the four deputies belonged to the main nationalist party, the Movement Démocratique de la Révolution Malgache. The French administrators favoured a rival party and used their influence, as in their other colonies, to direct the formal democratic processes in the way they wished. Friction rose to a head in 1947, although the actual cause of explosion is obscure. But a revolt broke out which the French blamed on the nationalists and put down with extreme severity. No-one knows the extent of the casualties. Many French planters and administrators were killed, as well as those Malgaches who collaborated with the administration. The Malgache national- ists claimed that 80,000 of their people died, and the French admitted to over 11,000. Much of the country was devastated, whilst the three nationalist deputies, including the writer, Jacques Rabemanan- jara, were imprisoned in France after being condemned to death. News of the rebellion and the loss of life was slow to spread overseas and had only a minor immediate impact on Africa. But Malgache nationalism, though inevitably cowed for a time, was not destroyed, and later was to turn to Africa for its natural associations.

Still farther away from Africa, well into the Indian Ocean, lies the island of Mauritius. Although its half-million inhabitants have had little Negro blood amongst their Indian, French and British elements, its political development has borne some slight relation to African affairs which is likely to increase in the future.

The island's economy had depended almost entirely on sugar growing, developing in consequence a plantation system. The French and British planters took on indentured Indian labour, which remained after the completion of indentures to form the island's labour force. There was a good deal of inter-mixing, from which a variety of racial types emerged.

The European planters held on to political influence through the early years of constitutional development. Franchise was limited by property and income qualifications, but until after the second war British colonial officials retained a majority in legislative and executive institutions.

In 1948, however, Mauritius participated in the constitutional liberalising process affecting most of the British Empire. Franchise qualifications were modified and women given the vote for the first time. In the Legislative Council thirty-one of the thirty-five seats were allocated to unofficial members, nineteen of them elected and twelve nominated. These unofficial members were also allowed to select four of their number to serve with the three officials in the Executive. Three years later they were associated with government departments in preparation for ministerial status.

Thus representative government was steadily growing. The real issue presaged by this advance was which group was to gain control of the new institutions. French and British settlers hoped to retain their power through political influence; but once the Mauritian working class overcame its internal racial suspicions and mobilised its strength organisationally, either it would gain power or representative government would have to be perverted to restrain it. In any case, it seemed certain that political, social and racial conflicts were rapidly approaching.

Nor need we spend long at this stage on the countries of the north-east. Ethiopia was re-taken from the Italians in 1941, ending the only years of foreign rule in its history. It was restored to the Emperor, Haile Selassie, who had become internationally renowned through his dignified protests against the Italian invasion and conquest of 1935-6.

Ethiopia remained after the war what it had been previously, a desperately backward country. The Italians had done some building, but had neglected education. There were hardly any recognisable roads in the country, whose people were not only cut off by their geographic position from the rest of Africa, but also from each other. Party politics were unknown, as were trade unions. The whole administration centred on the Emperor, whose energy and personality enabled him to control any conspiring factions. The ruling class and about half the population belonged to the Copt sect of the Christian church, which played a powerful role in government. The rest of the people were Moslem or pagan, but estimates of the total population were so uncertain as to vary between 10 and 20 million.

The Emperor chose and nominated his Upper House from the nobles, who, in their turn, together with the chiefs, nominated the Lower Chamber. The government itself used the services of a large number of foreign advisers drawn from all over Europe and North America. Indeed, Americans were more popular than the British, despite the Emperor's exiled sojourn in Bath. They not only contributed economic aid through Point Four, but it was remembered that neither they nor the Soviet Union had ever recognised the Italian occupation, as did the British and French. From 1947 the Americans also made the invaluable contribution, through Trans-World Airlines, of running an efficient Ethiopian Airline, which, for the first time, brought modern means of communication to the country internally and externally.

So for the first few years after the war Ethiopia remained remote from the African community. Parts of the country were extremely fertile and some excellent coffee was produced, but any modern kind of economic or social development had scarcely been visualised. Society remained primitive, its structure no more than feudal even in its most advanced sectors. The will and temper of the people could not be judged, for they had no means of expression. The Emperor believed in some forms of economic modernisation, and depended heavily on them for his favourite reform, an expanded educational system. But it would be a long time before the people of Ethiopia found the means to learn of events in the rest of the continent, still less to participate in them.

Closely connected with Ethiopia was the future of the million inhabitants of Eritrea. This Red Sea coastal strip next to Ethiopia, formerly an Italian colony, remained under British administration at the end of the war. Its people were divided between Coptic Christians and Moslems, the former anxious for unity with Ethiopia, the latter opposed to it. Other interested states held conflicting views. The Italians would have liked Eritrea to return to them; the Soviet Union and the Arab bloc, for different reasons, advocated its independence. Ernest Bevin proposed its partition between Ethiopia and the Sudan. The Ethiopians played a waiting game. They wanted Eritrea, as its two ports, Massawa and Assab, would give them alternative outlets to the sea than Djibouti, on which they had previously been forced to rely.

Eventually it was agreed that in 1952 Eritrea should be federated with Ethiopia. Its foreign affairs, defence, finance, customs and communications were consigned to the Ethiopians, but it retained its own assembly, which was divided equally between Copts and Moslems, and elected a chief executive to conduct government business. The people and land of Eritrea were poor, but under British administration they had begun to develop their own newspapers, had free elections, and had begun to form political parties. They hoped that this gradual enlightenment would enable them to build an education system, for although the Italians erected buildings in the capital, Asmara, and modernised the town, they had no interest in educating the Eritreans. There was therefore a good deal of discontent which was soon reinforced as the cost of living immediately rose after federation.

Finally, there were the 2½ million Somalis scattered over a number of territories and roaming indiscriminately between them. Although feuds amongst the rival Moslem factions were common, some feelings of belonging to one community existed amongst all Somalis. There were, in fact, four Somali territories; French Somaliland, an enclave around Djibouti, where Somalis were in a majority but not the only inhabitants; the Somaliland Protectorate, under Britain; Somalia, which had been Italian: and the Haud region of the Ogaden, inside the Ethiopian frontier, but administered by Britain. There was also a community of Somalis living in north-east Kenya. The objective of Somali nationalists was to unite these five communities into a single Somali state.

The French treated their Somali territory like the rest of their possessions. Its 60,000 inhabitants sent a deputy and a senator to Paris.

The British at first retained the war-time military administration over both their protectorate and Somalia, which they had captured from Italy during the war. When civil administration was resumed in the protectorate in 1948 it followed the pre-war pattern. The governor remained the sole legislative and executive authority over the 700,000 Moslem inhabitants. He had an advisory council, part of which was elected, but it had no power and could do no more than advise.

After many wrangles, Somalia, former Italian Somaliland, became a United Nations Trust Territory administered by Italy in 1950. It was laid down that the country was to become independent in 1960. Like the Somalis in the other territories, most of the 1¼ million inhabitants were nomads, constantly on the move in search of fresh grazing. The prospect of them being fitted to take over all government services within ten years seemed remote. Yet the Italians initiated a crash programme to train administrators to be capable of running the country at the end of the period and began to introduce representative institutions. Here they contrasted favourably with the neighbouring British administration, which, in similar circumstances and with similar people, continued to slumber undisturbed by the new conditions in Africa.

The fact that Somalis, even though mainly backward, primitive and scattered, could participate in public life had already been demonstrated. The Somali Youth League was founded in 1943 in Somalia. It became a modern popular party, with duly organised branches and an administration, maintaining its contacts with similar groups in the other territories. Its activities were stimulated by the presence of Kenya African troops and technicians during the war, and it developed into a widely organised radical nationalist party. Its main platform was pan-Somali nationalism and one of its leaders, Abdullahi Issa, demonstrated its sophistication by going to the United Nations to protest against the Italian administration, which he accused of persecuting his members.

So Somaliland revealed another form of post-war nationalism in Africa. Nationalist momentum was naturally greater amongst large urban groups, where political parties were based on economic and industrial organisations, but it could also appear in a well-organised movement amongst primitive nomads.

Communication between these various east African territories was still at a very rudimentary stage in the immediate post-war years. Few of the leaders had visited any of the other territories and there was no such unifying force as the RDA proved in French Africa, or even the looser pan-African movement in British West Africa. There was some little sense of fellowship between British East Africans, and a vague nationalist feeling amongst the Somalis. But there was virtually no contact between British East Africa and the north, although Jomo Kenyatta had shown interest in Ethiopian problems whilst in London. Any significant sense of an east African community, either of nations or of people, remained no more than a shadowy future possibility.

7

The Arab North

The final region in this continental study consists of the northern states bordering on the Mediterranean and the Red Sea. They have often been omitted from African studies as belonging more to Middle Eastern and European history than to that of Africa. Current events reveal this mistake. The Sahara is no longer a barrier between north Africa and the rest of the continent. Whatever the differences in culture, historical experience or ethnology, northern territories are now regarded and consider themselves as essentially part of the African continent.

The common features of these peoples are their Arab character and Islamic religion. These two features are not universal. There are important minorities, such as the Berber tribes of the north-west and the southern Negroes in the Sudan. Even the Egyptians are not pure Arabs, and Christians and pagans are to be found in every territory. Yet the dominant influences have been and still remain Arabic and Mohammedan.

The second world war made an important impact on this region. Contending armies fought each other over much of the area, and Cairo became one of the largest military centres in the conflict. In no part of the African continent was the conflict between rival imperialisms so apparent. Yet any hope that the contending imperial powers would exhaust each other and loosen the imperialist hold on the north African dependencies was soon extinguished. The defeated imperialists were simply replaced by the victorious; Algerians, Moroccans and Tunisians found as many French administrators in their midst in 1945 as in 1939; French and British took the place of Italians in Libya; a British Governor-General still ruled the Sudanese, whilst British troops remained in Egypt. No doubt the war had weakened the imperial powers and stimulated the forces of national resistance; but there was little overt evidence of weakening imperialism in 1945.

147

Egypt, at the end of the war, presented a classic picture of a society moving inexorably towards revolution. It is true that the country had been ruled by a variety of foreigners for almost 2,500 years, Turks, Arabs, Romans, Greeks and Persians, all leaving their impact, while a Nubian strain had also been added to the Egyptian bloodstream. Yet, for some reason, the sense of Egyptian nationalism had never been lost. There was little feeling for the country's ancient history and its ruling families were descended from foreigners. Yet the resentment felt towards British influence in Egypt had welled up into sheer hatred.

British imperialism was seen at its most cynical in Egypt. While it is true that British influence had modernised the administration and the economy, Britain had entered Egypt and remained there in the sole interests of her imperial power. She never annexed the country nor was it ever a British colony, and so the British never felt even the vague sense of responsibility for helping it towards ultimate self-government shown in other dependencies. Control of the Suez Canal was the prime purpose of the British presence, together with strategic considerations in the Mediterranean and in the Sudan. When national resistance became uncomfortably strong after the first world war, a sham form of 'independence' was conceded. But the 1922 treaty conditions made a mockery of the term 'independence', leaving ultimate authority in British hands. Even the 1936 treaty, supposedly granting full independence, still left British troops in the country. The pseudo nature of Egyptian independence was soon exposed when Cairo was needed by the British and American forces during the war; they simply occupied the city, despite Egypt's official neutrality.

Many Egyptian nationalists, including young army officers who were to become important after the war, hoped that Rommel would succeed in driving the British out of Cairo and ultimately out of all Egypt. Hatred rose to fever pitch amongst them when British tanks surrounded King Farouk's Palace in Cairo and forced him to change his Prime Minister. Despite the contempt later felt for the venal Farouk, this arrogant affront to Egyptian sovereignty was long remembered by every type of patriot.

So when the war ended Egyptians felt the same kind of shamed national pride as that experienced by defeated nations. The continued presence of British troops only exacerbated these feelings.

Thus xenophobia grew in a social situation displaying every element provocative to revolt. Less than 5 per cent of the total land area of Egypt was productively habitable, the Nile Valley alone providing means of life in this vast desert. Yet, not only were 85 per cent of the 19 million inhabitants landless, but over a third of the cultivable land was owned by one-half per cent of the population. There were 2,700,000 landowners in the country; of these over 2,000,000 owned less than an acre each. The Egyptian fellahin (from fellah, a ploughman) were amongst the most downtrodden peoples in the world. Living out their miserable short life in slime and squalor, racked by dysentery, bilharzia and trachoma, existence for the Egyptian masses reached the lowest depths of brutishness in human experience. Yet the ruling class, the land-owning pashas, descended from Turks and without interest in the country which gave them wealth, were amongst the most ostentatiously opulent group of human beings. King Farouk was the richest, grossest, and greediest of them.

This, then, was the back-cloth. But, in itself, it would have been unlikely to provoke more than a few short scenes of despairing violence. For, at all periods of human history, a few wealthy, powerful men have been able to maintain tyranny over illiterate, impoverished masses, at the price of no more than occasional, sporadic, easily quelled revolts. Additional factors are needed for the full drama of revolution.

Other factors were plentifully present in post-war Egypt. By African standards Egypt was a sophisticated country. It had an efficient railway system, many good roads, large-scale commerce, newspapers and radio. Cairo, with a population of $2\frac{1}{2}$ million, was the biggest city in Africa; Alexandria, with over a million, the second or third largest. Cairo had two universities, the Islamic Al Azhar, and the secular Fuad University, later re-named the University of Cairo. More than 20,000 students attended them.

So here were the foundations of a nation worth taking out of the hands of the effete, rapacious ruling class. Were there people sufficiently articulate, ambitious, idealistic and discontented to rouse and lead the masses?

To answer this question we must pause for a moment to look at the perspective of Egypt's political history. One would normally seek revolutionary leadership in a political party or group dedicated to overthrowing such a decadent ruling system. If we look back to the immediate post first world war period we find this factor. Under the inspiration of Zaghlul Pasha, the Wafd party became the spearhead of mass revolt against the British, culminating in the first 'independence' agreement of 1922. The following year, in the first elections held under the new constitution, the Wafd shocked the ruling nobility by gaining a sweeping electoral victory which turned them out of their traditional offices. But between 1923 and the second world war the character of the nationalist party fundamentally changed. From being a party led by intellectuals with mass backing, it became increasingly controlled by the same land-owning class it had been created to oppose. From being the main focus of anti-British effort, it became the party which arranged the spurious second 'independence' treaty with Britain in 1936, leaving British troops in occupation of the country. The supreme irony appeared in 1942; a Wafd government was forced on King Farouk by British tanks.

Moreover, by the end of the war, Egyptian faith in democratic processes had been completely destroyed. Between 1923 and the beginning of the war the Wafd party had been given a popular mandate whenever elections were held. Each time, however, either the king or the British authorities quickly dismissed its governments and restored the old ruling class. In the years immediately before the war the frustration thus provoked, together with the increasing failure of western European democratic systems, led to both the Wafd and its opponents organising themselves as para-military imitations of fascism. The exposure of corruption and profiteering, exploiting war-time shortages, completed Egyptian disillusion with political democracy. It was thus unlikely that, in the conditions of gross inequality and mass misery at the end of the war, the Egyptian masses would look to the politicians for revolutionary leadership.

Nor could the underprivileged in Egypt turn to the bourgeoisie, professionals or trade unions for leadership. The merchants and industrialists came mostly from the land-owning class, many of them retaining their stakes in the land. They were also largely dependent on the foreign capitalist concerns which took a major role in economic development. The principal ambition of professionals was to be accepted into the landed aristocracy through marriage or money. Trade unions were legally prohibited amongst the agricultural workers, whilst industrial unions were constantly weakened by the large number of unemployed.

For a time, the desperate forces of discontent were diverted into a semi-religious outlet. Apart from the brute power of the ruling class, the strongest anti-revolutionary influence in modern Egypt has been the Islamic faith. Islam is a 'revealed' religion, looking to the past and judging all issues by reference to precedent. Thus ortho-dox Moslem belief has had strong anti-modernising influence. At the same time, it was the British who were introducing the modernising features held to be inimical to Islam. Consequently, the Moslem movement was strongly nationalistic or anti-foreign. Paradoxically, the nationalist movement was thus composed of two mutually opposed elements, the modernist intellectuals fighting against a feudal ruling class and alien imperialism, and the conservative Islamists, combating the modernising influence of British and French.

The appeal of Islam was organised through the Moslem Brother-hood, originally founded in 1928, and first becoming prominent in the Palestine agitation of 1937. It began by preaching religious and ethical principles, but revealing the social and political concern characteristic of Islamic movements, soon began to declare political policies. It offered those suffering from poverty a collective respon-sibility for welfare. Politically it demanded an Islamic system based on the Koran. To the masses, sickened with the double-dealing and self-seeking of the politicians, oppressed under their load of misery, the chance to find a few moments' security in the Brotherhood's collective prayer meetings offered a welcome haven. Youth saw it as clean idealism challenging the degradation of Egyptian society; nationalists believed it to be a patriotic successor to the collabora-tionist Wafd; and opportunists sought their private purposes within its organisation.

During the war, the Brotherhood had abundant opportunities to exploit its anti-foreign appeal. After the war, ammunition for every form of nationalist and social appeal grew still greater. The war solved the unemployment problem, but only at the expense of greatly aggravating it once the war had ended. Many more people had been attracted into the towns, and, as war industries and services dried up, so the ranks of unemployed slum dwellers multiplied. Fortunes had been made out of war needs, but the rapid increase in population actually reduced the average standard of life, with the fellahin masses, as always, suffering most.

Immediately after the war, attempts were made to amend the 1936 agreement with Britain, but the bitter nationalist temper of the public was revealed when every effort made by the government to secure a compromise agreement was rejected by the people. Nothing short of the expulsion of all foreign forces would satisfy them. So another policy designed to direct people's attention from social conditions was initiated. Assistance was promised to the Palestinian Arabs in their revolt against the partition decreed by the United Nations in 1947. Along with fellow members of the Arab League, the Egyptian government first whipped up national enthusiasm for the war, encouraged volunteers whilst providing arms and supplies, and then committed its actual army. The subsequent débâcle, together with revelations of scandalous corruption in handling war supplies, shook the system to its roots. Egyptians could no longer be diverted from the domestic scene, with its proliferating social evils.

Meanwhile, the Moslem Brotherhood had been rapidly gaining strength in the midst of this chaos. It now had arms and trained forces, and the absence of the best part of the army gave it opportunities it was not slow to accept. After a reign of terror against Jews it turned its forces against foreigners and then attacked the police. The government eventually screwed up its courage to ban the organisation when it appeared about to overthrow the régime, but it dared not arrest its leaders. So the assassination of the Prime Minister by the Brotherhood was followed, not by arrests and trials, but by the counter-assassination of its leader.

With the collapse of the Palestinian campaign, increasing social crisis, and the activities of the Brotherhood, by the end of 1948 the situation had become desperate. The king, who had control over both the 100-strong Senate and the Chamber of 150 deputies through his executive powers, decided to hold new elections. He had dismissed the Wafd government in 1944, but now calculated that the desperate difficulties which had embarrassed its successors might destroy it finally. He was right, but only visualised a fraction of the consequences. The Wafd won the election, and, in a last desperate throw to save the situation, denounced the 1936 treaty and turned guerrilla forces against British troops in the Suez zone. Legal recognition was restored to the Moslem Brotherhood to enable it to participate in the nationalist struggle against foreign occupation. But the attempt to direct the wrath of ordinary people against the British failed. Nationalist and social revolts now merged. The fury of the masses overflowed after government bungling had led to the death of scores of police in the Canal zone. The king could dismiss the Wafd government as he had planned and appease some nationalists by assuming the title 'King of Sudan', but he could no longer direct mass passions. The mob turned against foreigner and pasha alike. Much of Cairo was burnt and pillaged; the social-nationalist revolution had burst on the old régime and foreign influences simultaneously.

The conception of the 'Unity of the Nile Valley' epitomised by Farouk's assumed new title had played an important role in Egyptian nationalism. From the time of the re-conquest of the Sudan by Anglo-Egyptian forces, Egypt had considered the Sudan to be rightfully under her suzerainty. She was affronted when the British virtually expelled all Egyptian administrators after the assassination of the Governor-General in 1924 and then had to watch Sudanese slowly introduced into the ranks of the administration. Although the Sudan was supposed to be ruled by an Anglo-Egyptian condominium, in practice it was the British who were in control. The slight on Egyptian administrative capacity gave further cause to anti-British feelings amongst Egyptian nationalists, inducing them to include a resumption of Egyptian rule in the Sudan along with their demands for the departure of British troops from their own country. This claim was, of course, further reinforced by knowledge that control of the Nile waters of the Sudan vitally affected Egyptian economic interests.

Yet the Sudanese themselves were not so sure that they wanted a resumption of Egyptian rule. After all, their war of liberation under the Mahdi in the nineteenth century had been against the Egyptians, and if it had not been for the involvement of General Gordon and the consequent support of British troops, the Egyptians would never have secured their revenge at Omdurman in 1898.

The Sudanese nationalist movement split on this issue during the war. The movement had developed from what was originally a cultural organisation, the Graduates' General Congress, founded in

1937. Within the Congress a movement known as Ashiqqa, demanding union with Egypt and led by Ismail al-Azhari, grew from 1942 onwards. It was loosely linked with the Moslem sect known as Khatmiyya, under the leadership of Sayyid Ali al Mirghani. The rival sect, Ansar, a neo-Mahdist movement under Sayyid Abd al-rahman al-Mahdi, backed the Umma party, formed from within the Congress early in 1945 to promote the aim of an independent Sudan separate from Egypt. Its leader was Abdullah Khalil. The British administration characteristically first supported the Mirghanist sect against Mahdism, and then switched to back the Mahdists against Ashiqqa's association with Egypt.

British administration had brought order, stability, honesty and a degree of economic advance to the Sudan. The civil service and co-operative scheme of cotton growing in the Gezira are lasting British contributions to the health of Sudanese society. At the same time, excellent though it was in many respects, the Sudan civil service was very expensive and extremely exclusive. Moreover, the administration had done virtually nothing to unify the Moslem-Arab north and the Christian or pagan negroid south. If anything, British rule had widened the gap, hindering inter-change between the two, maintaining a policy of indirect rule in the south calculated to keep the peoples there backward and separated from the modernising developments in the north.

Nevertheless, economic progress had led to the rise of a middle class of professionals, traders, farmers, small businessmen, who took an ever-increasing interest in public affairs. It also created a proletariat of wage earners who produced a remarkably virile trade union movement. The lead was taken by railway workers, but the development of a central organisation, the Sudan Workers' Trade Union Federation, and its success in calling a general strike in 1947, led to a general recognition of trade unions. The unions kept mainly clear from the political struggle before 1951, but the process of organisation and the experience in trade union activities undoubtedly assisted in the growth of a public awareness of political issues.

In line with its progressively developing constitutional policy, the British government introduced an advisory Council in 1944. This was the first form of representative body the Sudan had known under British rule; previously the Governor-General had possessed absolute power, advised only by his own small council. The new council was also only advisory, but it included twenty-four Sudanese, along with four members representing foreign interests, and was roughly a potential legislative assembly. Yet still its members were drawn only from the more developed, sophisticated north, the south remaining under its traditional rulers.

Soon after the war, in April 1946, a special conference was held to make proposals for further constitutional development. It proposed that a genuine Legislative Assembly be established, together with an Executive, partially drawn from the Assembly. After some modifications following Egyptian pressure, the two bodies were instituted in 1948, the Assembly consisting of seventy-five members and the Executive of fourteen. The franchise was limited to males with certain property and income qualifications, ten members were to be elected directly from the urban areas, forty-two through electoral colleges in the less populated areas, and thirteen chosen by tribal chiefs and councils in the southern provinces. The other ten were to be nominated by the Governor-General. In the Executive seven members were to be drawn from the Assembly, which would elect a leader, to be Prime Minister, who would propose his other Executive members to the Governor-General. The other seven were to be British officials and nominees. Ultimate powers remained with the Governor-General, who specifically reserved defence and foreign affairs for his own control.

The first elections under this new constitution were held at the end of 1948. But the Ashiqqa boycotted them. Amongst many of the younger nationalists in the towns, who supported Ashiqqa, there had emerged a form of nationalism at once suspicious of British constitutional offers and sympathetic to Egyptian anti-British nationalism. This group refused to have anything to do with the new constitution, relying instead on a joint nationalist effort with the Egyptians to expel the British from the whole Nile area. So the Umma Party, more conservative, pro-western and with stronger tribal links, won the first election in the absence of its main rival, Abdullah Khalil becoming the first leader of the Assembly.

This by no means ended the conflict. Religious rivalry would have kept it going anyway, but the issue of relations with Egypt ensured that Sudanese nationalism remained divided. The unilateral proclamation by the Wafdist government of Farouk as 'King of the Sudan' was repudiated by Britain, but it further stimulated controversy in the Sudan. The British began to prepare a draft statute introducing self-government, but the Egyptian revolution radically changed the circumstances. Only when the new Egyptian régime had emerged from the flames of Cairo would it be possible to envisage the future of the Sudanese peoples.

Before completing the picture of Arab Africa by looking at the Maghreb, we should spend a few minutes with Libya, an arid, largely desert country.

During the war, of course, British, American, French, German and Italian troops swept back and forth across the country several times. It was an Italian colony and during the desert war the British were considerably helped by King Idris, who had been in exile since 1923. With the final expulsion of the Axis forces in 1943, the king returned to his country. He was the head of the Senussi sect of Islam, and so both the religious and secular leader of his people.

Libya consisted of three provinces, Tripolitania, Cyrenaica, and Fezzan. At the end of the war the former two provinces were under British military administration and the latter under the French. Constant discussions took place among the great powers and at the United Nations as to how the provinces should be administered. British policy at first was to divide the country into two states centred on Tripolitania and Cyrenaica, but later, Ernest Bevin and the Italian Foreign Minister, Sforza, proposed trusteeship status for the three provinces, with Britain, France and Italy acting as trustees. The Americans also favoured a trusteeship supervision for ten years, but with a collective trust under the United Nations. The Russians envisaged themselves as the trustee power over Tripolitania.

None of these proposals was generally acceptable. In the meantime, little was being done for the country. The Italians had built Tripoli into a fine city and they had laid some good roads. But they suppressed all nationalism and did nothing for education. Britain had to spend considerable sums on her administration, but, so long as the wrangle continued about the future, neither Britain nor France could apply their particular colonial policies to the Libyans.

It was doubtful, too, whether any conception of a united Libyan nation existed amongst its people. The provinces were dissimilar, Tripolitania being mainly Berber, comparatively advanced and prosperous, containing two-thirds of the population, including 45,000 Italians; Cyrenaica, the home of the Senussi, was little developed and rather slummy; Fezzan was a desert oasis of the Bedouin nomads. There was little nationalist pressure, except what survived from the opposition to Italian rule, mainly originating with the Senussi in Cyrenaica. In Tripolitania, though, a political party of sorts grew up about 1947. It was called the National Congress Party, led by Bashin al-Sadawi, and strongly criticised both King Idris and the influence of Britain and America.

In 1949 Britain took the first step towards unification of the country by recognising Idris as Emir of Cyrenaica. A few months later the United Nations eventually made up its mind, passing a resolution declaring that Libya should be independent by the end of 1951 and sending a commissioner to prepare a constitution for independence. The following year a national constituent assembly proclaimed Idris King of all Libya, although some caustic opposition to this move remained in Tripolitania. The United Nations began a crash programme to produce the administration for an independent country within twelve months. On December 24, 1951, Libya assumed sovereign status.

A great deal now depended on the king, the mainly British civil servants who remained, and relations with the great powers, if independent Libya was to be sustained. Under the new federal constitution there was a Senate, half elected, half nominated by the king, and an elected House of Representatives. Each province also had its executive and legislative councils. In practice the king ruled the new state. He sanctioned and promulgated laws, exercising his power through his ministers. Meanwhile, Britain continued to subsidise the budget deficit, train the army and advise the administration. The Americans contributed large sums proportionate to the million or so inhabitants, through the Point Four programme, whilst maintaining their air base outside Tripoli. A new African state, largely composed of Bedouin nomads, had been born. Its survival appeared heavily dependent on outside good will.

The remaining area of North Africa is known as the Maghreb, which is the Arabic word for 'west'. This was the ancient Barbary coast, haunt of Mediterranean pirates for centuries, inhabited by Berbers, then Arabs, now mostly a mixture of the two, with both

Arabic and Berber languages surviving. It is the coastal belt which has been the home of most of the 20 million or so peoples of the three territories, Morocco, Algeria and Tunisia. In modern times all three countries have been ruled by France, with the Spaniards holding part of Morocco and an international zone established in Tangier.

Two main factors have linked the three territories and given them a certain common outlook; French rule and Islam. In north Africa there appears for the first time in this continental survey a conventional form of nationalism seeking to re-establish historical nation states. Egypt had an ancient historical experience for her people to look back to, but had been under foreign rule for so long that the nostalgic element in nationalism was almost entirely absent. It was more apparent in the Sudan, but the division between her two societies modified its effect. It was seen mostly clearly in the Maghreb.

French occupation never destroyed the sense of national community in any of the three Maghreb countries. It probably never could have done so, however long it lasted, for it is a basic tenet of the Moslem faith that Islamic peoples must never be ruled by non-believers. French rule provided a sophistication which enabled the nationalist leaders to learn modern tactics of resistance, to secure support in France itself, and to make international appeals. Meanwhile, the presence of over a million and a half French settlers, owning the best land, monopolising the social services, excluding indigenous Moslems from skilled jobs, and militantly opposing democratic reforms, offered constantly visible affronts to nationalist sentiments.

Once again, the effects of the war made a profound impact. There had been movements of resistance before the war, like Habib Bourguiba's Néo-Destour in Tunisia and the Parti du Peuple Algérien of Messali Hadj, but they were mainly composed of intellectual groups. The war affected all sections of society, for the first time arousing the masses. France suffered an enormous loss of prestige from her defeat, the Maghreb peoples were brought into contact with British and German troops, many had experience in the French armies, and the radio blared out propaganda of every conceivable character from Vichy, De Gaulle, the Italians, the Communists, the Arabs, the British and the Americans. Above all, they heard the inspiring appeal of the Atlantic Charter and recognised the relevance of its principles to their own circumstances. A meeting between President Roosevelt and the Sultan of Morocco during the war-time Casablanca conference was blamed by the French for the Sultan's conversion to nationalist ideas. The isolation of French Arab Africa from the ideas of the outside world was shattered. At the end of the war they learnt that the French mandates in Syria and the Lebanon had been ended and that the Arab League had been formed. The attractions of getting rid of French 'baby clothes' were increasing.

It was not only political stimulation which the war produced. A new proletariat emerged from war-time conditions, which had inevitably stimulated economic growth and industrialisation. The intelligentsia was augmented by new products of the educational system who had been in contact with non-French and non-Moslem ideas. The boom conditions of the war had given unprecedented numbers employment and the new needs induced by regular wages; but the end of the war brought immediate depression, aggravated by inflation and drought.

This economic crisis, in countries where there were two distinct societies, one alien, privileged, supported by the administration, Christian, and mainly wealthy, the other subject, Moslem, poor and persecuted, produced a situation openly inviting revolt. All the achievements of French administration in fields of economic development, efficient government, legal order, could not compensate for these stark social contrasts.

The first overt signs of revolt appeared in Algeria in May 1945. On VE Day a crowd in the town of Setif, near Constantine, took the opportunity of celebrating the end of the war to display nationalist flags. The police objected and in the ensuing riots about a hundred Europeans and a large number of Moslems were killed – the French admitted 1,500, the Algerians estimated between 20,000 and 30,000.

This massacre showed the French what violent feelings of revolt lay only just below the surface in their north African territories. Algeria had been under French rule since 1830, but it was obvious that French administration had not been accepted, at least in its previous form.

The northern territories of Algeria were considered to be part of metropolitan France and so did not qualify as an Overseas Territory entitled to the kind of constitution offered to the western and equatorial colonies. Nevertheless, Ferhat Abbas, who had served in the French army, had a French wife, and was organising his Union Démocratique du Manifeste Algérien, went to the Constituent Assembly in Paris. His new party had won eleven of the thirteen seats in the second Constituent Assembly of 1946. He had advocated recognition of a Moslem Algerian nation federated with France, and now put the proposal to the assembly. But he was ignored. Yet he still continued his moderate, westernised approach through his party organisation.

Instead, in 1947, the French offered a Statute for Algeria bearing some resemblance to the constitutions established in the Overseas Territories. Previously, the country had been administered by a Governor-General with a Consultative Council of fifteen officials and a Superior Council of sixty members. It had sent three senators and ten deputies to Paris, although it was not until 1946 that the first Moslems were elected. The new constitution increased the number of deputies to thirty, of senators to fourteen, and provided for eighteen members to the French Union Assembly. A half of each category were to be Moslems. At the same time, an assembly was created for Algeria itself, known as the Assemblée Algérienne. It was composed by an all-Moslem college elected by 1,300,000 voters, and a mixed Moslem-European college with an electorate of 370,000 Europeans and 60,000 assimilated Moslems. It was given powers over various local affairs, including the local budget, which pleased the French settlers, or colons. The million European settlers owned two-thirds of the arable land and the lucrative wine industry. They were no more enamoured of Paris control over their finances than white settlers elsewhere in the continent, and were confident that the administration would arrange the elections to these new institutions so that collaborationist candidates were elected. Their confidence was justified.

By this time, however, the nationalist movement was becoming more militant. Ferhat Abbas and Messali Hadj had tried working together in 1944-5 but, not only were the two men incompatible, their methods sharply differed. In 1945 their joint organisation, Amis du Manifeste et de la Liberté, replaced Abbas as leader by Hadj, repudiated the policy of federal association with France, and declared for an Algerian state free to order its own foreign policy.

Abbas proceeded the following year to create his own UDMA party, whilst Hadj's supporters, despite the deportation of their leader, transformed their Parti Populaire Algérien into the Mouvement pour le Triomphe des Libertés Démocratiques.

Discussion and argument between the legalists and the revolutionaries continued within the nationalist movement. But meanwhile, from 1948, a small group, amongst whom were to be found Ben Bella and Belkacem Krim, were building what they called the Organisation Secrète, collecting funds and arms for a future insurrection. In 1950 the police uncovered some of their caches. But neither the French administration nor the colons took heed. The Algerian nationalist insurrectionary movement gathered momentum underground, whilst on the surface the country appeared tranquil, held securely in the grip of Paris and the French settlers.

Morocco and Tunisia, the other two French north African territories, had a different status from Algeria. They had experienced similar unsettling influences during the war, but they were both protectorates, not parts of metropolitan France. This deprived them of representation in Paris, but left them both with indigenous institutions. Yet these institutions were severely controlled by the French and neither country could expect to participate in the constitutional developments offered to the rest of French Africa. They were, in fact, offered 'associated' status inside the French Union, but both refused, having fixed their eyes on complete independence.

It is quite conceivable that if French policy had been different, both protectorates would have been happy to continue some form of association with France, at least for a period. But even before the war the French had suppressed nationalist newspapers, ignored proposals for moderate social reform, deported leaders, banned nationalist parties and prohibited trade unions. Above all, they had convinced the intelligentsia that they were intent on undermining Islam, particularly in education, and replacing its culture with Christian teaching.

The final exacerbating factor was the rapid increase of French immigration and the active anti-reformist role taken by the new immigrants. Between 1926 and 1947 the number of French residents in Morocco increased from 74,000 to over 300,000 out of a total population of some 9 million. This was a much smaller proportion than the million Europeans in Algeria, where the total population was about the same, or the 250,000 in Tunisia, where the population was only about three and a half million. But the effects were similar in all three countries. The Europeans took the best land, capital was invested in their commerce and industry, and they insisted that social, economic and political policy be geared to European interests.

By the end of the war nationalist movements had developed in both protectorates determined to break the power of the settlers and take control from the French. Both countries had a much more distinctive national history than Algeria and it was only a matter of time before the nationalist spirit spread to the mass of their Moslem inhabitants.

In Tunisia, where development was much more advanced and the intelligentsia far more sophisticated than anywhere else in the Maghreb, the Néo-Destour party had existed since 1934. It was a modernist, militant party, closely linked with the Union Générale des Travailleurs Tunisiens, a powerful, well-organised trade union, whose leader, Ferhat Hached, played an important part in political as well as industrial organisation. Néo-Destour itself was mainly the creation of Habib Bourguiba, lawyer and journalist, who had been educated at the Sorbonne. The French attitude to Bourguiba could hardly have been better calculated to turn him against them. He was imprisoned from 1934 to 1936, and again in 1938, when his party was proscribed. During the war he was handed over to the Vichy régime, from which the Germans released him during their occupation of France. He was passed on to the Italians and fêted by them in the hope that he could be used against the Allies. Despite his treatment by the French, Bourguiba refused to be a tool of Axis propaganda, as they had hoped. In 1943 he returned to Tunis and assisted the Allies by urging his people to help the French, but with the *caveat* that a new world could be expected after victory. Yet the Free French seemed even less well disposed towards the nationalist leader than pre-war France had been. In 1945 he left his country again, this time to seek help in Cairo, where the Arab League had just been formed, from the Middle East, the Far East, and America. In his absence Salah ben Youssef was left in charge of the Néo-Destour.

Bourguiba returned to Tunis in 1949 and immediately renewed

his pressure on the French. The following year, the French Foreign Minister, Robert Schuman, included the term 'independence' in a statement of French aims in Tunisia. Bourguiba delightedly took up the expression and his party decided that on this basis they could participate in government. Moves were started to bring the country internal autonomy. This was a tremendous step forward. Since the war Tunisia had remained under martial law, there had never been elected legislatures, and civil liberties were unknown. There was a cabinet form of government, including Tunisian ministers, but each minister was supervised by a French director. Any kind of self-government might well harness nationalist energies to constitutional progress.

Once again, French policy destroyed the chances of a peaceful agreement. Pressure against the reforms was exerted by the settler community, and the administration in Algeria expressed its concern for the effects they might have on Algerian Moslems. The French government retreated, halted negotiations on reform, and again turned against the nationalists. At the beginning of 1952 the administration prohibited Néo-Destour from holding its congress and two days later arrested Bourguiba once more. Instead of completing the bridges it had begun to build, the French government had once more blown up their foundations. The Tunisians, exasperated by these equivocations, erupted into violent protest. The chances of retaining any Franco-Tunisian ties finally disappeared.

Tunisia had an intellectual élite leading its nationalist movement, with clear aims and the techniques for appeal to the masses. The country was economically advanced in agriculture, had a sophisticated bourgeoisie, and had moved out of the stage of Moslem feudalism. Morocco, on the other hand, was essentially an orthodox Islamic state, with its Sultan, Sidi Mohammed V, its feudal pashas, and its conservative attitudes to women and social reform.

So progressives and radicals had an indigenous feudal régime to face, as well as French colonial power. Yet there was a slowly expanding proletariat, centred in the mining region near Oujda, where Moroccan mineral wealth was being extracted with the aid of considerable American capital, and growing in the towns. The workers were not allowed to form their own trade unions, but could join European unions. As most of these were affiliated to the

French Confédération Général de Travail, dominated by the Communists, this French security prohibition was paradoxically helping Communist organisation in Morocco. There was also a small intelligentsia which had managed to find educational opportunities, usually in France, and had begun to take advantage of the country's economic growth during the war.

It was this group which had founded the main nationalist party, Istiqlal (Independence), at the end of 1943. It was led by Allal el-Fassi, who was only allowed to return home in 1946 after nine years in exile, and by Ahmad Balafrej. The party immediately declared its objectives by issuing a manifesto demanding renunciation of the protectorate treaty and recognition of Morocco's right to establish an independent state under the Sultan.

The nationalists had no love for the traditional feudal régime, but they realised that their first purpose must be to abolish French rule. To accomplish this task they needed a united national effort. So instead of fighting against the Sultan and his luxurious court, they wooed him. Instead of attempting to modernise traditional Moslem feudalism, they used the deep attachment to Islam in order to mobilise the orthodox against alien, infidel influence. They even compromised on the issue of women's status, lest they offend the people they needed to attract. Nor did they confine their activities to the towns; they made a strenuous effort to link the urban progressive movement with the largely Berber peasantry in the countryside and mountains. The fact that the country had been under martial law since 1914, with a complete absence of civil rights, gave them ample ammunition.

This policy of the nationalists was helped by the attitude of the Sultan. Before the war he had been pliable to French wishes, but by the end of the war he had become an overt sympathiser with the nationalists. He was not, of course, a radical; he had far too much of the extravagant life to lose. But he gave nationalism that support needed to provide the movement with a genuine national character. Whether this change in his outlook was induced by his famous dinner with Roosevelt or not, we shall probably never know. But he soon showed his genuine concern for the future of his people when he personally contributed 20 million francs at the end of the war to a massive campaign for education. The French, still cutting life-lines, responded by prohibiting the opening of private schools. The

Sultan replied by putting into operation a royal strike. As the fiction was maintained that Morocco remained an independent state under French protection, the counter-signature of the Sultan, as head of state, was required to legitimise decrees. Mohammed simply refused to sign.

In 1947 the Sultan declared himself to the world. He made a speech during a visit to Tangier which proclaimed his support for independence and his adherence to the policy of the Arab League. The French asked him to refrain from encouraging anti-French demonstrations, but they had now begun to realise that they had to deal with a nationalist movement and a politico-religious monarchy. They turned, as in Tunisia, to proposals for reform. And the nationalists, because any right of independence was excluded, quickly rejected them.

The Sultan made one strong personal effort to avoid an open showdown with the French. In 1950 he visited Paris to ask for a new protectorate treaty on improved terms. His approach was rejected, and both he and the nationalists turned to international opinion for support. El-Fassi was in Cairo and Balafrej went to New York where he was able to put the Moroccan case both to the United Nations and to the American public. The American reaction was particularly important, because they had large military installations and air bases in Morocco. It was one of the nationalists' complaints that negotiations over these bases took place between the French and the Americans, with no reference to Moroccan opinion. In fact, when they were built, it was actually the French flag which flew over them.

By now tension was rising as nationalist sentiment spread whilst the attitude of the French government and settlers grew more intransigent. The conflict also involved internal politics in Morocco. Some of the more conservative pashas were becoming frightened of the growing power of the nationalists supported by the Sultan. The Berber Pasha of Marrakesh, El Glaoui, was a close collaborator with the French, whose support now seemed necessary to preserve the old order. He threatened the Sultan in 1950, but was repulsed by him. Then the French Resident-General, Marshal Juin, thought he could use this Berber antagonism to get rid of Mohammed V. He gave him an ultimatum in 1951, demanding that he denounce Istiqlal and threatening to depose him if he refused. But this crisis was tided over. Then, when El Glaoui's Berber horsemen massed outside Fez, Rabat and other towns, Juin planned to use the occasion to expel the Sultan. He was refused support by the French government.

But the people were becoming angry, with strikes and riots ensuing, whilst the Sultan grew more politely defiant towards the French. In December 1952 the assassination of the neighbouring Tunisian leader, Ferhat Hached, reputedly by a white settler organisation, sparked off more riots in Casablanca. A general strike was called by the trade unions, crowds demonstrated in the streets, and the police were sent into the Moslem location to arrest the nationalist leaders. A battle broke out, with the troops using machine guns and the Arabs knives. A handful of Europeans and many Arabs were killed. Protests echoed from all sides, in Paris and elsewhere, with the French settlers given most of the blame. But the French government pressed on. Istiqlal was outlawed and its organisation smashed. The Sultan found himself isolated without his nationalist supporters.

The French had opened the way for a traditionalist Berber revolt against the Sultan by their destruction of the nationalist movement. El Glaoui saw his chance. By May 1953 he had persuaded 270 of the pashas and caids (local tribal rulers) to sign a petition to the French government demanding that the Sultan be dismissed. Again the cloaked Berber horsemen descended on Fez and Rabat. The Sultan's palace was defended by French troops, but the administration, under extreme pressure from the settlers, made new demands for the Sultan's collaboration. He had to submit. Glaoui was now determined to move in for the kill. He and his followers demanded that Mohammed be deposed, and they themselves deprived him of all spiritual authority. Nationalist feelings amongst the urban inhabitants broke out again, with rioting in Casablanca and Oujda. The French government, though divided, finally gave Resident-General Guillaume authority to depose the Sultan. Again his palace was encircled by French troops and this time he was formally deposed, deported to Corsica and later sent to Madagascar.

French government and settler policy had once more destroyed the bridges to the Arab community. It is significant that the Spanish government, which had already experience of nationalist revolt in their Moroccan zone in 1948, refused to recognise the deposition of Mohammed V. By doing so they retained the respect of their own Moorish leaders, who also continued to recognise the Sultan.

The French were now in open conflict with national forces throughout the Maghreb. Yet each of them would have been prepared to co-operate with the French government if it had shown any genuine sympathy for the national ambitions of the Arab people and less support for the irredentist activities of French settlers. Faced with the alternatives of constitutional reform leading to self-government, and support for the settlers involving war with the nationalists, the French had joined battle.

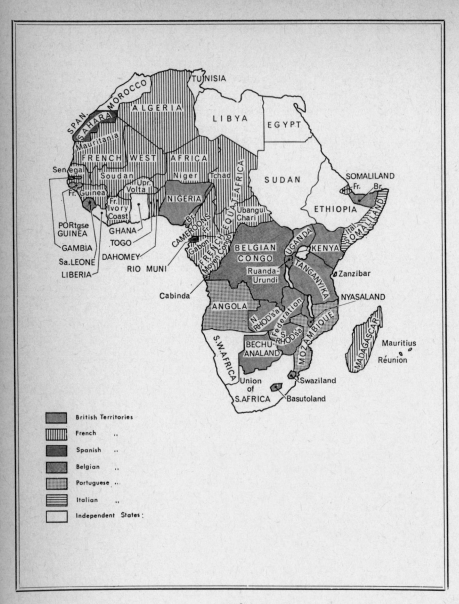

1958

8

The West Leads the Way

During the nineteen-fifties the Gold Coast (from 1957, Ghana) gained a dominant influence throughout the African continent. In west Africa events in the Gold Coast were not only more spectacular than anywhere else, but it was the policies of her leaders which eventually altered the course of history in the rest of the region. Nigeria had about seven times her population, whilst the area of federal French West Africa was incomparably larger. Yet, at the end of the decade a large proportion of Nigerians had adopted the policy of national independence which they had previously rejected, whilst French Africans had abandoned their assimilationist objectives and were racing each other to secure sovereignty. It was Kwame Nkrumah and his colleagues who had both set the compass and forced the pace.

Nigeria was too heterogeneous and divided to sustain the leading nationalist role she had played before the war. It might have been possible for either the eastern or the western region to do so, but efforts to bind these two progressive areas with the traditionalist north inevitably retarded the pace of advance. French West Africa was still concerned more with gaining equality with Frenchmen and participating in French politics than with the ideal of separate independence. Indeed, the two most powerful French Africans, Léopold Senghor and Félix Houphouet-Boigny, were both, for different reasons, definitely opposed to the independence objective.

The nationalist movement in the Gold Coast possessed the advantage of having clinched the leadership issue in the 1951 elections. It had now become clear that Nkrumah and his Convention People's Party were likely to win any democratically conducted election for the foreseeable future. Moreover, they were established in government, which would certainly give them the opportunity to strengthen the CPP vis-à-vis any other parties or groups. Nkrumah was now recognised as the chosen leader of his people and his party as the only agent capable of securing self-determination.

The Gold Coast, with its estimated population of under five million, its convenient size, its comparative wealth, and its popular nationalist party, thus seemed well placed to pioneer major experiments in nationalism. It might be held that the results were valid only for the particular circumstances of the Gold Coast itself; but as this was the first black African colony to test the strength of imperial power, they were bound to affect the outlook of every anti-imperialist movement.

The 1951 elections had given Nkrumah's CPP a widespread organisation and a parliamentary cohesion. It now had three major tasks to accomplish. It had to establish itself as the political authority of the country; to create an administration capable of replacing colonial government; and to persuade or coerce Britain to hand over power.

It was fortunate that at this critical point in Gold Coast history its governor was intelligent, imaginative and progressive. Sir Charles Arden-Clarke and Nkrumah established a relationship of trust and affection. Sir Charles was one of the few British colonial administrators who completely accepted the responsibility of a trustee in helping his wards to fit themselves for ending the trusteeship as quickly as possible. He thus made possible the remarkable paradox of colonial governor and leading African nationalist working in complete harmony to bring imperial rule to an end. Nkrumah harboured no resentment over his imprisonment, giving his complete confidence to the governor as soon as he recognised the sincerity of his objective.

Despite the fact that the constitution had been designed on the assumption that no genuine party system would emerge, the election results proved that one party was already established on a national basis. The Colonial Office expected that the new Executive Council would include a number of leading Africans drawn from various walks of life, probably holding different political views. The success of the CPP proved that the Gold Coast was ready for party government; unless the members of the new Executive were drawn from that party, the constitution was unlikely to survive.

The governor saw this political fact immediately. He released Nkrumah from gaol and offered to make him Leader of Government

Business. Nkrumah had to make the difficult choice between continuing his opposition to the 'bogus' constitution, which would probably have led to further violence, and gambling on British sincerity in granting him progressively greater powers if he worked within the constitution. He chose the latter alternative, accepted the post, and took office in an Executive Council still presided over by the governor, still including three colonial officials, but with most of its members drawn from his own party. He trusted the governor and the Colonial Office to allow him to travel to independence along the constitutional route.

Because Nkrumah was able to establish this rapport with Arden-Clarke, he was able to leave the issue of colonial rule in abeyance for his first two years in office. This left him free to devote his government's first efforts to the two problems of commanding authority throughout the nation and building an administration capable of taking over control from the colonial power.

The fact that the CPP had won the elections did not automatically give it the allegiance of the entire nation. Almost half the members of the new assembly were elected by territorial councils, heavily influenced by the chiefs and other traditional authorities. The habit of obedience to traditional rulers did not disappear simply because a new constitution had been introduced and representatives sent to an assembly in Accra. Many of the chiefly families and elders were contemptuous of Nkrumah and his 'verandah boys' from the southern Colony. They had no intention of abdicating their authoritarian heritage at the behest of new rulers introduced by the colonial administration.

Nkrumah's first major measure revealed that he also recognised the situation and was determined to establish his government's authority. Within a few months of taking office in 1951 he introduced a Local Government Ordinance, establishing local councils composed of two-thirds elected members and one-third traditionalists. Two years later a second ordinance extended the same procedure to town councils. The councils were designed to replace the system of native authorities which had provided the chiefs with their main focus of authority. The introduction of elective majorities would not only undermine the chiefs' power, but introduce ordinary people in the villages to the habit of thinking for themselves and participating in the direction of local affairs in place of merely referring to precedent or obeying the dictates of traditional authorities. It would also open the door for an introduction of party politics into local government, thus spreading the authority of the CPP still wider.

Nevertheless, it should be noted that Nkrumah did not mount an unrestricted attack on the chiefs. In fact, he always referred to 'the chiefs and people of the Gold Coast'. He was determined to place the reins of national authority in representative hands, but he believed in continuing to associate the traditional authorities with government during the process.

Yet the direct import of this ordinance was that the CPP intended to introduce modern methods of representative government throughout the country, encouraging the common people to assert authority through a party structure. Traditionalism, essentially conservative in its nature, would be given an opportunity to co-operate in the development of the new society. If it took the opportunity it would be tolerated; if it obstructed it would be removed. In either case it was to lose its power to order the life of the people. To modernise society required new methods of government capable of involving the masses in the national effort.

The first practical test of the extent to which Nkrumah and his party had succeeded in gaining authority came in the cocoa areas. A virulent disease known as 'swollen shoot' threatened to destroy the existence of the crop which provided the Gold Coast with the bulk of its revenue. The colonial government had failed to secure the co-operation of the cocoa farmers in measures to eradicate the disease. The only sure method of halting the spread of the disease was to cut down the infected trees. Nkrumah threw his party organisation into the task of educating the farmers into the necessity of destroying their own treasured trees. By a mixture of persuasion and coercion he was successful and the infection was stayed. Nothing could have demonstrated so dramatically the extent to which the new party government was gaining the confidence of Gold Coast inhabitants, even in the normally conservative rural areas.

The second major task of the government was to find and train personnel to take over the administration from the British colonial service. It was hoped that British officials prepared to accept African government would remain. But it was obvious that both policy and necessity demanded a great increase in the number of Africans for every branch of the administration, and particularly in the higher posts. By combining in-service training with overseas scholarships, the number of Africans in the senior civil service was more than doubled between 1951 and 1953, rising from 351 to 743. It was to double again during the next four years.

Once this first two years of intensive consolidation was over, the way was clear to return to the attack on colonial rule. The Colonial Office soon recognised the validity of party government established at the 1951 election by giving Nkrumah the title of Prime Minister early in 1952. But three colonial officials remained in the Executive Council, which was still responsible to the governor, who also retained powers over internal security, defence and foreign affairs.

In April 1953 the campaign for further constitutional progress was resumed with the emphasis on removing the ex-officio members of the Executive. In July Nkrumah introduced a motion demanding full responsible self-government, based on direct elections and universal adult suffrage. It further asked that the British government declare that independence would be granted soon after the new constitution came into force.

In reality, the Gold Coast nationalists were pushing at an open door. The 1951 election had been the real watershed. Once the CPP had proved itself a nationally-organised political party capable of gaining widespread electoral support, and as soon as Nkrumah's government had shown its ability to govern the country, the British grip on her colonial reins relaxed. The Indian precedent now inhibited any latent British inclination to try and maintain colonial rule once a colonial people had clearly shown its desire and capacity for independence. There were still forces within Britain which would try to retain imperial power for as long as possible; but once any colonial people had organised themselves for a united assault on imperial rule, such influence could do little more than delay or complicate the transference of power. The only serious remaining danger was that some discontented minority group within the colony might ally itself to the imperialist group in Britain and thus endanger independence by suggesting that the colonial people were not united in demanding independence. Apart from this possibility, political Britain was now ready to pursue a policy of decolonisation, at least so far as west Africa was concerned. Even though a Conservative government had now replaced Mr Attlee's

Labour administration, the two Colonial Secretaries, Oliver Lyttelton and Alan Lennox-Boyd, both became sincere supporters of decolonisation. On the west coast they recognised that this inevitably entailed black African government. Neither of them shrank from the prospect any more than they recoiled from their corollary of giving white inhabitants power in the eastern and central areas.

So when a new and more representative draft constitution emerged from a commission presided over by Mr Justice Van Lare, it was accepted almost without amendment by the British government. The number of seats in the Assembly was to be increased to 104, the ex-officio ministers were to be replaced by elected members, the Executive Council was to become a Cabinet, and its members would be chosen by the Prime Minister. Although the governor retained control over police and army, his remaining reserved powers were only to be exercised in an emergency. The constitution provided for virtually complete domestic self-government.

In order to put the new constitution into effect another general election was necessary. By now it was apparent to the traditionalist forces that they were facing the last ditch. If the CPP won another election on this nationally representative system the social revolution would be so accelerated as to leave them no further chance of defending their authority. After the previous 1951 election Danquah's United Gold Coast Convention had been left with virtually no base from which to recover its position. So it amalgamated with the conservative National Democratic Party and a number of CPP dissidents to form the Ghana Congress Party. But the new party was incapable of competing with the CPP for mass support and had to confine itself to associating groups of intellectuals, professionals and traditionalists under the leadership of Dr Kofi Busia, a university sociologist.

The prospects of opposition were much better in the north. Here meagre communications, the dominance of Islam, and the effects of British indirect rule had isolated a large part of the community from the influence of the new political forces in the south. Thus traditionalist rule had maintained a much stronger hold on the people. Faced with the prospect of an election which might give the 'upstart' CPP leaders control of an independent nation with the consequent loss of their British support, the northern chiefs formed their own party. They called it the Northern People's Party, and, under the leadership of S. D. Dombo, set out to mobilise the traditional allegiance of the largely illiterate villagers to their chiefs and elders.

The Moslems of Accra and Kumasi also organised their own party, the Moslem Association Party, designed to protect their communities against the dangers of the new secular politics. So the CPP was faced with all the conservative, traditional and particularist elements hostile to its modernising approach. The battle was joined to determine the basis of society in the future independent nation. Fortunately the channels had been cleared for the battle to be fought by constitutional means.

In the event, the CPP had greater difficulty in disciplining its own members than from the opposition parties. By now nomination as a CPP candidate was seen to be an almost sure guarantee of preferment. Defeated contestants for selection were therefore reluctant to accept rejection gracefully. Nkrumah had to expel 81 members of his party before the elections were even held.

The Northern People's Party was able to capitalise on the traditional authority of the chiefs and won twelve seats. The Congress Party, however, completely failed in its appeal to the Ashanti electorate, only Busia gaining a seat. The Moslem Association took one constituency, and the movement for the unification of the Ewe tribe, the Togoland Congress, gained two. There were a number of independents elected also, but the CPP, with seventy-two out of the 104 seats, both won a resounding victory and proved itself again to be the only existing mass party. In fact, when the Assembly met, Nkrumah refused to recognise an official opposition as he pointed out that it was in no position to offer itself as an alternative government.

It was now evident that in a democratic, representative constitution power would be secured only by a mass party with a national electoral organisation. The CPP was the only such party in the Gold Coast. It was using its organisation and governmental strength to undermine any alternative source of authority. It was rapidly teaching the masses the meaning of modern political activity whilst offering them new social and economic horizons. 'Freedom', the CPP rallying cry, implied more than emancipation from imperialism. It meant also freedom from traditional social authority; new opportunities in education, industry, the professions; the transformation of a static, backward society into a modern, progressive nation.

Moreover, the CPP was now on the last lap towards independence. In her message to the new Assembly the Queen referred to its opening as the last step before the goal of independence was reached. It was therefore clear that there was a strong prospect of an Nkrumah government taking complete control of the country within a short time.

Having failed to halt the CPP advance through the ballot box, the opposition elements now faced the alternative of accepting the prospect of independence under an Nkrumah government or finding some other means of defending their position. The approach of independence, with its consequent removal of British protection, was likely to prove the last opportunity to unite the various groups opposed to the government and the kind of society it was building.

The only common factor between the traditionalists, the intellectuals, the professional and middle class was their dislike of the CPP. An issue arose immediately after the election which opposition leaders thought might provide the unifying factor they sought.

Cocoa was marketed by the Cocoa Marketing Board, which accumulated reserves to ensure that the farmers were paid a steady price, irrespective of world fluctuations. After the election the government fixed the price at seventy-two shillings a load, hoping to use the surplus for its development plans. Despite the agreement of the opposition in the Assembly to the bill, the leaders of the various opposition groups saw this as their opportunity for mobilising hostility to the government. A new party, the National Liberation Movement, was formed, based in Ashanti where most of the cocoa was farmed. It brought together all the opposition elements, cocoa farmers, traditionalists, intellectuals, dissidents from the CPP, all under the umbrella of the Asantehene and the Asanteman Council, the heart of traditional authority.

The CPP had not been long enough active to change the habits of mind of many people in Ashanti and the north. The NLM could play on practical grievances, rumours of discrimination and the custom of deference to the chiefs. They also revived the old Ashanti hostility towards the south, dating from nineteenth-century days, when Ashantis believed that they would have conquered the southern areas if the British had not interfered. They mobilised feelings for Ashanti separation and declared for a federal constitution which would allow each region strong powers over its own affairs.

The NLM quickly went into the attack, demonstrating its determination to mobilise Ashanti public opinion and impress the British government with the dangers of granting independence under the current constitution. Ashanti chiefs who supported the CPP were destooled. The government retaliated by passing an amendment allowing appeals by destooled chiefs to the governor. Tension rose alarmingly, violence grew between government and NLM supporters in Ashanti, and Sir Charles Arden-Clarke found himself stoned on a visit to Kumasi.

In an attempt to calm the atmosphere and allay genuine fears of interference with local customs, the government invited Sir Frederick Bourne, an eminent constitutional lawyer from Britain, to visit the country and advise on a constitution best fitted to the needs of independence. The opposition boycotted his mission and refused to accept his proposals. Nevertheless, the government decided to put most of them into operation. For Sir Frederick agreed with the CPP that the unitary nature of the state should be preserved, with a strong central government, though with bicameral regional assemblies, each consisting of a house of chiefs and an elected council. They were to be financed by the central government, to deal with certain local affairs, and to be consulted on some forms of legislation.

So the government made its gesture towards reconciliation and yet secured its basic need. It had the authority of an independent adviser in support of its claim for power to govern the most important affairs of the whole nation and the retention of a unified system of government. Moreover, its control of regional finances left it secure against separatist ambitions from the regional assemblies.

Yet, although the modernist political approach of Nkrumah and the CPP had gained another victory over conservative traditionalism and the divisive influence of its opponents, victory had its price. British political opinion was impressed – and parts of it wanted to be impressed – with the division apparent in the Gold Coast nation. The British parliamentary system, with its opportunities for individual members to raise any matter of moment, and its opposition vigilant to scrutinise government policies, was bound to express concern when any section of colonial people opposed the independence arrangements. For the nation to which power was to be transferred was not an abstraction; it was a collection of people. And British anti-imperialists were always concerned to ensure both that it was the representatives of the majority of the colonial nation who received the transferred power, and that the minorities were guaranteed their rights. This concern was a natural product of the same democratic principles which inspired anti-imperialism.

So, when the Colonial Secretary insisted that another election be held before independence, British critics of Nkrumah were pleased, but those concerned with majority rule and minority rights also agreed.

Yet this decision was a blow to Nkrumah's prestige. He had fought the 1954 election in the belief that it was the penultimate step to independence. Now he had been forced by the actions of the NLM into a position of tacitly admitting that the people might have changed their minds during the ensuing two years. It was only after his two close friends, Kojo Botsio and Komla Gbedemah, had argued with Colonial Secretary Lennox-Boyd in London and been advised by the Labour opposition to hold the election, that Nkrumah agreed to swallow this bitter pill.

The 1956 election itself was inevitably fought with acrimony, particularly in Ashanti. Nevertheless, despite the violence and intimidation which had grown over the previous two years and the desperate efforts of the traditionalists in what they realised was their final stand, the CPP again emerged unmistakably as the only party capable of governing the country. They lost a few seats, the NLM winning twelve in Ashanti and the NPP fifteen in the north. Yet the government won seventy-two out of the 104 constituencies, eight of them in Ashanti. If the Gold Coast were to be regarded as a nation, its voice had spoken clearly.

The Colonial Secretary had promised that if 'a reasonable majority' in the new legislature passed a motion calling for independence he would declare a date on which the Gold Coast could become a sovereign state. So the independence motion was introduced. Opposition members boycotted the debate, trying to the last to persuade the British government to delay independence. They still believed that if they could gain more time, they might yet block the CPP advance to power. But they had been overtaken by events. The motion was passed by seventy-two votes to nil, and the Colonial Secretary named March 6, 1957, as the day on which the new sovereign state of Ghana would be born. As the Trust Territory, British Togoland, which had been administered as part of the Gold Coast, had voted in favour of continued integration in a United Nations plebiscite, the new Ghana state would also include this territory.

It would be difficult to exaggerate the impact of this achievement on the rest of Africa. To the vast majority of Africans Ghana was thought of as the first black independent state. Ethiopia and Liberia had never been regarded in the same sense, for the former was remote from the rest of the continent and the latter was considered to be an American satellite. To Africa, therefore, the birth of Ghana marked the beginning of the end of European imperialism in Africa, heralding the collapse of white rule. Nkrumah had always declared that he considered independence in Ghana as no more than a step towards the emancipation of Africa from imperialism and white domination. His words struck echoes to every corner of the continent.

Yet the success of the constitutional advance to independence was a victory for only one of the two fronts on which the CPP had been fighting. It did no more than provide further opportunities for mounting offensives on the other front. The multiple problems involved in building a modern state out of mainly tribal, rural societies remained. About sixty per cent of the population still lived a peasant, subsistence life, with less than twenty per cent urban workers. Amongst the rest, cocoa farmers predominated, and the country was still heavily dependent on cocoa revenues, largely influenced by world price fluctuation.

Ever since it first entered office in 1951, the CPP government had attacked this problem. Its first development plan revealed its thinking by devoting over sixteen per cent to economic and productive services and thirty-five per cent to communications, essential for economic development and distribution. Social services had been greatly expanded, particularly in the field of education, but they were allocated only a third of the capital investment. As a socialist, Nkrumah saw his government's first responsibility to be a raising of the common people's standard of life, but he realised that this would only be possible on a radical and permanent scale by laying strong foundations for economic growth. He laid great store by the plan to dam the Volta River and produce hydro-electricity capable of supplying a whole range of new industries. Yet this scheme would only be possible with the help of large-scale foreign investment. Here was a foretaste of the paradoxes Nkrumah would have to face after independence. How was he to combine his socialist and neutralist philosophy with the need for a degree of foreign capital which only the western powers could provide?

Yet, in one respect Ghana was much more fortunate than her sister African countries who were to follow her lead into independence. Her cocoa revenues had provided her with nearly £200 million in sterling balances and she could sustain considerable development plans from national resources. Apart from Colonial Development and Welfare money for education, most of her economic expansion had already been financed from domestic sources.

The other major problem facing independent Ghana was still political unity. National planning and reconstruction would be severely hindered if the conflict between the modernists and the traditionalists was not quickly resolved. To some extent government patronage could be expected to wean many opponents into the national effort, for government now held the keys to preferment, with many new posts to be filled. Yet this power contained its own dangers, for in the new atmosphere of expansion, nepotism and corruption had already appeared, whilst ostentatious affluence threatened to create new social divisions.

Yet Nkrumah knew that these problems, dangerous though they might be to the national effort, were not the only threats he had to meet. The most menacing issue was to be seen in the electoral figures. In both the 1954 and the 1956 elections the opposition groups had polled around 300,000 votes compared with the 400,000 of the CPP. And only between fifty and sixty per cent of the electorate had voted. It was clear, therefore, that more than half the population had not yet committed itself to the government's leadership. In view of the violent situation which many areas of the country had experienced in the years immediately preceding independence, it was apparent that the CPP government could not yet feel confident that its appeal to build a modern state had the support of the mass of the people. With the knowledge that transforming the social basis of a nation involves discipline and sacrifice, Nkrumah recognised that his most difficult task would be to attract those uncommitted sections of the community into a form of national unity capable of a united effort to achieve accepted objectives. Amongst the uncommitted he knew he had many bitter enemies. His régime could only survive by isolating them through massive popular support. Its democratic spirit could only survive to the extent that the forces of violence were contained and dissolved.

The history of the transformation of the Gold Coast into Ghana has been treated at some length because of its significance to the rest of Africa. Yet this experience had more impact on other African regions than in some parts of west Africa itself. There were sections in every west African nation who read of the Gold Coast's progress, felt a quickening of African pride and determined to follow her example. They usually came from the younger groups living in urban areas. But in the more conservative countries they had little immediate influence.

It could hardly be expected that Gambia, for instance, would find much practical inspiration from Nkrumah's success. True, she had a model to follow in gaining expanded representative institutions, but this would not solve the crucial issue of her relations with Senegal. The traditionalists, still wedded to the prestige of the chiefs in the Protectorate, agreed with the more advanced men in public life of Bathurst and the Colony on at least one issue. For their different reasons they did not want to become even a federal part of progressive, French-speaking Senegal. At the same time, their British administrators reminded them that Britain had to provide grants-in-aid, both for their tiny budget and to pay the expatriate officials. And, after the failure of the egg scheme, there seemed to be no reason to suppose that this dependence could be changed in the foreseeable future.

Still, progress could be made constitutionally, although Gambian demands for more representatives had to be pared down to what the country could afford. A ministerial system was introduced in 1954, with unofficial members given a seven to five majority in the Executive Council. In the legislature also, unofficials had a majority, with fourteen of their sixteen members elected, the four from Bathurst by universal suffrage, the rest indirectly.

This left one issue for those with modern ideas to fight. They began to concentrate, against the opposition of Moslems and chiefs, on extending the universal suffrage practised in Bathurst to the whole country. The lead was taken by Pierre N'Jie's United Party, mainly based in Bathurst, but it found a powerful rival in David Jawara's People's Progressive Party, which had greater support in the Protectorate. So when, in 1960, the next constitutional step was taken, the franchise extended to all adults and the Legislative Council increased to thirty-four members, it was the PPP which gained an electoral majority. Less than a year later, however, quarrels in the PPP and opposition to it from the chiefs, who were still directly represented in the Council, allowed N'Jie to take over from Jawara, only for their positions to be reversed again in the following year. In the meantime, there had been further constitutional progress, allowing for the appointment of a Premier and ministers drawn from the legislature, leaving the Attorney General as the only remaining official in the Legislative Council. In May, 1962, Gambia attained internal self-government; and in 1964 a conference was held in preparation for independence in 1965.

It was left to the Gambian people themselves to determine their future, and a UN study was made of the factors relating to some form of association with Senegal. Opposition to union with Senegal gradually modified as it was seen that colonial rule was fast disappearing from the whole continent. The value of the river and the importance of Bathurst as a port would obviously be greatly enhanced if used by the Senegalese as well as by the groundnut trade from the Protectorate. Slowly representative government began to bring the Gambian peoples face to face with the economic realities of their geographic situation.

Although Gambia was too remote from the main stream of African politics to be affected by Ghana's progress to independence, it might have been expected that Sierra Leone would have felt the repercussions much more strongly. In fact, this never happened. At one time Sierra Leone had been in the forefront of the nationalist battle, with its Fourah Bay College nurturing many leading west African leaders in their youth and its most famous son, Wallace Johnson, a companion of Nigeria's Azikiwe in the pre-war and immediately post-war west African nationalist movement. But a combination of social and political factors left Sierra Leone in the backwaters of progress during the nineteen-fifties.

Constitutionally the country followed the road hewn by the Ghanaians. After the elections following the introduction of the new 1951 constitution, responsibility for government departments was gradually transferred to elected members. A full ministerial system was introduced in 1953 and the following year Dr Milton Margai was designated 'Chief Minister'. In 1956 another new constitution enlarged the legislature and two years later Dr Margai became Premier, with a Cabinet of nine African ministers. Two years later again, in 1960, a conference in London agreed that Sierra Leone should become independent in April 1961, and in the interim the governor handed over the presidency of the Executive to the Premier. Independence arrived on the date agreed.

This sequence represented a classic example of peaceful, evolutionary transference of power from the British Colonial Office to African representatives. But it had virtually no effect on the life of the inhabitants, who remained almost entirely poor, illiterate, riddled with superstition and traditional deference. A few leading personalities made considerable fortunes from their new offices, but the mass of the people were unaffected, except that the administration was rather less efficient and more corrupt. Perhaps self-government and independence came too easily. The British had no reason to stay in control and after the Ghanaian example needed little pressure to hand over their powers when asked. In any case, the transference was to their traditionalist friends, whom they could expect to respect their interests, not to the brash upstarts of Accra. Dr Margai's Sierra Leone People's Party, which held office from its foundation in 1951 right through to independence, was based largely on the support of the Protectorate chiefs. And any chief who stepped out of line could always be dismissed.

There were, of course, a number of rival parties formed during this period. The United Progressive Party fought Margai's SLPP in the 1957 elections and won nine seats out of thirty-nine. Margai's own brother, Albert, co-operated with the labour leader, Siaka Stevens, to form the People's National Party in 1958, attracting most support from dissident members of the SLPP. The PNP did try to inject a more radical element into Sierra Leone politics, demanding immediate independence, but never secured any mass support. Still more radical was the All People's Congress, which Stevens and Wallace Johnson established after all the other parties

had joined a United National Front immediately before independence. The APC attracted some support from the younger men in
the towns, the trade union movement and discontented diamond
diggers. It demanded elections before independence and its leaders
were detained in prison during the independence celebrations. It
remained the only serious opposition party after independence.

Yet, over the whole scene hung the heavy hands of social respectability, conformity and deference towards the British. The few
aberrations in this pattern had no political significance. There were
labour troubles in Freetown in 1955 and mass large-scale discontent
when attempts were made to curtail illicit diamond digging and
sales two years later. Neither became serious political issues.

The fact was that the social fashions of Sierra Leone were set by a
combination of traditional chieftainship in the Protectorate and
Creole Victorianism in Freetown. It was characteristic that on the
occasion when Milton Margai was defeated for the leadership of
the SLPP parliamentary caucus by his brother Albert the decision
was reversed the same evening; to defeat the doctor 'just wasn't
done!'

So, when Protectorate workers came to Freetown in search of
employment and began to break away from their tribal background,
they did not find militant trade unions, social associations, intellectual groups or radical politicians waiting to welcome them. They
found instead the conservative conventions of inbred Creoles who
had used their economic and educational advantages to flood the
professions, despising manual labour. This prim community
slavishly imitated nineteenth-century England, contemptuously regarding African society as socially inferior.

When representative institutions were forced on the Creoles and
the Protectorate Africans began to enter political life, it was characteristic of the national outlook that twelve seats in the legislature
were reserved for paramount chiefs. This special representation of the
chiefs continued after independence.

Thus the twin influence of nostalgic Creoledom and traditional
authority pervaded social and political life. They prevented any
genuine nationalist movement developing and stifled any conception of changing social relations, planned economic expansion, or
association with the dynamic political ideas developing in the rest
of the continent. Sierra Leone continued to slumber, with some

black faces replacing white, but with most people's lives virtually unchanged.

Nor could one expect much impact from the momentous events in Ghana to be felt in west Africa's oldest state, Liberia. President Tubman showed his interest in the new Gold Coast developments as early as 1953. He invited Nkrumah to pay a state visit to Liberia, and sent his presidential yacht to fetch him. Incidentally, the upkeep of the yacht cost more than one per cent of Liberia's national budget. Indeed, over six per cent of the budget was allocated to the presidential administration.

But there was little overt criticism of presidential extravagance. After completing his statutory two four-year terms in office, the constitution was changed in 1951 to enable him to stand for election again. His personal dominance and executive power enabled him to continue securing election without serious opposition.

Yet, although this had now become virtually a personal dictatorship, its effect was to change the life of the country, albeit slowly, rather than to preserve the status quo. He was not content to rely on the support of the Americo-Liberians on the coast, perhaps one per cent of the million and a half inhabitants, who had traditionally ruled the country. He went into the hinterland, talked to the chiefs, and brought some individuals from the interior into his government. From 1950 onwards Point Four aid from America was combined with twenty per cent of the national budget in a development programme designed to tackle the immense problems of public health, agriculture, roads and education. The Firestone rubber company was persuaded to pay twenty-five per cent income tax on its profits to help to finance development. The Swedes were encouraged to pursue their interest in iron ore mining, with the result that the value of iron production eventually overtook that of rubber.

So, although there were no dramatic or fundamental changes as there had been in the Gold Coast, Liberians saw some prospect of a better life. The interior peoples participated for the first time in the affairs of the nation, women were given the vote, new economic and social developments began to appear. Monrovia continued to dominate the country to an unhealthy degree, whilst economic progress tended to be reflected too heavily in building in the capital. Inevitably economic progress attracted increasing numbers of Liberians to their only city, increasing the social and economic tensions there. The question posed for the future was whether Tubman's presidential system could meet the challenges provoked by his own gradual reforms, or whether some of his younger lieutenants, already attracted by the Ghanaian example, would demand swifter and more radical changes.

The only country in west Africa really comparable with the Gold Coast was Nigeria. The size of the country, both in territory and population, was so much larger than the Gold Coast that potentially it seemed likely to have an even greater impact on African society. It had also taken at least as important a role in the early nationalist movement and up to about 1950 might have been expected to attain independence as quickly as Nkrumah and his colleagues.

But constitutional evolution in Nigeria did not have a very smooth passage during the nineteen-fifties. A number of factors raised barriers to the dynamic drive seen in the Gold Coast. The whole socio-economic situation was much more complex than that which Nkrumah faced. Traditional power in the north was far stronger, with half the total population under its sway and the chiefs or emirs reinforced by the conservatism of Islam. In the west traditional chieftainship allied itself to a commercial class emerging from African traders, forming a strong bourgeoisie on the foundations of traditional forms. Whilst this allowed reform, it could never initiate a radical drive amongst the masses in the way shown by the CPP. The east was radical, but frequently torn by conflicts within itself which handicapped any ambition to become a genuine national party.

The fact that Nigeria was relatively much poorer than the Gold Coast did not encourage radicalism, whilst the graft, corruption and nepotism which inevitably accompany increased powers retarded progress more than would have been the case in a wealthier nation. Nor was there likely to be the healthy outcry against such practices in a country accustomed to more deference towards its rulers than arose in less traditionally-minded societies.

But the greatest handicaps to any dynamic national progress were the deep divisions between different sections within the country. Despite Azikiwe's valiant efforts during and immediately after the war, no genuine sense of Nigerian nationality had appeared in the early nineteen-fifties. Nor is it accurate to put all the blame for this lack on British imperial rule. It is true that the British administrators tended to favour the traditionalists, but they had brought the various elements of the country together for the first time in 1914 and were to make one major attempt to unite them politically after the second world war.

The fact was that the different societies brought together within Nigeria had too little in common, maintained too many mutual suspicions, and were each too large to be dominated by another as in the unifying drive in the Gold Coast. Nkrumah had faced similar problems, but never on such a large scale. Ghana was sufficiently compact to be made into a unitary state despite the differences between its societies; Nigeria was too large and diffuse.

This fact became apparent soon after the 1951 constitution came into operation. The constitution itself was an impossible amalgam of two contrary elements. The British wanted to lead Nigerians into a unified nationhood, but without giving power to the radical southerners. This policy contained a contradiction. Nothing less than a determined modernising drive from the south could have succeeded in creating a common national consciousness. So when the Macpherson constitution of 1951 came into force, it was un-acceptable to both traditionalists and modernists. It was designed to give considerable powers to the central government, but ensured that the central legislature was regionally controlled so as to avoid any danger of it being flooded with nationalists as in Accra. The central House of Representatives was elected by the regional legis-latures, and they indirectly, by electoral colleges. Moreover, the north, the home of traditionalism, was allocated sixty-eight seats to the thirty-four from each of the southern regions, reflecting population ratios. In the Council of Ministers, too, four members were to be drawn from each region, blocking any purely nationalist form of government.

So the constitution, which gave much stronger powers to the central than to the regional governments, limited the use of those powers by regional influence and preserved a strong element of traditionalist authority over the elections.

It was partly the effect of this constitution which diverted the attention of the politically-conscious to regional rather than national efforts. Azikiwe and Obafemi Awolowo had both favoured some form of federation to circumvent the deeply-rooted conservatism of the north. Now they recognised the danger of the Macpherson constitution giving the north full powers to determine national policy if it could find a few allies in the south. Both reacted in the same way, by concentrating their efforts on securing greater powers for their regions and organising their parties on a mainly regional basis.

So Azikiwe's National Council of Nigeria and the Cameroons, whilst never renouncing its claim to be a national party, found that it could only gain mass support in the Ibo-dominated East region. Awolowo based his Action Group on the Yoruba establishment in the West. The northerners founded their own party, the Northern People's Congress, led by the Sardauna of Sokoto. And the leaders of each party sought their power in the regional assemblies, leaving the central legislature to underlings. Indeed, this very fact brought schism to Azikiwe's party. When the NCNC decided to oppose the constitution it found its ministers in the federal house unwilling to resign. Supported by some members in the region they left the NCNC to form a National Independence Party.

But hostility between north and south soon undermined the constitution. In 1953 the southerners tried to get the federal house to approve a motion demanding self-government in 1956. They were baulked by the northerners, who would agree only to a request for independence 'as soon as practicable'. Northern members were insulted in Lagos, whilst tensions over activities of southerners in Kano led to riots. So new discussions were arranged, with all three parties, for their different reasons, insisting on a federal constitution with the balance of powers in the regions. The north feared that the better educated, more sophisticated southerners intended to disrupt and then control its society. The south, in both the western and eastern regions, feared that the conservative north would obstruct progress towards self-government and independence. And they knew that by this time the Gold Coast already had internal self-government.

By October 1954 a new constitution had emerged from the discussions. It was now frankly federalist. The three regions each had their Executive Councils and Houses of Assembly, with ministers nominated by the majority parties and strong powers over their regional affairs. The Southern Cameroons was given similar institutions, though the Northern Cameroons continued to be administered as part of the Northern Region of Nigeria. The Federation of the three regions and the Southern Cameroons had its own House of Representatives, now elected from federal constituencies by direct election in the south, but still through electoral colleges in the north. In a House of a hundred and eighty-four members, ninety-two came from the North, forty-two each from the West and East, six from the Southern Cameroons and two from Lagos, now, against the opposition of the Western Region, designated as Federal territory. The Federation also had its Council of Ministers, three drawn from each region and one from the Southern Cameroons.

This new constitution satisfied the desire of the nationalists to bring party politics into the arena, but demonstrated that henceforth they would have to be concentrated mainly on regional activities.

Each major regional party won the elections in its own region and formed its regional government, the NPC in the North, the NCNC in the East and the Action Group in the West. But in the federal elections the NPC won a much larger number of seats than the other two parties because half the total number of constituencies were in the Northern Region. Although they made half-hearted attempts, neither of the other parties could seriously challenge the NPC in its own region. The NCNC showed a final flicker of ambition as a national party by actually winning more federal seats in the West than the Action Group. This led to the bizarre situation in which the Governor General had to appoint six NCNC ministers, three from the East and three from the West, with only three from the NPC.

Yet the party leaders still remained in their regions, where they became regional premiers. A united Nigerian nation seemed farther away than ever. Each of the regions was going its separate way. The North was still feudal, run by the Fulani-Hausa emirs, with women in purdah and still denied the vote, the masses illiterate and deferential to their traditional rulers. There were a few signs of gradual reform, in education, communications and economic life, but they were scarcely perceptible, hardly scratching the surface of social or political relations. A group of the younger generation tried to pose the challenge of the modern world by forming an opposition party, the Northern Elements Progressive Union, led by Amino Kano, but it faced an enormous task in defying the might of centuries-old Islamic traditionalism.

The Eastern Region was always politically dynamic, but economically poor. Regional government produced progressive developments, particularly in education, and some centralised economic initiative. But political schism was frequent and financial corruption common. Azikiwe himself had to submit to an inquiry into his dealings with the African Continental Bank in 1956, and the following year faced a serious revolt against his leadership over his failure to introduce the promised universal free education. The Ibos found employment in all three regions, but suspicions of their ambitious nature prevented them making any serious in-roads into the established social system.

It was in the West that most progress was seen, for this was the cocoa region with sufficient wealth to contemplate seriously the building of a modern state. In education, commerce and productivity the West led the way, but to the creation of a bourgeois rather than a radical society. The Action Group was controlled by the Yoruba establishment. Government control of the economy widened opportunities for employment, stimulated public initiative in economic activities and gave some the chance to accumulate considerable wealth. But the society created was dominated by the professional classes and commercial leaders. It could not give a lead to the other regions, for the conditions in which it flourished did not exist anywhere else. And there was little sign that this successful commercialism would lead to a more radical transformation of society likely to affect the lives of ordinary people.

Having found themselves in the narrower channels of regionalism the nationalists of the East and West now mounted a combined offensive to secure regional self-government. This was quickly achieved in 1957, when it was agreed at a constitutional conference that both regions should become self-governing for those subjects of regional competence.

The North was still anxious to maintain British administration for a few years longer. But even the northerners had by now seen the inevitable pattern of the future. To general surprise the northerners participated in March 1957 in a unanimous motion of the Federal House demanding national independence in 1959. In August a federal Prime Minister was appointed and he immediately took two Action Group members into his cabinet to form a genuinely national coalition. The new Prime Minister was not one of the three main party leaders. He was the Sardauna of Sokoto's lieutenant, Alhaji Abubakar Tafawa Balewa, a reformist from the north, already a minister in the Executive, who was accepted because it was now obvious that only a northerner could hold the three regions together.

Here, then, was the turning point. In 1957 it became clear for the first time that the Nigerian regions were going to remain linked together in the same nation and that the new Nigerian state would be a federation. Economic realities, combined with a genuine desire to establish a Nigerian entity, had overcome the divisive forces. The Western Region, with its cocoa revenue and coastline, might have succeeded in creating a separate state. The North was large enough, but had no outlet for its exports. The East would have been very poor. Yet even the West was heavily dependent on good cocoa harvests and prices. In this same year of 1957 it was given a sharp reminder of how vulnerable it was to influences outside its control. Bad weather reduced its cocoa crop from 130,000 to 80,000 tons. In the same year there were record harvests of palm oil in the East and cotton in the North. Together with the constant supply of groundnuts from the North and palm kernels from the East, these products made up Nigeria's main exports. Almost all of them came from agriculture, in which four-fifths of the Nigerian people were engaged. Each region had learnt that the needs of economic development and international influence demanded that they hold together.

Yet their immediate ambitions were frustrated at the 1957 constitutional conference. Britain did not accept that they would be ready for independence by 1959. The conference was adjourned for further reports on the practical steps which still needed to be taken and did not reassemble until September 1958. The interim period was well spent, for Nigerian leaders now realised that independence could only be gained when they had reached agreement on the main issues still dividing them. So the resumed conference demonstrated a spirit of compromise and co-operation. The Northern Region asked for self-government dating from March 1959. The question of the minorities was settled by rejecting pleas for new regions to be

created, but leaving machinery for their creation in future. A single
police force was to be established, but some degree of control and
recruiting was left with the regions. A division of powers between
the regional and federal governments was agreed and a common
voting system based on universal suffrage was accepted, with the
proviso that for the time being women would not be given the vote
in the North. The new Federal House was expanded to 320 constituencies on a population basis, with 174 seats in the North, 62 in
the West, 73 in the East, 8 in the Southern Cameroons and 3 in
Lagos. Finally, the British Colonial Secretary agreed that if, after
new federal elections, the House were to request independence, this
would be granted on October 1, 1960.

The Federal elections were held in December 1959. They resulted
in the NPC gaining 142 seats, NEPU 8, the NCNC 89, and the
Action Group 73. Both the NCNC and the Action Group managed
to win seats outside their own regions, the NCNC 21 in the West,
the Action Group 24 in the North and 14 in the East. As both
Azikiwe and Awolowo had chosen to leave the security of their
regional governments for seats in the Federal House, it seemed as
though there were some prospect of the emphasis on regionalism
diminishing.

At first it might have been expected that these two leaders from
the south would have formed a progressive coalition, for their
combined seats just gave them a majority. But although Azikiwe
and Awolowo were willing, the battles between their followers had
been too bitter. The former NCNC ministers preferred to continue
serving under the northerner, Abubakar. So an alliance was formed
between the NPC, the NCNC and the NEPU, the government
consisted of nine NPC ministers and seven from the NCNC, with
Awolowo leading his Action Group as the official opposition.
Azikiwe himself refused to accept a ministry, preferring to become
President of the Senate. (After independence he was to become
Governor General, and in 1963, President of the Republic.)

Meanwhile there had been some confusion over what was to
happen to the Northern and Southern Cameroons. The Southern
Cameroons had not participated in the federal elections, for
its own 1959 elections had been won by the Cameroon National
Democratic Party which was opposed to union with Nigeria. The
United Nations decided that both Cameroon regions should have

plebiscites, which were held in February 1961. It had been expected that the more backward North would join the new Cameroon Republic, formed from the French mandate, and the more progressive South join Nigeria. In the event the reverse occurred. The North voted to continue its association with the Nigerians and the South became part of the Republic.

Now the Federal House was ready to make its formal request for independence. After further constitutional discussions this was duly achieved on October 1, 1960. It included an Anglo-Nigerian Defence Agreement which was strongly criticised by younger Nigerians. The largest country in Africa, with a population well over 50 million, had brought imperial rule to an end and become a sovereign state. It had still to become a nation. For regional loyalties remained deeper than any sense of Nigerian nationality. It had immense social and economic tasks to achieve, for its people were mostly poor agriculturists, whilst half its inhabitants still lived in a feudal society. The future of Nigeria and its impact on the world outside would depend on whether its social and economic problems could be overcome without the state fragmenting into semi-tribal, communal fractions. Independence provided no more than an opportunity for Nigerians to determine this issue themselves.

It is easier to follow the course of events in French Africa than in the British territories because French colonial policy has always been uniform. Although different attitudes have been shown in local situations, whilst protectorates and mandated or trust territories have been treated separately, constitutional advance has been achieved at the same pace and at the same time throughout the colonies. So, instead of the irregular pattern of British colonial history, with the various colonies negotiating in London each year and each progressing according to a complexity of factors, the French colonies took steps forward in unison, all with the same rights and almost identical institutions.

The first half of the nineteen-fifties is sometimes regarded as a period of political stagnation in French West Africa. This is something of an exaggeration. In 1951, for instance, franchise qualifications were reduced, increasing the total electorate from the figure of 1,362,763 in 1946 to 5,061,025. Now that the need to organise for elections had given the party system momentum, political awareness rapidly developed, and was mobilised for political action. More-over, the African parliamentarians, both locally and in Paris, were learning their arts, a few of them even being given experience as assistant ministers in the French government. The trades unions, too, helped by metropolitan unions, were learning the value of the strike weapon and industrial pressure. Their efforts were rewarded in 1952 by a 'Code du Travail', granting African workers certain minimum wages, reduced working hours, family allowances, holidays with pay and the right of collective bargaining.

Yet, in comparison with the spectacular progress of Ghana and Nigeria, these seemed minor advances in political responsibility. Moreover, they appeared to have no ultimate purpose. As inde-pendence had been ruled out in 1946, no amount of increase in political rights could ever lead to a transfer of executive powers. French policy seemed to be operating in a political cul-de-sac.

In addition to the extension of voting and trade union rights, an economic factor was also stimulating political awareness. In an attempt to ensure that the granting of French citizenship to Africans would be accompanied by the attainment of appropriate standards, French governments after the war had allocated considerable funds to increase production, raise living standards and increase social facilities, particularly in education. In April 1946 an organisation was set up called 'Fonds d'Investissement pour le Développement Economique et Social de la France d'Outre-Mer', colloquially known as FIDES. Three years later, after criticisms that Africans did not seem to see any direct benefits from the organisation, a second body was established known as 'Fonds d'Équipement Rural et de Déve-loppement Economique et Social' or FERDES. This was to develop the practical amenities of rural life – water supplies, primary schools, markets, dams and roads. The French spent much more on these projects than the British did on similar Colonial Development and Welfare Funds. More than two per cent of the French national income was contributed to overseas aid, and West Africa received nearly half this sum.

With the building of new universities and schools, the promotion of industry, commerce and agriculture, it was inevitable that public consciousness should grow. The effect was seen when investment and development suddenly slowed down in 1952–1954. Strikes spread throughout French West Africa in 1954 and 1955.

So beneath the apparent quietude there was activity and perhaps mounting discontent with the status quo. Houphouet-Boigny had to tackle the tough task of first purging his RDA of its communist elements and then rebuilding the party in support of his new conciliatory policy. In the process he lost considerable strength, even in his own Ivory Coast. In Upper Volta the all-Mossi party, Union Voltaique, led by Dr Joseph Conombo, and affiliated to IOM, replaced the RDA as the main party. Yet the younger évolués found the traditionalists uneasy bedfellows in this party and caused its dissolution in 1955. And when Conombo replaced it with his Parti Social d'Éducation des Masses Africaines, this new party was able to dominate the territorial assembly without relying on solid Mossi support. In Soudan, the troubles in RDA did not help Mamadou Konaté's affiliated Union Soudanaise, which continued to be out-voted by Fily Sissoko's Parti Soudanaise Progressiste, an affiliate of the French Socialist Party. Yet Konaté continued to organise the urban population and, as traditionalism gradually broke down, so the Union gained increased strength. By 1956, when the PSP split, it was ready to take over, despite Konaté's death. Mauritania and Niger remained political backwaters, the former under the traditionalist Moorish chiefs, the latter led by its IOM affiliate until 1956, when the labour leader, Hamani Diori, was elected and the IOM candidates lost their seats. In Dahomey powerful Catholicism was suspicious of the RDA and politics tended to avoid extremism from any quarter. Souron Apithy and Hubert Maga remained the outstanding political figures.

Whilst Houphouet-Boigny was occupied in trying to hold his RDA affiliates together under these extreme pressures, Senegal had its own troubles. Following the split between the older member of the French Socialist Party, Lamine Guèye, and the young intellectual, Senghor, in 1948, Senghor the Catholic and a Moslem schoolmaster, Mamadou Dia, formed the Bloc Démocratique Sénégalais. They claimed that it represented an African form of socialism, emphasising specifically African values, such as the extended family and clan basis of society. But the immediate appeal was on practical issues, prices, social welfare, co-operatives, and they gained wide support in the rural areas. Senghor's party defeated Lamine Guèye in the 1951 elections to the National Assembly, and again the following year in the territorial elections.

But it was not until 1953 that Senghor and his friends really showed where they stood in west African politics. In that year their association, Indépendants d'Outre-Mer, the rival inter-territorial body to the RDA, held a congress in the Upper Volta. It was here that the Senghor-led group first expressed their alternative policy to Houphouet-Boigny's plans for an individual association of each French African state with the French Republic. Senghor posed the sharp alternative of an African federal republic within the French Union. He was shortly afterwards to elaborate this proposal with the suggestion that French West Africa should be divided into two federations, one based on his own Dakar, the other on Houphouet's Abidjan, both being part of the Union.

Thus early the two contrary theories of French African progress were laid down; Houphouet visualising eight autonomous states in individual relationship with Paris, Senghor seeking larger units in African federations within the French Union. Both assumed that continued relations with France were essential for African development.

Despite the comparative calm of this 1950–1955 period, African pressure was mounting for radical amendment to the 1946 constitution. The effects of the United Nations influence in Togoland were seen in 1955 when France gave its trust territory virtually internal self-government. The French believed that with their control of the electoral system and Nicholas Grunitzky in office they could persuade the Togolese to join the French Union. A new statute was also drawn up for the other trust territory, Cameroun, and, despite fears aroused by severe rioting in Douala, it included universal suffrage.

With these examples of constitutional advance in French African trusteeships pressure for a new constitution in the West African colonies became irresistible. The main difficulty was to find a French government strong and durable enough to give serious, sustained attention to a colonial new deal. It was not until Guy Mollet formed his Socialist government in 1955 that conditions were fulfilled.

The presence of Houphouet-Boigny and Gaston Defferre, the socialist Mayor of Marseilles, in Mollet's Cabinet, provided the impetus and the local knowledge to draft a new constitution for the colonial territories. This came to be known as the '*loi cadre*', or 'skeleton' law. For the act, passed in June 1956, was really an enabling act, giving powers for the details of new constitutional forms to be filled in by decree.

This act marked a dramatic watershed in French colonial history. It discarded the two basic principles from which the colonial policy of France had been drawn – assimilation and centralisation. The conception that colonial subjects should become citizens of France was abandoned, as was the belief that French colonial government should stem from Paris. In their places France now recognised that the destiny of French Africans was to form individual nations, governed locally. There was some hope that they would remain in association with the French Republic and thus continue as a part of the French world. But the idea that a Greater France might be created was finally forsaken.

Under the new act the two great federations of French West Africa and French Equatorial Africa were virtually dismantled. Most of their powers passed to the separate territories, each of which was accorded semi-responsible government. The territorial assemblies were to be enlarged and elected by universal suffrage, including women, even in the Moslem areas. These assemblies were then to choose lists of candidates for ministerial office and to vote on them. The successful candidates would form the cabinet, the individual with most votes becoming vice-president, potentially prime minister. The Head of each territory, still appointed by France, was to be the president, but he had to consult the vice-president and take the advice of the cabinet on matters within its competence. The Grand Councils of the two former federations remained in existence, but were shorn of most of their powers. Each former federation was renamed a 'Group of Territories', and the former Governor-General became a 'Head' with reserved powers over police, foreign affairs and defence still retained by France. In all other matters he had to consult the Grand Council, but as this was elected by each territory, its affairs amounted to little more than co-ordination of common services.

Elections were also to be arranged for town councils, whilst the electoral college system for elections to the French parliament was abolished and universal suffrage introduced with direct elections.

The *loi cadre* represented a revolution in Franco-African relations. It is pertinent to consider why France should reverse all her previous policies at this particular moment. African pressure for reform had mounted, but was by no means unanimous. French government was certainly revealing weaknesses and shrank from facing the prospect of widespread colonial revolts. The defeat in Indo-China had shown what disasters could attend a policy of intransigence towards colonial demands. Tunisia and Morocco had just gained their independence out of nationalist resistance and the war in Algeria threatened to embroil French troops in another colonial war. In the face of these pressures the Mollet government felt itself impelled towards practising socialist principles of self-determination in the French national interest. Gaston Defferre was the man to put them into practice with the help of Houphouet-Boigny.

Yet the *loi cadre* was by no means welcomed by all French African leaders. It represented the Houphouet-Boigny conception of advance rather than that enunciated by Senghor and his supporters. There was a good deal of scepticism over the details of the scheme, many holding them to be based on the strategy of 'divide and rule', with dark suspicions of a plot to retain the hold of French capitalist interests over the colonies.

It was Senghor who made the most trenchant criticisms. To him the plan would lead to a balkanisation of African territories. He saw the dissolution of the federations as a retrograde step, weakening the future collective power of Africans. He put his criticism into two prophetic sentences in *Le Monde*: 'Dans le cadre d'une république fédérale française, une AOF de 20 millions d'habitants en face de la métropole peut constituer un ensemble équilibré et faire épanouir sa personnalité. Une Côte d'Ivoire ou un Sénégal de 2 million d'habitants ne le peuvent pas.' Nevertheless, despite Senghor's gloomy, but realistic fears, he concluded that the *loi cadre* could be an emancipating instrument if Africans wished it to be.

The *loi cadre* was passed through the French parliament with large majorities in 1956 and the decrees putting it into force were made in 1957. Its effect was to stimulate still greater political activity in the west African territories as preparations were made for new elections. Now every adult was directly concerned, whilst the knowledge that for the first time the candidates elected would be empowered to form governments legislating for matters of daily concern to the whole community inevitably increased popular interest. In general the new constitution acted as a special forcing house for the mass parties, leaving the sectional and tribal organisations steadily weakening.

Yet the policy battle over what would be the best structural relationship amongst African states and between them and France was not yet over. It was concentrated within the two regional political associations, the RDA, based on the Ivory Coast and the IOM, later to be succeeded first by the Convention Africaine and then by the Parti de Regroupement Africain, all led by Senegal. In particular, the argument waxed hot over what should be the future relationship with France, for it was generally recognised that the *loi cadre* could only be one step towards a more comprehensive settlement.

The RDA congress met at Bamako in September, 1957. It was dominated by the conflict between, on the one side, Houphouet-Boigny, its president, and his Ivory Coast contingent, supported by Léon Mba, from Gabon, and, on the other, the majority of the delegates, headed by Sékou Touré from Guinea and Modibo Keita from Soudan. The argument hinged on whether future relations with France would be better conducted by two federations of African states or by each state individually. With the exception of a few young delegates who took a violently anti-colonial line and left the conference to form an independence movement, the delegates at Bamako all accepted the need to build some kind of Afro-French association. Once again was revealed the sharp contrast between the outlook of British and French Africans at this time. Although in British territories the drive for independence was always seen in terms of joining the Commonwealth, this implied membership as fully sovereign and equal states. In the French colonies the objective was to create an association accepting that the French would retain major powers for a long period and in which the African states would not claim certain attributes of sovereignty. Even radical leaders like Sékou Touré and Modibo Keita accepted this assumption, a sharp antithesis to the approach of men like Nkrumah and Azikiwe and even of the more moderate nationalists in the Gold Coast and Nigeria.

The motives of those who accepted the need for continued French leadership varied. Certainly Houphouet-Boigny inside the RDA and Senghor outside it both felt an affinity with French life and culture. Both men, in their different ways, believed that Frenchmen and

Africans had contributions to offer each other which could produce a genuine Franco-African culture. Separation from France would destroy the opportunity for this to develop. Touré, on the other hand, without any deep experience of France, thought more in terms of strategy. He knew that all French colonies needed a continuation of French economic aid for many years and was prepared to pay a political price for it. He thus hoped to use French services in order to ensure that when the African states gained independence they would have strong, modern economic foundations. Keita shared this view, at least partially and with a good deal of scepticism as to whether the French would agree to a genuine association.

In the RDA debate at Bamako Houphouet-Boigny and Mba argued that each colonial territory should gain separate autonomy and then participate in a federal relationship with France. They advocated that the federal institutions be accorded certain powers in matters such as foreign, defence and economic affairs. It was perhaps no coincidence that these two leaders represented the wealthiest countries in French Africa, Ivory Coast and Gabon. There was resentment in each at the prospect of subsidising the poorer African colonies with whom they had been associated in the west and equatorial federations.

Touré and Keita took a position much closer to Senghor. They maintained that the federations still existed and should be brought under democratic control. They believed that the correct approach was to gain power for Africans over the internal affairs of each federation, leaving other affairs for the time being mainly in French hands. They saw this as a further step towards full independence for each federation. Their difference with Senghor was that they did not accept any association with the French as a permanent objective, whereas Senghor believed that an Afro-French community had an intrinsic value.

Touré and Keita had the majority of RDA delegates behind them. Yet there was no desire to lose the services of Houphouet. Despite the fact that he absented himself from the last two days of the debate and did not vote, the final motion deliberately avoided any appearance of defeating him, whilst he retained his position as president.

A few months later, in 1958, almost all the parties outside the RDA united in another inter-territorial association which they called the

Parti de Regroupement Africain. The initiative again came from Senghor, now reunited in Senegal with Lamine-Guèye in the Union Progressiste Sénégalaise. The PRA supported Senghor's plea for a strong west African federation, with its own executive, which could negotiate a new relationship with France as a single unit.

In May 1958 the French Fourth Republic collapsed and De Gaulle took over state powers. He immediately set up a commission to draft a new French Constitution. The Africans, therefore, were now forced to take a quick decision as to what plans they should put forward to define their role in the nascent Fifth Republic.

Recognising the importance of presenting a united front on this crucial issue, the RDA and the PRA held joint discussions in July 1958. The manifesto which emerged revealed Houphouet-Boigny's strength, despite his minority position in west Africa. The joint meeting called for a federal republic of autonomous states, leaving the question of groupings amongst the states to be decided by each individually. The PRA, although accepting that this plan represented the highest common factor of agreement, was not satisfied to remain committed only to a scheme which rejected their basic demand for a federation with its own executive. Immediately afterwards it held its own conference at Cotonou in Dahomey and laid down its distinctive policy. It demanded immediate independence, a constituent assembly of Africans to work out a confederal association with France (in which it wanted an African federation which would be sovereign on an equal basis with France) and a United States of Africa, linking all ex-colonial countries in one vast federation. This programme was obviously on a more visionary plane than that of Houphouet, its last proposal coming close to Nkrumah's outlook. It was the alternative which confederalism posed to federalism which was immediately relevant. As had now become habitual, it was Houphouet-Boigny who got his way.

When De Gaulle came to power Houphouet was appointed one of his four ministers of state. He was therefore in a position to influence the colonial proposals in the new constitution. His ideas appealed to De Gaulle who saw that to maintain strong links with Africa would aid his ambition of restoring French power. It would increase the population to be governed by him, provide him with minerals and probably oil from the Sahara, whilst extending the frontiers of French civilisation.

These were the thoughts which lay behind plans for the French Community offered for approval in September 1958. The African territories were no longer to be represented in the French parliament but would participate in the election of the President. The Community was to have its own Executive Council, presided over by the President, consisting of heads of government from each member territory together with other ministers concerned with matters within the competence of the Community. Its Senate was to represent the parliaments of each member in proportion to population and to discuss common issues before they were debated in the French and African parliaments. The institution was thus given only advisory powers. Each territorial member would have the right to change its status at the request of its legislature confirmed by a referendum.

The conception of the French Community represented a compromise which ignored political realities. It abandoned the concept of a legislative centre for both France and her colonies in Paris, for the French parliament was to confine itself to metropolitan legislation. It equally rejected full federal status, in which Community institutions would have been given legislative powers. Yet it also stopped short of offering sovereignty to the colonial territories in a voluntary association like the Commonwealth. Such an amorphous structure seemed unlikely to meet the challenges of the nationalist era.

Nevertheless, with the exception of Djiko Bakary in Niger, one minister in Soudan, and Sékou Touré of Guinea, all the leaders of both the RDA and the PRA called for approval of the constitution when it was submitted to a referendum in the African territories during September, 1958. The mass of the electorate followed their leaders, except in Niger. There Bakary, after trying to curb the influence of the chiefs, on whose support he had gained power the previous year, found his advice rejected. The chiefs were not prepared to contemplate independence, giving control to a man who obviously intended to destroy traditional authority. In a small vote, twenty-seven per cent followed Bakary's lead in rejecting the Community, but the vast majority obeyed their chiefs. Bakary of the PRA was replaced with Hamani Diori of RDA. In Soudan Keita thought it good tactics for the moment to follow the lead of Houphouet-Boigny and Senghor. For one thing, he realised that the economy of his country depended on the outlet to the sea through Senegal. Guinea was left as the only dissident.

The defiance of Sékou Touré was intended as a lead for the future. He hoped that the other territories would join him in gaining independent status prior to forming some type of federal union. Although none did so, both Senghor in Senegal and Apithy of Dahomey declared immediately after the referendum that they regarded the decision as a step towards full independence.

Touré had taken over the leadership in Guinea after the death of Yacine Diallo in 1954. A sudden boom in bauxite and iron mining created a new proletariat in Guinea which he, as a trade union organiser, was equipped to attract. He combined his trade union activities with leadership in the Parti Démocratique de Guinée, an affiliate of the RDA, but one based on more articulate popular opinion than most of the other members of that association. After the passing of the *loi cadre* he became vice-president of the Guinea Council and quickly set about destroying opposition to his PDG. In particular, he replaced the local authority of the chiefs with civil servants advised by elected councils. His object was to identify his party with the government, basing both on wide popular support. In the trade union field he demonstrated his pan-African outlook by establishing the Union Générale des Travailleurs de l'Afrique Noire as a federation of French African unions independent of external affiliation.

Once the people of Guinea had followed Touré's advice, with ninety-seven per cent voting against De Gaulle's constitution, they found themselves petulantly abandoned by the French. The sudden cessation of economic aid and the mass withdrawal of French administrators, some of whom stripped their offices of files, equipment, even electric light bulbs, left the country in a parlous situation. The immediate offer of assistance and association by Ghana had a greater psychological than practical effect. Sékou Touré was left to find economic aid wherever he could. He was often faced with obstruction from France's friends in the west, and although this offered an open invitation to the communist bloc, its aid was given more verbally than in practical or useful forms. Nevertheless, Guinea gave the lead in gaining independence, her bauxite deposits continued to attract international capital, particularly from America, and although administrative chaos inevitably followed the

French withdrawal, a basis for developing a modern economy remained.

The defeat of Senghor's plans for resurrecting the west African federation did not dissuade him from the need for such a structure. Three months after the referendum, at the end of 1958, he called a conference at Bamako to discuss the prospect. His object was to set up a new federation and the delegates who attended from Senegal, Soudan, Upper Volta and Dahomey agreed to participate in this venture. It was not long, however, before both France and Houphouet-Boigny were bringing pressure to bear on Upper Volta and Dahomey to withdraw their promises. In the former territory Maurice Yaméogo, a member of the RDA, had just succeeded to the premiership on the death of Coulibaly. It was soon firmly pointed out to him that his country depended on its outlet through the Ivory Coast to the sea and on the Abidjan-Ouagadougou railway. He submitted to Houphouet's pressure, lost his PRA supporters, formed a new party, the Union Démocratique Voltaique, and easily won a general election.

In Dahomey, Souron Apithy was never enthusiastic over the federation, particularly as Niger and Upper Volta were not members. Dahomey received an important part of its income from the passage of goods from these two countries through its ports. And Apithy, a member of PRA, had strong opposition from the RDA affiliate. The federation issue caused disturbances in Dahomey, leading to new elections. Further disturbances broke out over accusations of interference in the electoral processes, and Houphouet again intervened. Eventually both Apithy and the RDA agreed that Hubert Maga, leader of a third party from the north, should become Prime Minister; and Dahomey remained outside the new federation.

This left only Senegal and Soudan. The fact that the former was ruled by a PRA party and the latter by an RDA affiliate indicated the extent to which the federal issue cut across the two inter-territorial associations. It was now largely bound up with the rivalry of Dakar and Abidjan, Senghor and Houphouet.

So, in April 1959, the Federation of Mali was born, consisting of Senegal and Soudan, with Senghor as President, Keita as Prime Minister, and a common national assembly. Both its leaders were convinced that the first objective must be to gain independence for the new federal state within the Community. De Gaulle, now embroiled in the Algerian question, raised little objection, and, more surprisingly, Houphouet also agreed. The constitution of the Community was amended early in 1960 to allow for membership of sovereign states, and in June of the same year Mali was recognised as independent, though still a member of the Community.

In fact, the Federation only survived for three months after its independence. Senghor's gradualism and love of France were shown in sharp contrast to Keita's radicalism and pan-African outlook. After August 1960 Soudan retained the name 'Mali', Senegal reverted to its separate status and old name, and the federation collapsed with some loss of dignity.

In the meantime Houphouet had discarded his strong objections to the federal conception. Realising that Senghor might come to dominate French West Africa if his federation prospered, whilst the weaker states needed leadership and economic help, he gathered Upper Volta, Niger and Dahomey around his own Ivory Coast in what he named the Sahel-Bénin Union. This proved a much looser form of federation than Mali; it had no federal assembly, but only a council consisting of the four prime ministers and delegates from each of the national assemblies. But it agreed to co-ordinate policies on various public services, established a customs union and also a common fund from which the wealthier Ivory Coast sub-sidised development projects in the other three states.

The remaining territory, Mauritania, led by a chief, Ould Daddah, remained aloof from both associations. Its northern, Moorish nomads had no desire to come under Negro rule. They preferred to rely on the French administration and had to stake a claim to national existence against the ambitions of Morocco.

By now the momentum towards independence was gathering pace. Sylvanus Olympio, after years of frustration, during which the French administration kept him out of office, had become Prime Minister of Togoland. In the Cameroons, after a long struggle against Um Nyobe, Félix Moumié and their Union des Populations Camerounaises, a stable government had been formed under Ahmadou Ahidjo. Nyobe had been an original signatory of the RDA charter, and had refused to follow Houphouet's new moderate line when he broke with the communists. The UPC had tried to organise as a national party, but had been excluded from the 1956 elections and was carrying on a guerrilla war. Nyobe himself was killed by government forces in 1958, to be succeeded as leader by Moumié, then in Cairo. Yet when Ahidjo became Prime Minister he cut much of the ground from under the UPC's feet by demanding national independence from the French. Ahidjo could hardly claim to represent the Cameroons nation, depending on the Moslem north for almost all his personal support. But the other parties were prepared to unite behind him in the drive to independence, leaving the question of his conservatism and traditionalist sympathies to be settled later. His programme of independence and union with the British Cameroons ensured his popularity.

So Olympio and Ahidjo went to Paris to negotiate for independence. Their positions as leaders of Trust Territories gave their demands extra weight. When the United Nations debated the situation the only doubt expressed was whether the Cameroons should have new elections before independence. It decided that Ahidjo could fairly claim to lead a representative government. By 1960 both states were independent.

By now Houphouet was under heavy pressure. It had become clear that independence would not exclude any state either from membership of the Community or from continued French economic aid. The Mali Federation, Togoland and the Cameroons were seen to be gaining their sovereignty and would become members of the United Nations. No amount of argument from Houphouet could any longer persuade his associates that they had anything to gain by continued dependent status. If they were to maintain an equal stature with Mali and the Trust Territories they had to follow their example.

Eventually, with reluctance, Houphouet had to agree that events had overtaken his policy. In June 1960 the *entente* states, Ivory Coast, Niger, Upper Volta and Dahomey, requested France to accord them independence in August. They were not even to remain in the Community. Once the French had sponsored their membership of the United Nations they would be prepared to negotiate agreements on defence, economic aid and cultural matters with the Paris government. Despite the prevarications, doubts and deliberate obstructions, the logic of the *loi cadre* had been completed. The Community virtually collapsed, as its inherent paradoxes had always presaged.

In 1960 eight new French west African states took their seats in the United Nations. (This became nine when Senegal left the Federation of Mali and was recognised as a separate state. The tenth, Mauritania, also requested independence, but was temporarily blocked from membership of the United Nations by the opposition of Morocco, which claimed the territory as its own.) A combination of internal pressures, inevitably resulting from democratic government in an age of nationalism, and the pan-African campaigns of Nkrumah and Sékou Touré, had forced French African leaders to demand a status which most of them had previously rejected. They all remained heavily dependent on French economic help and military defence. These were to be features of their independence which continually invited criticism from the pan-Africanists. Most of their governments depended on traditionalist support, another target for attacks from the younger progressives, found particularly in the expanding trade unions, as well as from new militant African states like Guinea, Ghana and Mali. Yet, whatever the legacy of French civilisation, these French west African states had been brought into the arena of African nationalism despite the reluctance of some of their leading personalities. It would be in that African community that their peoples would henceforth seek their destiny.

9

The Final Laagers

During the nineteen-fifties the tide of black Africanism swept in from the north and west. Although Algeria and Kenya stood out as white islands, washed but not submerged by the tide, elsewhere in the north, west and east it was clear by the end of the fifties that African power had either swept away imperial government or was about to do so. It was at this point that African nationalism encountered the defences of southern Africa. Here it met a different kind of resistance. No longer was it faced with the simple barriers of imperialism. The Rhodesias and Nyasaland were nominally under British imperial rule, but in practice they were governed by their own white oligarchy. And these were but the outer defences. Beyond lay the Portuguese territories, Angola and Mozambique, the British High Commission Territories, South-west Africa, and ultimately South Africa itself. It was here that the last defences against Africanism were raised. Before Africans in the continent could consider themselves fully emancipated these had to be breached. The final chapter in the history of African political revolution would be written on this desperate struggle.

The defences of white southern Africa were stout and high, but never uniform. The areas within the region revealed sharp contrasts. The Portuguese territories were regarded as provinces of Portugal. At times miscegenation was positively encouraged in them, a social philosophy abhorrent to their South African neighbours. South-west Africa was still claimed in the United Nations as an international responsibility inherited from the League of Nations mandate. Despite its virtual incorporation into South Africa, it showed signs of playing the role of a Trojan horse. From a different angle, the High Commission Territories might play the same part, for they were still ruled by the British government, responsible to an electorate now hesitantly turning against the imperialist ethos. This left the Union of South Africa itself as the real heart of white African nationalism.

South Africans were not blind to what was happening in the northern half of the continent. Most of their English-speaking community were neither impressed nor particularly interested. They continued to make their money and live their lives secure in the conviction that such events could never affect their society. By contrast, the Afrikaners were deeply apprehensive. The independence of India in 1947 had shocked them, particularly when Dr Malan had to have his photograph taken beside Pandit Nehru at Commonwealth meetings; but India was an ocean distant. When independence was promised to the Gold Coast, in their own continent, consternation became almost traumatic. Within a few years this was followed by a growing momentum of African independence sweeping ever nearer the Limpopo.

Afrikaners realised that as black men were seen to be ruling their own countries in other parts of the continent, their own African inhabitants would grow increasingly discontented with their exclusion from any form of participation in South African government. At the same time, the National Party recognised that it represented less than half the South African white community. In the early fifties, in particular, it lived under the constant fear of being overthrown, either by the opposition United Party, or through a recurrence of the schisms within its own ranks which were traditional to South African politics. And the fear was heightened by Afrikaner conviction that the English-speaking community would grant concessions to the non-Europeans, thus opening a breach in the white front, inevitably leading to black power. Events in the northern half of the continent served as grim evidence for the reality of this threat.

But the Nationalists knew just what they had to do. This was their great advantage over their opponents, both white and black. Whilst others argued, fumbled and experimented, the Nationalists kept their gaze directly on their objectives, refusing to be diverted by doubts, criticism or opposition.

The Nationalist aim was twofold. They had first to establish themselves in power in such a way that the minimum chances of future defeat remained. This entailed mobilising all the forces of Afrikaner nationalism against the English-speaking community, weighting the constitution as heavily as possible in their own favour, and taking extreme powers to deal with those who might undermine the supremacy of the white race. Secondly, they intended to work out a strategy in racial policy which would enable them to remove the menace of African political pretensions without thereby destroying the African labour force on which the white community was dependent.

By the end of 1950 the foundations had been laid. The Group Areas Act, Population Registration Act, Citizenship Act, Mixed Marriages Act, the amendment to the Immorality Act, and the Suppression of Communism Act provided a firm base from which to advance. They gave the government stronger powers over opposition groups and individual citizens than existed in any other state which claimed to be a democracy. They gave clear warning that South Africa was to be fundamentally an Afrikaner society and that in it the racial groups were to be rigidly separated. Afrikaners alone were to be recognised as genuine South Africans, and only those Afrikaners who accepted the fundamental tenets of Afrikanerdom laid down by the party and its government. The rest, English-speaking, Afrikaner iconoclasts, Africans, Coloureds and Asians, were to be merely residents in the country, their personal and collective lives subject to the will of Afrikanerdom.

Politically, little obstruction stood between the Afrikaner nationalists and their objectives. The official opposition United Party was composed of a variety of conflicting elements never likely to form any unified barrier to the policy of white supremacy which underlay all Nationalist measures. Radical and liberal views appealed to only an infinitesimal proportion of the white electorate, whilst non-European opinions had virtually no constitutional channel of expression.

The main barrier to Nationalist advance was legal rather than political. Afrikaners held a profound respect for their Roman-Dutch legal traditions – but to most of them these applied only within the white community. The concept of the rule of law, brought into South Africa by the British early in the nineteenth century and applicable to all citizens regardless of colour, was alien to Afrikaner traditions. It was maintained by British South Africans, who saw in it the ultimate protection of their economic interests, and by those Afrikaners who recognised western democratic legal principles.

But to the Nationalists, where the rule of law obstructed Afrikaner racial convictions it must be circumvented. Thus their government spent the nineteen-fifties in continuous use of political power to alter any law obstructing their path, and legislating to provide themselves with powers to control the actions of the courts.

The most obvious example of this determination to steamroller Nationalist policy through every obstruction was seen in the prolonged efforts to remove the Cape Coloured voters from the electoral roll. In this instance the Nationalists were strengthened in their determination by the combined attractions of political advantage and racial ideology.

The right of non-Europeans in the Cape Province to vote on the same terms as Europeans had been entrenched in the 1909 Act of the British parliament establishing the Union of South Africa. Each province was to preserve its own franchise laws and in the Cape there was no colour discrimination in voting qualifications. The suffrage was open to all men who could pass certain property and educational tests. When European women were given the vote and all qualification removed from male European voters at the beginning of the thirties, the restrictions on non-Europeans were retained. The franchise was not extended to African or Coloured women, whilst non-European men still had to fulfil the previous qualifications.

Despite the fact that by dropping the qualifications and enfranchising women the European electorate increased enormously in proportion to the non-European, the campaign to remove African voters continued unabated. It is interesting to note that at this stage, Hertzog, as Nationalist leader and Prime Minister, and Malan, later to succeed him, were both adamant in assuring the Coloured community that their voting rights would never be jeopardised. Both men believed that the Coloureds were an inferior part of the European community.

The campaign against the African vote rose to a climax in 1936 when agreement between Hertzog and Smuts enabled the white parliament to remove all Africans from the ordinary voters' roll. As compensation, Cape Africans were allowed to elect three white members on a separate roll. This amendment to the constitution was achieved in the manner laid down in the Act, i.e. by a two-thirds majority of both Houses sitting together at a joint session.

By the nineteen-fifties the assurances previously given to the Coloureds were almost forgotten in the Nationalist camp. The object of the National Party was to extirpate every non-European influence from parliament, whether it came from the presence of non-Europeans intermingled with the white electorate or from direct representation of Africans. It was temporarily restrained after the 1948 election by its dependence on Havenga's Afrikaner Party, but after its victories in the South-west African elections of 1950 and its later absorption of the Afrikaner Party, it was ready to advance towards its objectives. As most Coloured voters supported the opposition United Party, to remove them would simultaneously strengthen the Nationalists electorally and remove an affront to white society.

The difficulty was that no possibility existed of securing the requisite two-thirds majority. The United Party had little moral concern as to whether the Coloureds voted or not, but it knew that it might lose certain Cape seats if Coloured voters were removed. So it could be expected that UP members would prevent the Nationalists from securing the majority constitutionally necessary.

As soon as it was known, early in 1951, that the Nationalists were seeking means to circumvent the entrenched clauses of the constitution, it became apparent that there was much deeper concern amongst the general white public than in the United Party itself. No doubt there was some fear that, if successful, this Nationalist move would lay open to attack the equality of the English language with Afrikaans, for language equality was entrenched in the same way as the franchise. It was also clear to the British community that once the Nationalists took powers to manipulate the constitution no protection would remain for any of their interests.

So a non-party movement designed to protect the constitution quickly sprang up. This became known as the Torch Commando, and was led by a war-time fighter pilot, 'Sailor' Malan, and an old Boer veteran, Commandant A. J. de la Rey. Its methods were to organise large processions and demonstrations in defence of the constitution and it quickly gained such wide support that United Party leaders became fearful of its rivalry to themselves. Yet, despite its public appeal and the financial support of the huge Oppenheimer mining concern, the Torch Commando achieved no

practical results. It was soon enmeshed in the chains of racial compromise which bound almost every opposition movement. Coloured
ex-servicemen expecting to march in its Alamein remembrance
were rejected. The Commando leaders, fearful about the effects of
the prejudiced white community of being seen with non-Europeans,
hedged and manœuvred, steadily losing respect from friend and
foe alike. The Torch Commando revealed the existence of a
widespread concern about the Nationalist attitude to the constitution, as was to be shown in the successor Black Sash women's
movement, but the government was undeterred by such demonstrations. Perhaps its only lasting effect was to add to overseas
awareness of Nationalist unconcern with democratic principles.

The Malan government still had to overcome the legal barriers.
When it introduced the Separate Representation of Voters Bill in
1951 and later passed it through the parliamentary processes by
simple majorities, the Appeal Court found the act to be *ultra vires*.
The government immediately claimed that this verdict had undermined the sovereignty of parliament and resurrected the complaint
that South African authority was being restricted by a British act.
So Dr T. E. Dönges, the Minister of the Interior responsible for
removing Coloured voters, brought in a High Court of Parliament
Bill in 1952, giving parliament powers to overrule the Appeal Court.
Again the court declared the act invalid on the grounds that its
sole object was to circumvent the government's constitutional
responsibilities.

At this point Dr Malan seemed inclined to accept the court's
verdict. He was a Nationalist from the Cape, usually less fanatical
than those from the Transvaal or Orange Free State. Moreover, he
was now an old man, subject to superstitions and more concerned
with foreign opinion than some of his younger colleagues. He
fought the 1953 election and allowed the 'sovereignty of parliament'
issue to assume an important role in it. But the year after his electoral
victory, in which the Nationalists increased both the number of
their seats and their votes, he retired. After a struggle between
northern and southern Nationalists, Johannes Strijdom, from the
Transvaal, defeated T. E. Dönges from the Cape for the succession.
The tight-lipped, sharp-featured 'Lion of Watersberg' (his constituency) was not likely to pay as much regard to the legal niceties
as his more pliant predecessor. He was a determined republican and

his racial outlook was summed up in the brief phrase, 'Either the white man dominates or the black man takes over ...'

Strijdom soon finished off the battle with the courts. He packed the Appeal Court, increasing its members from five to eleven, and then packed the Senate, swelling its membership from forty-eight to eighty-nine. This enabled him to hold a joint sitting of the two Houses, secure his two-thirds majority and obtain the legal sanction of the Appeal Court for his actions. The Coloureds were removed from the ordinary electoral roll, allowed their own roll on which to elect four separate white members to the Assembly and given a Coloured Affairs Council under a Sub-Department of Coloured Affairs in the Department of Native Affairs. The Cape Coloureds had been effectively amputated from the European society which was responsible for their existence. The Senate could now be restored to its previous size, whilst the United Party had to reconcile itself to the prospect of losing a number of Cape seats to the Nationalists at the next election.

This struggle over the constitution is significant because for the first time it fully exposed the ruthless nature of the Nationalists' determination to shape South African society in its own image. The organised opposition failed to meet this challenge and lost its political soul. Because it proved incapable of mounting a militant, principled defence when the constitution, the law and citizen rights were under fire, it emerged from the battle virtually emasculated. It could never again offer any serious opposition to the Nationalist plans. When the time came for further Nationalist advance against the remaining meagre white defences, hardly a whisper of protest was raised. The franchise was extended to eighteen-year-olds in 1958, the members representing Africans were removed in 1960, the Afrikaners gained their republic in 1961 and took their country out of the Commonwealth at the same time. As the Nationalists had consistently built up Afrikaner education, based on what they called the Christian National ideal, even insisting in certain areas on children being sent to Afrikaner-medium schools, whilst the narrow puritan authoritarianism of the Dutch Reformed Church increasingly dominated national social policy, it became increasingly obvious that South Africa was being transformed into a completely Afrikaner society. Behind the scenes the powerful Broederbond, a secret society pledged to enforce the practice of Afrikaner ideals, kept jealous control of public policy through a membership which included most leading figures in positions of influence.

Politically and socially, therefore, the Afrikaners were rapidly reversing the result of the Boer War. Economically, however, the reins were still firmly held in British hands, with a large share of ultimate control in London and New York. Afrikaners recognised this contrast and, although their main interest continued to centre on agriculture, they also made some positive efforts to gain footholds in finance and industry. The Volkskas, an Afrikaner bank, and finance concerns such as Saambou, together with small factories and insurance companies, demonstrated the efforts being made by the Afrikaner community to break British economic domination. But they gained no more than a minor influence, for the typical Afrikaner remained essentially a member of his isolated, remote community, suspicious of contact with people who did not accept his narrow, bigoted view of life.

The official opposition United Party made little effort to hinder the increasing domination of white society by Afrikaner ideals. Those sections of the white community with any kind of liberal outlook were therefore compelled to seek other means of opposition. Once convinced by the results of the 1953 election that there was no chance of returning to the ways of Smuts and Hofmeyr, liberals, who had previously supported the United Party, decided that they must establish a separate Liberal Party. Margaret and William Ballinger, who represented Africans in parliament, and Alan Paton, the writer, took the early initiative. But they found little response from their appeal to non-Europeans. It was too late for liberalism. The new party's proposed qualified franchise for both white and non-white seemed a tepid brew beside the policy of universal suffrage. And some whites, notably the Congress of Democrats, largely composed of ex-members or sympathisers of the Communist Party, were already supporting the claim for adult franchise. Moreover, most members of the Liberal Party came from affluent white families. They could not be expected to sympathise with the semi-socialist ideas now gaining currency amongst non-Europeans. After frequent quarrels, particularly between the Cape and the Rand sections, the Liberal Party advanced by 1959 towards an acceptance of universal franchise. But, although they were one of the agencies exposing the tyranny of apartheid, they never came to terms with the new radicalism which arose amongst non-Europeans as a natural reaction to apartheid.

A new party was also formed in Natal, under the inspiration of the old Senator and diplomat, Heaton Nicholls. But his Union Federal Party, based on the idea of reviving a federal structure for the provinces, never made much impact on South African politics. Meanwhile, the old Labour Party, after turning its back on its racialist past, was rapidly declining. Alex Hepple and Leo Lovell made some of the most effective parliamentary attacks on the government, but this attitude was bound to lose them electoral support. After the 1958 elections there were no Labour members left in parliament.

Yet attempts to combine attacks on the principles of apartheid with electoral support continued. In 1959 a dozen of the more liberal members of the United Party broke away to form a Progressive Party. They stood for much the same ideas as the Liberal Party had done originally, particularly in relation to a qualified franchise. But all except one, Mrs Helen Suzman, lost their seats in the 1961 election.

So, by the end of the nineteen-fifties, the Nationalists had established an iron control over white South Africa. Many of their apartheid laws and security regulations impinged on the personal freedom even of white citizens. But there was no organised, combined force to oppose them, although many courageous individuals, communists, clergymen, liberals, socialists, academics, raised their protests and tried to ameliorate conditions for the non-Europeans. But the Nationalists were shrewd enough never to tamper seriously with the economic life which had made white South Africa into an aristocratic society for labour, professionals and capitalists. Because the economy rested on gold, which could be mined by unskilled masses, an efficient, rational labour force was never as essential as in other industrial countries. For the time being capitalist industry and a feudal social system could co-exist.

Simultaneously with its inexorable advance to hegemony over white society, Afrikaner nationalism was steadily forcing the non-European communities into the subservient position reserved for them in the apartheid pattern. A number of Bantu Authorities Acts passed from 1951 onwards revealed the Nationalists' basic thinking on the correct place for Africans in South Africa. Tribal authorities were deliberately created in an effort to restore separate tribal communities and traditional discipline. Their authority was to extend to those Africans living and working in towns, who were to be grouped as far as possible in tribal divisions. The 1954 Bantu Education Act under-pinned this thrust back to tribalism. It destroyed the private mission schools which taught Africans dangerous notions, like human equality, and, through state direction, imposed an indoctrination of African children into their place in apartheid society. The Minister of Native Affairs, Dr Hendrik Verwoerd, put it quite bluntly in debating his bill in 1954, when he said, '. . . we want to indoctrinate the teachers (and children) – if we must use that term – with our spirit . . . they must not think that once they are educated they can leave their own people and seek equality with the European . . .' The curriculum was therefore centred on technical subjects, religious instruction, tribal and the two national languages, together with 'the Bantu's place in South African society'. As a logical corollary, the 1959 Extension of University Education Act prohibited the admission of any further non-Europeans to Cape Town or Witwatersrand Universities, which had practised a colour-blind policy of admission, and set up new universities, not only for each non-European group, but for separate tribes. Tribal history, languages, culture were to be the basis of teaching in each institution, which would be entirely under the Minister's control.

Despite this 'back to the kraal' policy, together with the attempt to control the minds of the next generation, the Nationalists were fully aware that a large number of Africans would still remain in personal contact with white society. Whatever laws were passed, the massive African labour force in the towns could not be dispensed with if the economic viability of white society was to be preserved. But contact with white society brought discontent and inspired dangerous ideas. So separation had to be enforced, at least outside working hours.

First, it was necessary to destroy another relic of British law. It had been legally established that a separation of amenities was permissible provided that equal facilities were provided for the different races. But the Nationalists had no intention of providing equal facilities when their apartheid practices enforced separation. So they overcame the legal obstruction by passing a new act in 1953, the Separate Amenities Act, allowing them to provide separate facilities for the races without the necessity of making them equal.

Having created this new legal protection, the Nationalists could make an assault on the habit of social contact between African and European in the towns. The most spectacular effort was made in Johannesburg, where a whole African community, which had lived for many years in the township known as Sophiatown, was forcibly removed to a new area called Meadowlands. It is true that the amenities in the latter district were generally cleaner, newer and more extensive than those in Sophiatown. But, whereas freehold was allowed in the old township, it was forbidden in the new, Meadowlands was much further from work places, and the removal was compulsory. Perhaps above all, Sophiatown had developed its own character, with Indians and Coloureds mixed with Africans, living proof that a detribalised, non-European urban community could exist. To the Nationalist this undermined the whole theory of apartheid and encouraged dangerous agitation. He substituted rows of clean, but identical, box houses, easily controlled and regimented, his conception of where urban Africans should be allowed to live.

Yet, so long as Africans remained in towns, there was a continuing danger of social contact between black and white. One of the reasons for the evictions from Sophiatown was that the township was only divided by a road from a white area, mainly inhabited by the poorer type of Afrikaner trying to change from country to town life. Not only did some of the whites covet the few better class houses in Sophiatown, but they often found it economical to cross the road to shop. This behaviour seemed to the Nationalists to be placing their own people in a position of no more than equality with non-Europeans. But they were even more concerned with the social mixing which took place in the houses of a few wealthier whites holding various liberal views. Here a deliberate attempt was being made to practise social equality, which was not only abhorrent to believers in apartheid, but could lead to the organisation of political subversion.

Only just below the surface of this hostility towards social mixing of the races lay the deeply-rooted sexual fear of the Afrikaners. The Afrikaner community was embarrassed after the passing of the 1950 Immorality Act amendment forbidding sexual intercourse between white and non-white by the exposure that more Afrikaners than British broke this law. The number of prosecutions steadily increased, reaching a yearly average of over 300. Here was overt proof of what had long been common knowledge in South Africa, that many white men, far from practising apartheid in their private life, enjoyed sexual relations with non-white women – and that most of these men were Afrikaners, some even Nationalists. Indeed, it seemed as though there were some connection between a vociferous contempt for non-whites, and an attraction to their women for casual sexual convenience.

The government tried to cover up this glimpse into the real nature of their society by blaming the liberal practice of mixed social relations for miscegenation. They took powers to prohibit social contact between white and black in a 1957 amendment to the Native Laws Act, and, at the same time, widened the criminal offence from actual sexual intercourse to 'any immoral or indecent act'.

It was also mainly concern for the position of the poorer section of Afrikaners which prompted the Nationalist government to deepen the division in employment between European and African workers. Ever since the nineteen-twenties, governments had used their powers in the public services and their persuasion amongst private employers to cure the 'poor white' problem and fix an unbridgeable gap between the jobs available to white and black workers. As industrialisation progressed, however, there arose the danger that some black workers would prove more intelligent and skilful than some of the white men and therefore be preferred in better jobs by employers. The Industrial Conciliation Act of 1956 removed this danger by giving the Minister of Labour power to reserve categories of employment exclusively for one racial group. The same act compulsorily segregated white and Coloured workers in separate trade unions. As African trade unions were not recognised, whilst the 1953 Native Labour Act made it a criminal offence for Africans to strike, the dignity of white labour was effectively safeguarded. African, Coloured and Asian labour was essential to white society; but it must never be given the dangerous opportunity to organise as a modern labour force.

The story of non-European attempts to stem this Nationalist advance to absolute power is mainly concerned with a search for the means of political action. White South Africa was a very heavily armed state, with its defences organised in terms of internal security. The powers taken by the government to punish those who opposed it were extremely strong, and whenever they were found inadequate, the government simply legislated itself greater power. Open defiance necessitated a spirit of martyrdom, which was apparent amongst few non-European leaders. Moreover, the urban African population, the usual source of revolt, was composed of many different groups, including men from the High Commission Territories, the Rhodesias and Nyasaland, and the Portuguese territories. The higher wages paid in a developed industrial society attracted them away from the mainly subsistence life in their own countries. These same comparatively high wages also induced a greater state of political apathy than was generally admitted. For when the Africans learnt of living conditions in most other parts of Africa, they realised that they had something to lose in South Africa.

Resentment strong enough to lead to revolt arose mainly from the middle class. The Asians and the Coloureds each produced a conventional bourgeoisie, with some property and professional qualifications. But the African middle class was almost entirely professional, teachers, lawyers, doctors and journalists, but with very few businessmen to provide economic strength. Social confusion generally kept the Coloureds apart, usually fighting internecine battles amongst themselves, but the Asians gave both economic and intellectual support to African movements.

Until the end of the nineteen-fifties, the African National Congress had the field virtually to itself. It was supported by the white Congress of Democrats and the Indian Congresses in the Transvaal and Natal. It had intermittent communications with the Liberal and Labour parties, although never with complete confidence.

Theoretically the ANC had a mass following, for it represented African hopes in both towns and reserves. Yet it was never able to find a method of mobilising its supporters. Partly, no doubt, economic conditions slightly better than utter desperation proved a handicap, although every survey conducted in urban areas or reserves showed that the mass of Africans were living below the poverty line. Partly the failure was due to the government's constant harassing, with every prominent leader frequently removed from public life. But these reasons only form part of the full explanation, for in similar circumstances elsewhere conspiracy and revolt have been organised against even more ruthless authority.

The idea of a 'day of protest', on which everyone was asked to stay away from work and remain indoors, was tried from 1950 onwards. It had a limited success in certain areas, but never gained genuine national acceptance. In 1952 it was widened into a deliberate passive resistance campaign in which volunteers were urged to break apartheid laws and court arrest and imprisonment. This was perhaps the high-water mark of organised resistance. During the second half of 1952 over 8,000 non-Europeans voluntarily went to gaol. Yet there was never any danger of the administration breaking down. The demonstration was effective as a cry of protest; it could never have become a serious revolutionary movement for it had no clear objectives, strategy or tactics.

The campaign was brought to an end by the enactment of two vicious laws, the Public Safety Act, giving the government emergency powers, and the Criminal Laws Amendment Act, imposing heavy sentences of imprisonment, fines and flogging for defying authority. The severity of these penal laws deterred further attempts to use this method of resistance – yet, in fact, the laws were certainly not as severe as those of Southern Rhodesia after 1960.

It was in 1955 that the ANC for the first time adopted a radical programme. Until this moment its aims had been the conventional liberal, bourgeois objectives of freedom of movement, the right to own property and to trade, political equality. It was in the Freedom Charter adopted by the joint Congress movement in 1955 that universal suffrage first became a stated objective. Economic aims were transformed from private ownership to 'ownership by the people as a whole' of minerals, banking, industry, land sharing amongst agricultural workers, and a national minimum wage. The government revealed how seriously it took this development in Congress by arresting 156 leaders at the end of 1956. They were charged with treason and their trial continued intermittently for four years. All were acquitted, but had been effectively prevented from engaging in political organisation during this period.

By this time the leadership of Congress had passed from the middle-class hands of men like Dr Xuma and Dr Moroka into those of Albert Luthuli. Luthuli was no revolutionary, but the example he set by defying the government and consequently being deposed

from his chieftaincy in Natal, his simple Christian belief in the need
to oppose apartheid, and his non-violent convictions, infused
Congress with a new sense of mission. With Walter Sisulu, from
Johannesburg, as the chief organising brains, Congress for a time
gained a cohesion never previously achieved.

Despite greater internal cohesion, the resistance movement remained on the defensive. Frequent banning of its leaders, including
Luthuli and Sisulu, disrupted its organisation, whilst ever-tightening
legislation constantly narrowed its field of action. In 1957 a bus
boycott against a penny rise in fares again revealed a collective will
power when Africans in their hundred thousands walked to and
from work in Johannesburg rather than pay increased fares. Single
day general strikes were tried again but failed to shake government
or industry. It was becoming increasingly clear that nothing short
of revolutionary conspiracy would undermine the government's
stronghold; yet revolution itself had scant chance of success against
the security forces unless external help could be secured.

It was the Sharpeville massacre which accelerated both the movement towards revolution and the chances of outside assistance. In
March 1960 at Sharpeville in the Transvaal police shot sixty-nine
Africans in a crowd peacefully demonstrating against the pass laws.
Horror at this act echoed round the world. In South Africa itself a
general strike of protest was largely successful in the main towns.
Outside, public opinion in the western world at last recognised that
persuasive words would not suffice to turn the Nationalists from
their authoritarian path. It certainly stiffened the resolution of
Commonwealth countries to face the issue of continued South
African membership. The following year, the new African member
states and Tanganyika, approaching the threshold of membership,
made it plain that they would leave the association if a South
African apartheid government were allowed to continue in membership. The technicality of the South African change to republi-
canism was used as the occasion to debate the issue, for it entailed
a South African application for renewed membership in her new
constitutional status. After the rough treatment meted out at the
Prime Ministers' Conference and realising that she would not be
accepted, South Africa left the Commonwealth on becoming a
republic in May 1961.

Yet increased Commonwealth and international sympathy for

the non-Europeans did not deter the Nationalist government from renewing assaults on those participating in resistance. After a short relaxation of the pass laws when the government seemed to fear that Sharpeville had broken African patience, more ferocious measures were taken to destroy non-European organisation. A state of emergency was declared, thousands of non-Europeans and their few white supporters were arrested and imprisoned without trial, even their names being withheld, and the two main African political parties were banned.

This ruthless policy had its effect on the African temper. Already, in 1959, a group had broken away from the ANC because they considered its policy both too moderate and too dependent on Europeans and Asians. Under the leadership of the Transvaal teacher, Robert Sobukwe, they formed a rival organisation, the Pan-Africanist Congress. It was this party which had organised the anti-pass campaign which led to Sharpeville. Sobukwe was arrested and sentenced to three years' imprisonment whilst the PAC was banned along with the ANC. (When Sobukwe was due for release he was detained indefinitely by the government on an island off Cape Town. If the Nationalists remain in power he is likely to spend the rest of his life there.)

The PAC was widely accused of being a racialist organisation because it criticised the association of the ANC with the European Congress of Democrats and the Indian Congresses. There was undoubtedly a certain attraction to black racialists in the movement, but this did not fully explain the motives behind the party. Its first objective was to create African self-reliance rather than racial exclusiveness. Its leaders believed that until Africans found the means to overthrow their white masters without help from other races, they would not be able to re-assert the dignity of the African peoples. Secondly, they considered that the non-violent, Christian policy of Luthuli was leading to appeasement in the face of white violence.

So, by the time of Sharpeville, African patience was wearing thin and more violent terms were being heard. This atmosphere was intensified by the series of events which immediately followed Sharpeville. An attempt was made by a white man to assassinate the Prime Minister, a revolt broke out in Langa, an African township near Cape Town, accompanied by considerable violence, and civil war erupted in the reserves, met by the declaration of a state of emergency in Pondoland, in the Transkei. Even some of the ANC began to despair of their non-violent policy ever prevailing over the draconian laws, police brutality and powerful security forces of the Nationalist government. Sabotage began to occur, with increased arrests, bannings, powers of imprisonment without trial and allegations of prisoners being tortured. Yet with security forces stronger than ever and the economy flourishing, white society felt that it could afford to scorn the criticisms mounting at the United Nations and the increasing threats of African states.

The Nationalists, however, made one concession to overseas criticism. They began to counter the almost universal condemnation of apartheid by describing their policy as an attempt to give Africans justice and self-government. To do so they revived the idealistic conception of apartheid produced in Stellenbosch in the nineteen-forties, claiming that the policy envisaged no more than separate self-government for the different races.

This new government attitude had been made possible by the increasing security now felt by Nationalist Afrikaners. The main objectives of the first two post-war Nationalist Prime Ministers, Nathaniel Malan and Johannes Strijdom, had been to secure permanent Nationalist power and to entrench the dominant position of the white race. These objectives had been largely achieved by 1958, when Mr Strijdom died. So his successor, Dr Hendrik Verwoerd, an ex-newspaper editor, a former anti-semite and Nazi sympathiser, who, as a northerner, again defeated Dönges for the premiership, was able to think more of the constructive side of Nationalist policy. He could take the country forward to the Afrikaner ideal of a republic, securing majority approval in a referendum. And he was able to consider how to create some kind of separate society for non-Europeans as an alternative to the traditionally negative policy of simply trying to expel them from the towns.

In 1959 the Promotion of Bantu Self-Government Act charted the way for this policy. It abolished the three seats for white African representatives in the Assembly and proposed to set up self-governing Bantu states based on the existing reserves. Whether these would ever become sovereign states was a matter of argument, though the question appeared hypothetical as their development was to be kept strictly in government hands.

In 1955 the Tomlinson Commission, appointed by the government to inquire into the feasibility of 'positive apartheid', had published its report. It had estimated that £104 million would have to be spent in the reserves over ten years, in addition to private investment, if they were to have any chance of becoming viable economic units. The Verwoerd government soon made it plain that its conception of apartheid did not envisage this kind of expenditure. White capital was not to be invested inside such Bantustans, industrial development being confined to the borders, where labour could be attracted. Public expenditure was to be only a fraction of the need revealed by Tomlinson.

It was not until 1962, when Dr Verwoerd announced his plans for the first Bantustan in the Transkei, that the pattern could be seriously examined. It was planned to establish a Legislative Assembly of 109 members (the first elections were held in November 1963), 64 of them ex-officio as chiefs, and the remaining 45 elected. Members of the Transkei tribes, whether resident in the reserve, in towns or on white farms, were entitled to vote. Its powers of legislation were limited by the exclusion of important subjects like defence, arms, international affairs, communications, banking and the higher aspects of justice. In its circumscribed field, the laws it passed would have to be submitted to the South African President, a Nationalist former minister, who could be relied on never to act contrary to the white government's wishes. Moreover, all existing South African laws applied to the Transkei. Thus white control was effectively maintained, whilst propaganda for overseas use could appear in a new specious guise.

Yet the appearance of this first Bantustan had some impact on the political scene. The Verwoerd government expected to be able to control all the chiefs because it paid their salaries. It did secure the collaboration of Chief Kaizer Matanzima, because he genuinely believed in apartheid – including the expulsion of all Europeans from the Transkei, which would certainly have shocked white South Africa. But Chief Sabata Dalindyebo of the Tembu tribe and Chief Victor Poto of the Pondos formed an alliance to use the new assembly with the objective of promoting a multi-racial form of government. Even though Matanzima, with the help of a majority of the chiefs, became the first Prime Minister, it seemed as though Verwoerd's Bantustan might become a Trojan horse, with increasing conflict between the new assembly and the white government.

The Bantustan policy, of course, ran directly counter to the economic realities of South Africa. Economic forces were unaffected by the words or feelings of the Afrikaner community. Industrialisation proceeded apace in the towns, demanding labour in such numbers as only the African community could supply. Simultaneously the eroded lands of the reserves proved increasingly incapable of feeding the growing rural population. No matter what political, social or mystical theories were voiced by white leaders, these two elemental forces both inexorably pulled the same way. Paths were worn hard from reserves to towns, and more feet trod them every year.

From the days of Smuts to those of Verwoerd white rulers refused to recognise that they could no more turn back the tide of economic forces than Canute could repel the waves. Yet this dichotomy between political and economic development did not necessarily nullify Nationalist attempts to produce an apartheid society. Under Verwoerd, government policy became more ruthlessly sophisticated. The need for African labour was accepted, but the racial separation of the population was vigorously pursued, whilst every attempt to oppose white domination was ferociously suppressed. Nor were the habitual predictions of economic collapse fulfilled. So long as gold remained to underpin the economy, it seemed probable that white prosperity and black subjection could continue to exist alongside each other.

Thus, so far as the domestic situation was concerned, it seemed that the Verwoerd government had accumulated sufficient powers to translate the Nationalist philosophy of life into practical form. Africans would be indoctrinated or coerced into the concept that their restricted rights stemmed only from their 'homeland' reserves. In the towns and cities or on the white farms they were to be treated as foreigners. They were entitled to vote for their Bantustan governments, but could claim no civic rights or protection where they actually lived and worked. The regions where almost all South African wealth was produced, mining and industrial areas and most farmland, belonged to the white community. To ensure the continued existence of this regimented, caste society, Afrikaner Nationalist governments would keep all the sources of power under their control, adding to them wherever a new threat appeared. White and non-white workers had been effectively separated, with the white workers' affluence apparently dependent on maintaining the industrial colour bar. The professional classes were equally separated by racial barriers erected by law. Tribal division within African society was actively encouraged and legalised, traditional authorities given disciplinary powers and created where they did not exist. Conventional sources of reform or rebellion seemed to have been efficiently blocked, whilst over the whole structure hung the enormous military power of a modern state, apparently capable of ruthlessly suppressing any revolt against this dictated pattern of society. It seemed that only external intervention held out any early possibility of severing the chains with which Afrikaner Nationalism had bound all other South African communities.

The area in which South Africa was most vulnerable to international intervention remained South-west Africa. Here, following the Nationalist assumption of power in 1948, the policy of apartheid was extended into government and social policy. Elections to the territorial assembly, which consisted of eighteen members, were confined to a white electorate. In the same way, when in 1950 South-west Africa was given representation in the South African parliament, the electorate for the six members of the House of Assembly and the two indirectly elected and two nominated members of the Senate, were likewise confined to the white community. The laws of South Africa extended to the ex-mandated territory whilst social segregation was enforced in a like manner. Throughout the nineteen-fifties the South African government consistently refused to heed orders constantly being given by the United Nations to abandon apartheid and place South-west Africa under a Trust agreement.

The main opponent of South African policy in this country was Hosea Kutako, Paramount Chief of the Hereros. Kutako had been asked to consider the resettlement of his tribe as long ago as 1946, as the South Africans wished to allocate his tribal area to white settlers. He refused to move his people and similarly resisted attempts by the South Africans to persuade him to accept the incorporation of his country into the Union. Instead, he petitioned the United Nations to bring South African administration to an end and take his territory under its own authority as a Trust Territory. He was to repeat this request at various intervals for the next fifteen years. In these petitions to the United Nations, Kutako was constantly assisted by the Reverend Michael Scott, an Anglican clergyman, who made the South-west Africa issue his own personal responsibility at the United Nations.

Despite the continual representations of the South-west African case at Lake Success and several references of it to the International Court, the South African government remained unmoved. Nevertheless, it gradually became evident that this issue might well prove the Achilles' heel of South Africa in international relations. Because the territory had been originally mandated by the League of Nations, international responsibility for it remained. This enabled the United Nations, without any question of interfering in the domestic matters of a member state, to investigate the racial policy conducted there by the South African administration. It also brought the South African Government to the bar of international opinion and forced it to defend its apartheid policy. As many African states became independent, so their membership of the United Nations was used increasingly to find the means of mounting attacks on South African policy. South-west Africa provided the best channel for this purpose.

After many debates, inquiries, and investigations, in October 1961 the special South-west Africa Committee of the United Nations resolved that South Africa was unfit to administer the territory, demanded that the South African government withdraw all troops from it and proposed that the General Assembly of the UN assume supervision of the mandate. Still the Verwoerd Government, like its predecessors, ignored the challenge, although flirting with ideas of inviting in the Western powers to save it from direct confrontation with the UN. The issue, however, remained one of potential international conflict, with the African states deliberately considering how it could best be used to embarrass the South African government and undermine its apartheid policy.

The second international issue which brought the Nationalists, however unwillingly, up against external opinion was that of the High Commission Territories. During the nineteen-fifties the Nationalists continued to hope that eventually the British Government would be either persuaded or coerced into handing over these three territories to the Union. They were not dissuaded from this ambition by forthright statements made in the British House of Commons, including one by Winston Churchill, declaring firmly that British responsibility for the three countries would not be handed over to the South Africans without consultation with their inhabitants. British spokesmen avoided the word 'consent', because this would have implied a power of veto in all circumstances. Nevertheless, it became quite clear that in practice no British Government could transfer authority for the three territories to a South African government pursuing a policy of apartheid unless there were a clear demand for such action from the people themselves. It was equally clear that the Africans in these countries had no desire whatever to join their brothers over the frontiers as further victims of the apartheid policy. Nevertheless, South African governments from Malan onwards argued that the British could consult the inhabitants of the territories without necessarily following their wishes. They, indeed, pointed out maliciously that this is precisely what had happened in the formation of the Central African Federation.

However thoroughly the British political parties might desire to preserve the High Commission Territories from apartheid, they could not escape the fact that each of them remained heavily dependent on South Africa. Basutoland was completely surrounded by South African territory and sent nearly half its able-bodied men to work on the farms and in the mines of the Union. The contribution sent back home from the wages of these men was a vital factor in the Basutoland national economy. Many workers came also from Bechuanaland and Swaziland. Each of the territories depended very heavily for its revenues on goods passing through Union territory. South African foodstuffs and manufactured goods, on the one hand, and South African markets, on the other, were vital to the economy of each country.

It was partly for this reason and partly because of the historical assumption that the three territories would eventually become a part of South Africa, that British policy towards them was quite different from that employed in her colonies. Instead of actively promoting evolution to self-government, the British, keeping the territories under the jurisdiction of the Commonwealth Relations

Office and of the High Commissioner for South Africa, left each of
them to slumber politically for as long as possible. Nor was there
any serious effort made to develop the individual economies of the
territories or to promote education and social welfare. In all things
the British government remained highly conscious of South African
objections to anything which seemed to be assisting their neighbouring Africans into the modern world.

Yet, eventually, it became impossible to insulate the High Commission Territories from developments in the colonial empire and
particularly in the rest of Africa. As early as 1952, Ntsu Mokhehle
founded the Basutoland African Congress. Basutoland tended,
indeed, to set the pace in political development, partly because so
many of its male inhabitants lived a large part of their life in South
Africa and associated there with African nationalists. So it was in
Basutoland that the first comprehensive constitutional inquiry was
made when the Moore Commission reported on constitutional
development in 1954. Immediately the Congress made its presence
felt. It had been widely expected and greatly hoped that the Moore
Commission would recommend the formation of a Legislative
Council to replace the advisory Basutoland National Council. The
hope was not fulfilled, the commission only recommending the
development of a form of local government. Under pressure from
the Congress, the National Council, consisting partly of nominated
and partly of elected members, rejected the Moore proposals, and
decided to appoint its own constitutional commission with Professor D. V. Cowen of Cape Town University as its adviser.

By 1958 Professor Cowen was ready to present his recommendations, which included a Legislative Council of eighty members and
an Executive Council of four British officials, four Africans, the
Paramount Chief and the Resident Commissioner. In fact, the new
constitution accepted the following year included a similar type of
legislature, dividing its members between chiefs, nominees of the
Paramount Chief and members elected from the district councils
sitting as electoral colleges. The Executive included three members
of the Legislative Council, four officials and one nominee of the
Paramount Chief. The influence which had been accumulated by
the Congress, now called the Basutoland Congress Party, was
shown when, in the first elections early in 1960, it won seventy-
three out of a hundred and sixty-two district council seats. When,

two months later, elections to the National Council were held, it gained twenty-nine of the forty elected seats. Despite this electoral success, divisions appeared within the party and its two main leaders, Mokhehle and Makola Khakela, parted company, the latter forming a Basutoland Freedom Party. Politics tended to fragment after the electoral system had been initiated. Nevertheless, most political leaders were agreed that Basutoland should march forward towards the independence being achieved in the rest of the continent. At an independence conference held in London in 1964 it was agreed that if the next elected Legislative Council should ask for independence within a year of its election, the British government would negotiate for this objective. The question as to how she could live and defend herself as an independent state within the frontiers of South Africa was given little serious consideration. But the Basuto delegates showed a realistic appreciation of the problems they would face after independence and revealed confidence in their capacity to negotiate with Dr Verwoerd.

Swaziland was a much wealthier country than the other two High Commission Territories. Its coal and iron provided it with a potential in mineral development which could bring considerable revenue. Its forests, particularly those initiated by the Colonial Development Corporation, added timber and wood pulping, whilst agriculture secured for it considerable capital investment from South Africa, accompanied by South African settlers amongst the white community.

Swaziland was more strongly traditionalist in its administration than even the other two territories. Its Paramount Chief, Sobhuza II, dominated political and constitutional life, including the two traditionalist councils, the Liqoqo and the Libandhla. The European community of something under 10,000 had its own Advisory Council with access to the Resident Commissioner.

Constitutional progress started on a local government level, with the establishment of rural district councils in 1956. It was not, however, until four years later that the first genuine political party, the Swaziland Progressive Party, was founded by John Nquku. Nquku had travelled widely over the previous few years and had talked with many politicians in Europe and America. He was a member of the Swaziland Progressive Association, which was mainly a cultural body for the educated élite, vaguely supported by both the British administration and the Paramount Chief. When the Progressive Party was founded, however, it initiated a political programme with the object of self-government and eventually independence. The development of modern political ideas was not to the liking of Chief Sobhuza. Although he nominated two of the members to participate in discussions on constitutional reform in 1960, it was quickly obvious that modern politics and traditional ideas of authority had nothing in common. The constitutional discussions continued between the Government, the Europeans and the Paramount Chief, together with his supporters. The politicians were frozen out.

It was at this point that the Progressive Party secured the advice of the same Professor Cowen who had played such a vital role in Basutoland's constitutional development. Nevertheless, early in 1962, Sobhuza's committee recommended that a Legislative Council should be established, divided between British officials, European representatives and members responsible to the traditionalist Swaziland National Council. This immediately precipitated a crisis between the politicians and those supporting traditional authority. The politicians demanded that they be given the right to participate in discussions and to make their own proposals.

In the meantime, the Progressive Party had begun to develop conflicts within itself. Its Secretary General, Ambrose Zwane, quarrelled with Nquku and fragmentation began. But there was sufficient in common between the rival political leaders for them to make a joint claim that some form of democratic representative elections should be included within the new constitution. Eventually it was left to the British Government to make its own proposals. It recommended a threefold division between traditionalist representatives, members elected on a qualified common roll, including European representatives, and directly elected members. The conflict continued, with traditionalists and conservative Europeans in alliance against the modern politicians, who were anxious to develop a Swaziland state with a progressive economic and political policy. After the 1964 elections had provided Chief Sobhuza with apparent wide national support, the political parties appeared to have lost the first battle. With support from organised European settlers favourable to South Africa it even seemed that Sobhuza's policy would be used by Dr Verwoerd as useful propaganda for his Bantustan ideas.

Nevertheless it seemed unlikely that this conservative traditionalism would survive against the forces of African nationalism as they developed within South Africa and in neighbouring Portuguese Mozambique. The election showed, however, that Swaziland had a long way to go before entering the modern African political world.

In many ways the third High Commission Territory, Bechuanaland, was the most interesting of the three. Not only was it spotlighted throughout the world over the Seretse Khama affair, but its size, strategic position and social structure gave it a special importance. It was a vast sprawling territory, much of which consisted of desert and swamp; it lay athwart the route from South Africa to the north, through the Rhodesias and on to black-ruled Africa; and its almost entirely tribal societies were engaged in finding a peaceful path to modern government.

The Seretse affair was not solved until the third quarter of 1956. Seretse and his white wife, Ruth, were compelled to live abroad after their banishment. They took up residence in London, hoping that one of the many attempts to secure their right to return home would succeed. When the Conservative government succeeded the Labour administration in 1951, however, it appeared to close the door on this hope. It announced that Seretse would never be allowed to return to Bechuanaland until his Bamangwato tribe had elected a new chief. The tribe had no intention of replacing Seretse and even when the British government appointed Seretse's cousin, Rasebolai, to a new post as Native Authority, the tribe never accepted the new ruler as a substitute chief.

It was when the Labour Party, now in opposition, took up the Seretse case officially, that the situation began to change. After holding an inquiry into the facts, the Labour Party began to press the government to accept a compromise solution which would allow Seretse to return home and participate in the life of the tribe. Eventually, in the course of a debate in the House of Commons in August 1956, Labour spokesmen announced officially that when they returned to office they would permit Seretse to return to his people. This declaration cut the ground from under the government's feet. The Bamangwato tribe now knew that, once the Labour Party had won an election in Britain, Seretse would be able to return. They therefore had no inducement to change their minds over their refusal to elect another chief. Less than three months later the government gave up its attempt to coerce the tribe, reversed its policy and Seretse flew back to Bechuanaland. His wife and children followed him a few weeks later. He was not allowed to assume the title of chief, but, because of his standing in the tribe, soon became its accepted leader, working with other prominent members to destroy the divisions which had followed his exile.

In Bechuanaland, as in the other territories, it was not until the end of the nineteen-fifties that any serious attempt was made to consider constitutional development. The Resident Commissioner had been advised by three councils, an African, a European and a joint body, which had worked harmoniously together. In 1958 both Africans and Europeans demanded that progress be made towards more responsible and democratic government. A year later a committee was set up to consider the problems of constitutional reform. Towards the end of 1959 the committee reported and a new constitution was announced in July 1960. This provided for a Legislative Council consisting of officials, equal numbers of elected Europeans and Africans, two unofficial Europeans, two Africans appointed by the Resident Commissioner and one elected Asian member. The Executive Council was to include six officials, two unofficial Europeans and two unofficial Africans. It was clearly a constitution designed to lead gradually to eventual democratic representation.

No sooner had the constitution been announced than a political party, the Bechuanaland Peoples Party, was formed to organise the political consciousness of the inhabitants. Its founder was Kgaleman Motsete, a teacher who, on being rejected as a candidate for the Legislative Council, quickly turned his party against the constitution. As in the other territories, however, it was not long before the party developed conflicts between different factions, partly caused by a reflection of the rivalry between the African National Congress and the Pan-Africanist Congress of South Africa. Most of the people in Bechuanaland, however, still looked to their traditional rulers for leadership, and Seretse Khama remained the dominant figure both in guidance and in consideration of future constitutional development.

From 1960 onwards, the British Government changed its attitude to the three High Commission Territories. In 1961 responsibility for them was transferred from the Commonwealth Relations Office to the Colonial Office. Once South Africa had left the Commonwealth, greater efforts were made to promote representative governments and to bring the three territories at least to the fringes of British colonial policy. The Morse Economic Commission recommended considerable economic aid to develop the life of the territories so as to lighten their dependence on South Africa. At the same time, however, each of the territories was involved in the flow of political refugees leaving South Africa, which both affected their internal political situation and brought them closer to the front of the international stage. Bechuanaland, in particular, became the main escape route for political refugees from apartheid, finding their way northwards to Tanganyika, Ghana and Europe. Meanwhile, the Verwoerd government was restricting the two-way passage across the frontiers, building a fence and control posts and threatening to limit the number of workers from the High Commission Territories allowed to enter South Africa. A war of nerves developed, with the High Commission Territories made more aware than ever of their vulnerable position vis-à-vis South Africa, aggravated by the lack of serious economic development which had characterised earlier British administration. Indeed, it became increasingly obvious in the early nineteen-sixties, that these three territories had been thrust into the front line of international conflict over South African apartheid, a position inevitably affecting their own internal development.

The final pieces of the southern jigsaw consisted of the Portuguese territories, Angola and Mozambique. They had an interest of their own, for their administration was unique; but their deeper significance lay in the part they were destined to play beside South Africa in the final defence of white men's power in Africa.

In June 1951, the Portuguese territories officially ceased to be colonies and became 'Overseas Provinces'. This decision from Lisbon reflected the Portuguese ambition to regain something of their long-lost national strength. Portugal had been so long neglected and ignored in Europe that Dr Salazar, her dictatorial leader, and his advisers saw their only chance of again becoming important in establishing what might be called a 'Greater Portugal'. Henceforth the Portuguese state was to include the African territories as provinces equally with the regions of the metropolitan country. This conception, of course, was something similar to that of the French after the second world war.

There were other similarities between Portugal in Africa and both French and Belgian colonial policies. The Portuguese theory of colonialism was based on the idea of racial equality with cultural inequality. This, of course, was observed more in theory than in practice. The Portuguese allowed the educated African to qualify for citizenship as an assimilado; but in 1950 only 30,000 out of a population of 4 million had qualified in Angola and 4,353 out of over 5,700,000 in Mozambique. Many literate Africans had no desire to become assimilados, either because of the extra tax burdens involved or because of the danger of separation from their own society. But, in any case, Portuguese policy avoided too much education for Africans, particularly higher education, and even if they had not adopted such a policy deliberately, with forty per cent illiteracy in metropolitan Portugal it would have been difficult to conduct any serious education programme in the colonies.

What differentiated Portuguese policy from French and Belgian was a belief in its permanency. There was always some vague idea in Paris and Brussels that ultimately the Africans would become responsible for their own future. This view was never shared in Lisbon. To the Portuguese the Africans were a part of Portugal and they could see no reason why their colonial peoples should ever desire to relinquish this honour.

The change to provincial status had some good effects. It enabled the African territories to participate in the national development plan, which during the nineteen-fifties considerably increased road building, bridges, dams, improved ports and produced some forms of co-operative production. Despite this improvement, however, both Angola and Mozambique continued to rely very largely on the income gained from increasing traffic through their ports and by the export of labour to South Africa. From Mozambique 300,000 workers and from Angola 100,000 were sent to the South African mines every year. Both territories secured a considerable revenue from this recruiting and made sure that if there were not sufficient volunteers African workers were 'persuaded' to join the recruiting drives. Indeed, despite a few modifications in labour laws, forced labour continued to provide the basis of active economic life in both territories.

The nineteen-fifties were also a period in which the Portuguese government succeeded in persuading its own swollen population to emigrate to Africa in considerable numbers, thus relieving the Portuguese unemployment problem. Between 1950 and 1959 the white population in Angola rose from 79,000 to something above 170,000. During the same period European inhabitants in Mozambique increased from 48,000 to about 85,000.

The movement of African labour through compulsory work legislation, recruiting for South Africa and for work in the expanded ports, together with the influx of white Portuguese, produced some of the major problems found elsewhere in southern and central Africa after the war. Urbanisation steadily increased, tribal disciplines began to break down, new ideas of society appeared, unemployment increased and competition between white and black workers led to a growth of colour prejudice and discrimination – a new factor in Portuguese Africa. Because most of the white immigrants were poor and illiterate, the tensions inevitably became heightened and the competition for employment served to aggravate them.

It is some indication of the nature of Portuguese dictatorship that when one of the Government's own colonial inspectors, Henrique Galvao, reported on the conditions of corruption, forced labour and maladministration in the African colonies, he was to find himself arrested by the political police and confined to gaol or hospital for several years. Yet discontent in these territories was shown through one small outlet when, in 1958, Portuguese citizens were allowed to vote for the Portuguese president. Humberto Delgado, the candidate opposing the government, actually received a majority of the votes in Beira, the Mozambique port, and considerable support in other African towns. The election showed that opposition to Portuguese centralised government, and particularly to the exploitation of colonial territories to bolster the metropolitan economy, was resented by both European settlers and educated Africans.

It was not until 1959, however, that the mounting feelings of revolt became clearly apparent. A strike for higher wages in the capital of Portuguese Guinea, Bissau, was ended by the police killing a number of African workers. Portuguese Guinea, though in west Africa, was linked politically and administratively with the larger Portuguese territories of the south. Police and troops began to round up opponents of the régime in Angola, including the African doctor and poet, Agostinho Neto, who had established an underground nationalist movement, the Movimento Popular de Libertacao de Angola. In the protests against his arrest, troops killed a number of demonstrators and destroyed villages. Meanwhile, suppression was so severe in Mozambique that it was eventually denounced by the Bishop of Beira.

By now, of course, the Portuguese territories could no longer be insulated against the growth of nationalism throughout the rest of the continent. The progress of representative government in the French equatorial territories, their independence in 1960 and then the independence of the Belgian Congo in the same year, were bound to have a profound effect in Angola. Early in 1961 came the spectacular event which seemed to provide a catalyst for the movements of resistance to Portuguese rule. Captain Galvao seized the Portuguese liner, *Santa Maria*, making this act a dramatic protest against Portuguese dictatorship. He originally planned to sail to the spice island of Fernando Po, off the west coast of Africa, and then on to Angola. Despite his short-lived success, Galvao's gesture certainly impressed international opinion.

It also seems to have had some effect in bringing about the African uprising in Angola a few days later. For the next few months rebellion burst out throughout the territory, with atrocious brutality between Portuguese forces, Africans and groups of white settlers. The well-publicised fraternalistic policy of the Portuguese had broken down in the face of African nationalism. Despite the eventual subjugation of the country by Portuguese reinforcements, who, incidentally, like Cromwell's soldiers, were invited to take land and settle, Africans under Portuguese rule had shown the world that their feelings towards European rule were no different from those felt in the rest of the continent.

It also became clear during this rebellion that Africans in the Portuguese empire could also organise political movements. In the north, the Union of Angolan People, led by Holden Roberto, had been in existence since 1954 and had built up a membership of around 40,000. The more radical group, MPLA, associated with Neto, Ilidio Machado and Mario Pinto de Andrade, took a prominent role in organising the African Revolutionary Front for the Independence of the Portuguese Colonies. It included some whites and mulattoes and was drawn across tribal frontiers. The MPLA was trying to build a single movement against Portuguese colonialism and for this purpose associated with the resistance movement in Portuguese Guinea, the African Party for the Independence of Guinea. Opposition groups in Mozambique, which based their operations in Dar-es-Salaam, were also being drawn into the united anti-Portuguese organisation.

These events had a considerable impact on international reactions to Portugal. The Portuguese had been able to count, first, on the support of most Western powers when attacked at the United Nations, and then, at least on their neutrality. Dr Salazar made the utmost capital of his value to NATO and the American bases in the Azores. The revolt in Angola, however, together with increasing signs of future resistance to Portuguese rule, faced the western world with the choice of supporting the Portuguese and alienating African opinion, or becoming critical of the Portuguese empire. The early nineteen-sixties began to show a move, particularly in America, towards the latter alternative.

So Southern Africa was left, by the early nineteen-sixties, as the last outpost of the theory and practice of white domination over African peoples. It was this determination to preserve white supremacy which was the common factor between the Portuguese and the South Africans. Portugal was determined to keep Angola and Mozambique within Greater Portugal, although she could have little hope of retaining Portuguese Guinea, now surrounded by newly independent African states. The South Africans had built up the strongest military and security forces on the continent and had every intention of using them in order to defend the form of society they had imposed on their country. Both South Africans and Portuguese were prepared to assist each other if necessary in this common interest. They saw increasing signs of independent black Africa building a strategy designed to destroy this final white laager. Africans in their own territories had been forced into violent revolt with increasing acts of sabotage and a growing number of trials and executions – Walter Sisulu and Nelson Mandela, the 'black Pimpernel', along with several of their nationalist colleagues openly admitted that sabotage was now being used as the last weapon in the fight for liberty.' In the United Nations and in other international assemblies the rest of the world was being increasingly challenged to choose between the southern whites and African freedom. Yet the whites believed that their military power was sufficient to maintain racial domination for the foreseeable future. The High Commission Territories and South-west Africa might act the part of the Trojan horse and were often cast for that role by those determined to destroy the last vestiges of white rule. It needed no clairvoyance to foresee the gathering clouds of a racial conflict in which finally black Africa would confront the white supremacists in an ultimate battle to decide whether white rule was to have any place in the African continent.

10

The Central Triangle

Central Africa may be said to consist of three regions where, as we have previously seen, different imperialisms met each other. The French in French Equatorial Africa, the Belgians in the Congo and Ruanda-Urundi, the British in the Rhodesias and Nyasaland, all took a part in the development of this central heartland of the African continent. These three regions are defined as Central Africa for the simple reason that they were each administered as units by the different imperial powers.

There is another reason, besides the administrative, which justifies considering these three regions as one central African unit. The activities and ideas of the peoples living under French, Belgian and British rule all influenced each other. The most obvious example was the division of the Bakongo tribe between the Belgian Congo and Moyen-Congo, under the French (another section of the tribe lived in Portuguese Angola). Brazzaville and Leopoldville are cities facing each other across the river. Inevitably there was much interchange between their inhabitants and they frequently interfered in each other's affairs. Then again, the Copper Belt was cut in two by the frontier between the Congo and Northern Rhodesia. Movement across this frontier was frequent, with steadily increasing mutual knowledge amongst the peoples on both sides. Above all, perhaps, this whole region stood between west and east Africa, on the one hand, and the south, on the other. It was therefore a kind of no-man's land, fought over between the rival policies of black and white nationalism. Although each region was different, and, indeed, there were many contrasting situations within the regions themselves, the area as a whole can be seen to have had some unity and many common problems.

French Equatorial Africa was often considered as nothing more than the poor relative of French West Africa. This was a false picture, for the equatorial countries had a character of their own. It is true that the same legislation from Paris applied to the central African region as to the west. The 1946 constitution, the expansion of the electorate in 1951, the *loi cadre* of 1956, the referendum of 1958 and membership of the community, were all measures common to the two regions. Yet the economic and social backwardness of the equatorial countries, their jealousy of their west African cousins and consequent reaction against them, together with the much stronger hold of the French concessionary companies and the French administration in central Africa, often produced sharp contrasts between the two regions.

Considered as a whole, the people of the equatorial regions remained much more conscious of tribal loyalty and authority than west Africans. The immediate post-war period had seen profound changes in the attitude of the French administration to its central African subjects. Their loyalty to the Free French cause during the war had completely changed the attitude of Paris. Forced labour was at least legally abolished, and the new constitution provided both African and European citizens with a limited form of representation. This was a fresh attitude, but it did not, of course, obliterate immediately the legacy of the past. In both local representation to territorial institutions and in elections to the French Parliament, Africans still looked largely to the Europeans as the people who best understood the responsibilities of government. They themselves tended to remain concerned mainly with their own tribal affairs.

Even in the fifties, after the expansion of the electorate in 1951, the growth of new institutions and the provision of wider forms of representation, this outlook changed only slowly. Urbanisation, which had been such a factor in west Africa, occurred in a much more modified form in the equatorial countries. There was some increase in the numbers of wage-earners in all four territories, but only on a minor scale. Between 1949 and 1958 the estimated total number of wage-earners in the whole region only increased from 150,000 to just under 190,000. This represented only about six per cent of the total population.

Moreover, amongst the working class, there was very little trade union organisation. The French trade union movement had attempted to extend its organisation to the equatorial countries, as to west

Africa. But although the socialists, communists and catholics all tried to develop their union membership in central Africa, none of them had any great success. There were never more than about ten per cent of the wage-earners in union membership. What unions did make any progress were usually much more on a tribal basis than affiliated to the French organisations.

This left weak foundations for the growth of political movements. In fact, the antecedents of political parties in this region were to be found far more amongst the pseudo-religious protest sects than amongst the trade unions. Consequently, political parties were also heavily coloured by tribal affiliations and tended to revert to inter-tribal violence rather than concentrate on modern political activity. Efforts to promote modern organisation were also gravely handicapped by the absence of any considerable educated community. Education had been grossly neglected before the war and, although much more money and effort were spent on it afterwards, there was a heavy backlog to remove. The educational services varied widely in the region, those of the Moyen-Congo being the best in all French Africa, whilst those in Tchad were the worst. But, as a whole, the region suffered from having few of the sophisticated, experienced men available as leaders in comparison with the outstanding individuals and the communities surrounding them in west Africa.

In politics greater remoteness from Paris prevented the metropolitan parties from gaining the same influence as in west Africa. The main party to benefit from this remoteness was the Rassemblement du Peuple Français, the RPF. It took advantage of the great popularity of De Gaulle, who was associated with the party, in equatorial Africa. It was also strongly influential amongst the administrators and so came to be linked with the French administration's pressures and manipulation of elections. Yet, eventually, the party's exploitation of De Gaulle's popularity and its close links with the administration repelled many Africans and it became very largely a Europeans' party.

The socialists, through the SFIO, never had much success in attracting members, though its parties in Moyen-Congo and Tchad gained some influence. It was not, however, until the socialist parties began to associate themselves with tribal organisations that they made any serious impact.

It was the RDA which had the strongest influence in the region, although it was not as well organised as in the west. It never found the outstanding leaders that emerged in the west African territories, but Gabriel Lisette, the West Indian in Tchad, took a leading part in its central organisation next to Houphouet-Boigny. There was always some fear that the RDA really represented the western territories, with the suspicion that the west was trying to dominate central African politics. This was particularly noticeable after the passage of the *loi cadre* in 1956. The central Africans refused to participate seriously in the debate which so profoundly divided the RDA, though Lisette supported Houphouet and there was a general rejection of the proposal to retain a federal structure. But as soon as it was thought that Houphouet and his supporters were trying to compensate in central Africa for their loss of support over anti-federalism within the RDA in the west, there was an immediate reaction against what was considered to be yet another attempt at western domination.

Whether it was in the RDA, or amongst the followers of Senghor's organisations, represented by Jean Aubame in Gabon, or amongst the other purely territorial parties, politics in French Central Africa remained largely attached to local feeling, based on tribal and regional foundations. Nowhere did a really strong radical group emerge and consequently the social struggle between modernism and traditionalism in politics was hardly apparent in any part of this area. Nevertheless, there were differences between the four countries comprising equatorial Africa and it will help to understand them, as well as to appreciate their reactions to the profound political changes of the fifties, to look at each country in turn.

Gabon was the smallest of the French equatorial territories, but its recent history was the most stable, and during the nineteen-fifties it developed the only strong economic momentum in the region. At first it depended largely on lumber exports, plus a little gold mining and cocoa growing. From these three sources it was able to show the only favourable balance of trade amongst the four countries. Later in the fifties the discovery of manganese and oil were to give Gabon an economic potential unrivalled in the whole area. They were also to provide the country with a higher rate of increase in the working-class population than any of its neighbours, although this was scarcely reflected in the strength of its trade union organisations.

Politically, the country was largely dominated by the Fang tribe, which comprised about a quarter of the total population, though more of its members lived in Cameroon and Spanish Guinea than in Gabon itself. From the time when new representative institutions were established after the war, Jean Aubame, a Catholic member of the tribe, was accepted as leader. Aubame had founded the party known as the Union Démocratique et Sociale Gabonaise in 1948 and, although Léon Mba, another member of the tribe, gained some rival support in Libreville, he was not to become politically important until later.

As early as 1950 Gabon began to show some restiveness over her position as part of the equatorial federation. It seemed to many of the leading Gabonese that her wealth was being used to subsidise the weaker members of the federation and that her people would gain economically by separation. Despite debates on this issue, the proposals for detaching Gabon made by Aubame were rejected. They were, however, to be revived later in the fifties.

Aubame himself was an individualist and, although he usually followed the lead of Senghor, his association with the IOM was hardly profound. In the same way, Mba looked towards the RDA, but his party was never firmly affiliated.

The relative prosperity of Gabon kept politics in a fairly tranquil state. Relations between the political leaders in the territorial assembly and the French administration were usually co-operative, whilst there was little tension between Africans and Europeans. Indeed, it was normal for Europeans to be elected as presidents of the territorial assembly and chairmen of its main committees.

Aubame spent a great deal of his time in Paris and by the mid-fifties was being overtaken in popularity by Mba. The latter became Mayor of Libreville in 1956 and in the municipal elections began to attract support from outside the Fang tribe. He also included Europeans amongst the candidates of his party, now named the Bloc Démocratique Gabonais. Following the passage of the *loi cadre*, elections were held in March 1957 to the new expanded and more powerful territorial assembly. Aubame's UDSG and Mba's BDG secured almost equal representation, but it was Mba who now found himself able to form a government, with the support of some opposition members, and who took the new office of Vice-President of the Government Council.

It was almost entirely local and personal conflicts which separated the two parties. These did not go so deep as to prevent co-operation between the two, although in 1958 there was some political unrest amongst rival student groups. But the government continued as a form of coalition, with Mba in charge, but some of Aubame's members as his ministers.

The relations between the two men and their parties and the extra-territorial groups also revealed the strength of their common approach towards the interests of Gabon. Aubame followed Senghor from the IOM into the Convention Africain and then to the Parti du Régroupement Africain. He attended the PRA conference at Cotonou in 1958, but he did not accept the policy on demands for independence and renewed federation agreed by the congress. Similarly, although Mba still followed the RDA and was at the Bamako 1957 congress, he was part of the minority group, led by Houphouet-Boigny, who resisted the majority aim of establishing a strong federation. Both men, in fact, reflected the separatist, but pro-French, outlook of Gabon; both believed that their people would gain more by becoming autonomous whilst retaining strong links with France, than by either becoming a part of a federation or seeking independence.

By now iron, manganese and oil had been discovered and the Gabonese had no desire to share the profits they envisaged with their neighbours. A Franco-American consortium was established, known as COMILOG. This consisted of forty-nine per cent United States Steel and fifty-one per cent French, divided between private companies and the French government. The Germans also were brought in by the French to share in the development of iron ore, whilst uranium deposits had begun to be exploited at the same time.

The appearance of these new riches served to bring the two parties closer together, rather than dividing them on conflicting policies as to how they should be exploited. Both leaders agreed in September 1958 to advise their supporters to vote for autonomous membership of the French Community in the referendum. Although a small new party opposed the affirmative vote, 97·7 per cent voted 'yes'.

The coalition continued with Mba as President and later as Prime Minister. Although opposed to federation, the Gabonese were not averse to some form of economic association with their neighbours. So in January 1959 a tariff, trade and transport union was negotiated between the four equatorial states in which Gabon participated. This loose form of association suited Gabonese purposes without endangering their autonomy to the extent implicit in a federation.

Mba continued as Prime Minister until Gabon joined the rush towards independent status in 1960. The country became independent in August of that year and Mba became head of state. By this time, however, signs of tension had appeared within his party, particularly over his pro-French attitude. It was not long after independence before several members of his own party, including the President of the Assembly, were imprisoned. Although still largely wedded to traditionalism and tribal affiliations, the economic development of Gabon, with its accompanying increase in the number of wage-earners, suggested that the somewhat complacent conservative coalition régime might well be challenged in the future by more radical forces.

Ubangui-Chari, along with Tchad one of the two northern territories in the equatorial region, did not find the same economic opportunities as Gabon. It was a much poorer country, depending almost entirely on the production of cotton for its economic life, about a quarter of its people being engaged in this pursuit.

Most of the inhabitants remained in agricultural life, and their lack of economic development inevitably led to the maintenance of traditional society. The country was not only underpopulated, but its people showed little sense of national purpose in working for improvements. So much so that, despite the abolition of forced labour by the French government soon after the war, a form of compulsory work was later introduced by its own African government in the form of work camps and penalties for those refusing to work. The legacy of the depredations ensuing from the rule of concessionary companies before the war produced greater racial tensions in Ubangui-Chari than in most other French African territories. Consequently there was constant conflict between the African inhabitants and the French administration in the post-war period.

The backwardness of the people in Ubangui-Chari at least partially explains the dominance of individuals in political life. Antoine

Darlan, the first post-war leader of protest, was supplanted in the early nineteen-fifties by Barthélemy Boganda, who had trained and practised in the Catholic priesthood until he married his French secretary. Boganda, who had originally been elected with the support of the French MRP, continued the Darlan tradition of attacking the French administration, which was largely dominated by the RPF, until the mid-fifties. Then he realised that if he was to secure the French aid needed for the development of his country, he would be more likely to succeed through co-operation. After the 1952 elections his party played a dominant role in the enlarged territorial assembly, although balanced by the RPF candidates elected from the first college and a number of independents. Yet politics in Ubangui-Chari were still sufficiently primitive to allow Boganda's party, the Mouvement pour l'Évolution Sociale de l'Afrique Noire, or MESAN, virtual control over local affairs. The party, as its name indicates, had pretensions to become a wider movement than one simply confined to the single territory. Indeed, Boganda used the prestige he had gained as the outstanding personality in central Africa and President of the federal Grand Council, to propose a United States of Latin Africa, including all the French territories, the Congo and Angola. He made little progress on this grand design, but did constantly try to persuade his fellow leaders in the equatorial countries to rebuild their federation. Boganda, indeed, stood head and shoulders above any other personality in French central Africa during the fifties and organised his party separately from any affiliations in order to dominate the political life of Ubangui-Chari.

After the *loi cadre* became operative Boganda attempted to persuade the equatorial federation to become a member state of the Community. But, like Senghor in the west, he was unsuccessful. Inevitably, as such an outstanding personality, he provoked jealousy amongst his contemporaries and was strongly opposed by the RDA. Nevertheless, he called on his people to support membership of the Community in the 1958 referendum, and demonstrated his hold on them when 98·8 per cent followed his advice. He then became Prime Minister and renewed his attempt to establish a wider association of states. He could find no support from Youlou in Moyen-Congo or Aubame in Gabon, and that which he secured from Opangault and Tchicaya in Moyen-Congo was insufficient to build his dream. Eventually, although a Central African Republic was declared in December 1958 as a member state of the Community, it only consisted of Ubangui-Chari with Boganda as President and David Dacko as Minister of the Interior. The new republic acquired a strongly centralised form of government, for Boganda was now supported by an almost entirely MESAN assembly. There were some few signs of opposition still existing, but all attempts to organise it failed through intimidation by the single majority party.

The early part of 1959 was spent in preparation for new elections. It was in the midst of this campaign that Boganda was killed in an air crash, so that the keystone of the country's political life was lost.

Despite this disaster, MESAN won almost a clean sweep of the assembly seats. Yet it still had to find a new leader. After the elections the new assembly chose David Dacko, a cousin of Boganda, born in the same village, as the great man's successor. Yet although he secured almost unanimous support in the assembly, Dacko was not given the same virtually unrestricted powers as his predecessor. Indeed, factional conflicts broke out within the party and although it held together until Ubangui-Chari, now known as the Central African Republic, attained sovereign independent status in August 1960, the tensions had become clearly apparent. Only a few months after independence the main opposition party, which had been formed as a breakaway from MESAN, was banned and its leaders, including Boganda's lieutenant, Dr Abel Goumba, were arrested.

The second northern equatorial territory, Tchad, had a population consisting of more than half the total French central African inhabitants. Yet, in such a huge territory, it was totally inadequate for the needs of the country. The division between the Moslem nomads of the desert north, derived from the same stock as the tribes of Northern Nigeria, and the mainly Christian Negroes of the south, played an important part in the political development of the territory. The northerners used their cattle not only as beasts of burden, but also as meat exports, an unusual feature in this part of Africa. The other main marketable product was cotton seed, grown extensively, but mainly concentrated in the south-west. Traditionalism, both amongst the nomad tribes of the north and the powerful Sara tribe of the south, remained the predominant social factor, and partly explained the unstable character of political development during the nineteen-fifties.

Until the year before independence, much of the political history of Tchad was controlled, though not dominated, by Gabriel Lisette, a French Negro born in Panama and leader of the Parti Progressiste Tchadien, affiliated to the RDA. Yet always Lisette had, behind his shoulder, the powerful but curious figure of Ahmed Koulamallah, a socialist, but often the spokesman of some sections of the Moslem north. The northerners, although all Moslem and traditionalist, were nevertheless constantly divided between a variety of Islamic sects. Yet if anybody were entitled to speak on their behalf it was usually Koulamallah, socialist follower of Lamine Guèye, constantly emphasising his connections with the SFIO.

Lisette usually followed Houphouet-Boigny, and in 1950 moved from the previously radical position of the RDA to Houphouet's more moderate outlook. Despite this change, the French administration was able to prevent his re-election as a deputy in the following year. They secured his replacement by RPF candidates until 1956, when Lisette regained his seat as a deputy. In the meantime, he had spent his time in the territorial assembly. Yet the RPF, with the support of the administration, remained dominant in the territorial elections and was in full control of the local assembly. It was as a result of these elections and the strong suspicion that the administration had gerrymandered them, that violence broke out in 1952 in the Logone region. Following his electoral defeat in 1952, Lisette linked up again with Koulamallah who had previously been associated with him. For the next few years there was constant movement and manœuvre between the various political parties, which prevented any single national party emerging, but nevertheless strengthened the forces of African opposition to the French administration. It was some sign of the changing mood of the country that, whilst in 1947 Tchad was the only French African nation to support the retention of the double electoral college system, by 1955 it had changed to strong support for the single college.

By 1956, Lisette's PPT was winning majority support in the southern Sara area, defeating the administration's candidates and those supported by the chiefs. It was now clear that Lisette and the PPT were on the verge of taking over control of the country from the French administration and its RPF party. Lisette himself became Mayor of Fort Lamy and in the post-*loi cadre* elections the PPT, now forming a coalition with minor parties and campaigning against 'the white man and the chiefs', gained a considerable majority in the new expanded Assembly. Lisette became Prime Minister, and although his coalition did not survive long, he remained the key figure in the various alliances between the different parties formed over the following two years.

Lisette and his PPT could never form a cabinet on their own, for they drew their support almost entirely from the rural Negroes of the south-west. Some kind of accommodation had to be made continually with other groups including some from the north. There were also frequent criticisms of Lisette, not least because of his non-African descent and his association with French West Indians. He often had to face the opposition of Koulamallah, who although defeated in the 1957 elections, still remained a political force. Indeed, when Koulamallah alleged unfair electioneering in one region new elections were ordered to be held. In these elections in 1958, Koulamallah was successful and formed a socialist coalition against Lisette's government.

Lisette allied himself with Houphouet-Boigny in the argument which developed at the Bamako Conference in 1957. Despite the fact that he had been somewhat sympathetic to the federal ideas of Boganda from Ubangui-Chari, Lisette now supported Houphouet in the argument against a strong federal executive and in his conflict with Sékou Touré.

The following year, Tchad, like the rest of French Africa, had to decide its attitude towards membership of the Community. Here Lisette and Koulamallah were in sharp opposition. Although Lisette had not pursued his sympathetic attitude towards reconstituting the federation, he nevertheless wanted to take advantage of the opportunity to achieve autonomy as a member of the Community. On the other hand, Koulamallah was anxious to break as far away as possible from the rest of French Equatorial Africa, and even to retain the status of an overseas territory, like French Somaliland. But the Assembly decided to advise in favour of membership within the Community, and the 98·7 per cent vote in the referendum showed the hold it had over the electorate.

Tchad became a republic and a member state of the Community. In 1959 it joined the customs, trade and transport union with the rest of French central Africa, and Lisette was left with a fairly flexible mandate to decide what future co-operation there should be with its neighbours. In particular, Tchad wanted and needed to continue receiving French financial and technical assistance.

By now, however, any form of unity left within the government coalition was rapidly disintegrating. The absence of Lisette in Paris was taken as an opportunity for ministerial resignations and his government quickly fell. After a number of minority governments had lasted for very short periods, a new administration was formed by François Tombalbaye, a colleague of Lisette's and a former trade union leader. Tombalbaye tried hard to rally the country, which had been almost immobilised by a succession of government crises and quarrels within the Assembly. In the elections of 1959 the PPT still retained its popularity, winning fifty-seven of the eighty-five seats. Yet confusion continued and efforts to promote political unity all proved in vain. Fighting broke out shortly after the elections and new party alliances were continually being made. When the various Moslem parties of the north came together early in 1960 to form a common organisation, the Parti National Africain, it seemed for a moment as if the country might split in two. Tombalbaye saw the danger, and quickly initiated discussions with the Moslem leaders in the following year, resulting in a fusion of the new Moslem party with the old PPT.

In the meantime, Tchad followed the example of the other French African territories and attained its sovereignty in August 1960. Tombalbaye had by this time been persuaded by Koulamallah to remove Lisette from his cabinet and then deport him from the country. He himself took the new position of President of the Republic and, recognising the needs of a land-locked country, showed much greater sympathy than his predecessors to the conception of reviving the federation. Yet it had become quite clear at the time of independence that the future of Tchad was bound up with the necessity to induce some form of genuine unity between the Moslem, nomadic north and the more settled, Negro south. With such endemic poverty in the country, little social or economic progress could be expected without a genuine effort based on national unity. There could be no chance of invoking the spirit of nationalism until the deep social, ethnic and religious divisions had been bridged, giving some chance of political cohesion.

The history of Moyen-Congo during the nineteen-fifties was

largely dominated by rivalry of three tribal groups. In the north the M'Bochi tribe was led by Jacques Opangault, in his Mouvement Socialiste Africain, an affiliate of the SFIO and originally founded by a Frenchman. On the coast, at Pointe Noire, Jean Félix Tchicaya, the first African member of the National Assembly, led the local RDA affiliate, the Parti Progressiste Congolais, supported by members of the Vili tribe. From the mid-nineteen-fifties onwards, the Balali section of the wider Bakongo tribe gave Abbé Fulbert Youlou an opportunity to challenge the position of the two older leaders. The country was poor, with its northern half covered with dense forest in which about a third of the total population lived in small villages. It had few natural resources, depending largely on the railway and river communications, whilst its exports consisted almost entirely of agricultural produce. Yet, instead of developing a strong national drive for economic progress, most of the time was taken up with conflicts between racial groups, often resulting in extreme violence and many deaths.

Until the middle of the decade, Tchicaya's PPC retained majority control in the Assembly, with the MSA as a minority group. The Assembly criticised the administration for ignoring its resolutions, as in other parts of French central Africa, but there was little serious political activity at this time. It was not until the 1956 elections and the emergence of Youlou that the mood began to change. Youlou had trained in the priesthood, along with Boganda of Ubangui-Chari, and although dismissed by the Catholic Church he continued to wear clerical dress and retain the title 'Abbé'. He decided to stand against Tchicaya and Opangault in the elections for the assembly and secured the support of most of the Balali. Some of them accepted him as the messianic Matsoua's heir, and it soon became obvious that the elections had a strongly tribal and religious flavour. On election day itself there were riots between supporters of the various candidates, and when the results were announced voting was so close that although Tchicaya retained his seat, both the Balali and M'Bochi demanded that the election be annulled. Youlou's support continued to grow, for in November of the same year he was elected Mayor of Brazzaville, and in alliance with the Opangault socialists his candidates won a complete victory over the PPC in Pointe Noire.

By this time Tchicaya's support was dwindling, and Youlou,

advised by some Europeans, formed his own party, the Union Démocratique de la Défense des Intérêts Africains. He based his appeal on the need for social reform and national unity, although there was some considerable irony in the latter claim.

In the elections of March 1957, following the *loi cadre*, Youlou and his former ally Opangault, split and really fought the election between them. The PPC had now almost disappeared, and it was Youlou's UDDIA and Opangault's MSA which each gained twenty-one of the forty-five seats, the others being held by independents. A coalition government was formed, led by Opangault, who was able to secure the support of two of the three independents.

Youlou now saw the need to associate with one of the interterritorial movements and approached the RDA. Cynically, but realistically, the RDA dropped the weakened Tchicaya and accepted Youlou as an ally. It was now clear that the battle for national leadership lay between the defrocked Abbé and his rival, the socialist Opangault.

Before the end of 1957 the UDDIA ministers resigned, following a virulent article in Opangault's newspaper and an anonymous letter circulated to members of the assembly denouncing the four ministers. After some tension, Opangault and Youlou agreed to work together again. For one thing, the French were at this moment considering building a new hydro-electric dam on the Kouilu river and would obviously be reluctant to commit themselves in the midst of political uncertainty. No sooner was the agreement for the dam signed, than supporters of the two leaders were again at each other's throats. Rioting broke out once more, and when Youlou tried to discuss pacifying measures with his rival, Opangault refused to receive him. So the uneasy association continued, whilst preparations were made for the referendum over membership of the French Community. Here there was little dissension and Moyen-Congo voted by 99·1 per cent to join the Community.

No sooner had the assembly proclaimed membership of the Community than one of Opangault's followers announced his defection to Youlou. The latter immediately claimed the right to become Prime Minister and form a new government. Chaos broke out, with a public invasion of the assembly building and vain attempts by the police to restore order. Eventually the defecting member was actually covered by Youlou's revolver as he retreated from the hall, and was quickly flown back to Brazzaville. Rioting continued, but the UDDIA had the bare majority and immediately transferred the capital from Opangault's stronghold at Pointe Noire to Youlou's Brazzaville. Youlou was now firmly in the saddle, despite his bare majority. Yet rioting continued sporadically, exacerbated by the trouble at the beginning of 1959 in Leopoldville, just across the river from Brazzaville. The following month, when Youlou presented his first budget, the riots reached a new ferocity, when over 500 people were killed and only the appearance of French troops prevented still further slaughter. Youlou now took this opportunity of crushing his opponents completely by sending Opangault to gaol and virtually destroying his party. So, when the next elections were held in June, Youlou's UDDIA secured fifty-one of the sixty-one seats. Nevertheless, Opangault had been elected, even though still in prison, and was shortly afterwards released without facing a trial.

Youlou's next move was to get the assembly to grant the government powers to ban meetings, impose curfews and establish a special court with the power of imposing the death penalty on anyone convicted of fomenting trouble. He then proceeded to secure a new constitution, allowing him to become both President and Prime Minister. The full reins of political power were now in his hands. When, in 1960, he reached agreement with Opangault for a merger of their two parties, with his former rival as a minister of state under him, it simply served to tighten his personal hold further.

In 1960 Youlou flirted for a time with the idea of reconstituting the equatorial federation and applying for its independence as a federal group. The opposition of Gabon and the lukewarm attitude of other leaders prevented this plan coming to fruition. Meanwhile, the approach of independence across the river in the Belgian Congo inspired a new idea. Youlou saw that if he could unite his Bakongo tribe in his own country, the Belgian Congo and Angola, this could form the core of a richer, stronger area, even perhaps including wealthy Gabon and approaching the imaginative conception of Boganda of a United States of Latin Africa. President Youlou, however, did not prove as powerful a leader of the Bakongo as his fellow-President Kasavubu in the Congo. Youlou had to content himself with following the fashion in the rest of French Africa and taking his Republic of Congo into independence in August 1960. Time had still to show whether this political supremacy would be sufficient to overcome the disintegrating forces of tribal conflict which had dominated life in the country for the previous ten years.

French central Africa is one example of an area becoming independent by external pressures rather than by its own intent. Each of the four countries was so accustomed to relying on European guidance and direction that very little indigenous pressure developed for self-government. Indeed, it was not until the late fifties that the African leadership turned against the double college electoral system. For almost ten years after the war they were quite happy to accept representative institutions through which Europeans retained a powerful political influence by nomination in the first college.

It was only after the passage of the *loi cadre* in 1956, a law which owed little to central African pressure, that the strong European influence disappeared. Even then, Europeans were not driven from the political field, but rather voluntarily left it. After 1956, most of them believed that their responsibilities lay solely in the technical and economic fields. Those few who still retained a political interest did so through advisory positions to African leaders, rather than by representing specifically European interests.

Even after 1956 most of the African leaders would have preferred to retain strong links with France than to take the independence path. Boganda, with his ambitious federal schemes, was the main exception, but he found little support in either central or west Africa. Each of the territories was to a greater or lesser degree constantly aware of its economic weakness and desperately anxious to retain French economic, technical and military support. Three of the four states tried hard to bolster their strength by joint links – the exception being the wealthier state of Gabon. They succeeded in mid-1959 in forming a customs union and in maintaining certain common services, even Gabon realising the disadvantages of complete separation from her neighbours. But the opposition of Gabon was sufficient to prevent the resurrection of the equatorial federation, though something similar was proposed by the other three states as a 'Union des Républiques d'Afrique Centrale'.

It was obvious that nothing less than some sort of federal union could produce a viable economic unit in this region. Nevertheless, the centrifugal forces were stronger than economic common sense. It was not only Gabon that opposed close association, for in Moyen-Congo many of the powerful Bakongo tribe looked more across the river to their fellow-tribesmen in the Belgian Congo and to those who lived in Angola than to their neighbouring French Africans.

So in 1960, the four states now separated but linked by agreements on common services, customs and defence, were swept by the west African independence fever into a sovereignty few of them really desired. They put much more store by association with Paris, and were assured by De Gaulle's ministers that French aid would continue. In fact, the French continued to provide a much higher rate of economic aid than Britain and maintained much stronger defence agreements. The four French central African states attained sovereign independence in August 1960, but they remained essentially French African states, heavily dependent on French support. The interesting query, left for the future, was the extent to which the leadership groups in each of these territories, with their close French links, would remain acceptable to popular opinion as economic development gradually threw up potentially rival leaders. This would depend on the reputation achieved by the existing leadership in their local communities and the effects of ideas and propaganda imported from other parts of Africa.

If French central Africa was bedevilled by a surfeit of politics, neighbouring Belgian Congo suffered from the opposite malaise. Until the mid-nineteen-fifties it remained Belgian policy to govern from Brussels, with no more than minimal advice from the Congo peoples themselves, both white and black in the Congo being debarred from political representation or serious activity. Belgian theory was that to lay the foundations of a healthy democratic political system required first a sound economic and social basis. The Belgians therefore concentrated on social and economic development. In theory they believed that eventually the Congolese people might be given a representative policy system, but that prospect remained an unconsidered cloud on the distant horizon. They were still thinking in terms of something like thirty to forty years' evolution. Two main forces caused a profound upheaval in all Belgian plans.

First, Belgian policy was based on a fallacy. Intelligent and thoughtful Belgian colonial administrators believed they could produce an African community with an upper crust of skilled technical workers alongside a highly paid, sophisticated, white community, whilst still insulating both white and black from politics. So, after the war, the process of introducing social benefits and promoting economic development was accelerated and this policy continued until the mid-fifties. There was, for instance, forty-two per cent literacy achieved in the Congo, a higher figure than perhaps anywhere else in the continent. Yet it was not until 1956 that the Congo secured its first university, the Catholic University of Louvanium, fathered by Belgium's Louvain. And it was three years later before the first state university was established in Elizabethville. In the same way, both state and companies provided excellent social services and fringe benefits, housing, pensions, health insurance, family allowances – but allowed practically no genuine African trade unionism. Or again, the big companies, Union Minière du Haute Katanga, and Huileries du Congo Belge, greatly increased wages after the war and gave excellent technical training to Africans; but there were very few Africans promoted to the higher administrative ranks.

Meanwhile the Belgians maintained their previous policy over the immigration of whites. They deliberately controlled immigration policy so that only skilled workers went to live in the Congo and there was no possibility of a 'poor white' problem developing. Nor was there any chance of competition between white and black in the lower grades of skilled work, or in business and commerce within the African market. Indeed, Africans in the Congo were not only to be seen in skilled technical work in charge of machines and using skilled tools, but they also owned most of the small businesses in their own townships, whilst considerable numbers of them were to be found as clerks in government offices. On the other hand, apart from the African teaching community, there were almost no African professional men, doctors, lawyers or higher civil servants.

This was the first fallacy. Keeping Africans away from academic studies and particularly from the intellectual life of universities in Europe did not prevent them from developing political ideas, nor did the character of the white community avoid racial tension. It was inevitable, as Africans gradually earned more money and gained more skills in the decade after the war, that they should begin to consider the idea of running their own country. As the white community grew more cohesive and recognised the signs of expanding African ambitions, so it began to act more like white settler communities elsewhere.

Thus it was Belgian colonial policy itself which provoked the beginnings of African nationalism in the Congo. To try and continue on pre-war lines by preventing political activity and yet advancing the Africans economically could only produce an accumulated head of political steam eventually bound to lead to an explosion.

The second fallacy led to the same consequence as the first. Belgian colonial policy was founded on theory presupposing a sociopolitical vacuum. It took no cognisance of events or influences from other parts of the African continent. Yet by the mid-fifties the French territories, separated only by the river from Leopoldville, had been accustomed to exercising political responsibilities for ten years. The *loi cadre* of 1956 served to increase these responsibilities to the verge of autonomy. Meanwhile, across another border in the Rhodesias, the hostility aroused among Africans to the Central African Federation had led to the growth of African nationalist parties, to determined political action and to heated political debate. By the mid-fifties, also, Britain had announced her intention to grant the Gold Coast independence by early 1957. It was impossible to keep the Congo Africans in ignorance of these radical developments in the rest of their continent. It thus became inevitable that the Congolese would begin to rebel against the continued refusal of the Belgians to allow them political opportunities similar to those of their neighbours. Indeed, Belgian policy itself logically led to political demands. If, as the Belgians claimed, their colonial subjects in the Congo were given better economic and social facilities than Africans in other territories, they were surely better fitted to govern their own country.

Thus the ground was prepared from the mid-fifties onwards for the growth of African political activity in the Congo. The first serious political expression dated from the publication in 1954 by Professor A. A. J. van Bilsen of a treatise entitled 'Thirty Years Plan for the Emancipation of Belgian Africa'. The ideas in this article were taken up by a group of Congolese intellectuals who had been supported by Catholic missionaries since 1953 in publishing a journal called *Conscience Africaine*. In mid-1956 they published a special issue of their journal in the form of a manifesto calling for ultimate independence for the Congo. They still believed, as did Professor van Bilsen, that it would take several decades to establish a sovereign state in Belgian Africa. Their conception of such a state included Belgian as well as African residents, but on an equal, non-racial basis. Despite the moderation of their aims, this first serious, overt sign of political ambition amongst Africans threw the Belgian administration into panic. The degree of myopia toward African realities among both administrators and Belgian settlers may be judged from the fact that this very mild manifesto caused a serious drop in colonial stocks and a readiness amongst many white settlers in the Congo to sell up and leave the territory. Yet, in fact, the manifesto itself was scarcely perused by those who supported it. Although M. Ileo was to achieve some political prominence after 1960, few others in the group ever became politically effective.

On the other hand, this moment marked the end of the Congo's isolation from African nationalism. Ever since 1950 an association of the Bakongo, known as ABAKO, had been in existence for the purpose of preserving and developing the culture of the Bakongo tribe. ABAKO was now stimulated into further activities by the publication of the manifesto and by the results of the French *loi cadre* amongst members of the same tribe across the river in Moyen-Congo. They followed up the manifesto with emphasising their demands in a more forthright manner. In particular, they coupled with their demand for independence the immediate right to form political parties. The leading force in ABAKO had now become Joseph Kasavubu, who was to rival Fulbert Youlou in Moyen-Congo for leadership of the Bakongo.

By this time, too, some of the Congolese intelligentsia had begun to recognise that divisions within white society were affecting the Congo situation. The Belgian elections of 1954 had brought into office a coalition between the liberal and socialist parties. Although this did not radically disturb the even tenor of Belgian colonial policy, it did raise one comparatively new issue. The liberals and socialists both tended to take an anti-clerical line, both in cutting subsidies to the Roman Catholic mission schools and in setting up separate lay institutions. This at least shook the stability of the alliance between church and state in the Congo. It was followed, to perhaps a lesser extent, by a growth of mistrust between the state and the companies, particularly accentuated when government looked to America for capital to develop hydro-electric power. There was no doubt, either, that by this time many of the members of the Belgian socialist party who had made colonies their particular concern foresaw that the Belgian paternal attitude must come to an end. In such circles an awareness was growing that unless there were a radical change in Belgian colonial policy an explosion was imminent.

At the beginning of 1957 elections were held in the municipalities on a limited representative system. This was the beginning of the Belgian answer to accumulating African political pressures. Elections were held first in Leopoldville, Elizabethville and Jadotville, each town being divided into European and African communes. Male suffrage at the age of twenty-five was instituted for the election of communal councils, which in their turn were allowed to choose a mayor, though still subject to the veto of the divisional governor. These elections illustrated the fact that under the leadership of ABAKO the Bakongo had become more cohesive and better organised than any of their rival tribes. Although they comprised only slightly more than half the electorate, they gained 129 of the 270 seats in Leopoldville. Elections in all three towns were conducted largely on a tribal basis, an attitude repeated in the following year when further elections were held in other urban areas.

This lesson was not lost on the rivals of the Bakongo. In 1958 their chief competitor, the Bangala, took the lead in organising a rival political party, the Mouvement National Congolais. But this party was not simply a tribal association; for the first time some of its leaders, particularly Patrice Lumumba, realised that if the Congo was ever to become organised for a united drive to independence, tribalism could not form the basis of political parties. The MNC, therefore, set out from the start to establish a nation-wide organisation, with the attainment of independence as its central object.

By this time, political relations between Belgium and the Congo were developing fast. There were influences below the political surface which decided the Belgians to adopt a completely new policy based on de-colonisation. This reversal of traditional Belgian policy produced political activity so feverish as to approach panic.

The major factor undermining Belgian confidence in its imperial destiny was the sudden fall in copper prices in 1957. The heavy dependence of the country on copper exports, and consequently the precarious nature of the Congo's value to the Belgian business world, was suddenly apparent. Investment quickly dried up, and, as the new signs of developing nationalist ambitions appeared among the Congolese themselves, the Belgian government and business world suddenly and astonishingly reversed their entire previous attitude. It became accepted that the Belgian stake in the Congo could only be retained by rapid progress to independence.

This new policy was put into effect by a succession of colonial ministers. In mid-1958 the liberal-socialist coalition in Belgium fell and a new coalition government under Gaston Eyskens took office. The new Colonial Minister was Leo Petillon, who had just completed his term as Governor-General in the Congo. Petillon believed in constitutional progress, although on a rather conservative basis. He immediately announced that a policy of de-colonisation would now be followed, and set up a working party to study what constitutional reforms should be recommended. It was not long, however, before Petillon was replaced by a much more liberal minister from the Christian Socialist party, Maurice van Hemelrijck. Hemelrijck continued his predecessor's policy of reform and the government accepted the proposals made by the working party. All the institutions were to receive a new injection of democracy in which, for the first time, elected councils were to have some executive reponsibility instead of simply acting in an advisory capacity.

During 1959, however, M. Hemelrijck gained the reputation of being pro-African and consequently became correspondingly unpopular amongst white settlers in the Congo, who by now were raising political barriers against African constitutional advance. It was on these grounds that M. Hemelrijck was forced to resign in September 1959, his cabinet colleagues feeling that they could not accept the rapid pace he was setting for Congolese self-government. He was replaced by Auguste de Schrijver, who again continued his predecessor's work, announcing that local elections would be held at the end of the year, provincial councils established the following spring and central legislatures before the end of 1960.

By now the pace had become almost frenetic. By January 1960, a round-table conference had been called to sit in Brussels; within a week of its opening it was announced that independence would be granted. It had taken the Belgians less than three years from the time when they first doubted their prized colonial policy, the subject of fifty years' boasting, to accept its complete reversal.

While these rapid changes had been taking place in Brussels, the political flood in the Congo, so long dammed, had now burst. At the end of 1958 Patrice Lumumba visited Accra as a delegate to the All-African Conference. In Accra he met leaders of the other nationalist parties in Africa and heard discussions on the continental drive towards total national independence. On his return to Leopoldville at the beginning of January 1959, he forthrightly announced that his objective was immediate independence.

His declaration was made in circumstances which by now bordered on the revolutionary. The recession had caused large-scale unemployment, which particularly hit the urban workers. Leopoldville itself could find work for no more than about 50,000 Africans, but seven times that number lived in the city. Immediately after Lumumba's declaration the cancellation by the authorities of an ABAKO meeting and a march of the unemployed through the city sparked off riots and looting which lasted for several days. At least fifty Africans were killed and about the same number of Europeans injured, although no white person lost his life, partly because of the protection given them by some of the Africans. Nevertheless, these riots had shown an ugly African hostility to the Europeans and their property, whilst, on the other side, the authorities had displayed an attitude bordering on panic in the deployment of troops. A few days later Joseph Kasavubu was arrested along with other ABAKO officials and shortly afterwards the party itself was proscribed.

Despite these disturbances the constitutional reforms were pursued and came into effect during 1959 and 1960. They were accepted by all the political parties except ABAKO, which was re-formed after Kasavubu's return in May 1959. Kasavubu himself was, in fact, never charged, being sent instead to Belgium on a government-sponsored tour. By now ABAKO was demanding a separate state for the lower Congo region.

The stimulation of elections and the sudden appearance of political activity where previously there had been none, now induced a variety of tribal groupings to establish their own parties. Confusion was only aggravated by outbursts of inter-tribal conflicts, with rioting in Stanleyville, tribal fighting in Kasai and civil disobedience campaigns in Bas-Congo.

By the end of the year Kasavubu took the initiative in trying to bring some of the groups and parties together in order to avoid complete disintegration. He secured the support of Antoine Gizenga and his Parti Solidaire Africain, Albert Kalonji's Kasai faction of the MNC and other groups now supporting a federal structure. Kasavubu led this association to the round-table conference in Brussels in July 1960.

The conference was attended by representatives from fourteen Congolese parties, by delegates from traditional chiefs, by members of the Belgian government and by representatives of the socialist party. A decision on independence was soon reached, but it then became clear that the central issue was what form the independence constitution should take. Kasavubu and his supporters were now demanding a federal state, representative of provincial and tribal groupings, whilst the MNC and Gizenga demanded a centralised system. This latter structure was eventually adopted, after Kasavubu had withdrawn from the conference, the constitution providing for a central bicameral legislature and provincial governments and assemblies with powers restricted to local affairs. This constitution was promulgated by the *loi fondemental* of May 1960.

It was agreed that further discussions should be held on economic affairs and the drawing up of a treaty of friendship between Belgium and the new independent Congo. The Belgian government agreed to give continued support to the Congo by supplying it with administrative, judicial, military, cultural and educational personnel, whilst leaving Belgian troops in the country, to be used only at the request of the Congo government. By these means it was hoped to bridge the yawning gulf which had now become apparent between the needs of an independent state and the existing supply of trained people. The Belgian policy of training artisans, but no professional class, and of restricting its African subjects to the lower reaches of all forms of national life, had left the country in a vacuum so far as the needs of a nation-state were concerned. There were no African army officers, no African higher civil servants, no African doctors, to mention only three categories of essential occupation in a national community. Having deliberately avoided the contemplation of any possibility of African self-government throughout the period of its colonial rule, the Belgians now ignored the fact that they had done nothing to supply the Congo with the basic needs for independent existence. Once their confidence began to break in 1957 they rushed headlong and panic-stricken into abdication of all responsibility for the consequences of their previous policy.

Nor was the transition to independent status helped by the attitude of the African leadership. Elections to the Chamber of Representatives were held in May 1960, with results which probably gave Lumumba's MNC a majority, but the affiliations of the elected members were so indeterminate that no one could really decide what the final result showed. Lumumba was first asked to form a government, but failed to secure a vote of confidence from the Chamber. Kasavubu was likewise unsuccessful because Lumumba's MNC demanded that he include their leader within the government. It was as late as June 12th, only eighteen days before independence, that a government was eventually formed, with a coalition between Kasavubu as President and Lumumba as Prime Minister.

But already in these last days before independence the shadow of future tragedy was cast across Congo politics. The ABAKO called for an autonomous government in the Bas-Congo. Moise Tshombe, who had formed a party supporting a federal constitution, the Confédération des Associations Ethniques du Katanga, CONAKAT, cabled the Belgian parliament demanding that the constitution be revised. Both these parties and others representing provincial tribal groupings were to try to proclaim secession within a few weeks of independence.

In the midst of the Force Publique mutiny and widespread violence which broke out immediately after independence on June 30th, the Congolese people, having virtually no experience of national administration or feelings of national loyalty, reverted to their only known haven of security; they went back to their tribal centres, instinctively feeling that here alone would they find protection against the incomprehensible forces of violence which had been unleashed amongst them. The complete failure of the Belgian colonial principles could hardly have been more brutally exposed.

The Belgians themselves recognised the failure of their policy in the Congo and learnt something from this lesson when they came to deal with the neighbouring territory of Ruanda-Urundi. This United Nations Trust Territory benefited, as other trust territories had done, from UN supervision. The Belgians were anxious to show themselves as progressive colonial administrators to the outside world. They had believed for long that they were doing so in their distinctive policy in the Congo. In Ruanda-Urundi, however, they had to answer to the UN Trusteeship Council, which regularly sent visiting missions to report on their administration.

The territory was small, over-populated and very poor. It was, in fact, a burden on the Belgian economy. It remained largely feudal under the rule of two kings, each known as a Mwami. The people remained almost entirely agriculturalist, the only important export being coffee, most of which was sent to America.

Despite this economic and social backwardness, Ruanda was used by the Belgians for pilot schemes in constitutional development, later to be applied to the Congo. Indeed, the fact that elections were allowed earlier in Ruanda-Urundi than in the Congo itself produced resentment in the latter territory and helped to provoke political activity there. In 1956, the year before any elections were held in the Congo, the Belgians experimented with elections for various advisory councils in Usumbura, the only considerable urban area in Ruanda-Urundi, and in the rural districts. Up to this time Belgian administrators had governed the country by the indirect method, almost entirely through the power of the two kings and their chiefs. Despite this, as soon as ingenious electoral methods were introduced for the largely illiterate population, considerable political interest was shown.

Yet politics still very largely stemmed from tribal loyalties. Of the two tribes, the Tutsi, the traditional rulers of the country, consisted of only about twelve per cent of the total population. The Hutu formed the majority, did all the work and were treated virtually as serfs. In Ruanda there was growing tension between the two tribes, but in Urundi the wise, genial populist, Mwami Mwambutsa, who had ruled since 1915, had succeeded in bringing them both into co-operation. In the middle of 1959 the Mwami of Ruanda suddenly died, and was replaced by Kigeri V, chosen by the tribesmen themselves. Kigeri was much less popular than his predecessor, who had been making some efforts to raise the standards of the Hutu people. His election was followed by serious tribal warfare which led the Belgians to fly in troops. Sacking and burning of Tutsi villages continued and many Tutsi were killed, injured or fled into Uganda. A demand for the deposition of the new Mwami became widespread throughout Ruanda.

Meanwhile, in 1960, a visiting mission from the UN recommended that elections be held the following year with independence following shortly afterward. Having learnt their lesson in the Congo, the Belgians now greatly accelerated the training of Africans to take administrative charge of their country. They also took the precaution of granting internal self-government six months before independence was due.

Yet, despite the persuasions of the UN and the Belgians and the obvious economic interests involved, the two sections of the Trust Territory decided to become separately independent. There was some hope that re-unification with Tanganyika would follow independence, for the whole of this area had been united as German East Africa up to the time of the first world war. These hopes were not fulfilled.

In Ruanda the Hutu rising had been successful in gaining control of the country and Mwami Kigeri fled from the country. When independence came, therefore, the Belgians handed over power to a renamed Rwanda with a republican régime under President Kayibanda, an austere leader who eschewed the ostentation found in other parts of independent Africa, insisting on an austerity régime for members of the government as well as for the people. He was supported by the Parmehutu party, which won the elections and firmly established Hutu domination.

In neighbouring Burundi – the name taken on independence – the Mwami's régime was maintained with the support of the Uprona party, led by the Mwami's own son, Prince Louis, until his assassination in 1961.

Independence was thus achieved by the two territories by 1962 with far less disturbance than in the neighbouring Congo. The Belgians remained in the territories as technicians, administrators, military and police advisers after independence. Although both countries suffered from budget deficits and declining production, particularly of coffee, the fears entertained of a repetition of the Congo tragedy proved unjustified. Nevertheless, grimmer economic prospects and the fact that about 100,000 Tutsi refugees were living in the surrounding countries left danger signals for future peace.

During the nineteen-fifties and early sixties profound and radical changes took place in the constitutional life of French and Belgian central Africa. In many cases these political changes vitally affected the life of the ordinary inhabitants, if only by bringing violence and disorder into their communities. Nevertheless, it was in British central Africa that the most significant conflict occurred, for here, between the bastion of white autocracy south of the Limpopo and the ever-widening black rule north and west of the Great Lakes, the two contending nationalisms of Africa came to grips. On the outcome of the battle between white oligarchies and black nationalism depended far more than the character of government in the two Rhodesias and Nyasaland. The real issue in this conflict was whether those countries where white settler communities had been founded during the twentieth century were to participate in the new trend toward democratic, representative government in colonial Africa, or to follow the precedent of South Africa and the older dominions, where self-government was granted to the European immigrant communities. If the former alternative were accepted, it would inevitably entail a bitter racial battle, though probably mainly confined to political weapons. This choice would foredoom the eventual end of white oligarchic domination throughout Africa. If the latter alternative prevailed, the rest of the continent would see it equally as an affront to African nationalism as the maintenance of white power in South Africa and the Portuguese territories. They would never rest until it were removed, and this could probably only be accomplished by some form of violence. It would certainly become a bitter international incident of even greater danger than the Congo itself was to prove.

The first battle over the Central African Federation was opened in 1951. The war itself did not conclude until the last day of 1963. The issue thrown into the arena was produced by a conference of officials meeting in London during 1950. The moving spirit in this conference was Sir Andrew Cohen, later to become Governor of Uganda. Cohen was a leading intellectual in the Colonial Office, with deep, liberal sympathies towards Africans. Yet it became clear from his work in the conference and from the influence he exerted over ministers in the Labour Government, particularly Colonial Secretary James Griffiths, that he lacked any real understanding of the harsh facts basic to the racial struggle. Thus the federal plan which emerged from the officials' conference was no doubt designed to combine economic progress with a gradual evolution of African political power. Yet the fact was that the scheme itself provided the white community with just that opportunity it sought to fix its political control in perpetuity over the whole area of British central Africa. The strength given to the white community in comparison to that of the Africans was so great that only by waging a racial war could the Africans hope to break white settler control. This reality of the political situation in Central Africa seemed to have escaped Cohen and his colleagues.

The publication of the federal scheme proposed by the conference of officials was seized on by Sir Godfrey Huggins, Prime Minister of Southern Rhodesia, and Roy Welensky, the leading European in Northern Rhodesia, as the opportunity they had been seeking. They had by now abandoned the hope of amalgamation, recognising the virtual impossibility of persuading any British government to support it. Federation, however, provided them with most of what they sought, together with the possibility of securing British government support.

Some form of closer association between the two Rhodesias was seen by these two leaders as imperative for both the preservation of white leadership and the opportunity to develop the economic potentials of their area. They were prepared to accept the adhesion of Nyasaland in addition, for although little wealth was to be found in that small territory there was an abundance of labour, which the Southern Rhodesians especially needed. By now white immigrants were pouring into Southern Rhodesia at the rate of 16,000 a year, and, although there was considerable emigration, the white populations of both Rhodesias had tremendously increased since the war. Provision for the new white residents aggravated the economic problems of Southern Rhodesia, which now had regular budget deficits and grave problems of social resources. If the means were found to link the expanding manufacturing industries of Southern Rhodesia to the copper wealth of Northern Rhodesia, these problems could be solved and a rosy economic future visualised. Huggins, in particular, recognised these possibilities, for he had been offered a large loan from the Americans for railway construction, and had seen the possibilities of large-scale electric power from the waters of the Zambezi.

In Northern Rhodesia there was not the same enthusiasm amongst the white community. The highly-paid copper miners, who comprised a large and most vocal section of the European residents, had no desire to subsidise their brothers in the south. Nevertheless, both white societies agreed on one major danger to their future. In Northern Rhodesia, with the help of the British Trade Union Congress and the support of the British Labour Government, African trade unionism had begun to develop a strength greater than anywhere else in the continent. The African Mineworker Union had now about 25,000 workers, whilst teachers, railway workers and catering employees had also formed unions. During 1951, for the first time, a Trade Union Congress was held to which seven African unions affiliated. The strength of African industrial organisation provided a more direct menace to the continuation of white power than any political activities. The white communities in both Rhodesias expected a high standard of living and a social status far superior to any they could expect in Britain. The white miners on the Copper Belt were reasonably secure for the time being, for they had taken advantage of the pre-war shortage of labour and wartime conditions to secure such contractual protection as would enable them to maintain both their high wages and barriers against African dilution for the foreseeable future. Nevertheless, they knew that one of the large copper combines, the Rhodesian Selection Trust, with American capital behind it, was concerned to break down the industrial colour-bar in order to secure greater efficiency in its labour force. Although the other concern, the Anglo-American Corporation, did not share this progressive outlook, being more strongly influenced by the policy of its business in South Africa, many white miners feared that unless their political power were quickly entrenched, the security of their labour aristocracy might be threatened.

The threat was much greater in Southern Rhodesia, where although African workers were not organised in anything like the same strength, the white inhabitants 'in more diversified industries' were much more vulnerable.

This combination of economic interest and socio-political defence against the menace of African advance convinced the majority of white inhabitants in both Rhodesias that federation offered the best solution to their problems. The small European population of Nyasaland mainly associated itself with this attitude in the belief that their future would be more assured as part of a wider federal community than in isolation. There were doubters, not only amongst those Northern Rhodesians who objected to a part of their wealth being used to subsidise a federal state, but also in Southern Rhodesia, where a considerable proportion of Afrikaners from South Africa were intermingled with the mainly British immigrants. The Afrikaners, who at one time formed their own party, paradoxically named the Democratic Party, hoped that Rhodesia would follow the policy of apartheid and perhaps link herself with the Union south of the Limpopo.

Huggins and Welensky, however, confidently pursued their goal, and were usually supported by the major influences in the white community. After the publication of proposals for a federal constitution in mid-1951, the two Labour Secretaries of State, James Griffiths, the Colonial Secretary, and Patrick Gordon Walker, Commonwealth Secretary, decided to visit the territories concerned in order to gauge opinion there. Griffiths went to Nyasaland and Northern Rhodesia and Gordon Walker to Southern Rhodesia. The two men received varying impressions, Griffiths being influenced by the weight of African opposition to Federation, whilst Gordon Walker broadly accepted the view that it would bring important economic benefits. It was decided that a conference should be held at Victoria Falls, with the three territories and the British Government represented, to discuss the whole question of federation. The conference itself was inconclusive, because the handful of African delegates were opposed to the scheme, and the British ministers were non-committal. Immediately afterwards, however, in October 1951, a British general election saw the defeat of the Labour government and the return of Winston Churchill to office. Churchill's Colonial Secretary, Oliver Lyttelton, was a fervent supporter of the federal idea, and immediately took a more positive line than his predecessors. He pressed on with discussions and conferences, eventually producing a federal constitution, debated in the British parliament in the spring and summer of 1953.

In the meantime, African opposition to federation had grown. The two National Congresses in Northern Rhodesia and Nyasaland mobilised opinion against it, and although their resources were scanty, they found a great deal of support amongst the chiefs, particularly in Nyasaland. Delegations of protest were sent to Britain, where they were particularly well received in Scotland, for the Scottish Church had a long paternal interest in Nyasaland's affairs. Perhaps more seriously menacing the position of white domination was the growing proof that African trade unionists could organise in a manner which would often have been envied in other parts of the world. This became clearly apparent in October 1952, when the African Mineworkers Union in the Copper Belt led 37,000 African workers in a strike for a wage increase. The discipline shown by the Africans over a three-week period of strike, and the fact that they unanimously returned to work as soon as the Union declared it had succeeded in securing arbitration, was the surest demonstration of a new discipline established by African leaders. The following year violence broke out in Nyasaland, in which a number of Africans were killed, but at this stage it was the industrial organisation of Africans rather than their political activities which was most seriously challenging white supremacy.

At the beginning of 1953 the final federal conference was held in London. Its members were all white, and included representatives from the British government and the three constituent territories. No Africans could be prevailed upon to attend from Northern Rhodesia and Nyasaland, and none were invited from Southern Rhodesia.

The federal constitution provided for an Assembly of thirty-five members, twenty-six of whom were to be elected, and nine to represent African interests. Of the twenty-six elected members fourteen were allocated to Southern Rhodesia, eight to Northern Rhodesia and four to Nyasaland. There were to be three members representing the interests of Africans from each territory, two chosen by each of the Representative Councils and one nominated European in the northern territories, two Africans and one European elected in Southern Rhodesia. There would thus be twenty-nine Europeans and six Africans in the new Assembly, though two of the Africans, those elected in Southern Rhodesia, would represent more European than African electors. As a protection against discrimination, an African Affairs Board was to be set up, with six members, nominated by the Governor of each territory, to examine legislation and report on it to the British Government if it was considered to discriminate on racial grounds. The franchise for the elections was in the first place to be the same as for the territorial elections in the two Rhodesias, and as there had been no elections in Nyasaland, a new franchise was designed there, heavily weighted in favour of the Europeans. In fact, although at this time the total population of the three territories consisted roughly of 200,000 Europeans and 6,000,000 Africans, no one could doubt that legislative control of the new federation was almost entirely in the hands of the white community.

In April 1953 the Southern Rhodesian electorate was asked to approve the constitution by referendum. At this time the Southern Rhodesian electorate of roughly 50,000 included fewer than 500 Africans. Despite some opposition from the Afrikaner section of the white community and those frightened that federation might eventually bring Africanisation, the constitution was approved by an almost 2 to 1 majority.

The scene now moved to Westminster. By this time the Labour Party, although responsible for producing the original scheme, had recognised the violent opposition of the African population to it. Despite the use of the term 'partnership' to describe the principle on which race relations in the new Federation were supposed to be based, the Africans had clearly demonstrated that they considered the new scheme to be a blatant imposition of white-settler rule. In particular, the Africans of the northern territories strongly objected to being placed under any kind of Southern Rhodesian control. Many of them had worked for periods in Southern Rhodesia, and knew how the hated pass laws worked in that country, how the Land Apportionment Act enforced racial segregation and what a mockery of democratic representation was provided in its electoral system. They were accustomed to various forms of social discrimination in their own countries, in the use of separate entrances in shops and post offices, for example, but saw the legislative discrimination applied in Southern Rhodesia as of a more permanent character.

So the Labour Party now condemned federation, mainly on the grounds that no constitution should be imposed on a dependent people against their will. A small section of the party, though one including prominent figures such as Gordon Walker, took a different view, based on the belief that the economic advantages of federation would be found to outweigh the original political disadvantages. What was largely neglected at Westminster was the hard political fact that once a section of a colonial community is given strong powers over the rest, it is very difficult to make changes except by revolutionary means. South Africa had taught this lesson.

The Conservative government, however, was by now completely wedded to the federal idea and after a number of debates the con- stitution was finally approved by parliament in July 1953. It came into effect in September, and in the first election for the Federal Assembly the party led by Godfrey Huggins and Roy Welensky, the Federal Party, won twenty-four of the twenty-six seats. Only one went to the party opposing federation, the Confederate Party, the other being gained by an independent.

Thus Huggins and Welensky and their supporters had eventually won the battle they had been waging since before the war. They had established a political system which gave them power to entrench the hold of the white man over capital development, labour, social relations and political authority. Behind them, they now had the support of the British government.

At this early stage of federation there were few Africans in any of the three territories with political experience or ability to organise political action. Constitutional opportunities for political activities were very scarce. In Southern Rhodesia the white community had shown its future intentions when, in 1951, it raised the voting qualifications from the possession of property to the value of £150 or an annual income of £100, to property valued at £500 or an annual income of £240. The Southern Rhodesian electoral system had been based on the old Cape principle of a non-racial franchise with property and educational qualifications. As soon as an attempt was made by the Southern Rhodesian Labour Party to organise African registration on the electoral roll, the Huggins government took fright and introduced these steep increases in qualification for the franchise. It was no secret that the reason for this move was to keep Africans off the electoral roll. Even though Huggins resigned from the premiership of Southern Rhodesia in 1953 to become fede- ral Prime Minister, and was replaced by a more liberal colleague, the missionary Garfield Todd, it was doubtful whether any less

prejudiced policy would gain support from the white electors. In
Northern Rhodesia the franchise was restricted to British subjects.
So virtually no Africans in Northern Rhodesia had the vote; as late
as 1957 only eleven Africans were on the electoral roll. The four
African seats on the Legislative Council were filled by indirect
election through the African Representative Council and the twelve
elected seats were all filled by Europeans, elected almost entirely by
the white community.

In Nyasaland there were no elections at all to the Legislative
Council before 1956. Until that date the unofficial members of the
Council were all appointed by the Governor.

So there was almost no constitutional political activity open to
the Africans. Each territory had its African Congress, although in
Southern Rhodesia it was practically moribund. In Nyasaland the
leadership still depended very heavily on the advice given by Dr
Hastings Banda, who was practising medicine in London and had
not been in the country for twenty years or so. In Northern Rhodesia, Harry Nkumbula's Congress had gained some strength from
the development of organised trade unions, although at first there
was no direct affiliation between political and industrial organisations.

All the Congresses were stimulated into activity by the federal
issue. But there was little they could do about it except make protests, send delegations to London and hold meetings. When the
African members of the first Federal Assembly were chosen, in the
northern territories by the Representative Councils and in Southern
Rhodesia by the mainly European electorate, they were largely un-
representative of the African community. Indeed, there was continual debate in African political circles as to whether the African
federal seats should be filled or the whole federal system boycotted.
In Nyasaland particularly, the Congress turned against federal
representation at an early date, strongly condemning those Africans,
like Manoah Chirwa, who consented to fill the federal seats.

The first few years in the life of the Federation saw a variety of
often contrary influences at work. The Federation itself satisfied
none of its inhabitants. The European political leaders constantly
grumbled that the preservation of protectorate status for the two
northern territories raised a barrier against the achievement of complete independence. A number of their white opponents, like
G. F. M. van Eeden and John Gaunt from Northern Rhodesia, never

accepted federation, believing that it would undermine white control; some of them began to propose the alternative of partition between black and white states. The Africans were convinced that federation had been imposed on them by the British government in order to perpetuate white rule. The two northern territories continued to fear the encroachment of Southern Rhodesian practices, and always suspected that the expansion of economic life which followed federation was directed for the benefit of Southern Rhodesian industry at the expense of the less developed economies of Northern Rhodesia and Nyasaland. These suspicions were only heightened when the Kariba hydro-electric scheme, based on the Southern Rhodesian side of the Zambezi, was given preference over the Kafue scheme in Northern Rhodesia.

Meanwhile, in each of the territories conflict increased over the social aspects of race relations. Although officially racial partnership was the declared policy of the federation, few white inhabitants in any of the territories were prepared to accept that partnership implied equality. In Southern Rhodesia many Europeans watched the establishment of the multi-racial University College in Salisbury with grave suspicions. Any suggestion that the Land Apportionment Act, on which social segregation was based, might be modified, aroused strong racial passions, and in 1958 the Prime Minister, Garfield Todd, was removed because of his suspected liberalism being replaced by Sir Edgar Whitehead.

In Northern Rhodesia the African Congress took action against the social colour bar, whilst the mine workers waged a battle against industrial discrimination. Congress organised boycotts of shops and beer halls, even attempting to break segregation in the Dutch Reformed Church. As a result of their efforts, Harry Nkumbula, the Congress President, and Kenneth Kaunda, its General Secretary, found themselves in prison. The mine workers had the sympathy of the copper companies – particularly of the Rhodesian Selection Trust – in trying to break down the industrial colour bar, shown by providing for Africans to be trained for skilled jobs. They also secured the support of the Mineworkers' International, whose representative, the Labour MP, Ronald Williams, gave them invaluable guidance. It was the white Mineworkers' Union which formed the chief stumbling block, and it took several years after federation before the white miners could be persuaded to allow even a few skilled jobs to be broken down so that Africans could participate in them.

In Nyasaland, Congress opposition to federation continued unabated, concentrating all the time on the demand for withdrawal and a return to British rule. At the same time the Nyasas were mounting a campaign for elected African representation in their own Legislative Council.

The first constitutional changes after federation were made in Nyasaland. In 1955 a new constitution was introduced which, for the first time, provided for direct elections. Six of the twenty-two members of the Legislative Council were to be elected on a constituency basis, but the franchise was restricted to Europeans and Asians. The five African members of the Council were to be indirectly elected through the Provincial Councils. This naturally infuriated the politically-conscious Africans, who rejected the whole scheme. They demanded not full representative government but, for the time being, simply equal representation between the $2\frac{1}{2}$ million Africans and the 9,000 Europeans and Asians.

Two years later it was the turn of Southern Rhodesia. Here new franchise qualifications were introduced with two electoral rolls. The ordinary, or upper, roll required much higher qualifications for registration, although proof of a secondary education was combined with a lower monetary qualification. The special, or lower, roll provided franchise rights to those with an income of £240 a year or £120 a year combined with proof of two years' secondary education. The number of voters on the lower roll was never to be allowed to exceed one-fifth of the upper roll electorate. Here was a clear attempt to combine a superficial appearance of racial partnership with the actual maintenance of white domination. A certain number of Africans would be able to qualify as electors, but there would be no danger of the all-white Southern Rhodesian parliament losing its European character.

By this time, too, constitutional discussions had started in Northern Rhodesia, but there was to be considerable delay before they came to fruition. In the meantime, the Federation had been strengthening its control over its own affairs and creating a new electoral system designed to protect still further the domination of the white community.

First, in April 1957, Sir Roy Welensky, who had succeeded Sir

Godfrey Huggins, now Lord Malvern, as federal Prime Minister, held a conference with the British in which a convention was agreed by which the British government promised not to legislate for the Federation except at its request. Federal ministers were thus given the assurance that they could conduct their affairs without the threat of interference from London. In the same year, too, a new constitution for the Federation was proposed, on the same general principles as that of Southern Rhodesia. There were to be two electoral rolls, a higher and a lower, on the Southern Rhodesian model. The Federal Assembly was also to be increased from thirty-five to fifty-nine, forty-four of its members to be elected from the general, or upper, roll, twenty-four from Southern Rhodesia, fourteen from Northern Rhodesia and six from Nyasaland. These were, in practice, all European members. The four specially elected African members from the northern territories were to be retained, along with the three European members representing African interests. In addition, eight new African members were to be added, four from Southern Rhodesia and two from each of the northern territories. These new African members would be elected by the two electoral rolls combined, thus giving a dominant influence to European voters over their election. In short, the new Federal Assembly would consist of forty-seven Europeans and twelve Africans, eight of the latter dependent on European choice.

Again the appearance of multi-racial partnership was portrayed, but the reality of European control was not only maintained but strengthened. The African Affairs Board now stepped in and suggested that this was a case in which Britain should decide whether discrimination was involved. There were passionate debates at Westminster, but the Conservative government's majority was used to override the fears of the African Affairs Board and to approve the new constitution. Elections under it, held in November 1958, were won easily by Welensky and his United Federal Party; Africans expressed their protest through a policy of boycott.

Meanwhile, after long discussions and delays, the British Government announced its constitutional proposals for Northern Rhodesia. Again, an attempt was made to provide some evidence of African progress towards political influence, but pressure from the white settlers and the Federal government was enough to ensure that white control remained virtually unimpaired. The new Legislative Council was to include twenty-two elected members. Of these twelve were to come from constituencies mainly near the railway line where Europeans were largely settled; six would be allocated to other constituencies from the rest of the country. In practice this would mean that twelve Europeans and six Africans would be elected. In addition, two Europeans were to be elected from the mainly African areas and two Africans in European districts. Again there were to be two electoral rolls, one with higher and the other with lower property, income and educational qualifications.

If this hybrid political arrangement was intended as a compromise between European and African claims, it completely failed. Both the Europeans and the Africans condemned it, the former for providing too great an African advance, and the latter as completely inadequate to their claim for democratic representation. The Africans also strongly objected to the clause that African candidates had to secure the approval of two-thirds of the chiefs in their area before they were allowed to stand. As the chiefs were appointed by the government, this was clearly a crude attempt to control African politics and prevent the political leaders from gaining parliamentary influence.

The Northern Rhodesian constitution of 1958 had a special significance. In 1960 a conference was due to review the federal constitution. The Northern Rhodesian delegation to this conference would be drawn from the new Legislative Council. It was clear from these constitutional proposals that the delegation would be dominated by Europeans supporting Sir Roy Welensky in his claim to sovereign status for the Federation. African opinion thus recognised this as its last chance to stave off white domination. They rallied to the slogan of 'one man, one vote', and prepared to mount an even more radical opposition to the new constitution. Yet differences of practical policy allied to personal antipathies led the African nationalist movement to divide at this critical point in its history. Kenneth Kaunda split away from Harry Nkumbula and, assisted by others dissatisfied with Nkumbula's leadership, formed a new party known as the Zambia National Congress. Nkumbula was prepared to fight these new, complicated elections; Kaunda declared a total boycott of them.

By this time it had become clear that the political tempo was rapidly accelerating. In July 1958 Dr Hastings Banda had returned to Nyasaland after his long sojourn abroad, had been hailed by the mass of his people as a messiah, and become president of the National Congress. His immediate tactic was to increase pressure on the British government for a new constitution allowing Africans direct election to the Legislative Council. In Southern Rhodesia the defeat of Garfield Todd and his replacement by Sir Edgar Whitehead was seen by the Africans as the end of any chance of government liberalism. In Northern Rhodesia the campaign against the new, undemocratic constitution was gathering momentum. In both Rhodesias attempts by liberal elements in the European community to bridge the racial gulf by forming multi-racial parties had little effect.

The storm broke early in 1959. In Southern Rhodesia a state of emergency was declared in February and the leaders of the African National Congress were arrested. The president, Joshua Nkomo, happened to be abroad, and escaped imprisonment by remaining in exile. The government took drastic powers to control political activity and banned the Congress. In Nyasaland riots and disturbances occurred at the same time, and a state of emergency was declared early in March. Congress was banned, federal troops sent, and more than fifty Africans lost their lives. The British government decided to appoint one of its judges, Mr Justice Devlin, to investigate the whole situation. In Northern Rhodesia, although no state of emergency was declared, there were political disturbances, accompanied by the banning of Kaunda's Zambia Congress and the rustication of its leaders to remote areas. Kaunda himself again spent some time in prison.

It was becoming clear that the whole future of the Federation was in the balance. The white leaders had believed that, once the initial opposition to the scheme died down, they would be able to persuade sufficient Africans to act as junior lieutenants and secure the acceptance of the new régime amongst enough of their followers to isolate the African politicians. It was now apparent that they had failed in this attempt and that those Africans with education or wealth on whom they had counted for support had almost entirely taken the nationalist path. The régime could therefore be maintained only by force or by a radical revision of its political basis. But the latter would clearly necessitate a federal state ultimately dominated by the superior numbers of the African inhabitants. It was doubtful whether in any of the three states there were sufficient liberal Europeans to make such an approach possible. In any case, the European political leaders were not prepared to reverse their previous policy. They therefore had to rely on force, and for the time being were supported in their attitude by the British government.

When the Devlin Commission reported on the disturbances in Nyasaland and declared that for the time being Nyasaland had become a 'police state', the British Colonial Secretary, Alan Lennox-Boyd, rejected the judgment of the Commission he had appointed himself. Even Conservative opinion was troubled, both by this apparently cynical attitude of the British Government, and by growing evidence that racial conflict in the Federation was reaching dangerous proportions.

Although the Conservatives won the general election of October 1959, they became aware during its course that many sections of British public opinion considered colonial policy to be the weakest element in Mr Macmillan's stewardship. The conflict in Cyprus, the scandal of Hola Camp in Kenya, and now the allegations made by Devlin, had begun to cause some fears for British reputation in the world. After his electoral victory, Mr Macmillan, always a pragmatist, changed both his Colonial Secretary and his colonial policy. Lennox-Boyd was replaced by Iain Macleod, and the Prime Minister himself made a tour of British Africa, during which he criticised apartheid in South Africa and referred to the 'wind of change' blowing through the African continent.

This marked a decisive moment in British policy. The succession of Macleod to the Colonial Office brought to an end the previous policy of supporting the claims of white communities in Africa at almost any cost. But Macleod's mandate extended only to Northern Rhodesia and Nyasaland. In Southern Rhodesia Sir Edgar Whitehead pursued a dualistic policy, alternating between liberal exhortations and legislating himself draconian powers to suppress African political activity. This policy was followed by riots in Salisbury in 1960 in which twelve Africans were killed, and the resignation of the federal Chief Justice as a protest against Whitehead's severest laws, the Unlawful Organisations Act and the Law and Order Maintenance Act.

In the countries where he could take executive action, Macleod soon revealed that much of Lennox-Boyd's policy was to be reversed. On April 1st Macleod released Hastings Banda from prison and he returned home in triumph to become leader of the Malawi Congress, successor to the banned National Congress. Four months later Macleod was negotiating a new constitution with Banda in London. This completely broke the deadlock which had gripped Nyasaland since federation. Although the double roll system of franchise was to be introduced here, as in the other territories, twenty of the twenty-eight members of the Legislative Council were to represent lower roll voters. Only eight were to be elected by the higher roll. As qualifications for the vote were much lower than in the other territories, it was clear that Africans would secure a substantial majority, though Europeans would still be able to have some small influence in political life. In the Executive Council five unofficial members of the Legislative Council were to hold office, bringing Africans into positions of responsibility from the start of the new régime.

Early in 1960 the British cabinet had sent a commission, including federal members, under the chairmanship of Lord Monckton, to tour the Central African territories. It was to prepare a report which would serve as the basis of discussions at the constitutional review conference, due to be held before the end of the year. In September 1960, the Monckton Commission published its report, revealing that a majority of its members considered that each constituent territory within the Federation should have the right to secede, whilst representation of Africans should be rapidly increased. In the following month the British government announced that the constitutional review conference would be held in London in December and that, simultaneously, conferences would be held to discuss constitutional changes in Southern and Northern Rhodesia.

Macleod's new initiative had completely transformed the situation in Central Africa. Although in Northern Rhodesia suspicions remained that the strong white community might persuade the British government to avoid the democratic progress offered to Nyasaland, the agreement between Macleod and Banda, followed by the Monckton Report and the expressed intention of discussing constitutional changes, demonstrated that previous policies had now been accepted as having failed.

No one could yet tell in what direction the peoples of central Africa were to advance, although it was now fairly clear that

Nyasaland would become an African-governed state. Yet what had become apparent was that the attempt made by the white political leadership of the two Rhodesias to establish permanent control in British central Africa was breaking down. They had shown themselves incapable of securing the confidence of the African peoples, and by now it was apparent to the British government that any attempt to repeat the South African form of settlement would result in the collapse of the Commonwealth, violent criticism at the United Nations and possibly armed revolt in central Africa. The real problem now facing British ministers was how to extricate themselves from a situation in which they had led central Africans to believe that they would permanently support federation, no matter what its political character.

When all the central African leaders met with British ministers in London at the end of 1960, the question of changes in the federal constitution was postponed until the affairs of the separate territories had first been settled. The conference on the Southern Rhodesian constitution was adjourned and resumed in Salisbury in February of 1961. There, with the assistance of Duncan Sandys, the Commonwealth Secretary, new constitutional proposals were made, including an increase in members of the Legislative Assembly from thirty to sixty-five, with fifteen of the seats reserved for the lower roll electors. This, in fact, meant that the Africans were to be offered fifteen seats and the Europeans fifty. As future constitutional changes would require a two-thirds majority, this arrangement left the Europeans not only with immediate political power but with control over the future. After some suggestion that Joshua Nkomo, the African nationalist leader who was present at the conference, had accepted the proposals, he and his National Democratic Party (the successor to Congress) came out strongly against them. Whitehead promised his electorate that they would be allowed to decide on the new constitution by referendum, and when this was held in July 1961 the new constitution was approved by a large majority. The Africans organised a rough-and-ready referendum of their own as part of their campaign against the new constitution, and proved that the mass of the African community followed the leadership in rejecting the proposals.

Yet it had always been in Northern Rhodesia that the fate of the Federation seemed destined to be settled. Nyasaland was certain to be governed by African leaders, for there were simply not enough European residents to challenge their power. Southern Rhodesia had such a strong European society that it seemed bound to continue in control for many years. Northern Rhodesia was the real enigma. Could the 75,000 European inhabitants, many of them entrenched in their strong copper-mining union, maintain the link with Southern Rhodesia, and so prevent the weight of African numbers breaking through to power?

The Africans of Northern Rhodesia had the strength of their own trade union organisation and a rich prize to win. With its copper wealth Northern Rhodesia could clearly stand on its own and would not present the poverty difficulties to an African administration that were certain to be faced after independence by Dr Banda in Nyasaland. The weakness of the African position was the split which had occurred in the nationalist movement, with Kaunda now leading the United National Independence Party, successor to his Zambia Congress, and Nkumbula still in rivalry as leader of the African National Congress.

Yet the two men and their parties co-operated in the constitutional conference opening in December 1960. After a number of tactical moves between the African leaders and the Northern Rhodesian section of Welensky's party, led by John Roberts, including a walk-out, it became clear also to the British government that this was the core of the federal problem. What was decided in the new Northern Rhodesian constitution would determine whether the two Rhodesias would be kept together, whatever happened to Nyasaland. It had become virtually certain by now that they could only be retained as one unit by force, so the Northern Rhodesian constitution was also destined to determine the issue of peace or war in central Africa.

Macleod could not rush his decision in the same way as his colleague Sandys had done in Salisbury. The white miners from the Copper Belt had threatened to take their guns on the streets if Africans were given power. The Africans themselves had shown their impatience by frequent disturbances, particularly in the northern provinces.

So Macleod took his time, making his proposals in two instalments. In February 1961 he announced his first constitutional suggestions, which provided for a new Legislative Council of forty-five members and six officials, the elected members to be divided equally between upper roll, lower roll and 'national' constituencies. The fifteen upper roll seats would probably go to Europeans, the same number of lower roll seats would be won by Africans, but the hope was that the national seats would force Europeans and Africans to vote together, with the possibility of either Europeans or Africans securing election.

This attempt to find a transitional method from European control to African by combining the two communities for electoral purposes did not satisfy the Africans, although they were prepared to work the system, and it infuriated the Europeans. As a result of bitter denunciation from Sir Roy Welensky, threats from the European community, and vituperation in the House of Lords from Lord Salisbury and one or two supporters of the old Conservative imperialist policy, Macleod came under extreme political pressures. In June he announced his additional proposals, somewhat amending his former suggestions. His amendments were clearly designed to appease European and Conservative pressure. Eight of the national members were to be elected now in double-member constituencies, with one member African and the other European. Moreover, candidates in all the national constituencies, except the one reserved for Asian and Coloured voters, would have to secure at least twelve and a half per cent of the votes of each race, or 400 votes from each race. The fact that there would be such a small European electorate, very few of whom would be prepared to vote for African nationalist candidates, meant that the nationalists would almost certainly be unable to win national seats. Probably the seats would remain vacant for want of any candidates capable of securing this qualification, though Europeans would have a better chance.

So the argument continued, with further disturbances in the northern areas and the Africans now beginning to lose faith in Macleod. However, Macleod himself was replaced in 1961 by Reginald Maudling, who immediately visited Northern Rhodesia and Nyasaland in order to see the situation for himself. Having assured the Nyasas that they would have the right of secession from federation, he went to Northern Rhodesia to talk to all the parties concerned.

Again the British decision was delayed. It was not until 1962 that the constitution was finally approved. Maudling had recognised some of the African objections as valid, had reduced the percentage demanded in the national constituencies from twelve and a half to ten and abolished the 400 alternative. Eventually elections were able to be held under this new constitution at the end of October 1962. As had been forecast, several of the national seats remained vacant, as the elections were void – no candidate obtaining the requisite number of votes from the other race. Again there were many manœuvres before, towards the end of the year, Kaunda and Nkumbula agreed to form a coalition government. The alternative would have been for Nkumbula to have combined with John Roberts and his white UFP candidates. Nkumbula had indeed come to an arrangement with Roberts during the elections, but realising how angry the Africans would become if they were now prevented from gaining majority control in the new government, he finally agreed to throw in his lot with Kaunda.

Meanwhile, in Southern Rhodesia, Whitehead had been continuing his 'hot-cold' policy towards the Africans. In December 1961, he had banned the National Democratic Party, only to find Nkomo forming a new party, known as the Zimbabwe African People's Union, a week later. The new party was not to live very long. By September 1962 it followed the fate of its predecessors, was outlawed and its leaders again arrested. This time Whitehead made certain by law that no succeeding party following the same policy and with the same leadership could replace it. On the other hand, the Southern Rhodesian Prime Minister had also announced his intention of repealing the Land Apportionment Act and abolishing racial discrimination wherever possible.

By the end of 1962 Whitehead's policy was proved a failure. He had tried, at one and the same time, to convince the European electors of his ability to control the ambitions of African nationalist politicians while still initiating a sufficient degree of African advance to prevent a nationalist explosion. The fact that this policy had not convinced the white electorate was shown in the Southern Rhodesian elections of December 1962, when Whitehead found himself defeated. He was beaten by a tobacco farmer, Winston Field, leader of the Rhodesian National Front, which was the successor to the Confederate Party, the Dominion Party and other right-wing opposition to Welensky and Whitehead's United Federal Party. Whitehead found himself in the curious position under the new electoral system of having won fourteen European seats, fourteen African

seats (all with tiny votes as the nationalists had boycotted the elections) and one Coloured. But Field had had an overwhelming success in the European constituencies and so obtained a majority
sufficient to enable him to form a new government. It had become
clear that politics in British Central Africa were becoming as
polarised as the various constitutions would permit.

The year 1963 was to be a year of decision for British Central
Africa. Already, in December 1962, R. A. Butler, the British minister who had taken central African affairs out of the hands of the
Commonwealth and Colonial Offices, had conceded Nyasaland the
right to secede from the Federation. This was the decisive crack in
the federal ice, inevitably leading to complete collapse. If Nyasaland
could secede, no reasonable objection could be made to extending
the same right to Northern Rhodesia. Welensky and his supporters
recognised this political logic. They had fought a bitter battle with
British ministers to maintain the principle that no right of secession
could be granted without the consent of all four Central African
governments. But the turning point had come at the time of decision over the Northern Rhodesian constitution. In 1961 Welensky
had foreseen that once Africans were admitted into the halls of
power in Northern Rhodesia, the whole existence of the Federation
would be endangered. Political momentum would be bound to
give them ever-increasing powers, eventually leading to their
demanding secession. Nyasaland might be jettisoned, but if Northern
Rhodesia set foot on the same path, the days of Federation were
numbered. Military action was contemplated in the Federation at
this crucial moment, but the British government called the bluff by
making its own military dispositions. Once this shadowy battle
was lost, Federation could only have been saved by such radical
constitutional changes as would have given Africans a major share
of power. This would have been to lose the principal raison d'être
of the federal system for the Europeans – the maintenance and extension of their privileged way of life – and was thus unthinkable to
the Welensky government. But the British government had now
learnt that the bluff of white settler military revolt could be called.
Its threat would not have the same effect again.

So Welensky could protest furiously at the 'betrayal' represented
by Britain's recognition of Nyasaland's right to decide her own
future; but he could do nothing effective to counter it. The British

government could afford to break previous pledges to him with the utmost cynicism, and with impunity.

In any case, as 1963 opened, Welensky found himself isolated, without power in any of the three constituent territories. In Southern Rhodesia, the Whitehead branch of his party had been defeated by Field's Rhodesian Front. In Northern Rhodesia, the Roberts branch could only form the opposition to the Kaunda-Nkumbula coalition. In Nyasaland, Dr Banda was in firm control. Welensky was left with his Federal government and a parliament which had gained its seats at an election boycotted by the opposition.

It was thus clear that in the two northern territories African nationalism had broken the back of resistance. It had been enormously helped by the destruction of the sacred white citadel in Kenya at the 1960 Lancaster House conference. But its own resolute tactics, together with the discipline shown in both Dr Banda's and Kenneth Kaunda's parties, had pressed home the advantage against irresolute and divided white forces fighting without sufficient defences against the prevailing African tide.

So Nyasaland achieved internal self-government in February and Dr Banda became Prime Minister. The following month Mr Butler acceded to the demand of Kenneth Kaunda, Harry Nkumbula and their supporters, that Northern Rhodesia should be granted the same right of secession as Nyasaland. This marked the end of the road for Federation. Welensky and those who sympathised with him in the British Conservative Party could again make appropriate protest noises; but they no longer had the power even to delay the Federation's demise. The Africans had been antagonised by the original federal scheme, outraged by its imposition on them and infuriated by the prospect of permanent rule by a white-dominated Federal government. They had used the opportunities offered by their relationship with Britain and shrewd political strategy to break away and build their own African states. They were fortunate that their efforts coincided with the great African independence revolution sweeping the continent. And they had won their battle.

Henceforth, all that remained was to divide up the assets, liabilities and responsibilities of the Federation, to allow Nyasaland and Northern Rhodesia to proceed to national independence, and to face the dangerous problems left in Southern Rhodesia. At a conference at Victoria Falls in June and July, agreement was reached on the dismemberment of the Federation and its death was arranged for December 31, 1963. The way was thus cleared for the now customary graduation of Nyasaland from domestic self-government to full sovereign independence, and for Northern Rhodesia to proceed along the same path a short step behind.

Nyasaland ultimately achieved independence on July 6, 1964, taking the name of Malawi. Dr Banda and his ministers then took responsibility for the tremendous task of finding an economic policy capable of providing their more than 3 million people with a modern standard of living in a land-locked country almost totally dependent on agriculture. Their Malawi Congress Party provided them with a national movement capable of mobilising a development effort right down to the village level. The Banda government was even prepared to negotiate with the Portuguese in order to facilitate access for their exports to the coast. But, in the shadows, some of Banda's young men were talking of a more radical Pan-African policy. They had fought for nationalism before the Doctor's return. They might not always follow his westernised lead.

Meanwhile, Northern Rhodesia proceeded along the same constitutional road. A new constitution enabled her to hold another election in January 1964, when Kenneth Kaunda's United National Independence Party won a clear majority, with fifty-five of the seventy-five seats. Europeans were allotted ten reserved seats in the new Assembly and UNIP fought them all with white supporters. But still the majority of Europeans, unfortunately frightened by the East African mutinies which occurred during the election, refused to back Kaunda.

The reserved seats were all won by John Roberts' National Progress Party, the old branch of Welensky's United Federal Party under a new name. This refusal to support the African majority party and co-operate in building a new national government representative of all races was an unhappy augury for political race relations after independence. Nevertheless, the fact that Europeans made no serious protest against progress towards independence under African government represented a revolution in outlook comparable with that in Kenya. There was also reason to hope that the inter-African conflict would soon disappear. Nkumbula's African National Congress won only ten seats, mainly in the southern, Tonga, province. It seemed likely that, once Northern Rhodesia became independent,

Kaunda's efforts to avoid tribal dissension would succeed in persuading the Tonga to join the nation-building effort, particularly if Nkumbula, as one of the nationalist pioneers, were found some prominent place in the new nation's life.

Kaunda thus became Prime Minister, and his government was accorded powers of internal self-government. On October 24, 1964, Northern Rhodesia became the second unit of the extinct Federation to gain independence under African government. She took the name Zambia, becoming the first state to adopt a republican system on independence. With her rich copper resources, her improving race relations, the trust built between Kaunda and the principal copper companies, and her strong trade union history, the country began her national life with better prospects than most other African states. Much leeway had to be made up in education, technical and administrative training, and development of the rural areas, where most people still lived. Yet Kaunda and his team had already recognised these needs and prepared to face them realistically. They also realised the strength which a wider international association could bring and had explored the ground for closer links with Tanganyika. In economic strength and political maturity the new Zambia seemed to have the resources to become a powerful influence in the counsels of the continent.

This left Southern Rhodesia as the sole residual problem of the Federation. Southern Rhodesians suffered from being on the border line between black Africa and apartheid. The white population was more numerous than in any part of Africa north of her frontiers, with the exception of Algeria. She had between 200,000 and 250,000 European inhabitants when the Federation died, a considerable proportion of them third and fourth generation Rhodesians. They were unlikely to accept African government as easily as the 60,000 whites of Kenya, or the 75,000 in Northern Rhodesia. Already they had dismissed two Prime Ministers, Garfield Todd and Edgar Whitehead, for proposing to make too many concessions to the Africans.

Moreover, it was the white Southern Rhodesian high standard of life which was most directly threatened by the end of Federation. One of the main objectives of Federation had been to link the copper wealth of the north to thriving industry and commerce in the south. Huge building projects in Salisbury and Bulawayo had followed the establishment of the federal link. The white community doubled and the prospects of maintaining this privileged position in business, the professions and amongst artisans seemed rosy.

When the blow fell and the Federation disappeared, with African governments succeeding in the north, many Europeans left the country, usually to settle in South Africa. Unemployment of both Europeans and Africans rose dangerously, building ceased and the props beneath white living standards seemed to be splintering. Sudden insecurity is a dangerous influence on political temperature.

Winston Field was left in a hopeless position. When the right of secession was accorded to Northern Rhodesia both he and Welensky immediately demanded that Southern Rhodesia be granted independence. They claimed that she had been internally self-governing since 1923, had shown an ability to provide good government far more clearly than the new African governments in the north, and would have become independent previously if the Federation had not been created.

But by now the British government had felt the influence of African and Asian opinion on the issue of majority rule in African states. It had been expressed within the Commonwealth and in the United Nations. It could count on American as well as communist support in an issue of this kind. Mr Butler tried to persuade the Southern Rhodesian Prime Minister that he must reform his constitution so as to allow Africans much more influence than their fifteen out of sixty-five seats represented if Britain was to be expected to give independence.

Winston Field had made an electoral promise not to alter the constitution during the life-time of that parliament. He also knew that most of his cabinet would oppose any such policy and that the majority of Europeans were equally determined to resist concessions which they saw leading directly to African government. They much preferred the government's extension of Whitehead's tough line towards the Africans – the introduction of a mandatory death sentence for throwing petrol bombs, whippings and life sentences. A section of white opinion in Southern Rhodesia favoured a unilateral declaration of independence, in defiance of the British refusal. This would have been tantamount to rebellion. It would have put a strain on the loyalty of the armed forces, have led to exclusion from the Commonwealth, with its important imperial preferences for

Rhodesian tobacco, and might have resulted in active UN inter-vention. The suggestion alarmed the business community, but, with all its dangers, it remained popular with a considerable section of the European community.

During the fifteen months following his election, Mr Field made strenuous efforts to persuade the British government to grant him independence. He even agreed to attend the Victoria Falls conference and co-operate in the dismantling of Federation, despite the fact that he had made independence a condition of his attendance. But he received little satisfaction from Britain. Indeed, after Sir Alec Douglas-Home replaced Harold Macmillan as British Prime Minister in October 1963, Conservative opinion in Britain tended to harden against the white Rhodesian case. Although previously identified with opposition to the liberal trends in his party, Sir Alec made more definite committals to majority rule as a condition of independence than his predecessor. The British government would not state its specific requirements for the grant of independence lest these be used by the Southern Rhodesian government to mobilise white support for unilateral action on 'Boston Tea Party' lines. But it certainly indicated the need to broaden the African franchise and increase the number of African seats. It was particularly anxious to ensure that the Africans had a minimum of the one-third of the total seats required to block constitutional changes.

Meanwhile, this Southern Rhodesian issue took on an ever-increasing significance amongst African states. They raised it at the UN, and those who were members of the Commonwealth took the opportunity of pressing Britain to take more decisive action to increase African rights and protect the nationalists. They were par-ticularly incensed by Field's policy of continuing to harry the nationalists, with both Joshua Nkomo and the Reverend Ndaba-ningi Sithole as the chief victims of prosecutions and detensions.

Yet both African and British pressure for increased African rights would have been strengthened if the nationalists had been more united and politically sagacious. But Nkomo was not a very skilful leader and lost much respect amongst his colleagues for his frequent absences from the country during crises. This eventually led in 1963 to a split in the nationalist camp, with a number of leading figures breaking with Nkomo to form a rival Zimbabwe African National Union under the leadership of the Reverend Ndabaningi

Sithole. After the banning of his Zimbabwe African Peoples' Union by Whitehead, Nkomo had been reluctant to form a new party which he had every reason to expect would suffer the same fate as his others. But he now created a People's Caretaker Council as a substitute. The supporters of Sithole and Nkomo began to make violent attacks on each other, especially in Harare and Highfields, the African townships in the suburbs of Salisbury. Nkomo tended to retain the support of the masses, whilst Sithole appealed more to the intellectuals. Leaders of other African states tried to heal the breach, but without any immediate success. There even seemed a danger that divisions would arise between the African states as to which to support. But certainly the split made it easier for the Rhodesian Front government to refuse all concessions. The white population could point to this inter-African violence as an indication that African government would lead to a repetition of the Congo disaster.

So Southern Rhodesia was left, along with South Africa, Angola and Mozambique, as one of the problems still to be solved after the independence revolution had captured the rest of the continent. The white community was less than a tenth the size of South Africa's European population and could not expect to hold out against African nationalism for as long. It was significant that, despite appeals from Welensky and Field, Dr Verwoerd refused to commit himself to their aid. He had no desire to extend his defensive lines and add another three million Africans to his problems. The Rhodesians were comparatively well armed with both an army and an air force. There was considerable determination to resist compromise with African nationalism, and even Winston Field was dismissed in April 1964 for lack of toughness. Yet, if anything, this made the task of his successor, Ian Smith, even more difficult. It deepened the division in white Rhodesian society between those who would sacrifice all economic prospects on the altar of racialism, and those who were prepared to compromise in order to avoid a violent confrontation. The former Prime Ministers, Garfield Todd and Sir Edgar Whitehead, along with the former Federal Chief Justice, Sir Robert Tredgold, gave public warnings against the dangers involved in a unilateral declaration of independence. There was even some talk of recalling Sir Roy Welensky to lead a united opposition, but of course this raised the difficulty of his previous illiberalism and unpopularity with the Africans. The worsening situation also dissipated further Conservative sympathy in Britain. But even if the whole quarter million whites had been united, there were simply not sufficient of them to offer a South African-type resistance. With Britain still holding ultimate constitutional authority, with the rest of Africa and international opinion against them, they would eventually have to accept African government. The real issue was whether they would compromise in time to salvage the chance of inter-racial co-operation or destroy their own future by permanently antagonising the Africans.

By the end of 1964 this crucial decision had not yet been taken. Increased support for Ian Smith among the whites was shown by two defeats for the opposition in bye-elections. In one Sir Roy Welensky, who had now taken over the opposition leadership from Whitehead was baulked in his attempt to return to parliamentary life. Smith also held an indaba of chiefs to convince the British government that responsible Africans supported his claim to independence. But, although they expressed support, everyone knew they had only heard the government case, were under government control, and were anxious to obstruct the nationalists. And only the white community was represented in the referendum which came out overwhelmingly for independence.

In 1964 Harold Wilson, the new British Prime Minister, publicly warned Southern Rhodesians that a unilateral declaration of independence would amount to rebellion and lead to expulsion from the Commonwealth with all its economic consequences. He was supported in Washington and the Commonwealth capitals. Smith was now in a desperate situation. If he backed down he would suffer the fate of Field; if he pressed on he would find himself alone with South Africa and Portugal.

So the choice was still undecided. Were white Southern Rhodesians to try to build a non-racial society in harmony with Zambia and Malawi; or would they gamble on alliances with South Africa and Portugal, becoming the bulwark against the southward tide of African nationalism?

11

Conflict and Decision in the East

East Africa during the nineteen-fifties and early sixties was the scene of a conflict with decisive significance to the whole continent. The battle was fought mainly in Kenya and Tanganyika, though it had echoes throughout British East Africa. The issue was simply whether the Africans could achieve political power in countries where considerable European communities had settled. A subsidiary question involved was whether, in the event of Africans gaining power, Europeans would still be able to live securely on their farms or in the towns they had built. Could they make the profound psychological adjustment needed to live under African governments?

The outcome of this conflict was to influence attitudes and events far beyond east Africa itself. The struggle had not only a practical importance in determining the constitutional future of Kenya, Tanganyika and Uganda. It had an equally profound symbolic significance. From the time of the first world war, both in multi-racial Africa and in Britain, Kenya was considered the keystone to the white settler position. Southern Rhodesia was virtually run by its white community, who had the special power of conquerors. No one envisaged their authority being seriously challenged in the foreseeable future. Northern Rhodesia remained wild and undeveloped, except for the Copper Belt, which was governed by expatriate companies. Even Tanganyika, being an ex-German colony, now partially under United Nations authority and with only a small, nationally mixed white population, was rarely thought of as a white settler country. Uganda was even less of a test, for the Africans there had both a highly developed social structure and a considerable share in wealth, whilst few Europeans ever adopted it as their permanent home.

Kenya thus remained the focus of argument, surrounded by more passionate and contrary advocacy than any other African country.

It was not until the decisive year of 1960 that the spotlight of world attention moved to the Rhodesias, Algeria and South Africa. The fluctuations of the Kenya battle had affected developments in each of these territories; the 1960 crucial decision foreshadowed the ultimate destiny for the rest of multi-racial Africa.

A second feature of east Africa during this period was the gradually increasing communication between its constituent parts. As we remarked in Chapter VI, this particular delineation of east African territories is quite arbitrary. Certainly in the early fifties there was little relationship between them. Yet before the end of the period most of them had begun to develop some form of relations, either in friendship or hostility. In the early fifties many politically-conscious Africans feared that their European politicians had ambitions to build the same kind of federation which was then being established in central Africa. This fear was one of the principal causes for the Uganda crisis of 1953, for African politicians demanded that each of their countries be treated separately. Yet by the end of the decade African leaders were seeking means to create their own federation. There was virtually no contact between Kenya, on the one hand, and Ethiopia and the Somalilands, on the other, until the early sixties. Yet the plans for federation embraced the possibility of both Ethiopia and Somalia becoming member states while violent conflict was mounting between Somalia and her two neighbours. Although under British rule like the mainland territories, Zanzibar had little contact with either Tanganyika or Kenya, except for the link with Kenya's coastal strip, but she also came to contemplate membership of the proposed federation. Mauritius toyed with the same idea, although her relations with the rest of east Africa scarcely existed. Madagascar was the exception. Her interests tended to veer towards the French-speaking African states, but only after independence. Although after the war her representatives had mixed with African deputies in Paris, her nationalist activities developed largely independently from those of Africa. With this exception, the late fifties and early sixties saw a slowly growing sense of community amongst those states we have placed together in an east African context.

Madagascar spent most of the fifties in efforts to repair the devastating damage caused by the rebellion of 1947 and its suppression.

Whole areas were ruined and as the export crops, coffee, rice and tobacco, had never sufficed to pay for much more than half the imports, the need for external aid was greatly increased. Heavy budget deficits, restoration work and new development were financed by the French, and the island became a heavy financial burden on the metropolitan taxpayer.

The Malgaches developed one of the few genuine indigenous nationalisms in the African orbit. The 5 million inhabitants possessed their own language, culture and identity. The fact that they lived on an island gave them a geographic unity which owed nothing to imperialist decisions. Their desire to bring French rule to an end was induced, not simply by negative xenophobia, but by a positive ambition to provide their nation with the powers of sovereignty.

Thus, despite the catastrophic loss of life and the widespread devastation resulting from the rebellion, Malgache nationalism was never subdued, still less suppressed. For some years after the rebellion the French administration ensured that representatives approved by them were elected to Paris, but the *loi cadre* provided the opportunity for a reassertion of nationalism. This centred around the personality of Philibert Tsiranana, a French-educated schoolteacher and lecturer on education. Tsiranana made his name through membership of the Majunga Provincial Council, becoming a deputy in the French Chamber at the beginning of 1956. There he joined the SFIO during the period of Guy Mollet's government and, with SFIO help, formed his own socialist party in Madagascar, the Parti Social Démocrate. The *loi cadre* established a form of federal government for the island with provincial and central institutions. Tsiranana became both president of his provincial assembly in Majunga and vice-president of the federal cabinet. His party quickly gained widespread support in the countryside, though faced with considerable opposition in the towns.

Tsiranana was thus in a position to give a decisive lead on the De Gaulle referendum of 1958. He decided that the time was not yet ripe for complete independence, fearing, like the French central Africans, the dire economic consequences of any breach with France. In the two main towns, Tananarive and Tamatave, however, nationalists, socialists and communists amongst the younger intelligentsia called for a negative vote and complete independence. Tribal feelings also entered into the division between the two views, for many of those supporting separation from France belonged to the Hova tribe, the traditional rulers of Madagascar, whose reputation among non-Hovas was no better than that of the French.

Tsiranana's advice was followed by seventy-seven per cent of the voters and Madagascar became the Malgache Republic within the Community. The new republic was accorded somewhat greater powers than other Community members, being allowed its own flag and national anthem. Moreover, a Constituent Assembly drew up a presidential constitution similar to that of De Gaulle, giving the president powers to select his own ministers and dissolve the assembly. He was advised by a senate, the first one being entirely composed of Tsiranana supporters. Tsiranana himself was elected as the first president in 1959 and immediately had to use the powers accorded him in the constitution to deal with the disastrous effects of cyclones and floods which devastated his island. These tragedies only increased the Republic's economic dependence on French aid, for it was clear that the island's weak economy would take years to recover to even its previous precarious position.

Despite this reverse, Tsiranana steadily pursued his goal of sovereignty in association with the French. He was always aware that in his shadow lurked the threatened return of the three nationalist deputies exiled in France ever since the rebellion. Meanwhile, the opposition was trying to consolidate its forces by coalescing under the leadership of the popular Protestant minister, Richard Andriamanjato, Mayor of Tananarive. It had now established a party with a coherent nationalist and socialist policy, based on demands for immediate independence and industrial nationalisation. The party gained considerable popularity amongst urban workers, but they were not sufficiently numerous to provide more than a handful of municipal or parliamentary seats.

Tsiranana handled these problems with skill. He and the PSD maintained a vaguely moderate socialist programme, based mainly on the egalitarian concept. They concentrated their organisation on the rural inhabitants forming the bulk of the population, and proceeded to negotiate with the French for complete independence. Their policy was wholly successful. Independence for the Malagasy Republic was agreed for June 26, 1960, setting the pattern for the rest of French Africa. It did not involve leaving the Community, though this association quickly withered. Tsiranana felt himself sufficiently strong to grant an amnesty to the three exiles. He then showed his political skill by persuading the most famous and popular of the three, the poet Jacques Rabemananjara, to join his government. In the September elections after independence the PSD won 75 out of the 107 seats; any formidable opposition to it or to President Tsiranana would clearly be unlikely until the urban areas had developed closer to parity with the large rural population.

At first sight it might seem common sense for Madagascar's two small neighbouring islands, Réunion and Mauritius, to have associated with the development of the Malagasy Republic. All three were outside main trade routes, remote from mainland Africa's progress and apparently in economic need of association with some larger area. Yet the different racial composition of their inhabitants prevented this solution ever being seriously considered. The large French element within the population of Réunion induced continued close association with Paris. The island became an Overseas Department of the French Republic, represented within French institutions. Mauritius, on the other hand, clung to the British connection, its large Indian population remaining entirely averse to associating with either French rule in Madagascar or an independent Malagasy Republic.

Despite this aversion, French culture remained a strong influence in Mauritian society. The commonest language was a French patois, whilst Franco-Mauritians maintained powerful economic and political positions in the island. Indeed, much of the history of the fifties consisted of conflict between the Franco-Mauritian sugar planters and the urbanised Indians, with the sugar workers, usually employed for only part of the year, divided between the two camps.

Under the 1948 constitution the franchise was qualified, constituencies were multi-member, and election was by simple majority. The Mauritius Labour Party won the 1953 elections, securing thirteen of the nineteen elected seats in the Legislative Council. Unofficial members of the Council joined officials in the Executive and were associated with government departments in a pre-ministerial system.

But the Labour Party, led by Dr S. Ramgoolam, was alleged to be an Indian party and felt by many sugar planters to threaten their economic domination. The party actually had a multi-racial membership, but naturally consisted mainly of Indians, who formed the bulk of the population and the majority of manual, clerical and professional workers. Yet the allegation impressed the British Colonial Office, which attempted in 1956 to introduce a single transferable vote system of elections in multi-member constituencies on a list basis in place of the simple majority method. The object was to prevent any party securing an overall majority. The Labour Party was naturally furious and pointed out that such a system would actively encourage communal politics, with all their dangers to social peace, whilst preventing the formation of a strong government capable of dealing with the economic needs of the island.

The Labour Party won a famous victory. An independent commission supported its argument and the island was divided into forty constituencies with twelve extra members appointed to ensure adequate representation for all communities. The Labour Party demonstrated its popular support by winning twenty-three of them in the 1959 elections. Nine of its members became ministers and in 1961 provision was made for the office of Chief Minister.

Yet, despite these successes, the Labour Party and the government it formed faced formidable difficulties. Internal troubles and friction with certain trade union factions weakened its cohesion in an island community still remaining very parochially minded. Two severe cyclones within a few weeks of each other in 1960 severely damaged economic prospects. Population increase in a small island already inhabited by over half a million people threatened to retard economic and social progress. Valiant efforts were being made to diversify the economy and reduce dependence on sugar, but when the government tried to introduce birth control clinics in 1960, religious opposition overbore economic needs. Yet when Professors Mead and Titmuss of London University were asked to examine the economic and social problems of the island and suggest how higher living standards could be achieved, they both emphasised that population control was the vital factor. The choice was stark; birth control or lower living standards. The mounting numbers of unemployed and under-employed bore witness.

Yet the most profound problem for the future lay in the constitutional destiny of Mauritius. Even internal self-government was postponed because the ultimate climax of independence seemed impossible for this small island to achieve. Developments else-where, independence promises to the West Indies, Zanzibar and Malta, began to change this outlook. Yet Mauritians knew that however well their imaginative economic planning succeeded, any real prospects of economic prosperity depended on their ability to join a larger unit. They began to talk in terms of approaching the East African Federation, which had yet to be born. In the meantime, Dr Ramgoolam and his colleagues concentrated on planning economic advance in their island, hoping that new horizons would appear in the future.

One man dominated events in Tanganyika during the nineteen-fifties to a degree unparalleled in Africa outside the Gold Coast. During this decade a constitutional revolution transformed the country from almost complete British control to the threshold of independence under African government. All the early steps taken in this direction were instigated by Julius Nyerere; all the later ones were guided by him. When he began his political campaign he was almost alone; when he saw it reach fruition he had built up a cadre of experienced associates. But no one doubted that overseas confidence and internal security alike depended on the continued presence of Nyerere as the guiding influence.

The Tanganyika revolution was almost entirely political. Few noticeable changes occurred in the life of its nine million inhabitants, except that they found more black faces in the seats of administration. For a tiny proportion, of course, there were ever-widening opportunities for the prestige, power and rewards of office. But these affected few, and, in any case, were scarcer and less remunerative than elsewhere in the continent. Opportunities for education slowly increased as Africans gained wider responsibility in government, but they still affected only a very small proportion of the population.

For most Tanganyikans life remained elemental, a search for sufficient food to appease hunger. The one genuine change was a growing consciousness of African dignity, of responsibility for the local and national affairs of their own country, a dawning awareness that the white rulers were not a permanent feature of Tanganyikan society.

This profound change in outlook was almost solely due to Nyerere. There were no forces within Tanganyika capable of producing a

social or economic revolution, nor even of raising the standard of
political revolt out of economic or social discontent. There were
never more than about 400,000 wage earners in the country, most
of them in agriculture and half employed only on a temporary basis.
Trade unionism increased rapidly in the second half of the decade,
but to no more than about 80,000. The growth in working-class
organisation followed rather than preceded political activity. Moreover, it tended to create social divisions within African society, for,
though badly paid, the small wage-earning section of the community gained a much higher standard of life than the vast majority.
They therefore discovered that their organised pressure for increased wages brought them into conflict with the masses who
resisted the growth of a labour aristocracy. The few landowners
and capitalists were of different race, often expatriates, and so far
removed from the African social scene as to be remote from any
possibility of challenge. Coffee growing around Moshi on the slopes
of Kilimanjaro brought wealth to the Chagga tribe, but without
affecting more than the fringes of national social life. The sisal
plantations, on which most of the export trade depended, and the
diamond mines, were in the hands of non-Africans; as African
technical training was still in its infancy, thoughts of taking them
over were unreal, although the trade union movement cut some of
its first teeth in agitating for better conditions on them.

So the focal point of African effort was confined to political
change. A few of the more thoughtful leaders may have considered
political revolution an essential precursor to new social and economic
conditions. But anti-colonialism was the emotion which stirred the
mass of the African people and it was anti-colonialism which provided almost the sole inspiration of the nationalist movement. This
movement was founded, inspired, controlled and led by Julius
Nyerere at every stage of its progress.

Nyerere had been educated during the war at Makerere, the
University College in Uganda. His early political instincts were
demonstrated when he founded there a branch of the Tanganyika
African Association, a discussion group which began to take an
active concern in politics after the war. As a devout Catholic he
then taught in a Roman Catholic mission school in Tabora until
becoming, in 1949, the first Tanganyika African student to attend
a British university. He went to Edinburgh, where he found a

lively concern for colonial issues and African affairs in particular. After graduating three years later, he returned home to resume teaching, again in a Catholic school, outside Dar-es-Salaam. But by now he was convinced of his political mission. In Edinburgh he had fitted himself intellectually and emotionally for the task of organising and leading his people to self-reliance, with the ultimate objective of governing themselves. He immediately began to follow his teaching duties with a twelve-mile walk into Dar-es-Salaam to participate in political activities, returning the same distance for his next day at school.

As a result of this work Nyerere was soon elected President of the Tanganyika African Association, but this organisation, with its mainly intellectual tradition, did not seem to him capable of accomplishing the revolution he sought in national life. When he founded the Tanganyika African National Union on July 7, 1954, it was in order to create a mass party which would fertilise the roots of Tanganyikan society with his nationalist ideas.

For Nyerere was fundamentally a political man. He saw the poverty and often the misery of his people as evils which were his responsibility to change. He attended Labour Party conferences in Britain and learnt something of the social and economic struggle there. At the United Nations, where he appeared on behalf of his people before the Trusteeship Council, he talked with delegates about the needy two-thirds of the world's people. He used to stay in New York with a trade union leader deeply involved in American working-class conditions.

Yet, although Nyerere felt the needs of his people and set an example to other African leaders by living a notably frugal, abstemious life, he basically agreed with the Nkrumah doctrine: 'Seek ye first the political kingdom'. Nyerere was under no delusion that political independence would in itself solve any of his people's problems, save only to give them dignity. But he believed that Tanganyikans would never experience the feeling of national dynamism essential to change their social conditions until they had discarded colonial rule. So he applied himself to the task of undermining imperial authority and leading his people to battle for the right of governing themselves. Only then would he and they gain the opportunity to attack the roots of poverty.

Nyerere found that his main barrier was less imperial domination than paternalism. The British had ruled the country on the principle of indirect rule. They had given authority to the chiefs, and where chiefs were not to be found, they had appointed them. They encouraged the chiefs to develop advisory councils which might become the nucleus of local government. When Africans were introduced into national government through appointment to the Executive Council, the administration drew on the chiefs again, grooming men like the young Chief Kidaha to take leading roles. But the imperial administrators relied on co-operative traditionalists or government-appointed chiefs. They were immediately suspicious of African politicians with ambitions to undermine such co-operation through introducing political parties.

So when the new constitution, which had been recommended four years previously, was introduced in 1955, it was not Nyerere and his political colleagues who were given office. The constitution was based on a principle which was to become particularly Tanganyikan, i.e. equal representation from each of the three main races. The Governor nominated thirty members to the Legislative Council, ten Africans, ten Asians and ten Europeans, after consulting their respective communities. There they joined seventeen official members and fourteen unofficial ones, all pledged to support the government. In the Executive, also, each of the three races was represented by two unofficial members.

Nyerere and his party, TANU, naturally seized on this system as their first point of attack. They criticised the inequity of the same number of members representing 9,000,000 Africans, 100,000 Asians and 20,000 Europeans respectively. They also took up the criticisms of the UN Visiting Mission, which had vainly urged the British administration to declare that Tanganyika was an African country and would eventually be ruled by a primarily African government. It was some measure of Nyerere's moderate ambitions, as well as an indication that even he did not fully comprehend the forces he had set in motion, that his own demand to the UN in March 1955 was merely for a guarantee of independence in twenty to twenty-five years.

But Nyerere and TANU were already under fire from the government. The party had spread extensively throughout the remote countryside in this huge country, with its scanty communications. Inevitably, members and officials of branches were difficult to control from the central executive and, predictably, some of them behaved irresponsibly. The government, and certain journalists, blamed TANU and Nyerere, suggesting that the imperial mystical slogan, 'law and order', was threatened. Nyerere was described as 'a dangerous agitator' and certain TANU branches were proscribed.

Perhaps Governor Twining and some of his administrators were secretly pleased with the responsible progress which Nyerere was making with his party. Nevertheless, they had committed themselves to a multi-racial political balance which TANU was determined to upset. The strategy designed by Twining was to attempt an evolutionary process which would gradually accustom Europeans and Asians to African representation without provoking the racial hostilities witnessed in neighbouring Kenya and Central Africa. But the unreal conception of the evolutionary pace may be judged from the outraged protests made against Nyerere's declared ambition for independence in a quarter of a century.

Meanwhile, in 1956, some of the administrators encouraged the formation of a rival party, the United Tanganyika Party, with a multi-racial membership, emphasising respect for established government and partnership between the separate racial communities. At one time the UTP claimed 10,000 members, two-thirds of them Africans; TANU was soon in the hundred thousands, all of its members African.

At this stage it was considered by some people inside and outside Tanganyika that the multi-racial character of the UTP gave it an advantage over TANU. Nyerere himself believed in the non-racial approach and assured the Trusteeship Council in 1957 that his party was about to open its doors to non-Africans. But he encountered such opposition from within TANU that he had to postpone the move. The fact was that Africans had been treated as inferior for so long, that, for the time being, they had to cling to the security of exclusiveness. Only when they had convinced themselves that equality as individuals and communal superiority from their numbers had been secured could they contemplate genuine non-racialism.

But the UTP proved no more than an insignificant incident in Tanganyikan history. Despite the restrictions and disabilities placed on Nyerere and his colleagues, TANU quickly became the party of the people to an extent rarely witnessed in Africa. From the start it worked closely with the trade unions and co-operatives, the only other organised groups in the nation. There were simply not enough Europeans to resist the surging force of nationalism it brought to town, village and hut. Apart from the administrators, a nomadic section of the community, only a few thousand Europeans had made their homes in the country. Some of the richest Asians backed the UTP for a time, but the Asian intelligentsia quickly recognised political realities and gave valuable support to TANU leaders.

The pretence of multi-racialism continued throughout 1957, during which the Governor nominated Nyerere and the trade unionist, Rashidi Kawawa, to the Legislative Council in an effort to secure nationalist co-operation. But by now political momentum had carried the party into a demand for immediate universal suffrage with parity between Africans and non-Africans in the Legislative Council. The goal of independence had been advanced to 1969. Finding these conciliatory proposals rejected, Nyerere resigned from the Council. But when the government accepted alternative constitutional proposals, made by a committee presided over by Professor Mackenzie of Manchester University, Nyerere again showed his co-operative spirit by persuading his colleagues to operate them whilst still retaining the right of criticism. Mackenzie was still trying to devise methods which would lead voters from each race to think of people from the other communities as members of the same nation. So he proposed that the country be divided into ten constituencies, each to elect three members, an African, an Asian and a European, with every voter compelled to vote for three different racial candidates. TANU strongly objected to the compulsory three votes, but Nyerere persuaded his colleagues to operate this tripartite system rather than boycott the elections.

This was the decisive moment in Tanganyika's political history. A boycott decision would have led inevitably to a breach between TANU and the government, which would have resulted in the kind of political conflict experienced in the Rhodesias. The example of peaceful negotiation set by Tanganyika to the rest of British East Africa would then never have been possible. It was a measure of Nyerere's courage and intelligence that he saw how to use his strength constitutionally in order to attain a position from which further pressure would be irresistible. For when the elections were held, the first half in 1958 and the second in 1959, TANU virtually swept the board. Once his party had thus proved that it genuinely represented the mass of the people, no British government could deny it a more democratic system of representation.

Just before that moment arrived, another influential change occurred. In mid-1958 Sir Edward Twining was succeeded as governor by Sir Richard Turnbull. Twining had laid the foundations of inter-racial communication. The three races had learnt to speak to each other in reasonable terms under his guidance, but he never saw beyond the multi-racial system. Perhaps he was encouraged in this myopia by his Colonial Secretary, Alan Lennox-Boyd. For the Colonial Secretary steadfastly retained the conviction that each racial community should share in political power, not by virtue of their skins, for he was never colour prejudiced, but by reason of their status; he was an aristocrat.

Turnbull started with a serious disadvantage. He had been personally responsible for many of the measures taken against the Mau Mau movement in neighbouring Kenya. Yet he overcame the suspicions inevitably felt by Africans in Tanganyika, proving exactly the right man to take the country from Twining's multi-racialism into the era of non-racialism. His one weakness, no doubt derived from his Kenya experience, was extreme sensitivity towards security dangers. Consequently, TANU's organisation still suffered some interference when branch activity seemed to be undermining local authority. But Turnbull never allowed his fears to divert him from the conviction that African responsibilities must be quickly increased, that Tanganyika was destined to be ruled by Africans within his term of office.

Both the governor and the country were fortunate that in the year after his arrival a change took place also in the British Colonial Office. The succession of Iain Macleod to Lennox-Boyd after the 1959 British election removed the last barrier to democratic representation in Tanganyika. It had seemed in 1959 that progress in Tanganyika to full non-racial democracy, now accepted by all races there, might be restrained lest its example undermined the quite different multi-racial policy of Sir Roy Welensky's Federation. The 1959 Post Elections Committee under Sir Richard Rammage, for instance, was expressly forbidden to consider universal adult suffrage. Lennox-Boyd was a convinced supporter of the Welensky policy and there was even some coolness between Governor

Turnbull and his Colonial Secretary over this issue. Macleod's accession to the Colonial Office removed this obstacle.

Turnbull's first, and most profoundly important step, was to gain the confidence of Nyerere. The latter made a striking gesture to extend the hand of friendship to the new governor. At the time of his arrival, Nyerere was under a charge of sedition. All African experience pointed to the advantage of the martyrdom to be gained by going to prison. Nyerere, however, realised that his imprisonment would sour the start of Turnbull's governorship and might deny the new governor any chance to associate himself with African advance. With remarkable magnanimity, he chose to pay the fine. From that moment, the relation between Turnbull and Nyerere resembled that of Arden-Clarke and Nkrumah in the Gold Coast, with equally rewarding consequences for the country's peaceful development.

Constitutional progress from the time of Turnbull's arrival in mid-1958 to independence on December 9, 1961, was smooth and almost devoid of conflict. The elections of 1958 and 1959, under the tripartite system, showed that the UTP could not compete with TANU anywhere once a reasonable number of Africans were given the vote. They also demonstrated that the splinter African National Congress, which Zuberi Mtemvu had formed in protest against TANU's co-operation with Europeans and Asians, had gained no following in the country. It was thus obvious that, with such a widely representative national movement as TANU had become pressing for additional reforms, further constitutional advance would have to be granted quickly.

In 1959 the governor invited five elected members to join seven officials in a new Council of Ministers – an embryo cabinet. Nyerere decided that at this stage he should not become a minister himself, for he wanted to keep his hands free to continue the pressure for a more representative system, based on adult suffrage. But he agreed that three members of TANU, and an Asian and European who supported TANU, should accept ministries. He had already been promised further reforms once this system was in operation.

So the new constitution had only been in effect for just over a year when it was replaced by Tanganyika's first genuinely representative structure. This provided for a Legislative Council of seventy-one elected members and nine nominees, a Council of

Ministers in which ten of the thirteen ministers would be elected members, and reduced franchise qualifications, which would greatly expand the electorate. Of the seventy-one constituencies eleven were to be reserved for Asians and ten for Europeans, though it was significant that this arrangement was proposed by the Africans against the wishes of Asian and European spokesmen. In August 1960, new elections were held under this constitution. So strong was the hold of TANU, however, that fifty-eight of the constituencies returned unopposed the TANU or TANU-supported candidates. In the thirteen contests TANU lost only a single seat, thus controlling seventy of the seventy-one seats in the new Council. In September, Nyerere was asked by the governor to form a government and became Chief Minister. Within seven months the Colonial Secretary, Iain Macleod, was in Dar-es-Salaam for final constitutional discussions. It took only two days to agree that full internal self-government should be assumed on May 1, 1961, with the governor withdrawing from the Council of Ministers and Nyerere becoming Prime Minister, and that independence should be achieved in December of the same year. Nyerere's successive demands for independence by 1975–80, 1969 and, as late as in 1959, for it to be granted by 1964, had all been overtaken by the momentum of the nationalist forces he had unleashed and then organised.

Meanwhile, a number of domestic and international issues had arisen as Nyerere and his colleagues assumed increasing responsibilities. In late 1960 there was a clash between the TANU government and the Tanganyika Railway African Union, led by Kasanga Tumbo, and supported by other unions, over the pace of Africanisation in the public services. Throughout 1961 relations between government and unions remained uneasy, for TANU was now having to face the social and economic, as well as the political problems, of the country. With a limited national income and little chance of early growth, the ministers knew that an increase in wages to the organised workers, a small proportion of the total population with a considerably higher than average standard of life, would reduce the resources available for social welfare and economic development. The former union leader, Kawawa, now Nyerere's chief lieutenant, declared that the unions should now accept a part in nation-building, but there were inevitably difficulties involved in directing trade union activity from the central object of improving members' conditions.

Nyerere also had trouble during 1961 over the provisions of his Citizenship Bill. The opposition he had formerly encountered within TANU against his attempt to open its ranks to non-Africans was now resurrected amongst some backbenchers over the government's decision to allow resident Europeans and Asians the right of citizenship. It was only when Nyerere threatened to resign that the Bill was pushed through without amendment.

On the international scene Nyerere's impact was of a happier character. In 1960 he squarely committed his country to the idea of an East African Federation with Kenya, Uganda, Zanzibar and anyone else who wished to join. He was prepared not only to sink Tanganyikan sovereignty in the wider federal association, but even to postpone his own country's independence if it were possible to secure simultaneous independence for all east Africa. For he realised that it is much more difficult to merge national sovereignty into a federal state after it has been attained than before. Nyerere was unsuccessful in this effort, mainly because of the difficulties in Kenya; but he maintained his efforts for closer association between the emerging states of east and central Africa through the pan-nationalist organisation, the Pan-African Freedom Movement of East and Central Africa.

It was in March 1961 that Nyerere made his most dramatic appearance on the international stage. The occasion was the meeting of Commonwealth Prime Ministers in London to consider the South African application for continued membership after she had declared herself a republic. The real issue, as everyone knew, was whether the rest of the Commonwealth wished to continue the membership of a country following the apartheid policy, or whether this opportunity would be taken to exclude Dr Verwoerd's South African republic.

Nyerere was not present at the conference, for Tanganyika was not yet an independent state. Nevertheless, his intervention was decisive. He informed each of the Prime Ministers that if South Africa was allowed to remain in the Commonwealth Tanganyika would not wish to join on attaining independence. His voice tipped the balance. Opposition to South Africa became so apparent that Dr Verwoerd withdrew his application and left the Commonwealth.

Tanganyika became a sovereign state on December 9, 1961. Its constitution detailed individual rights, provided the qualifications for citizenship, entrenched the right of universal adult suffrage, laid down the duties of the High Court and Civil Service Commission, and provided for constitutional amendment by a two-thirds majority of the National Assembly. The political revolution had been completed (with the minor addition of republican status in 1962). Unity had been forged to a degree unknown in the rest of Africa. But the tough social and economic tasks lay ahead, increased rather than decreased by independence. It remained to be seen whether the political unity organised to abolish imperial rule could be maintained for an attack on the basic problems of the Tanganyikan people – appalling poverty, widespread malnutrition, debilitating diseases, ignorance and superstition; above all, lack of either national resources or even a skeleton modern economic organisation capable of giving Tanganyikans a higher way of life.

In many respects Uganda showed marked contrasts during this period to her British East African neighbours, Tanganyika and Kenya. The issues she faced and the character of her struggles bore little relation to those of other territories in east Africa, often more closely resembling conditions in the western side of the continent. Yet her geographic position, communications and membership of the East African High Commission all tied the country to the east, which resulted in her own progress being strongly influenced at times by events in neighbouring territories.

Uganda did not face the same problem of national poverty as Tanganyika, nor the white settler ambitions of Kenya, nor the struggle waged against imperial rule in both her neighbouring territories. On the contrary, her cotton and coffee, reinforced by developing mining, industry and hydro-electric power, ensured national prosperity by African standards. Moreover, the absence of white settlers, the protection of land for African use, together with the encouragement of co-operative production and marketing, ensured that much of her wealth found its way into African pockets. It is true that Asians dominated a large section of the commercial life, but equally true that they added to the economic wealth of the country and thereby assisted in providing economic opportunities for the Africans themselves.

Yet this comparative prosperity did not lead to any rapid growth of an urban proletariat. Most African producers remained peasants,

and where a demand arose for industrial labour, it was largely satisfied by immigrant workers from outside Uganda. Thus the trade
union movement grew very slowly and never played an influential
part in politics. Moreover, the intelligentsia, a considerable section
of the community with the advantage of several famous schools and
Makerere University College, found opportunities which largely
diverted them from the national political struggle. Each province
had its own traditional establishment and administration. The chiefs
were often drawn from the educated class and it seemed to many
of the younger generation that there were better prospects in working
with the traditional authorities than in bearing the standard of revolt.

So, during the nineteen-fifties, Uganda never had the strong
nationalist movement which arose in other African countries. Indeed,
its major problem was not to find the means of abolishing imperial
rule, but rather to come to terms with the modernising process
offered by colonial administrators. For often, it seemed that British
colonial policy was socially and politically in advance of the outlook
of a considerable section of the population, and particularly of those
with most influence in the country. On any objective test, Uganda
had the means to become the first independent state in British East
Africa. That she did not do so was entirely due to the brakes applied
by her traditionalist leaders when greater representation and responsibilities were offered.

From 1950 Uganda acquired her own particular form of 'parity'
in racial representation. The new Legislative Council introduced in
that year gave Africans eight seats, alongside four Europeans and
four Asians. These sixteen unofficial members, nominated from the
various provinces or by their respective communities, were balanced
by a like number of officials. Two years later the Executive Council
was reconstituted on a different basis of 'parity', with each racial
group represented by two of its unofficial members. Two years
later again, in 1954, yet another constitution was introduced, with
one more new feature. This time, whilst the balance between
African and non-African in the Legislative Council was maintained,
with fourteen Africans, seven Europeans and seven Asians, a different kind of member was created. He was to sit on a cross-bench,
to vote automatically for the government on confidence motions,
but otherwise to be free to make up his own mind. There were to be
eleven such members, six of them Africans, and together with

seventeen officials they would ensure that the government could not be defeated on a major issue by a combined vote of the unofficial members. But the main idea of their introduction was to initiate an escape from purely racial politics, whilst reducing the official element in the legislature.

The following year still further amendments were agreed. Now the Legislative Council was to be increased to sixty members and a Speaker. Of these, thirty were to be indirectly elected representative members, eighteen Africans, six Europeans and six Asians. There would also be thirteen cross-benchers, including seven Africans, nominated by the government, together with fourteen ministers and officials, and three ex-officio members. Thus the thirty representative members would again be balanced by an equal number of government supporters. The Executive Council of thirteen was to include eight officials and five unofficials, three of the latter Africans. Ten members of the Executive would become ministers. It was announced at the same time that there would be no further constitutional changes for another six years.

So, although by the mid-fifties Uganda had not acquired a modern electoral system based on constituencies and direct elections, within a short period she had progressed far on the road to African political control. Meanwhile, increasing numbers of Africans were being trained and taken into the administration. It was thus only the step to direct representation which remained to be taken for Uganda to start on the last cycle of constitutional changes leading to self-government and independence. She had not advanced as far as the Gold Coast or Nigeria, and certainly had never known as representative a system as French Africans; yet, by the mid-fifties, Africans in Uganda had been accorded far greater influence than anywhere else in British east or central Africa. If they wished to take the opportunities offered, it was now obvious that the road to self-government lay clear ahead.

Paradoxically, it appeared that they did not want to take their opportunities. Whilst the rest of British Africa was mounting its assault against imperial rule and French Africans were about to attain a considerable degree of autonomy from the *loi cadre*, most of Uganda's Africans were fixated on parochial issues. The Buganda Lukiko continually refused to nominate its members to the Protectorate Legislative Council for fear of that body becoming too powerful and too representative of Africans! Many of the leading politicians appeared more concerned to boycott Asian traders than to prepare for self-government. In place of organised political activity cultivating national consciousness, virtually all politics were concentrated for two years on missions to the exiled Kabaka of Buganda, then living on a tax-free grant of £8,000 a year in London.

Uganda was reasonably prosperous but still sunk in feudalism. The British policy of indirect rule had strengthened the already powerful hands of kings and chiefs, the prosperous Africans growing cotton or coffee were content to have their commercial activities fostered and protected by the British, the intelligentsia was absorbed into education, administration or court posts under the feudal régimes, and the peasants remained in awe of their traditional over-lords. Even the absence of white settlers, whilst improving race relations, took the cutting edge out of the political situation.

After the confusions of the 1945–50 period, the nationalist move-ment never attained either coherence or organised strength. Its main weakness remained infirmity of purpose. To gain any con-ventional nationalist ends demanded direct opposition to the traditionalists. No nationalist party was ever prepared to face the hostility which this would have provoked from the largely servile masses or the dangers of personal attacks from the traditional authorities. In 1952 Ignatio Musazi returned to the political fray by founding a Uganda National Congress, a non-racial party aiming at the achievement of self-government. But although it gained some support in the few urban areas, the opposition of all traditional authorities in Buganda successfully restricted its appeal.

Thus, in the nineteen-fifties, it was neither nationalism nor de-mands for political progress which dominated the scene in Uganda. What stirred the emotions of most people was the struggle between traditional rulers and the imperial power. Ironically, in the context of African nationalism, it was the colonial administration which was trying to develop modern centralised government and create a sense of national unity, whilst the African traditionalist leaders were continually manœuvring in centrifugal directions. In this instance it was Africans who had followed the policy of 'divide and rule'. They feared that in a centralised state under democratic methods of election they would lose their power. So they used every available tactic to frustrate the progress offered by the colonial government.

This central feature of public life in Uganda and its effects on the nationalist movement were best illustrated in the cause célèbre of the Kabaka of Buganda, an affair which dominated political life for several years. The young Kabaka, Frederick Mutesa II, educated at a British public school and Cambridge University and an honorary captain in the Grenadier Guards, came from an ancient dynasty of rulers and inherited their aristocratic pride. The Governor, Sir Andrew Cohen, appointed by a Labour Colonial Secretary, had a radical, restless personality. The two soon clashed – Cohen was impatient with the feudal practices which were obstructing progress towards representative government. The Kabaka considered himself to be king of his people, the governor no more than an official of the British government. The personality clash could hardly have been sharper and was accentuated by the physical contrast of a slim, slight, reserved African faced by the broad, tall, extroverted Englishman.

At first Cohen seemed to be succeeding, when he persuaded Mutesa to implement former promises to introduce a larger number of elected men to his own parliament, the Buganda Lukiko. But then a tiny incident started a chain reaction which was to bedevil Uganda politics for the next decade. Oliver Lyttelton, the British Colonial Secretary, made a passing reference to the possibility of an East African Federation when speaking at a London dinner. This was in mid-1953, the very moment when Central African Federation was being imposed on reluctant Africans in the Rhodesias and Nyasaland. Immediately a tremor ran through African society in the east, a fear that it was to suffer the same fate. In Uganda apprehension was particularly severe. Having escaped the racial conflict which then had Kenya gripped in the Mau Mau struggle, Uganda Africans saw federation placing them under the control of Kenya's white settlers. There was immediate revulsion against the prospect, ending cooperation between Kabaka and governor. The former made three immediate demands on the British government: transfer of Buganda from the Colonial to the Foreign Office, an undertaking that racial 'partnership' was not to be introduced into Uganda, and consent to Buganda independence separate from the rest of the protectorate.

These demands and the attacks made on British policy in the Lukiko revealed considerable confusion of thought. The fear of white domination from a federation similar to that in central Africa was natural, but Britain soon gave an undertaking that federation would never be introduced against the will of the people and this satisfied the Kabaka and his ministers. If this had been the only fear, the incident would have closed. It was not. On the one hand was the dislike of an imperial presence which endangered traditional social forms; on the other was the apprehension that developments within the Protectorate might see the end of imperial rule, but would subject traditional authorities to government by commoners. Throughout the nineteen-fifties traditionalists in Uganda and many of their associates became quite neurotic from the impact of the fate of chiefs in the Gold Coast, war and liberal progress in Kenya, federation in the Rhodesias and Nyasaland, and constitutional advance in Tanganyika.

So the Kabaka adamantly refused to co-operate with Governor Cohen, thus breaking the 1900 agreement by which Kabakas were bound to co-operate with British governments. Cohen banished Mutesa from his country, exiling him to England. The shock to Uganda, and Buganda in particular, was catastrophic.

Apart from the personal shock felt by people in Uganda at the forcible removal of Mutesa (his sister dropped dead on hearing the news) its impact on the political situation was disastrous. Every political group concentrated on securing his return, normal political activity virtually ceasing for two years. Even Congress followed the common trend, for during this period everyone with political ambitions was forced to jump on the Kabaka bandwagon. Consequently practically no thought was given to the real political problems of the country, nationalism was distorted into a negative form of anti-colonialism and the prestige of the Kabaka and his feudal court became extravagantly enhanced. The result was that nationalists concentrated solely on the indignity suffered by Mutesa at the hands of the colonial power, whilst the traditional elements, who were offering the major resistance to modernisation, national unity and democracy, were given a new lease of life by their natural opponents.

The effects of this diversion of normal political activities were soon apparent. The British government was unable to gain any serious support for its effort to secure the election of a new Kabaka and began to prepare the way for Mutesa's return. It appointed

Sir Keith Hancock, the constitutionalist, to assist in drawing up a new agreement with the Baganda people. After many delays this agreement made it possible for Mutesa to return to his Kampala palace in October 1955. He was supposed now to have been transformed into a constitutional monarch without political power, but in fact was soon seen to have greater influence than ever. His return initiated a new and more virile phase of Buganda separatism, with the traditionalists, under his leadership, in almost unchallenged power.

The parties also suffered from confused political thought and objectives. Musazi and his young general secretary, Abu Mayanja, were both out of the country for some years during which Congress declined and then began to split into factions. The Progressive Party, organised by Eridadi Mulira, never appealed to more than a group of intellectuals, but its fervent adherence to the Kabaka's cause led it into a political cul-de-sac. Fear of communism then induced the Roman Catholics to form a new party which they christened the Democratic Party. They tried to attract non-Catholic adherents also and represented themselves as the spokesmen of the underprivileged. But even when Matayo Mugwanya, previously Chief Justice of Buganda, was replaced as leader by the more modern-thinking lawyer, Benedicto Kiwanuka, the party made little more appeal than any other to the Baganda. The Baganda were now wedded to their own tribalism, identifying their security after the shock of the exile with the authority of the Kabaka and his entourage.

So, instead of progressive constitutional development towards national independence, Uganda found herself in a dilemma created by her own people. The Protectorate could not advance towards nationhood without the adherence of Buganda, its most developed province and the centre of its economy. Yet the Baganda were set on a separatist path, despite the assurances of 1955, and were prepared to hinder constitutional advance in order to prevent domination by modern, representative politicians.

In 1957 the announcement that a Speaker was to be appointed to the Legislative Council was made the excuse for renewed Buganda obstruction by the Lukiko. Once again the cry of separate independence was raised and when, in the following year, elections were held for the Legislative Council, Buganda again refused to fill its allotted seats. The influence of Buganda traditionalism was now being felt in other districts where traditional authorities envied the extent of the Kabaka's powers. So, although direct elections for African members were permitted for the first time, only ten of the eighteen seats were actually filled by this method. Nevertheless, where elections were held, the mass interest of the people was demonstrated by eighty per cent registration and heavy polling.

By now the Buganda attitude had begun to arouse resentment in those parts of the country where the hold of traditionalism was not so strong. Congress won four of the ten seats, but after the election anti-Buganda members formed a new party, the Uganda Peoples' Union, which drew off some support from Congress and became the majority party. Congress was further weakened shortly afterwards when most of its non-Baganda members broke away under the influence of the young radical, Milton Obote, who had learnt his politics in Kenya.

Despite continued obstruction from the Baganda, the British administration, in co-operation with non-Buganda parties and elected members, pressed on with constitutional reforms. After the elections a committee was set up under the chairmanship of the Administrative Secretary, J. V. Wild, to recommend what electoral system should be prepared for the next elections in 1961. The Lukiko refused to nominate members even to this constitutional committee. Indeed, by 1959, so overpowering had become the resistance in Buganda to development of representative government that both Musazi and Mulira joined with the traditionalists in protests against the Wild Committee. They seized on the section of the committee's terms of reference which asked for recommendations on representation for non-Africans and organised a boycott of European and Asian shops. In fact, this was a tactic to exploit African hostility to Asian economic activities for political advantage. The campaign led to a reign of terror in Buganda, resulting in the movement being banned with Musazi and Mulira rusticated to a remote district.

By now Baganda obstruction had begun to stiffen the determination of non-Baganda politicians to lead the country to independence, no matter how much criticism might be provoked from inside Buganda itself. In February 1960, non-Baganda parties coalesced under the leadership of Milton Obote as the Uganda Peoples'

Congress with independence as their objective. The Wild Committee had made its recommendations for the next elections, the majority report proposing an expanded Legislative Council, compulsory direct elections, universal suffrage on a common roll, and a Council of Ministers responsible to the legislature. July 1961 now became the independence goal. Although Iain Macleod, as Colonial Secretary, did not accept all the proposals of the majority report, he declared that progress towards internal self-government and independence would be facilitated after the elections. He also appointed a Relationship Committee to report on future relations between the provincial and central governments.

The traditionalists had now begun to realise that they were losing the battle to prevent the country from being ruled as a single unit by representative government. The Kabaka led a Baganda delegation to London to demand that elections be postponed until the future structure of the state was settled. The rulers of Ankole, Bunyoro and Toro made the same demand. Rebuffed by Macleod, the Kabaka's government ordered the Baganda to refrain from registering for the elections, whilst the Lukiko petitioned the Queen for secession and passed a resolution declaring Buganda independent from the beginning of 1961.

No one paid very much attention to this resolution, for preparations were now in full swing for the elections. It was expected that the Uganda Peoples' Congress would win the elections, for it was the only party with considerable support outside Buganda, whilst its chief rival, the Democratic Party, was handicapped by its close association with the Roman Catholic church. These expectations proved false. The DP secured twenty of the twenty-one seats in Buganda on a tiny poll, most of those qualified to vote declining to register on the instructions of the Lukiko. Together with seats gained in other parts of the country, this enabled the DP to secure forty-three members to the thirty-five of the UPC, which, however, had attracted a majority of the votes. The governor thereon formed a government after consulting with the DP leader, Benedicto Kiwanuka, who became Leader of the Legislative Council, with Obote as Opposition Leader.

It now remained to be seen whether the final constitutional stages to independence could be achieved without a confrontation with the traditionalists, particularly with the Kabaka and his medievalists. In June 1961 the Relationship Committee recommended a strong central government, with Buganda in a federal relationship and Bunyoro, Toro and Ankole in semi-federal relationship, to the centre. The new National Assembly should be elected on a common roll of universal suffrage, the Lukiko directly elected, but given the option to decide between direct and indirect election of Buganda members to the National Assembly. Kiwanuku was appointed Chief Minister – another milestone.

So the way was prepared for the next constitutional conference, held in London in September 1961. This was to lay the foundations on which an independent state could be constructed.

To the general surprise, the constitutional conference succeeded. It agreed on the general line of approach recommended by the Relationship Committee, named March 1, 1962, as the date for internal self-government and October 9, 1962, as the date for independence, with new elections held to the National Assembly in April 1962.

The key to this success was a new political tactic adopted by Milton Obote and his Congress. Realising that without support from Buganda he was unlikely to defeat Kiwanuka, and that the continued obstruction of the Baganda might well delay independence, Obote decided to do a deal with the Kabaka's supporters. This was a complete reversal of previous policy, for the UPC had grown on the support of radical forces angered by Buganda's obstruction. Nevertheless, the new tactic paid dividends. In November 1961 a new organisation called Kabaka Yekka (Kabaka Only) was formed in Buganda. An electoral alliance was arranged between the KY and the UPC in the elections for the Lukiko in February 1962, attracting all the anti-Catholic vote, assisted by suspicions of clerical interference in politics, and winning sixty-five seats to the DP's three. The new Lukiko then decided to select Buganda's members to the National Assembly itself, in effect allowing the Kabaka to choose them. Thus Kiwanuka's chance of gaining a majority by winning the Buganda seats as in 1961, disappeared. The UPC, with its strength outside Buganda, gained thirty-seven seats in the April Assembly elections to the DP's twenty-two, enabling Oboto, with the support of the Kabaka Yekka, to form a government. Internal self-government had been granted on March 1st, with Kiwanuka as first Prime Minister, an office he held for under two months before being replaced by Obote.

It was thus possible to proceed to the final pre-independence conference in July 1962 with the obstruction of Buganda already removed. The rulers of the other monarchies showed some jealousy of the special privileges accorded Buganda and Bunyoro was particularly incensed that its claim to certain areas previously incorporated in Buganda had only been referred to a future referendum. But none of these provinces had the strength to raise the dangerous barriers previously erected by the Baganda. Independence arrived peacefully on October 9, 1962, with Milton Obote as Prime Minister. The question of a future head of state after Uganda became a republic was left in abeyance, for it might well resurrect Baganda fears for their Kabaka's status.

Obote had taken his political life in his hands by making this agreement with the Baganda. His party had a radical basis, seeking to establish a welfare state and lead Uganda into association with the rest of newly independent Africa in the Pan-African movements. Much of his strength had been gained through his opposition to the very Baganda traditionalism with which he had now allied himself. In the 1962 elections it was apparent that some supporters turned away from him because of his alliance with Kabaka Yekka, although he was able to counter-balance the loss partially by offering the radicals in Buganda a new political home.

But Obote gambled shrewdly. The central Government's relationship either with Buganda or with the other monarchies was not truly federal. In effect, they were allowed to maintain their traditionalist forms and ceremonies in exchange for association in a basically unitary state. The fact that the major towns, including Kampala itself, were brought under the control of the central government, insured the centre against a repetition of earlier Baganda economic blackmail. Obote no doubt hoped that the alliance with the Baganda would enable him gradually to erode their obsession with traditionalism and attract their support for building a modern centralised state. The Baganda traditionalists, now assured that their forms were protected, doubtless expected that Obote's need of their support would enable them to retain their power. The issue of modernism versus traditionalism was not decided by the constitutional agreement nor by independence; but it could now be contested within a sovereign state insulated from the dangers of interference by external influences.

Zanzibar spent most of the fifties and early sixties both in developing representative institutions and gradually working out a relationship with the African mainland. It might be thought that these two islands, Zanzibar itself and Pemba, a single administrative unit with a population of about 300,000, would have little significance in this time of continental revolution. Yet so sensitive was the whole African area during this period that events anywhere remotely connected with the continent instantly took on an importance out of all proportion to the numbers of people involved. This was particularly true of matters concerning the contact of racial communities, and almost everything in Zanzibar touched race relations. Arabs, various types of Africans, and Asians, both Hindu and Moslem, lived side by side in a confined space. The history of this period is almost entirely concerned with the relations between these communities and the impact of political activities on them.

In the early fifties political activity scarcely existed, although the Arabs, with their long contacts with the middle east, always took some political interest. But, in general, Zanzibar slumbered, concerned only with its trade, its visiting dhows, its cloves and the dignity of its Sultan. Where political ideas began to develop they were usually closely attached to racial groups. The Indian, Moslem, Arab, Shirazi and African Associations presaged some of the racial influences which were to bedevil politics later.

It was the Arabs who made the first overt political moves. Although much less numerous than the Africans, the Arabs had a longer tradition of political discussion, were wealthier, for they owned most of the land, and usually better educated. From 1954 onwards they took their stand on a claim for common roll elections with universal franchise, a ministerial system, and an elected majority in the Legislative Council. It seemed strange that these demands should emanate from the Arabs, a permanent minority in the population, who seemed certain to be outnumbered in any such system. Yet the Arabs were intensely political, proud of their ancient heritage and resentful of British control. They believed that they could lead the country into a more representative system under the benevolent authority of their Sultan. When the British Resident refused their demands and fixed the proportions of unofficial representation in the Council at four Africans, four Arabs, three Asians and one European, the Arabs withdrew from the legislature and all other representative bodies.

In 1956, despite Arab opposition, a new constitution was introduced, providing for six elected unofficials, six appointees of the Sultan, after consultation with the racial communities, and twelve officials, with the Resident as President of the Council. Franchise was restricted to males with certain economic and educational qualifications. Three of the unofficial members were also to join the Executive.

By this time a number of political parties had begun to sprout. The Arab Association laid the foundations for the Zanzibar Nationalist Party whilst the African and Shirazi Associations fathered the Afro-Shirazi Party. In the elections the Arab origins of the ZNP told against it, whilst the British administration appeared to favour the ASP as the more moderate, less nationalistic party. The ASP won all six elected seats, and they were joined in the legislature by four Arabs and two Indians nominated by the Sultan.

During the few years immediately following the election, party politics waxed furious. If the battle had been fought over policies it might have had a politically educative effect on the population. But it was so closely related to personalities and race as to become dangerously explosive, an effect considerably aggravated by the limited area in which it was fought and the close proximity of the combatants.

The ZNP began as a sophisticated, radical, nationalist party, led by the political element amongst the Arab community. Close links grew between it and Cairo, whilst the Chinese communists also showed some interest in it. The ASP tried to organise the two African groups, drawn largely from the working class. Its organisation was always weaker than that of its rival and it initially suffered from suspicions of being supported by the British. Later these same suspicions were transferred to the ZNP. In 1959 the Zanzibar and Pemba Peoples' Party was formed by some Shirazi dissenters from the ASP and by those in Pemba who felt that the needs of their island were not receiving sufficient attention.

Thus racial, social and economic elements all formed parts of this combustible situation. It was further complicated by the intervention of the Tanganyikan national party TANU. Nyerere himself never openly interfered, but some of his leading figures took an active role and there was no doubt that TANU hoped for the success of the ASP. It may be that the party felt the pull of African solidarity against the Arabs. But whatever the attraction, TANU made a tactical error in supporting the weaker party and some of its members undoubtedly poured vituperative petrol on smouldering racial fires.

The consequence was that in the ancient, narrow streets of Zanzibar town, in the coffee houses and in the countryside, political emotions began to boil over into violence. Every semi-public occasion was turned into a political demonstration. Before long Arab shops were being boycotted on the one hand, and on the other, African squatters turned off land they had occupied for years by Arab landlords.

The full tragic effects of this mixing of racial and social tensions with politics were not seen until 1961. In that year two elections were held under a new constitution proposed by a constitutional adviser, Sir Hilary Blood. In the first election, in January, a democratic nightmare became an actuality, when in one constituency a candidate was elected by a majority of one vote, and the balance of parties depended on the adherence of that single candidate. To the expanded Legislative Council of twenty-two members the ASP won ten seats, the ZNP nine, and the ZPPP three. As the members of the latter party divided in their allegiance, two supporting the Nationalists and the other one the Afro-Shirazis, there was stalemate. An interim government was set up and new elections planned for June, with one additional constituency. The deadlock between the parties only served to inflame passions still further, with allegations of communist sympathies and religious prejudice against the ZNP, and accusations of racial propaganda against the ASP. The presence of an American rocket tracking station in the island had also become a matter of controversy, with suspicions that it was to be used for military purposes. The agitation against it certainly helped the Nationalists, but raised yet another element of contention.

The second election produced almost the same result as the first, but as the Nationalists gained one extra seat, this left the ZNP level with the ASP with ten seats each, and the ZPPP again held the balance with its three members. The Resident, anticipating a coalition between the ZNP and ZPPP, already arranged, it was said, through one of the Sultan's sons-in-law, called on Ali Muhsin, the Nationalist leader, to form a government. Muhsin revealed his political sagacity by inviting the ZPPP leader, Mohammed Shamte, to become Chief Minister, with the other ministries filled by Nationalist members. The Afro-Shirazis, after protests which reached the point of boycotting the Legislative Council, became the opposition, led now by Othman Shariff, an ex-government servant, who had replaced the former leader Abeid Karume.

Yet the election results paled into insignificance beside the appalling violence which accompanied them. All the accumulated emotions of the past years burst out during the election campaign, and sixty-eight people were killed during several days' rioting. This horrible experience in Zanzibar proved, if proof were needed, that race and politics can only be mixed in an explosive amalgam.

Yet the hostility between the two main political parties continued, now further exacerbated by the suspicion that it was the Nationalists who had begun to collaborate with the administration, whilst the ASP became much more radical in opposition. The antagonism of landowner and worker or peasant remained only just below the surface, although it was obvious from the voting figures that the ZNP was attracting considerable numbers of Africans, particularly among the urban dwellers in Zanzibar town. This continuing hostility brought further deadlock in 1962 when another constitutional conference in London attempted to prepare a constitution which would lead to self-government and independence. Although government and opposition parties reached some agreement over broadening the franchise rights and arranging constituencies, they could not agree on the conditions for internal self-government and independence. The opposition ASP demanded new elections before independence, reasonably calculating that they stood a better chance of gaining power under colonial rule than after the ZNP had gained the prestige of governing an independent state. Equally reasonably, the ZNP, having gained power, saw no reason to surrender it before the next elections were due in 1964.

So internal self-government and independence were postponed solely because the Zanzibar politicians could not reach agreement. It was not until the following year that outside events forced a decision. Once it became clear in 1963 that Kenya would gain independence within a few months, pressures for a decision in Zanzibar became irresistible. The first issue which demanded attention was the future of the coastal strip of Kenya, still under the Sultan's authority, although leased to Britain. The British Colonial Secretary, Duncan Sandys, visited the Sultan in February 1963, and by agreement the strip was handed over to Kenya in October.

The Zanzibar government, realising that Kenya's progress left them with little time, now agreed that elections should be held in July. In June internal self-government was attained, with Mohammed Shamte as first Prime Minister. In the elections of the following month the government coalition won a majority of seats, although the ASP attracted most votes. The ZNP won twelve seats, the ZPPP six and the ASP thirteen. It was clear that the organisation of the ZNP had enabled it to supplement its traditional Arab and Indian support with many African votes, whilst the conservative Shirazis of Pemba were still backing Shamte, the ex-headmaster whose quarrel with the ASP remained bitter. The ASP itself had done well in voting strength, but its large majorities in its own seats were wasted by their concentration. It still had the confidence of most trade unionists, but the division between feudal landowners and plantation workers was not entirely reflected in the rival parties. Ali Muhsin, who now became Foreign Minister, had shown himself to be the shrewdest and probably the most progressive politician in the island. The ASP, now led again by Karume, went into opposition mollified by entrenched clauses in the constitution protecting civic and political rights and strengthened by the knowledge that it represented the majority of the population.

So Zanzibar attained independent status with the Sultan as constitutional Head of State on December 10, 1963, with an apparent atmosphere of greater racial and political tolerance than for some years. The government was faced by heavy economic tasks, with clove exports depressed through Indian and Indonesian restrictions and many difficulties before diversification could succeed. It seemed likely that the future of the islands would be strongly influenced by their relations with the rest of east Africa and the outcome of the project for federation. Over this issue Zanzibaris were in two minds. They needed a continuation of the common services with east Africa and the opportunities of its wider market, but some feared domination from the strong mainland parties. Nevertheless, politically and economically, it appeared certain that an independent Zanzibar could only become viable by finding some role in the greater east African scene.

With this history of racial, social and political strife, and with scanty security forces, it was hardly surprising that the ZNP-ZPPP coalition government survived for only a few weeks after independence. A revolution in January 1964 brought the Sultanate to an end, with the Sultan himself exiled, dismissed the Shamte-Muhsin government and instituted a republic. Abeid Karume became President, with Kassim Hanga as his Prime Minister and Mohammed 'Babu' as Foreign Minister. Hanga had some Russian experience, and an American Negress wife who had sought refuge in Russia. 'Babu', formerly a prominent member of the ZNP who had resigned in June 1963 to form his own small UMMA party, also had considerable contacts with the communist world. The revolution itself was easily accomplished after a raid on a police armoury led by the curious figure, John Okello, an African from Uganda, with Mau Mau experience, who had visited Cuba and apparently been refused promotion in the Zanzibar police force. With no army to call on and resentment amongst the police over the introduction of Arabs, the Shamte government offered virtually no resistance. The revolution itself was a military rather than a political coup, Karume and his colleagues being placed in office by the revolutionaries, though it was doubtful whether power lay with the ministers or Okello. That this was possible, however, was clearly due to anti-Arab resentment, accompanied by social and economic discontent. Whatever the political sympathies of the new ministers or their relationship with 'Field-Marshal' Okello, their social and economic problems remained the same as had faced their predecessors. Even after army mutinies spread to Tanganyika, Uganda and Kenya, it still remained obvious that some form of federation in east Africa alone could begin to solve them. Although some lessons might be learnt from Russian or Chinese experience, communism, in itself, was irrelevant to African problems. It would be firmly resisted from the mainland countries which had no desire to replace capitalist with communist imperialism. Karume, Hanga and 'Babu' would depend for their future on the relations they established with Nyerere, Kenyatta and Obote, or their successors. The 1964 union with Tanganyika, as Tanzania, brought Zanzibar into the mainland context.

The focal figure of Kenya in the nineteen-fifties was Jomo Kenyatta, despite the fact that he spent most of these years in prison. Kenyatta is an intriguing personality, composed of many contrasts and con- flicts. He is rational and mystical; analytical and superstitious; westernised and tribal; intellectually introverted, yet a social extro- vert. He made the most of his personality contrasts. Because of his long European sojourn and academic distinction, he won the prestige amongst his own Kikuyu people of being an educated man, capable of holding his own in European society. At the same time, because he held close to the roots of tribal tradition, he could speak to them as one of their own community, understanding and appre- ciating the deep significance which their tribal upbringing maintained over their lives.

On his return from London, Kenyatta hoped to take an imme- diate part in the political life of Kenya. A bold and imaginative governor might have nominated him immediately to the Legisla- tive Council. Such an action in 1947 would have completely changed the future history of Kenya. Phillip Mitchell, however, was no Arden-Clarke or Richard Turnbull. He told Kenyatta to start first in local government, where in fact there was little opportunity for his energies or ideas.

The social conditions in Kenya at this time forced the choice between either decisive constitutional executive action or revolution. Unemployment, overcrowded conditions and homelessness had reached mammoth proportions in Nairobi. Several of the reserves, including the Kikuyu, were overpopulated, alongside some un- cultivated areas of the White Highlands. Overstocking and erosion were rapidly making it impossible for many African areas to support their increasing populations. When the political tensions were added to these social evils, it was clear that an explosive situation was being reached. The maintenance of extensive colour prejudice and many legal forms of racial discrimination, together with the fact that only four out of the twenty-two unofficial members of the Legisla- tive Council were Africans, representing a total population of over 5 million, inevitably provided ammunition for political agitation. The authority vested in chiefs and administrative officers enabled many of them to interfere with African political activities, banning meetings and prohibiting demonstrations, thus adding more com- bustion to the smouldering discontent.

Above all, the government was identified in many African eyes with the white settlers. It was held to be protecting their exclusive land-holdings and guarding their privileged political position, with eleven elected representatives in the Legislative Council. Thus, even when the government took remedial action, such as organising terracing and conservation to improve agriculture, African confidence was not sufficient to induce co-operation. In fact, many Africans in the countryside believed that these improvements would be followed by the seizure of their land by European farmers once it became more productive.

On the other hand, there were Europeans who saw the dangers for the future and tried to act in time to avoid them. They were few in number, drawn mainly from civil servants, technicians, educators and some businessmen in Nairobi. Their leading figure was Ernest (Verrey) Vasey, who, after being Mayor of Nairobi, became one of the unofficial members in the Legislative Council and tried to organise co-operation between the unofficial members of all races. But Vasey was the exception. He was able to secure little support and was rarely listened to by the governor or senior civil servants.

So the ground was ripe for Kenyatta's political experience when he returned to Kenya. Having been rejected by the governor, he devoted his energies to building up the political party, the Kenya African Union. He took over the presidency of KAU from James Gichuru, and, together with Peter Koinange, set about making the party a truly national organisation. This work he directed from his luxurious house at the teachers' training college in Githunguri, symbolically 'facing Mount Kenya'.

The character of Kenyatta's political activities over the next few years until 1952 is still shrouded in mystery. Various pieces of evidence are available, but they are by no means sufficient to establish a definitive picture. He certainly surrounded himself with those in KAU who had formerly been leaders of the old Kikuyu Central Association, banned during the war. He was also constantly aware of the presence of the 'Forty Group' at his elbow. This body was formed by a number of young Kikuyu belonging to the 1940 age group. In other words, they were initiated together in the year 1940. Some of them had served in the army during the war and, returning to Nairobi afterwards, became a kind of gang, organising violent crimes mixed with some element of politics. They became virtually the self-appointed violent section of the nationalist movement. It is still uncertain as to what extent the group was used by Kenyatta or how much he was pushed into actions by its pressure.

On the other hand, Kenyatta was the one individual in Kenya at this time who could speak directly and critically to his own people. He did this frequently, telling his African compatriots bluntly that they had themselves to blame for many of their difficulties. He particularly attacked corruption among African officials and dishonesty amongst African traders. He urged his people to improve their farming methods and to co-operate in measures for the conservation of the soil.

At this stage official KAU policy was no more extreme than the demands of liberals in Britain. When the Colonial Secretary visited Kenya in 1951 KAU submitted to him claims such as an increase in representation of the Legislative Council from four to twelve, elections for African members to the Council, opposition to the European objective of equal representation with all the other races combined, and equal African representation with Europeans and Asians in the Executive. It also demanded the prohibition of racial discrimination by law, greater expenditure on African education, support for trade unionism, increased agricultural education and greater opportunities for Africans in the higher grades of the civil service. It complained of the restrictions imposed on African meetings and denounced the authority accorded to administrators and chiefs. It significantly claimed that it was the use of this authority in banning legitimate political meetings which was encouraging the secret societies. The whole of this programme would have been considered unbelievably moderate ten years later.

It seems that in Kenyatta and his followers there was a profound dichotomy between western methods of political pressure and the secret organisation of violence, traditional to tribal revolution. There is every reason to suppose that if the government had accepted and encouraged the normal political activities of KAU and shown some sensitivity to some of its more constructive demands, reasonably peaceful constitutional progress would have resulted. But in the troubled circumstances of Kenya during this period, with rapidly growing African frustration, particularly among the Kikuyu, the appearance of semi-religious, semi-political bodies and vociferous pressure by the European settlers for greater political control, the government tended to see only the violent, negative character of the nationalist movement and ignore its genuine political objectives.

It was the Kikuyu who felt the racial, economic and political tensions in their severest forms. The Kikuyu lived alongside the White Highlands and around the outskirts of Nairobi. A higher proportion of Kikuyu than of any other tribe actually heard the threats of white settlers, which culminated in a demand during the visit of the Colonial Secretary that any suggestion of African nationalism of the kind that had developed in west Africa being British policy for Kenya 'should be considered as seditious'. They declared that if the British government would not give an assurance on this policy, they themselves would 'take matters into their own hands.' It was the Kikuyu too, who were generally the most advanced tribe, with more educated members and a higher degree of political consciousness. Inevitably, it was those who had approached to the frontiers of western society and then found themselves rejected, who felt discrimination most sharply. It was the Kikuyu, also, who formed the largest contingent of the unemployed, homeless and starving in the African locations of Nairobi.

From 1950, onwards, tension rapidly mounted. The words Mau Mau were heard for the first time, acts of violence increased and the administration of oaths, of which the most extreme were profoundly bestial, began to take the form of incitement to murder Europeans and chiefs collaborating with the government.

Oathing, secret societies, witchcraft and superstition are not peculiar to African society. They are known in societies throughout the world and usually appear at moments of intense social frustration and insecurity. These features of the Mau Mau movement, accompanied by violence against persons, property and cattle, certainly arose from the frustration of the Kikuyu and a few associated tribes, together with their fear of being placed, as in South Africa, under the permanent domination of an alien race.

Yet the Mau Mau movement only broke out in its most violent form after attempts had been made to avoid disaster. There was a section of KAU, led by Tom Mbotela, which was strongly opposed to violence and attempted to commit the movement against it. They failed to do so and were eventually defeated, but not before strong efforts had been made to disassociate KAU from Mau Mau.

Kenyatta himself declared Mau Mau to be a bad thing at a public meeting in February 1951. Whether he eventually connived at the subsequent organisation of violence, whether he was forced into accepting it, or whether it developed despite his opposition, may never be known.

What is certain, however, is that the circumstances of 1951 and 1952 made violence almost inevitable. Efforts were made, for example, in the Kenya Citizens' Association, which brought Europeans, Asians and Africans together, to avoid racial conflict, but the European politicians were still vociferously demanding at least the preservation of the status quo and, more usually, increased powers to govern the whole country. After the visit of Colonial Secretary James Griffiths, in May 1951, it was announced that there would be no major change in the constitution until after the election due in 1952, but that then there would be a constitutional conference. In the meantime, the first African would be appointed to the Executive Council, African membership of the Legislative Council increased from four to six, the Asians and Arabs would have one extra member and European representation rise from eleven to fourteen. For the time being, Europeans, who had feared that the Labour Government was intent on advancing African influence, were pacified, but the preservation of European parity with the other races could not be expected to appease the Africans. Even though they had their first representation inside the Executive, with the appointment of Eliud Mathu, they still saw their 5 million-strong community having to take a minor place compared with the less than 50,000 Europeans.

Moreover, in 1952, European ambitions were again voiced, accompanied by obstruction inside the Council. They were also becoming increasingly fearful of the attacks from Mau Mau, fears which were hardly stilled by the minimising of its dangers from the lips of the governor, Phillip Mitchell. Mitchell seemed to think that Mau Mau was nothing more than one of the religious cults previously seen in the colony. When he left Kenya at the end of his term of office in June 1952, the British government allowed a dangerous interim gap of three months before the next governor, Sir Evelyn Baring, arrived. During this time Europeans had begun to demand emergency powers to deal with growing violence. Meanwhile, since the constitutional disappointment, Kenyatta's speeches had become increasingly anti-European, whilst his Independent School Movement was clearly developing subversive activities throughout the Kikuyu area.

By the time that Baring arrived, tension had mounted to fever point. Early in October attacks were made on European farms and when Chief Waruhiu, one of the senior Kikuyu personalities, was assassinated only a few miles outside Nairobi, Baring decided that a state of emergency had become essential. This was declared on October 20th and the following day Kenyatta, along with ninety-eight of his followers, was arrested. British troops were flown in, marking the direct involvement of the British government in the whole Kenya issue.

For the next few years Kenya was given over to the horrors of civil war, further aggravated by the overtones of colonial military rule backed by imperial forces. This was not simply a black-white conflict. According to the official figures, during the whole course of the emergency to the beginning of 1960, 7,811 Mau Mau were killed and 844 wounded and captured. The security forces lost 470 Africans, 2 Asians and 38 Europeans killed, together with 392 Africans, 12 Asians and 62 Europeans injured. Amongst civilian casualties, 1,316 Africans, 30 Europeans and 19 Asians were killed. It is obvious from these figures that the African community, particularly the Kikuyu, suffered far more bitterly and widely than any other race. The small proportion of the wounded and captured compared with the numbers killed bears witness to the brutal nature of the war. When is added to these casualties the picture of massive round-ups of Kikuyu in Nairobi and in the rural areas, the detention of about 100,000 of them and their forcible return to the already overcrowded Kikuyu reserve, some conception can be gained of the manner in which the very foundations of this million-strong tribe were shattered during the period.

During the war, of course, the most ghastly atrocities were committed by both sides, often by neighbouring Africans on each other, no doubt taking the opportunity to pay off old scores, as in the notorious Lari massacre in 1953. The African communities in the whole country were torn between those who saw the Mau Mau forces as 'Freedom Fighters', battling for a free Kenya against a combination of colonial power, white settlers and African collaborationists, and those who believed that the Mau Mau movement was destroying any chance of political progress in Kenya. Thus Africans within the Kikuyu tribe fought on both sides, as did those most closely associated with them in the Meru, Embu and Kamba tribes. Most of the other tribes in the country remained passive, some doubtless with vague sympathies for Mau Mau, but on the whole only anxious for the war to be brought to a speedy end.

The arrest, trial and conviction of Kenyatta at Kapenguria for managing Mau Mau certainly removed the one African personality in the country who might have been capable of negotiating peace. The validity of the trial and conviction will always remain a matter of argument. The result of it was certainly to banish the only man accepted as even potentially a national leader into imprisonment in the far north of the colony during eight crucial years.

Whatever one may think of the brutalities and bestialities perpetrated during this civil-cum-colonial war, there can be no doubt that historically it increased the pace of African political advance. It is hypothetical to speculate whether constitutional progress during the nineteen-fifties would have evolved in a more healthy way towards African self-government without the violence of Mau Mau. What seems certain is that once the British Government had to find the troops and the money to combat African violence, the ambitions of the white settlers to gain the kind of political control which had been accorded to South Africans were finally destroyed. The British government now recognised that to hand over political power to the white settlers would be to provoke further outbreaks of this kind, with continuing demands on British money and military aid.

Thus, both British and settlers were forced by the revolt to reconsider their attitude towards the future government of the colony. The nineteen-fifties became a period of continuous and vociferous argument about constitutions and political powers, conducted against the dark background of war in the forests.

It was only a little over a year from the start of the emergency that discussions on constitutional change began. When it is remembered that during these bitter first few months of the war Kenyatta and most of the Kikuyu leaders had been removed, the KAU had been proscribed and Eliud Mathu, the Kikuyu member of the Executive, had been almost completely ostracised by all sides, the early re-opening of constitutional discussions is all the more remarkable. In April 1954 the Colonial Secretary, Oliver Lyttelton, made proposals for reorganising the government and the Legislative and Executive Councils. In the legislature Europeans were to retain their parity with the other races amongst the unofficial members, but a Council of Ministers was to be set up in addition to the Executive Council. In this three elected Europeans from the legislature would sit with two Asians and one African, together with the official members. The Executive Council would consist of all members of the Council of Ministers, but, in addition, one Arab and two Africans were to be included. A beginning was also to be made in introducing members of the different races to government responsibility, by giving four unofficial members in the Council of Ministers government portfolios and appointing three Africans, one Asian and one Arab from the Executive Council to be Under-Secretaries. Although the African members of the legislature were still to be appointed, a commission was to be set up to investigate the best method of choosing these members in future; the following year the Coutts Commission was established for this purpose.

The sharpest effect of these proposals was felt in the European community. There was widespread hostility to the idea of non-European ministers, particularly to the appointment of two Asians. But Michael Blundell, who had led the European demand for settler participation in the war operation, now joined the government and formed a European party, the United Country Party, for the purpose of supporting the multi-racial principle. At the same time, his party pledged itself to defend the White Highlands and the communal form of representation. In reaction to his moves, another section of Europeans established the Federal Independence Party, which proposed provincial autonomy, or a modified form of apartheid, as the solution for Kenya.

The Africans were not very interested in the appointment of their first minister. The Europeans, including Blundell, made it impossible for the governor to appoint the leading African, Eliud Mathu, because he was Kikuyu. Instead, the Ministry of Community Development, which concerned Africans alone, was given to B. A. Ohanga, a Luo. The refusal to appoint Mathu had serious effects on African confidence that the Europeans had any serious intention of sharing power with them, and was an equally serious drawback to the chances of building bridges between the Europeans and the politically-conscious Kikuyu.

By this time, there was very little coherent African political activity. Nevertheless, African organisation had not come to a complete halt. The emphasis had moved from political parties to the trade union movement. Here Tom Mboya made his first public impact as general secretary of what was first called the Kenya Federation of Registered Trade Unions and later the Kenya Federation of Labour. It was from this trade union movement that the sharpest criticism came when, for example, the Coutts report was published at the beginning of 1956, proposing the first of what came to be known as the 'fancy franchises'. The government, however, now under the direction of a new Colonial Secretary, Alan Lennox-Boyd, was determined to prevent any colony-wide African political body coming into existence. In mid-1955 Africans were again allowed to form political organisations, but these were restricted to a district basis and were excluded from the Central Province where most of the Kikuyu lived. This insistence on confining political organisations to districts, which inevitably coincided largely with tribal groupings, laid the foundations for the later division of African politics in Kenya along tribal lines.

Elections for the new legislature under the Lyttelton Constitution were held in two parts, the European and Asian in September 1956 and the African in March 1957. In the European elections Blundell and those who supported the multi-racial approach to government gained only six of the fourteen seats, the other eight being won by Group-Captain Briggs and his associates, who were opposed to the constitution. Nevertheless, after the election Briggs and Blundell came together in government and Blundell dissolved his UCP.

The African elections were held under a most complicated system, in which amongst the Kikuyu, Meru and Embu 'loyalists' alone were allowed to vote, whilst varied qualifications were needed amongst other tribes, allowing in some cases up to three votes per elector. Before the elections were held, there was considerable debate amongst Africans as to whether the election should be boycotted in protest against the basis of the Lyttelton Constitution, or whether it was better to use what constitutional means were offered to press for further reforms. Although the Africans had now been allocated eight seats in place of the original six, they all regarded this as totally inadequate representation for their massive population. They also considered that the complicated system of

voting was expressly designed to prevent genuine African representatives from being elected.

Early in 1957, an important private meeting took place between
Tom Mboya, now moving towards African political leadership,
and Aneurin Bevan, who had recently been made Labour Party
spokesman on Commonwealth Affairs at Westminster. Mboya was
inclined to adopt the policy of boycotting the elections. Bevan,
with his long experience of political life and shrewd insight into the
realities of political power, advised him that even if he were only
offered one seat in a parliamentary system he should accept it.
Bevan argued that such were the pressures within British political
life that, as soon as a community of 5 million secured any form of
elected representation alongside that of a minority community
consisting of only 50,000, British political opinion would begin to
demand fairer proportions. Mboya was impressed by this advice,
and began to adopt a policy of accepting inadequate reforms in
order to use the influence they offered for the purpose of securing
greater progress at a later date.

In the African elections two main leaders clashed with each other.
Mboya was not yet accepted by the Africans as an established
leader. He had already been challenged by the first African lawyer,
C. M. G. Argwings-Kodhek, who had first tried to form a National
Congress and then, when prevented by the government, established
the Nairobi District African Congress in 1956. Owing to a split in
this Congress, Argwings-Kodhek and Mboya fought each other
in the elections in Nairobi. Mboya won the battle and formed his
own party, the Nairobi Peoples Convention Party. The other
significant result in these elections was the defeat of Mathu in the
Central Province, largely due to the activities of the local administrators, who encouraged a high registration from the Meru tribe,
thus enabling its candidate, Bernard Mate, to be elected. This
association of the Kenya government with white settler hostility
towards Mathu, not only the first but the ablest African political
representative, revealed the myopia which had arisen from the bitter
conflict of the previous few years.

Despite all the efforts made to secure the election of African
members prepared to co-operate in this multi-racial system, each
of the successful African candidates had campaigned against the
Lyttelton Constitution. Now, under the leadership of Mboya,

they immediately demanded further increased representation in the Legislative Council and refused to accept ministerial office. Their policy made it impossible to work the constitution and again forced the onus of political decision on the British Colonial Office. Six months after the African elections, when it was clear that the constitution had broken down because of African obstruction, Colonial Secretary Lennox-Boyd had to visit Kenya, listen to the contending demands of the rival communities and shortly afterwards agree that six additional African members should be elected, bringing African representation on a par with that of the Europeans. Africans were also to have one additional minister, whilst there were to be twelve specially-elected members of the legislature, four from each race, elected by the whole Council sitting as an electoral college. Finally, a Council of State was to be set up for the purpose of preventing any discriminatory legislation being enacted.

The Africans were strongly opposed both to the Council of State and to the specially-elected members. They saw the former as too closely modelled on the African Affairs Board in the Central African Federation, whilst they recognised that in a Legislative Council electoral college the combination of European officials and unofficials would control the elections.

When the time came for these new elections, all six African members supported their colleagues in opposition to the new constitution, whilst the election of the specially-elected members exposed the shallowness of European commitment to multi-racialism. The leading proponent of the inter-racial principle, Ernest Vasey, was defeated in these elections, through the opposition of European officials and unofficials, and the effect of a boycott organised by the Africans. Shortly afterwards Vasey left Kenya to assist Julius Nyerere in neighbouring Tanganyika.

By this time, the balance of political initiative was tilting swiftly from the European to the African side. Africans now had an equal number of unofficial elected members with the Europeans in the Legislative Council, although the official element gave white members a considerable majority. In the Council of Ministers the two Africans and two Asians balanced the European unofficial members. More important than figures, however, was the fact that the Africans had shown that through their pressures they could break constitutions imposed by the Colonial Office and were determined to pursue the path of full democratic government. This meant that any hope amongst the Europeans of a white governed Kenya had disappeared, whilst it was clear that the British Colonial Office would be unable to maintain its authority against revived African nationalism for many more years. It now became European policy, as previously it had been African, to demand continued protection from Britain. Moreover, the Asians, recognising the way in which politics were tending, gave ever more positive assistance to the Africans in seeking democratic representation. Lennox-Boyd had declared that there would be no further increase in communal representation, whilst the racial proportions of communal seats were to be frozen for ten years. This was clearly an unreal outlook. The Africans had no further interest in multi-racialism now that the momentum of their political attack was succeeding. They demanded an African majority in the Legislative Council and a further constitutional conference to discuss new advances.

By this time, too, Kenyatta's name had re-entered the political arena. Although the Colonial Secretary had declared that Kenyatta and his colleagues would never be allowed back into the Kikuyu area, as the time approached for his release from prison, a number of Africans, led by the Luo, Oginga Odinga, began to make favourable public mention of Kenyatta's name. There was still considerable opposition to Kenyatta within the African community, particularly amongst those who had fought against Mau Mau. Nevertheless, once his name was being used in public, the old magic began to return and it became important for anyone with political ambitions to demand his release. By April 1959, when he had served his term of imprisonment, Kenyatta was released, but had to remain restricted to Lodwar, in the remote Northern Area.

Pressure for further constitutional talks rapidly increased, until in January 1959 the African elected members declared another boycott of the Legislative Council until some assurance that they would be held had been given. Shortly afterwards, Michael Blundell resigned as Minister of Agriculture and formed a new multi-racial group in the Legislative Council which he called the New Kenya Group. This also supported further constitutional talks and in April of 1959 Lennox-Boyd promised that there should be another conference before the next elections in 1960, adding certain conditions which he considered should be fulfilled before political power was transferred.

This new political initiative immediately precipitated divisions within both European and African political communities. Blundell was now calling for the abolition of racial barriers and the opening of the European Highlands. His European opponents, collected again behind the banner of Group-Captain Briggs, who now formed a new United Party, determined to resist any further retreat from white privilege. At the same time, another multi-racial party was formed in the legislature, named the Kenya National Party, with African and Asian members, plus one iconoclast European. This party was headed by Masinde Muliro, with backing from the less nationalistically-inclined African members. The more determined nationalists formed a rival party, the Kenya Independence Movement, with a clear objective of independence and an added demand for Kenyatta's complete release. The KIM was led by Odinga, with Mboya as its general secretary.

By October 1959, the Kenya government had been persuaded to accept the removal of racial barriers in the Highlands and in the educational system. It was able to base its recommendations on the land issue on the report of the East African Royal Commission, which had recommended in 1955 a complete reappraisal of land holding. Inevitably, this raised bitter anger among settlers, who declared that the decision broke pledges given to them by previous British governments. By this time, however, a decisive change was taking place in British political life. After the general election of October 1959, Lennox-Boyd was replaced as Colonial Secretary by Iain Macleod. Lennox-Boyd had always been a firm protagonist of the multi-racial idea. By this he had understood permanent separate representation of each racial community in legislature and government. This had never been accepted by the African political intelligentsia, who had always held that complete democracy, with guaranteed individual rights, regardless of race, formed the only genuine basis of a democratic system. This they termed 'non-racialism', as distinct from 'multi-racialism'.

Moreover, Lennox-Boyd's last months as Colonial Secretary had been marred, so far as his Kenya administration was concerned, by the Hola Camp scandal. In Hola eleven detainees had been beaten to death for refusing to obey orders and it seemed, in the debate held in the British Parliament in July 1959, that the Colonial Secretary was trying to escape from his own responsibility for these brutal murders. He was strongly denounced for this attitude by a prominent member of his own party, Enoch Powell, a former minister, who later rejoined the Macmillan government.

Macleod, however, took a radically different line on African affairs from his predecessor. By this time it was fairly clear in French, Belgian and British Africa that African nationalism based on non-racialism was in the ascendancy. Macleod wasted no time in announcing that a constitutional conference on the future of Kenya would be held in London early in 1960. This conference was to be decisive, not only for the character of future politics in Kenya, but for the destiny of all British multi-racial Africa.

The Lancaster House conference, which met for the first two months of 1960, confirmed that the balance of political initiative in Kenya had now moved to the Africans. It also showed that Kenyatta had again become an important figure in the political scene. At the very start of the conference these two features became apparent. The nationalists were now demanding that Kenyatta should be released and had asked that he attend the conference. Although this request was refused, Odinga and some of his followers immediately insisted that Kenyatta's former associate, Peter Mbiyu Koinange, be attached to the delegation as adviser. The refusal of this demand led to an African boycott of the first few days of conference meetings. The government then had to capitulate, with the result that the Africans took the initiative from the start.

The two groups of African leaders co-operated for the purpose of negotiation and elected Ronald Ngala, who had been a leading member of the Kenya National Party, as their chairman and Mboya as secretary. On the European side, Blundell led his New Kenya Group, whilst Briggs led the United Party, now fighting a last-ditch battle for the European position. The central objective of Colonial Secretary Macleod was to find the means of evolving from communal to common representation without making any substantial section of the community feel so insecure as to resort to open opposition. After several weeks' negotiation, a new constitutional plan emerged, based on Macleod's policy.

In the new constitution the Council of Ministers was to consist of four officials, four Africans, three Europeans and one Asian. Thus, both the minority communities were to lose one minister, while the Africans increased their number from two to four. The Legislative

Council was to be composed of sixty-five members. Thirty-three of these were to be elected on a common roll with a qualified franchise. The twelve specially-elected or 'national' members were still to be elected by the legislature acting as an electoral college. A common roll was also to elect ten Europeans, eight Asians and two Arabs, but each of these candidates would first have to be selected by primary elections from their own communities. There was no provision for a Chief Minister and no intention yet of giving powers of internal self-government.

The publication of this new constitution made it clear that the policies of white leadership and multi-racial politics had come to an end. It was also plain that the political power of the European community was finally broken. Although the Europeans had apparently voluntarily abandoned their previous claims and agreed at Lancaster House to a constitution placing the Africans in a paramount position, this impression was false. Michael Blundell and his supporters did not represent the majority of the European community. Group-Captain Briggs, though more representative of the European outlook, had not been able to make a very strong stand. Once the British government decided to remove its backing from European political pretensions, they virtually collapsed. Around the table in Lancaster House, Iain Macleod, with the assistance of Michael Blundell, was able to guide the negotiations so as to avoid an open clash and make it appear that all races were agreed on the new proposals.

The Europeans themselves recognised that their era of political power had come to an end, and when Blundell returned to Nairobi he was abused as a traitor. For it was clear from the constitutional provisions that all the members of the new Legislative Council would depend on African approval for their election. Despite the restricted franchise, the majority of electors for every seat were bound to be Africans. The message that the British government was now encouraging African majority government in the country which had always symbolised white settlement rang throughout east and central Africa and was even heard in the Cape. An era of British policy had been abruptly ended, however many euphemistic words might cover the fact. In future, no British immigrant community would be able to count on British Conservative support to maintain its power over African majorities.

The Europeans in Kenya raised one last spark of resistance, when Major Cavendish-Bentinck resigned as Speaker of the House, attacked the British government's reversal of policy, accused it of breaking its pledges to the settlers and rallied some Europeans round him in the formation of a new party, the 'Kenya Coalition'.

But the die was cast. Indeed, even this victory was insufficient to satisfy the Africans. It was now that Tom Mboya put into practice a policy he later described as 'growl now, smile later'. On his return to Nairobi he declared that he would refuse to accept office and attacked the new constitution as already outdated. At the end of March, at a meeting in Kiambu, the Kenya African National Union was formed as a mass party. Kenyatta was nominated as president, but, as this caused the Kenya government to refuse to accept registration, James Gichuru took the presidential chair on the understanding that he would hand it over to Kenyatta as soon as possible. Odinga became vice-president and Mboya the secretary-general.

Yet already tensions had begun to develop within African politics. Fears grew that the new KANU organisation was dominated by the powerful Kikuyu and Luo tribes, with too much control in urbanised Nairobi. The pastoral tribes, the Masai and Kalenjin group, became restive over this leadership issue. As usual in Kenya, it was the land question that appeared most important, smaller tribes fearing that the Kikuyu intended to monopolise the White Highlands as soon as they were opened to African settlement. So, after some small tribal parties had been formed, a joint meeting was held in May 1960 at which a rival to KANU, the Kenya African Democratic Union, was established, with Ngala as leader and Muliro as his deputy.

There were economic as well as political problems to face. The decline of European political power, the abolition of restrictions around the White Highlands and the political maelstrom which surrounded the Lancaster House conference, inevitably reduced confidence in Kenya's economic future. An outflow of capital began, unemployment rose and white farms began to be sold, the more intransigent settlers finding their way to Southern Rhodesia or South Africa. Increasing suspicions of a Mau Mau revival, renewed oathings and the operations of a Freedom Land Army, all aggravated the fears now besetting the white community.

Meanwhile, preparations were made for the elections which would give Africans an absolute majority in the Legislative Council for the first time. Governor Patrick Renison continued to refuse the release of Kenyatta, whom he referred to as 'the African leader to darkness and death'. Yet KANU was now making the demand for his absolute release a major political issue.

In the communal primary elections at the beginning of 1961 it became clear that Blundell and his group could not claim to represent European opinion. Blundell himself just scraped through the primaries, enabling him to stand on the common roll, on which, with African help, he was able to defeat Cavendish-Bentinck decisively. In the elections proper, it became apparent that neither African party had established firm discipline, for many who were refused the official party nomination nevertheless stood as candidates. It also seemed clear that KANU could count on the support of the Kikuyu, Luo, Meru, Embu, Kamba and Kisii tribes, whilst KADU represented the Masai, the Kalenjin group and the smaller, mainly pastoral tribes. KANU, using Kenyatta's name freely, won the election decisively, gaining eighteen seats to KADU's eleven. Nevertheless, on the governor again refusing to release Kenyatta, KANU decided not to form a government.

Here the governor and his advisers made a serious mistake. There had been many leadership conflicts within KANU and the government estimated that the party was likely to break up under these rival pressures. They thought that if the minority KADU were allowed to form a government, the new prestige would help it to become a more nationally-representative party. This policy flew in the face of all historical evidence, for, inevitably, when Ngala became Leader of Government Business and his party, in association with Blundell and some Asians, formed a government, this was their kiss of death. They were considered by many Africans to be collaborators with the colonialists and betraying the cause of Kenyatta's freedom.

By now Kenyatta had been moved from Lodwar to Maralal, nearer Nairobi, and was in touch with the political leaders. In August 1961 he was released from all restrictions, but the governor immediately announced that his prison sentence debarred him from becoming a member of the legislature. On his release, however, he immediately made strenuous efforts to bring the two parties together, hoping that a coalition government could be formed in preparation for a new constitutional conference. After acrimonious discussions, KADU eventually rejected Kenyatta's leadership and the talks broke down. By now, KADU, recognising the greater power of organisation and electoral attraction of its rival, had begun to concentrate on a regional plan which would allow the smaller tribes a considerable measure of self-government in their own areas. KANU rejected this approach, continuing to demand sufficient centralised powers to plan the country's future. When Kenyatta eventually despaired of bringing the two parties together and accepted the presidency of KANU, the chances of a single national party disappeared.

Kenyatta now visited London for the first time since 1946, leading a delegation demanding independence by early 1962. Iain Macleod had been succeeded as Colonial Secretary by Reginald Maudling, who now made a gesture of reconciliation by declaring that the constitution would be amended to permit persons imprisoned for more than two years to stand for the Legislative Council. He then visited Kenya himself, announcing on his departure from the colony that another constitutional conference would be held in London in February 1962 and indicating at the same time that some process of devolution could at least be considered. The following month, at the end of 1961, Kenyatta became a member of the Legislative Council at an uncontested by-election and was immediately adopted as leader of the Opposition.

So once again, Kenya politicians, officials and the British government representatives, led by Colonial Secretary Maudling, met round the table at Lancaster House. This time, however, there was one significant difference. Jomo Kenyatta was leading the KANU delegation.

The main problem of this conference was to devise a constitution which would both give a government sufficient powers to organise the new state after independence, and, at the same time, allay the fears of the smaller tribes that a strong central government would produce Kikuyu-Luo domination. In the event, Ronald Ngala and KADU got much of what they were demanding. When the constitution was published, well after the conclusion of the conference, it was seen to provide for strong regional governments as well as a central government. Six regions were to be established, in addition to Nairobi, and there were to be two parliamentary chambers, a House of Representatives, on a national constituency basis, and a Senate, with equal representation from each region. The regional assemblies were to have considerable powers over local government and to have their rights entrenched, important changes needing a ninety per cent vote in the Senate.

On this basis, a coalition government was set up, though it was always an uneasy alliance. The fact that members of both parties were in the same Council of Ministers did not prevent them from attacking each other bitterly in public meetings. Moreover, political tolerance was not helped by the dissensions within both parties, and particularly inside KANU. Mboya and Odinga were continually jockeying for power, whilst at one time a separate Luo movement broke away and later Paul Ngei, who had been convicted and imprisoned with Kenyatta, took his Kamba group out of KANU to form an African Peoples' Party. All this confusion led to ever more extreme speeches as the various figures concerned vied with each other to convince their supporters of their uncompromising policies. As, by this time, many of the most intransigent detainees were being released and also joining in the chorus of political demagogy, sometimes verging on racialism, intelligent politics were at a premium. Indeed, it seemed at one time, towards the end of 1962, that KANU, seemingly the strongest party, was breaking up as a result of these dissensions. It was at this moment that Kenyatta, recognising the danger, acted decisively by reorganising the party and bringing its dissentient factions under his discipline.

At the beginning of 1963 the British government demonstrated a determination to pursue its policy to its logical end by appointing Malcolm MacDonald as governor in place of Sir Patrick Renison. This was generally accepted as an earnest of British intentions to force the pace of political development so as to avoid the growing dangers of disintegration.

By the time of the first genuine general election in May 1963, KANU had largely recovered, whilst KADU was unable to put sufficient candidates in the field to secure a majority even if all of them should win. Ngala of KADU and Ngei with his APP eventually made an electoral agreement, but only after nomination day when rival candidates were already in the field, and never on a very secure basis. In these circumstances KANU, after a most sophisticated campaign on a platform of national unity and a national effort to raise the standards of the country, won 72 of the 117 seats in the lower house and 18 out of 41 in the Senate. The six regional assemblies were divided equally between the two parties. In the new seventh region, the Northern Frontier Region, the shadow of future difficulties had already fallen. Here the large Somali community was demanding secession from Kenya and incorporation into the Somali state. It boycotted the elections, refusing to send representatives to any of the Kenya institutions.

On June 1, 1963, Jomo Kenyatta became Kenya's first Prime Minister. The *bête noire* of the settlers, the 'African leader to darkness and death' of Governor Renison and a man who the British Colonial Secretary had declared would never be allowed to return to public life, was invested with greater responsibility than any other individual in Kenya's history. He soon showed that he was a big enough man to forget the past. He offered white settler farmers hospitality at his own farm at Gatundu, and was then accorded a most remarkable standing ovation by white settlers in the former Mau Mau centre of Nakuru. He also made sure that his ministerial offices were spread beyond the Kikuyu and Luo tribes, including a Kamba, a Kisii, a Maragoli and even a Masai in his government team. Odinga became Minister of Home Affairs and Mboya Minister of Justice and Constitutional Affairs. Peter Mbiyu Koinange and Joseph Murumbi, who had both spent most of the emergency in London, also became important ministers.

Immediately after the formation of his government, Kenyatta entered into earnest discussions with Julius Nyerere of Tanganyika and Milton Obote of Uganda, in the hope of establishing an East African Federation by the end of 1963. The hope was eventually to be dashed, partly through the obstruction of Uganda and largely from the fact that it is easier to talk about surrendering national sovereignty than actually to achieve it. This had always been Nyerere's fear, when he had desperately attempted to achieve federation before each constituent territory secured the appurtenances of sovereignty.

The Somali question also continued to plague Kenyatta's government, as it had the British administration. The Somalis maintained their adamant refusal to participate in Kenyan institutions and began to organise forcible resistance to rule from Nairobi. Raiding parties from over the border attacking police posts only added to the tension, and before the end of the year the Kenyan and Ethiopian governments agreed to sign a defence pact after Kenya independence to resist Somali claims on their territories.

In July, plans for independence were published, with the date declared as December 12th. It was agreed that the British military base in Kenya should be evacuated by a phased withdrawal over the twelve months of 1964.

By now the success of KANU had led to a number of Opposition members crossing the floor and eventually to Paul Ngei and his APP members rejoining KANU forces. Kenyatta's government was thereby strengthened as the country approached independence.

But there was one hurdle still to be jumped before the way to independence was entirely open. At the end of September a final constitutional conference met in London. The KANU government strongly pressed for increased central government powers at the expense of the regions and a modification of the difficult provisions for amending the constitution. These demands were sternly resisted by KADU.

During the course of the conference, with Duncan Sandys, Maudling's successor as Colonial Secretary, in the chair, both sides attempted to bring their utmost powers of pressure into play. First KADU threatened to set up a separate independent state within Kenya, consisting of the regions they controlled. Then this was countered by a KANU threat to declare the whole country independent unilaterally.

Eventually, most of the awards favoured KANU. A single civil service commission and one national police service commission were to be established, whilst the central government was to have powers to draft its security forces to any part of the country without having to secure the approval of regional councils. Yet the rights of both individuals and regions remained strongly entrenched, still requiring a seventy-five per cent vote in the lower house and a ninety per cent vote in the Senate. Less fundamental changes in the constitution were now to be permitted by only seventy-five per cent of both houses or a two-thirds majority in a national referendum. KADU returned to Kenya declaring these amendments to have been 'a breach of faith' by the British government, but their threats of independent action did not seem to hold out much menace, at least for the immediate future. Nevertheless, they left open the issue as to whether the centrifugal forces of tribalism in Kenya could be prevented from leading to national disintegration once the unifying element of opposition to colonial rule had been removed.

On December 12, 1963, Kenya Colony and Protectorate, the chief symbol of British white settler rule in the African continent, became an independent state under a mainly African government elected by universal franchise. The dream of a country shaped by a white settler community holding economic, social and political power, had been shattered. The chimera of a multi-racial system, in which each community maintained an inalienable right of political influence, had hardly been conceived before it was destroyed. Kenya was to be ruled by democratic representation. How this would affect relations between the large African population and the smaller Asian and European communities was yet to be seen. The paradox of a centralised socialist planned economy, in which the KANU government believed, and the necessity of preserving large-scale European capitalist farming, had still to be resolved. The problems of the unemployed in Nairobi, the shortage of land, competing tribal and national loyalties, the integration of hard-core detainees and men still returning from the forests into the new community, government control over the security forces, the attraction of overseas capital for essential development, the maintenance of the high standards of a society built by Europeans, and the external relations with Ethiopia and Somalia, exacerbated by the opposition of the Somalis inside Kenya – this multitude of problems challenged the skill and integrity of Kenyatta's government. Nevertheless, in the history of Africa the achievement of independence in Kenya had a very special significance; more than any other single event it presaged the establishment of black African government throughout the continent.

The history of the Somalilands during the nineteen-fifties was a continuing story of the search for unification. Somali nationalists believed that the Trust Territory, where most Somalis lived, the British Protectorate, French Somaliland, the Haud and Ogaden Regions of Ethiopia and part of the Northern Frontier District of Kenya, were rightly all constituent parts of a Greater Somalia. Certainly, in each of these regions Somalis formed a majority of the inhabitants. Yet Ethiopia had no intention of surrendering Somali areas, whilst neither the British administration nor any of the Kenya Africans intended to reduce the area of Kenya and its population by allowing the Northern District to become a part of Somalia. Theoretically, it would have been possible after 1956 for French Somaliland, the Djibuti enclave, to have joined the wider Somalia. After the passage of the *loi cadre*, elections were held in French Somaliland, as in the rest of French Overseas Africa. The elections were won by Mahmoud Harbi, who was in favour of joining the other Somali territories. In the 1958 referendum, however, he was unable to secure more than a quarter of the votes for his proposed rejection of membership of the Community. Shortly afterwards, Harbi fled to Cairo and was deposed by the French. In new elections, no doubt influenced by the French administration, an Assembly was returned which voted for continuing status as an Overseas Territory. There was little attraction for the Somalis in Djibuti to dispense with the economic aid provided by Paris and join their much poorer brothers in Somaliland proper. Yet the machinery to make the choice remained available in French Somaliland.

This left the Italian Trust area and British Somaliland to determine whether there should be any unified Somali state. The Italians, with 1960 fixed as the deadline for independence by the United Nations, did much more to prepare their country for self-rule than the British. Although there had been considerable opposition to the return of the Italians as the administrators of the trust, there is no doubt that Italy was aiming to train sufficient administrators and to provide the machinery of government for a peaceful transfer in 1960. The opposition to the Italians was led by Raji Mohammed Hussein, one of the founder members of the radical Somali Youth League. As president of the SYL, Hussein led this opposition from 1950 to 1953, when, after serious rioting against the Italian administration, he left the country for Cairo to pursue academic studies. His absence from the scene allowed Abdullahi Issa to assume the leadership and begin co-operation with the Italians. After the 1956 elections, in which the SYL won forty-three of the seventy seats, Issa became Prime Minister, pursuing the task of modernisation in co-operation with the Italian administration. Issa was re-elected in 1959, but by this time Hussein had returned and was making bitter attacks on him for his failure to promote Somali unification, meanwhile trying to organise violent resistance to the Italians. The executive of the SYL suspended Hussein, whereupon he founded a rival party, the Greater Somalia League. In 1959, however, following further rioting, the new organisation was banned and Hussein arrested.

In the March 1959 elections the SYL won eighty-three of the ninety seats. But by the time that independence was attained in July 1960, Issa had become too controversial a figure to remain Prime Minister. He was attacked on various counts: for lack of enthusiasm for unification; for his friendship with the west and particularly with Italy; and for trying to change Moslem traditionalism too quickly. He was therefore replaced as Prime Minister by Aden Abdullah Osman, who had opposed Hussein along with Issa, but was more acceptable to orthodox Moslem opinion. Issa became Minister of Foreign Affairs.

Meanwhile, the British did virtually nothing before 1958 to prepare their Protectorate for self-government. In that year, riots and demonstrations drew attention to the fact that only two more years remained before the neighbouring Italian Trust Territory would become independent. Already Somalis under the British had been deeply antagonised by the return of the Haud district to Ethiopia in 1955. This district was an important grazing area for Somali nomads, had been incorporated in the Italian Empire and then reconquered during the war. Somalis expected that it would be retained after the war, but, in 1955, the British government, by agreement with Ethiopia, returned it to the Emperor. All sections of Somali opinion in the protectorate saw this as a lack of concern by the British for the interests of the country they were supposed to be protecting.

In 1958 a commission was set up to study political development. It was decided that elections should be held in March 1959 for a new Legislative Council which would have thirteen elected members and three nominated unofficials, but still with an official majority of seventeen members. Unofficial members were to be brought into consultation on the working of certain government departments. Despite the fact that in both neighbouring French Somaliland and Somalia universal franchise was now practised, voting in the new elections in the British Protectorate would still be restricted. On the grounds that these elections would not provide for an unofficial majority in the Legislative Council, the main Somali party, the Somali National League, decided to boycott them. This allowed the less radical party, the National United Front, led by Michael Mariano, to gain a majority. He immediately proposed talks between the Protectorate and Somalia. Even before these elections, however, the British Colonial Secretary had suddenly recognised the urgency of preparing the Protectorate for self-government and made a speech in Somaliland explaining that there would be further progress after the elections. He promised an elected majority in the Legislative Council by 1960 and Somali members of the Executive. He also assured Somalis that if the Legislative Council wished to discuss the union with Somalia, Britain would assist in the negotiations.

In the meantime, another commission was appointed and this time recommended the election of another Legislative Council composed of thirty-three elected and three ex-officio members, with four elected members becoming ministers, together with three officials, in the Executive. When the new elections were held in February 1960, the Somali National League confirmed its hold on the country by winning twenty of the thirty-three seats, whilst the Somali United Party, which had an electoral alliance with it, won another twelve.

The National United Front, considered to have been too moderate in its demands for Somali self-government, could only win the remaining single seat. In April 1960 the new Council passed a resolution demanding independence on July 1st, the same day on which Somalia was due to become independent. Actually, British Somaliland became independent on June 26th with the SNL leader, Mohammed Hadji Ibrahim Egal, as Prime Minister. His term of office lasted only four days, for on July 1st the two territorial assemblies merged and the two countries united, with Osman as President of the new Somali Republic, Abdi Rashid Ali Shermarke as Prime Minister and Abdullahi Issa as Foreign Minister in a coalition government.

Thus another African sovereign state was created, still heavily dependent on outside aid to balance its budget and support its meagre exports of hides and bananas. It was significant that the new Republic adopted a national flag with a five-pointed star. Two of the five points of Somali national ambition had been united. The future history of Somalia would centre on attempts to regain the other three points and the relations with other states in Africa consequent on such efforts.

The last country in the East African mosaic is Ethiopia. There is little new to be said of it during the nineteen-fifties. It proceeded in its archaic way without political parties, trade unions or, outside Addis Ababa, any of the facilities of modern life. In 1955 there was some revision of the constitution, through which the Emperor became the head of government and head of state, with a cabinet responsible to him. A pseudo-parliamentary system was introduced, the upper house or Senate being appointed by the Emperor and the lower house or Chamber of Deputies being elected (in 1957) by the people, but remaining nothing more than an advisory council still under the control of the Emperor and his court.

Nationalism played little part in Ethiopia. In one way, the country remained one of the oldest nationalisms in the continent; in another, there was no nationalism, for outside Addis Ababa the state retained a provincial feudalist structure.

Yet this does not imply that there was no opposition to the anachronistic form of government. The Emperor continued his interest in education and social services, the results of which were seen in the growth of an educated student group inevitably discontented with the nepotism, corruption and inefficiency of the régime. Demands for land reform and economic development increased with the growing numbers of the educated younger generation.

Yet the Emperor himself retained a mystical reverence from the majority of his people. It was not until December 1960 that this was first seriously challenged. In that month part of the Imperial Guard revolted under General Neway and placed the Emperor's son, the Crown Prince, on the throne. At this moment the Emperor himself was paying a state visit to Brazil. He returned immediately and, finding the army and air force loyal to him, led his troops in triumph into Addis Ababa only four days after the revolt. General Neway was executed for his part in the revolt and when sentenced to death declared that he had acted because 'Ethiopia has been standing still, while our African brothers are moving ahead in the struggle to overcome poverty'.

Although large sums of money were being spent on government buildings in Addis Ababa, virtually nothing was being done in the country itself. The increase in education applied almost entirely to children in the capital, whilst the few social services which had been developed hardly extended to the country areas.

It was not therefore surprising that a revolt should have taken place and the Emperor saw the danger signals sufficiently clearly to begin appointing some younger, more progressive ministers. He was, however, still largely restricted in these efforts by the heavy hand of the feudal nobility dominating his administration.

One of his efforts to escape from domestic problems was the initiative he took from 1960 onwards in African politics. The second conference of independent African states was held in Addis Ababa in 1960 and in 1962 the Pan-African Freedom Movement of East and Central Africa not only held its conference in the Ethiopian capital, but secured the attendance of both Ethiopia and the Somali Republic. Indeed, this conference between the nationalist parties of the east and central African territories, now joined by the South African nationalists, gained greater publicity for itself in Addis Ababa than in all its previous activities. Its object was first, to unite the nationalist movements of these areas, and secondly, to promote closer association leading to federation from the Red Sea to the Cape.

In 1963 the Pan-African Conference of Heads of State from all independent African countries, by meeting in Addis Ababa, gave Ethiopia a central position in the pan-African movement. All this was good for the prestige of the Emperor and his country, but it had very little relevance to the needs of his people. Administration remained so sketchy that the national population could be variously estimated between 10 and 20 million.

The nineteen-fifties and early sixties saw, in general, a rapid, determined movement in east Africa towards the creation of new independent states governed by Africans, drawing their authority from the universal voting right of their people. Little progress was to be seen in any profound attacks on the roots of poverty or any new social orientation away from traditional life. In one or two large urban areas a proletariat and an intelligentsia had begun to appear, but they made more vociferous protests than constructive plans for the future of the masses. The focal emphasis had been on race relations, with the triumph of African nationalism in Kenya, in particular, in Tanganyika, Uganda and the Somalilands, breaking the foundations of white settler political domination.

The main ideas that had emerged from this period were, first, the paramountcy of political democracy, which had even survived the disasters in Kenya and established itself in principle as a basis for each state except Ethiopia. Secondly, there had developed, largely under the inspiration of Julius Nyerere, a new concept of international association which, in the long term, looked for some form of federation between all the states in east Africa, central Africa, ultimately, even in southern Africa. This new concept was inevitably vague, but practical efforts were made to create its first base founded on the British territories of Tanganyika, Kenya, Uganda and Zanzibar. Certainly, the conception itself and the discussions held about it gave a new confidence to the nationalist movements throughout the area and farther south. It was hoped, too, that federation could solve the major problems of tribal conflict in Kenya and Uganda, and the frontier disputes between Somalia, Ethiopia and Kenya. Above all, of course, federation or some form of international co-operation between these countries was essential for an attack on the basic economic problems of the whole region. Nothing less than co-ordination of economic planning and economic investment could seriously approach the problem of endemic poverty amongst the east African peoples. The sovereignty which had been gained during this period of political struggle provided no more than an opportunity to tackle the basic social and economic issues. To their great credit, most of the principal African leaders recognised this hard fact of African life, symbolised in the slogan offered by Julius Nyerere to his countrymen, 'Uhuru na Kazi' – 'Freedom and Work'.

12

The North Becomes African

The history of north Africa during the nineteen-fifties was only unevenly related to the African independence revolution. Already, at the beginning of the fifties, Egypt was formally independent, whilst Libya attained that status in 1951. Five years later, the Sudan, Morocco and Tunisia had all achieved their sovereignty. Thus, before the great rush towards African independence was initiated by the example of Ghana in 1957, all but one of the north African countries was already a sovereign state.

Moreover, the Arab outlook of each north African state still tended to separate them from the ideas and events developing south of the Sahara. The progress of the Arab League, internal pressures within the Arab world and relations with Israel formed much more important parts of the north African perspective at this time than the affairs of black Africa.

Nevertheless, two central issues in this region attracted African attention and played a major part in building communication across the Sahara. The Egyptian revolution of 1952, followed by a four-year struggle to overthrow the last remnants of European imperialism, were seen in other areas of the continent as an integral part of the African anti-colonial revolution. Secondly, although the independence movements of Morocco and Tunisia did not appear to have any profound influence on the rest of French Africa, the liberatory war in Algeria certainly did. By the late nineteen-fifties, the Algerian question had become a major issue in African relations with Europe, whilst it also caused considerable tensions between African states themselves.

Thus, in the context of the African continent, the nineteen-fifties saw Egypt repelling the last violent efforts of the European imperialists to maintain their control over the Suez area, with Cairo becoming an important centre for nationalists from various parts of the continent; in Algeria a bitter struggle was seen to be taking place to defeat that combination of European colonialism and white settler power which also remained the main obstacle to African nationalism in the east, centre and south of the continent.

The Egyptian revolution had two formidable obstacles to overcome. First, the forces of change had become identified with the foreign occupying power and, secondly, the Mohammedan religion was deeply rooted in the political and social structure of the country, intent on resisting any changes which appeared to weaken its traditional influence. In Europe it had been the growth of democracy which produced modern nationalism; in Egypt it was the nationalist movement which had promoted democratic ideals. The failure of social development to produce a bourgeoisie interested in and capable of challenging the land-owning class had prevented the liberal democratic constitution from being used to transplant the roots of social, economic and political power. Thus liberal democracy came to be identified both with the foreigners, who had introduced it, and with those Egyptians who would preserve the existing class structure. Nationalism had originally made use of the constitution, but, because it lacked any social dynamic, it ended by discrediting it.

Meanwhile, the acceptance of Islamic doctrine as divine revelation and perfect truth constantly restrained any search for new political and social ideas. The preservation of traditional Mohammedanism could only hinder those changes in Egyptian life essential to construct a modern state.

Both the identification of liberal democracy with the foreigner and with Egyptian conservatism, together with the fear that the forces producing economic change were European, imperialist and anti-Islamic, had prevented the old order from being either reformed or overthrown during the past thirty years. But, at the same time, a gathering storm of revolt had been mounting as nationalist and social ambitions found themselves obstructed by the same forces.

In the absence of a dynamic bourgeoisie, the only element capable of effecting radical change was the army. In the Egyptian army there was a considerable group of young, educated officers, who took a similar role to the bourgeois progressives in other societies. What is more, they held a strategically vital position in the monarchical régime, for without their support the king and his court, together with the discredited politicians, would be exposed to the mounting anger of the Cairo masses. It was this military group who had felt most keenly the shame of the Palestinian war and who had suffered personally from the corrupt munition profiteers.

During the months following the Cairo riots of January 1952, the Farouk régime was rapidly disintegrating. Desperate changes of government and political leadership could not seal the cracks. The Wafd had become completely ineffective, whilst galloping corruption only accelerated political chaos.

By this time Lieutenant-Colonel Gamal Abdel Nasser, in 1952 just thirty-four years old, had organised his Free Officers Committee. Nasser had been an anti-colonial nationalist since boyhood. He had spent much of his time, when in military college and serving at El Alamein, in the Sudan and in Palestine, in working out a theory of revolution and the tactics to put it into effect. His object was both to replace the effete régime of Farouk and to expel the British. By July 1952 he and his committee were ready to move. The Farouk régime had almost completely disintegrated and when, in the early hours of July 23rd, tanks were moved to strategic places in Cairo, the centres of civil administration were taken over and the radio announced that the army was in the process of purifying itself and the nation, there was virtually no opposition or disorder. Farouk was forced to abdicate in favour of his son and left for exile three days later. An elder, respected officer, General Mohammed Neguib, was brought in to become chairman of the Revolutionary Command Council, with Nasser himself as deputy chairman. Aly Maher was made Prime Minister, but only for a few weeks, Neguib replacing him in September. The following year, in June 1953, the monarchy was brought to an end, Egypt became a republic and Neguib was made both President and Prime Minister, with Nasser as Deputy Prime Minister and Minister of the Interior.

Neguib, Nasser and the military junta now had to face two immediate and desperately difficult tasks. Nasser described them as the two revolutions, political and social. The political objective was to unite the nation in assertion of its independence; socially, the task was to shake the ideas of the past, seeking to release people to feel their individuality. It was soon clear from the massive

demonstrations of support from the ordinary people that the revolutionary forces could count on popular acclaim. Yet this in itself
posed a heavy responsibility. After their long years of degradation,
the Egyptian masses expected a new deal from the revolution. The
slogan 'Unity, Order, Work' might attract the enthusiasm of the
people, but of itself could not provide them with more food, land
or houses.

The critics of the revolution declared that the military junta was
based on fascism and communism. Certainly the measures taken
were totalitarian and, in the circumstances, nothing less could have
succeeded. The new régime also took some of its ideas from both
fascism and communism, establishing a form of state capitalism,
underpinning it with military power, and breaking up large estates.
Yet this was a purely pragmatic policy. Neither Nasser nor his
colleagues had any clear idea of what political philosophy would
serve the situation. They had to live from day to day, their main
objectives being to clean up corruption and organise the state on
such a basis as would allow it to benefit its citizens. Certainly nothing
approaching the terrorism of fascism or communism was employed
in Egypt.

The first major action of the revolutionary government was to
break up the estates of the large landowners, establishing a ceiling
for land-holding and distributing the rest amongst the landless. By
the Agrarian Reform Law of September 1952 land ownership was
restricted to a maximum of 200 acres, releasing land which over the
following years was used to resettle 150,000 families.

Domestic policy was based on a conception of 'Arab socialism'.
Measures were taken to increase industrialisation and reduce the
dependency of the economy on cotton. Both industry and agricultural development were assisted by firms in Europe and aid
secured from both America and Russia. The major hope for future
development was based on the building of the Aswan High Dam,
300 feet high and three miles long, designed to irrigate a million
new acres and increase cultivation of other areas then only seasonally
farmed. It was the Soviet Union which, from 1958 onwards, lent
the first two-fifths of the capital needed for a project which was
estimated to cost one billion dollars.

Yet these domestic plans have always been handicapped by
Egypt's age-old problem of rapid population increase. The annual

expansion of the population by 2·5 per cent never allowed the expansionist plans to do more than maintain the social status quo. Meanwhile, the increased bureaucracy needed for state control and the drain of heavy military expenditure both handicapped economic progress.

Thus the hopes that Egypt's revolution would create a genuine and healthy social democracy never approached fulfilment in the nineteen-fifties. State control, based on military power and authoritarian discipline, had to be maintained to preserve national unity for the purpose of economic reconstruction. National organisations like the Liberation Rally and its successor, the National Union, were formed with the purpose of supervising the revolution and guarding the principles of national development. They were hierarchical bodies designed to involve the masses, under strict control, with national development. In the same way, the trade unions were controlled by the government and, although some workers were selected to join with government nominees in the management of state-controlled industries, the unions were not allowed any independent activities such as the right to strike.

Politically, the first two years of the new régime were marked by stresses and strains within the military government as an intense struggle for power was fought. Various changes took place within the Revolutionary Council, but it was at the top that the main conflicts occurred. Neguib was anxious to return quickly to a parliamentary régime, whilst Nasser considered that the people were not yet ready for it. As the result of various pressures from within the army, a demand for revolutionary momentum and the clashing of personalities, the two men were frequently in and out of office during the early months of 1954. In February Neguib was forced to resign all his offices. Nasser took over as Prime Minister, but was faced by such a wave of opposition in the streets of Cairo that within three days Neguib was restored as his President. On March 9th, Nasser threw down the gauntlet by resigning his offices of Prime Minister and President of the Revolutionary Command Council. Later in the same month he pressed his challenge home by testing reactions to the proposal of restoring the political parties and making preparations for new elections. The revolutionaries in the army recognised that this would restore the pre-revolution situation. They showed their unmistakable support of Nasser's claim that the revolution must be pursued to its completion before liberal democracy was restored, and rejected Neguib's proposals for reintroducing a democratic régime. In April, Nasser was reinstated as Prime Minister and immediately rescinded his resolution permitting a restoration of parties and an electoral system. The final act in the drama was played out later the same year, after an attempt by the Moslem Brotherhood to assassinate Nasser in Alexandria. There was no reason to suppose that Neguib had been privy to these plans, but the Brotherhood was hoping to restore him to power after eliminating Nasser. In November Neguib was put under house arrest and disappeared from the scene. His value as the only leader really close to the people was felt to be no longer needed by the revolutionary movement.

It was in this same year of 1954 that Nasser not only took over supreme control from Neguib, but, with his colleagues in the Revolutionary Council, destroyed the influence of the only two other movements which might have challenged the military junta. The Communist Party was proscribed and about 250 of its leading members imprisoned. This was done not so much because of its political ideology, but because Nasser was not prepared to have within his country a political movement controlled by a foreign power.

Even more threatening than the communists was the Moslem Brotherhood. At first the Brotherhood supported the military revolution, believing that it would accomplish one of its own particular objectives, the expulsion of the British. But it then expected that it would itself take over control of the country. When it found that the basic objective of Nasser was to create a secular society, an Arab rather than an Islamic state, it turned against Nasser and his council. Nasser himself was an orthodox Moslem and had indeed been a member of the Brotherhood, but he could not afford to have two mass national movements in rivalry with each other. Perhaps he vaguely recognised that the Brotherhood stood for the strict form of Islamic society which was bound to obstruct the reforms essential for him to retain the support of the masses. So the Brotherhood was suppressed in January 1954, 450 of its leaders arrested, its local headquarters shut down and its funds confiscated. Despite this proscription, in October of the same year its members attempted to assassinate Nasser and this time the government completely crushed the movement, six of its members implicated in the assassination plot being hanged.

Although these dramatic events in Egypt brought Nasser and Egyptian affairs to the attention of Africans in other parts of the continent, it was in his foreign policy that Nasser first really came into prominence in Africa south of the Sahara. In 1955 he attended the Bandung Conference in Indonesia and proclaimed the country's support for the policy of neutralism. This only added to the growing hostility being shown towards him by the western powers. The Americans withdrew their loan offer for financing the Aswan High Dam, followed by cancellation of British and World Bank loans. When, on June 26, 1956, Nasser retaliated by nationalising the Suez Canal Company and declaring that its profits would be used for building the dam, the breach with the west became open.

In October 1954 Nasser had been successful in negotiating an agreement with Britain by which the British army was to evacuate the Canal Zone, the last area of the country occupied by British troops. There were qualifications in the agreement, but this seemed to mark the ultimate attainment of Egyptian sovereignty, freed from future interference by the British. Nevertheless, when the Nasser government announced the nationalisation of the Suez Canal, an action which any sovereign state was fully entitled to take, fierce denunciation arose from the British government. Britain and France began to prepare for war.

The Arab–Israeli conflict had never been settled. Indeed, one of the handicaps to Egyptian influence in Africa was the fact that many African states and leaders were friendly to Israel, having received considerable help from Israelis, whereas Egypt was in a state of continued war with her.

On this occasion, however, the whole of Africa condemned Israel when her forces invaded Sinai on October 29th. This attack was used by Britain and France, who demanded that Egyptian and Israeli forces should both withdraw ten miles from the Suez Canal. The Egyptians naturally rejected this affront to their national sovereignty. British and French bombers began raiding Egyptian territory and their forces effected landings at Port Said three days later. Following pressure by America, Russia and the United Nations, these forces were withdrawn, but not before severe damage had been caused and many lives lost. For Britain, this was perhaps the final fling of imperial arrogance in Africa, a reversion to the days of gun-boat diplomacy. The French had still to learn the lessons of Bizerta and Algeria.

Following the British and French withdrawal a UN force occupied the area and confirmed Egyptian sovereignty over the Suez Canal. Nasser became the anti-colonialist hero of the African continent. Whatever may have been the doubts about the character of his régime previously, the fact that he had withstood European imperialist military forces now banished criticisms and gave him high prestige throughout Africa.

So far as Africa was concerned, this Suez affair provided Nasser with a base from which to spread his influence to other areas. He now began to give hospitality and active support to a variety of nationalist movements from various parts of the continent. Yet his foreign policy, despite his adherence to the Casablanca Bloc, never had much effect in Africa itself. It was the Middle Eastern aspect of Egyptian foreign policy which led to the attempt to form a United Arab Republic with Syria from 1958 to 1961 and later a form of union with Syria and Iraq. These efforts had little impact in Africa. Nor were Africans particularly interested in the new Egyptian constitution which came into effect in 1956 and led to elections in 1957. The 350-member National Assembly, which was then elected, never had much power and was always controlled by the National Union, a government-organised body replacing the political parties. The Union was, however, useful in stimulating greater national unity and popular involvement in government policy. This was particularly so during the period of nationalisation, when, from the middle of 1961, the state took control of most industry and financial concerns throughout both Egypt and Syria. This was, indeed, one of the causes for the collapse of the United Arab Republic.

So, by the early sixties, it could be said that although the future of Egypt was still indeterminate, Nasser had destroyed the power of the three elements which had cemented the old régime – the monarchy, the Wafd and the British presence. He had also broken the Moslem Brotherhood and thereby opened the way for a secular state. He had at least reduced the power of the great land-owners, and involved the state in the reorganisation of industry, finance and agriculture. He had achieved these aims by using authoritarian methods, whilst, by refusing to seek any peaceful solution to the conflict with Israel, he had never been able to halt the drain of valuable resources for military purposes. Nevertheless, from the end of the nineteen-fifties, Nasser was accepted in Africa as one of the leading radical nationalist figures who could always claim to be included in any plans for the new Africa emerging out of the imperialist era.

The Egyptian revolution directly affected not only Egyptians, but also affairs in neighbouring Sudan. When, in a last desperate effort to divert attention from internal shambles, King Farouk's government attempted to abrogate the treaty providing for joint Anglo-Egyptian administration of the Sudan, the British rejected his claim to be King over the whole Nile valley. In the following year, 1952, the British government prepared its own draft statute to introduce self-government into the Sudan, but agreement with Egypt was not possible until after the Egyptian revolution. Neguib, in particular, was interested in the Sudan, having been brought up there himself, and after the revolution he and his government put forward a number of amendments to the draft statute. The attitude of the Neguib government, combined with nationalist pressure within the Sudan, led to agreement being reached with Egypt in February 1953 by which the Sudan was to be granted virtual autonomy. New elections were to be held and within three years the Sudanese people were to have the right of deciding whether to become separately independent or to join Egypt.

In November 1953 the general election was held, largely by means of symbols, because most of the electorate was illiterate. This time Azhari's Ashiqqa, now joined with some other groups in the National Union Party, participated in them. Azhari was still strongly supported by the Khatmiyya sect, led by Mirghani and supported both financially and politically by the Egyptians. He won the election with a clear majority, Khalil and his Umma Party, still backed by the Mahdists, becoming the opposition. In the parliament which opened in 1954 the National Union Party held fifty seats and Umma twenty-three; Azhari became Prime Minister.

The nationalist movement in the Sudan showed profound differences from nationalism in the rest of the continent. In sharp contrast to almost everywhere else, there was very little anti-colonialist content in Sudanese nationalism, at least during its later years. This was not simply because of the strength of the well-organised civil service, trained by Britain, nor yet only from appreciation of schemes like that at Gezira bringing new wealth to the country. The fact is that there was very little real national feeling in the Sudan itself. Most of the population continued to live in primitive conditions and there was very little preparation for active participation by them in political life. In the deserts of the west and north and the tropics of the south, life remained within a tribal structure. Towns were few, less than four per cent of the population living in urban areas. There was also only a tiny literate section of the population, whilst the political intelligentsia had been deeply divided on religious, rather than political, issues.

Only Azhari gained any considerable support from townspeople and it was clear that in the towns and among organised workers most hopes for the future lay in association with Egypt. The trade unions were, indeed, comparatively strong. The Sudan Workers Trade Union Federation, set up by the railway workers in 1950, associated with both the communist-controlled World Federation of Trade Unions and with the International Confederation of Arab Trade Unions dominated by the Egyptians. Later, it was also to become a member of the All-African Trade Union Federation. Not until 1956 was a rival trade union centre established, sponsored by the government and affiliated to the International Confederation of Free Trade Unions.

But certainly the most profound division within Sudanese society was that between the north and south. Of the 12 million Sudanese people, about $3\frac{1}{2}$ million were southern Negroes, quite different from the Moslem Arab northerners. The more sophisticated northerners tended to look down on the southerners, whilst the latter strongly opposed attempts to unify the country under Arab or Moslem domination. One political party, the Southern Liberal Party, founded in 1953, tried to organise this resistance into political forms. It found strength to force changes of government but never really established itself as a representative political party.

In the two years after the formation of Azhari's government, this factionalism, based on religious and political differences, seemed to become endemic. It was accompanied by a certain amount of violence. In both 1954 and the following year, supporters of the Umma Party led riots when President Neguib made a state visit, whilst Negro troops in the south also used violence to express their opposition to the prospect of northern rule. Azhari now began to recognise the strength of opposition to his pro-Egyptian policy and changed his ground. He led parliament in adopting a transitional constitution and laying down conditions for allowing a transfer of power to an independent Sudan. He was also successful in persuading his parliament to alter the plan for holding a referendum on a choice for the country's future and instead, the two houses of parliament, the House of Representatives and the Senate, joined together to declare the Sudan independent on January 1, 1956.

Thus independence was gained partly in conjunction with the British administration and partly in association with the Egyptians. But the independence movement had completely failed to unify the country whilst gaining its objective. Hostility was still evident between Mirghani's Khatmiyya sect and the Mahdist Ansar group, whereas the south, pagan and Christian, was increasingly suspicious of northern intentions to introduce Moslem rule. The political parties were largely governed by these sectarian religious considerations and the communists, although officially proscribed, were active in the trade unions and in support of the Anti-Imperialist Front. It was no surprise when, a few months after independence, the Khatmiyya group shifted its allegiance from Azhari and the National Union, replacing him with Khalil and a new coalition government.

Without ethnic, religious, social or economic unity, and in the absence of any national leader, it was no wonder that in 1958 parliamentary government collapsed and a military coup placed General Ibrahim Abboud, the Kaid or Commander-in-Chief of the Sudanese Army, in control. The army had stepped in to save the country from the politicians and their destructive factionalism.

Libya, having, as we have seen, gained independence in 1951, does not properly come into this story of independence. Yet, because it played some little part in African affairs during the nineteen-fifties, we should perhaps just glance at what Libyans were doing during this period.

From the start the position of King Idris was deeply entrenched in the constitution. He had executive power through his ministers and legislative power in association with parliament, which he had the right to dissolve. All laws came into force through him and he could issue decrees when parliament was not in session. He had the power of vetoing legislation, but could be overridden by a two-thirds majority vote in the two houses. The King, in fact, being constitutionally above the law, had absolute powers in his hands if he wished to take them.

King Idris had no desire to see his country divided by rival political parties. The fact that the three provinces had been brought together in no more than an uneasy federal system, clearly offered opportunities for factious political activity. In the first elections, in 1952, the National Congress Party, based on Tripolitania, demanding a unitary state and challenging the power of the Senussi, won only eight seats, but these were in Tripoli and the surrounding areas. During the elections the NCP attracted support from pro-Egyptian and Arab quarters, along with some communist sympathy and the backing of the rather weak trade unions. Elections were followed by violent rioting, the party was banned and its leader, Bashir as-Sadawi was exiled to die in Egypt.

And so this backward, mainly desert country continued its independent life very largely under the control of King Idris, sustained by its military value to the western powers. A treaty of alliance with Britain afforded the right to maintain a British army establishment in exchange for underwriting the continual budget deficit. The United States maintained a large air force base at Wheelus Field near Tripoli, spending large dollar sums each year. The great shortage of technicians and trained people of every kind was partially offset by United Nations aid. But the life of the people generally remained hard and often short, with a very high infant mortality rate and only a tiny area of the total country suitable for cultivation.

Nevertheless, at the end of the nineteen-fifties, there were signs of some change. In June 1959 oil was discovered, which completely altered the future economic prospects of the country. Within a short time, spending by the oil companies and their staffs had tremendously increased the demand for imports, but their operations, together with the revenue from the military bases, completely covered the balance of payments. The issue which then arose was whether the new oil revenues would be put into national development, so very badly needed, or, as in so many Middle Eastern countries, would be controlled by a handful of very rich men. The first effect of the oil discoveries was to widen the gap between the few rich and the many very poor. The fact that there was a high degree of urbanisation in Libya, with about a fifth of the total population in Tripoli and Benghazi, and another tenth in small towns, suggested that the absolute power of the monarchy might be defied as soon as any serious form of industrialisation began. Political consciousness was growing slowly, having begun after, rather than before, independence. It found avenues in small discussion groups, in the business world and in the professions, rather than in political parties. A business community and a wage-earning working class were beginning to develop towards the end of the nineteen-fifties and to move away from traditional Libyan life. The oil companies and the military bases gave employment, the civil servants provided a growing foundation for the middle class, but increasing numbers of those leaving the oases to seek work in the towns were swelling the ranks of the unemployed and extending the boundaries of the shanty-town slums.

One straw in the political wind was seen when, in October 1960, members of parliament for the first time took independent action to defeat the government over a scandal concerning the building of the Fezzan Road. They forced the Prime Minister to resign and a new government to be formed. Then again, in February 1962, eighty-seven people were sentenced to prison on a charge of organising a branch of the Arab Socialist Ba'ath Party. These were small signs, but, in combination with expanding economic prospects, they could be seen as presaging a change in the dominant monarchical form of government. Libya remained economically tied to the west, with western military power clearly visible in her midst. Yet the necessity for new government activity in an expanding economy and her increasing involvement in African affairs made it likely that voices would be raised against this commitment to one side of the Cold War. The backlog of poverty, the absence of national economic foundations, the continuation of provincialism and the gap between rich and poor, together with the new economic activities consequent on the oil discovery, seemed to suggest that the régime of King Idris would not suffice to meet national needs or popular demands for many more years.

And so we return finally to the struggle of the Maghreb to wrest independence from the French. The two protectorates, Tunisia and Morocco, and the officially integrated state, Algeria, had all to face the same kind of conflict as Kenya and Central Africa. They had to destroy at one and the same time the power of their own European settlers and that of the imperial government based on Paris. Although the indigenous population of these three countries was a mixture of Arab, Berber and various other communities, their struggles form a genuine part of the African independence revolution.

By the beginning of 1952 it appeared that Bourguibism, the attempt of Habib Bourguiba to find a conciliatory path between dominant European colonialism and intransigent nationalism, had failed in Tunisia. Bourguiba was arrested and imprisoned at Tabarka, close to the Algerian frontier. The violent protests following his arrest culminated in a general strike, and towards the end of March the Prime Minister, M. Chenik, and four other ministers were also arrested. Bourguiba himself was then sent into a still more remote area of the Sahara and a few weeks later to La Galite Island off the coast of Tunisia. Meanwhile, protests, rioting and terrorism increased, whilst the Tunisian issue became really prominent at the United Nations. The fact was that Bourguiba's party, Néo-Destour, had succeeded in uniting the intellectual, politically conscious élite with the masses, many of whom were now living in Tunis and the coastal towns.

Ben Youssef escaped to Cairo, where after the July military coup he worked closely with Neguib and Nasser. So the leadership of the nationalist movement passed to Ferhat Hached, the trade union leader. Hached was the leading figure in the Union Générale des Travailleurs Tunisiens, a well-organised trade union with nearly 100,000 members, affiliated to the International Confederation of Free Trade Unions. Hached had taken his union out of the communist-dominated French CGT control at the end of the war. He was still opposed by the communist trade unionists, who formed their own rival union, affiliated to the WFTU, but never gaining the strength of the UGTT. Hached himself had made contact with the American trade union movement, particularly with leaders like William Green of the AF of L and James D. Carey of the CIO.

In December 1952, however, Hached was murdered by the extreme settler organisation known as the Red Hand. He was caught in an ambush when driving during the day and machine-gunned to his death. The settlers, having destroyed the French initiative for making progress in association with Bourguiba, thus deliberately struck another blow against moderate nationalism and destroyed the last chance of peaceful evolution to self-government. They had shown a fanatical hatred of Hached, of his American associations and of the United States, which they considered to be supporting him. With his assassination, they started a train of events which could only lead to further bloodshed and ultimately to the defeat of their own ends.

Recognising the threat which the Tunisian situation presented to their own foreign policy, the French administration now organised elections for local councils in April 1953. They followed this with the appointment of a new Resident-General, Pierre Voizard, hoping to appease the attacks planned for the next meeting of the UN General Assembly. By this time Pierre Mendès-France had become Prime Minister of France and he appointed the French Commander-in-Chief to replace Voizard, clearly basing his policy on protection for French interests, whilst working out acceptable reforms.

By this time, however, security had almost disappeared in Tunisia. Inevitably, in a country dominated by nationalist uproar, violence was at a premium and many ruffians took advantage of it for their own ends.

The nationalists were being supported by the Arab world and by both Asian and Arab countries at the United Nations. The Mendès-France régime now recognised that it was, in fact, risking destroying their whole international position unless it could find their way out of what was rapidly becoming a colonial war. Bourguiba was removed again, this time to Groix, an island off the Brittany coast, and then to Chantilly, near Paris. The moves were part of the search for a path of reconciliation, bringing Tunisian nationalist leaders back into French confidence.

At the end of July 1954 Prime Minister Mendès-France announced that he would visit Tunisia and declare internal self-government for the country. Bourguiba recognised this as a step back towards evolutionary progress to independence. He warned, however, that in future that road should not be fraught with conflict between French and Tunisians. Having established a special government department for Tunisia and Morocco, Mendès-France flew to

Carthage in the following month and declared internal autonomy for Tunisia. A new government was formed with Tahar ben Ammar as Prime Minister and three members of Néo-Destour included in the ten-man cabinet. Bourguiba was now allowed to negotiate a settlement in Paris and, by the following April, agreement had been reached on the form of internal self-government. On June 1, 1955, Bourguiba made a triumphant return to Tunis, being greeted by enthusiastic crowds and two days later the agreement with France was signed.

By now, however, Bourguiba had to face internal attacks on his conciliatory policy. From the beginning of 1955, Ben Youssef had been attacking the Mendès-France proposals and in September he returned to Tunisia. Now influenced by his association with Nasser, he was adopting a policy which mixed Pan-Arabism, neutralist militancy and Islamic traditionalism, in rivalry with Bourguiba. In particular, he denounced the close ties with France involved in the agreement. But Bourguiba had the confidence of most of his party, and in the following month, October, Ben Youssef, its secretary-general, was expelled, an action supported by the Néo-Destour congress in November. Ben Youssef's followers then began a guerrilla movement in the southern part of the country, sternly suppressed by the government, whilst he himself left for Libya and eventually returned to Cairo.

In the same month that the Néo-Destour congress was held, it was announced that Morocco was to be given complete independence by the French. As was to be apparent a few years later in the rest of French Africa, once internal autonomy had been gained, full sovereignty became inevitable. The half-way house in which an indigenous government controlled domestic affairs but remained under French authority in its foreign relations, could never be sustained. Having tasted the wine of power, the glass had to be drained.

So Tunisia immediately demanded the same rights as the Moroccans, and, following further negotiations, attained sovereign status on March 20, 1956. A week later a Constituent Assembly was elected, Bourguiba was chosen as first Prime Minister and entered office on April 12th. Just over a year later, in July 1957, the monarchy was abolished, a republic established and Bourguiba naturally became president. Once again the combination of a charismatic leader, an organised nationalist party and the provocations of imperialist obstruction to representative government, had forged an independence movement whose momentum became irresistible.

The announcement of independence inevitably increased the national problems facing Bourguiba and his people. About 100,000 Europeans, mostly French, left the country, whilst the French army bases were cut, although the navy remained in Bizerta. Many of Bourguiba's plans for modernisation remained dependent on French capital, whilst the progress of the Algerian war, forcing Bourguiba to adopt the uncomfortable position of keeping a foot in both camps, continually endangered the continuation of French aid. Although without the minerals of Morocco, Tunisian agriculture was well organised, still occupying three-quarters of the population. Unemployment and under-employment were the main threats to the economy, particularly as the high degree of urbanisation meant that there was a continual attraction into the towns. Yet this fact of urbanisation itself formed one of Tunisia's strengths. The country had developed one of the strongest indigenous middle classes in the continent, controlling a high proportion of commercial enterprise and developing a sophisticated character unique in north Africa. The balance between towns, villages and rural areas bridged the gap between urban and rural populations to an extent unusual in African countries. Thus, contact between the middle class and the peasants was much closer than elsewhere and avoided some of the worst social stresses. Cementing this bridge was the Néo-Destour party, an organisation which combined the features of a national movement with those of a political institution. The party mobilised the nation in almost every quarter of the country, giving leadership, providing political education and offering a national consciousness which could bridge social gaps. How long this social collaboration would last when the vital economic problems of population growth, unemployment and economic development had to be faced, not to mention the issues of association with France, Algeria, the Arab and African worlds, remained a matter for the future.

The history of Morocco during this period followed parallel lines to that of Tunisia, with the major exception that the character of its actual society was completely different. Morocco had little of the sophistication of Tunisia, and no large bourgeois element. It remained a traditional Islamic society, centred on the Sultan, with the majority of its inhabitants still living under Moslem feudalism.

Nevertheless, the deportation and exile of Sultan Mohammed V in 1953 provoked the nationalist movement to the same kind of violent protests as in Tunisia. The French, with eighteen months' experience of the dangers to which frustrated nationalism could lead, tried to appease nationalist sentiments by promising reforms. They had appointed a new Sultan, Sidi Mohammed ben Moulay Arafa el Alaoui, known as Mohammed VI, an uncle of the exiled Sultan. But the new Sultan was a colourless, weak personality, never accepted by the Moroccans, who would not recognise any right of the French administration to select their Sultan for them.

The French tried to appease nationalist wrath by ending the absolute monarchy, overhauling the government in an attempt to introduce modern methods, merging the French and Moroccan administrations and laying the foundations of a semi-parliamentary system. They promised a new labour charter, reforms in the judicial system and the introduction of some civil liberties.

These promises generally fell on deaf ears. The nationalist movement, baulked of progress under its own Sultan, resorted to violent methods, forming a National Army of Liberation. Many people were killed and injured and on two occasions attempts were made to assassinate the new Sultan. When the French threatened to punish the rebels they were met by nationalist threats of passive resistance.

Meanwhile, the Moroccan issue, like that of Tunisia, had become an international issue, debated at the United Nations. The Americans had originally protested when Mohammed V was exiled, but their attitude and that of the west in general was equivocal when it came to United Nations debates. The Americans, in particular, were in a difficult position because of their large military installations in Morocco and the doubts as to whether they would be better defended in the long run by the French or by a Moroccan nationalist group.

But the Moroccan issue, taken in conjunction with the question of Tunisia, was rapidly bringing France into international disfavour, particularly within the Arab world. The Mendès-France régime decided that some attempt would have to be made to solve the problem, although it was bitterly opposed by the French colons in Morocco itself. Eventually, indeed, the colons' lobby was successful in defeating the Mendès-France government.

In the meantime, however, the military Resident-General, Augustin Guillaume, was replaced by a civilian, Francis Lacoste, in an attempt to find a political, rather than a military, solution. Mendès-France promised political reforms with the eventual objective of internal autonomy, but he refused to restore Mohammed V to his throne and tried to ride both horses by declaring that French interests would be safeguarded. Despite the promises, nationalist hostility continued, and by November 1955 the French administration was forced to abandon its vendetta against Mohammed V and allow him to return home from Madagascar. His return was hailed with tremendous popular enthusiasm. It was also accompanied by French acceptance of the independence principle.

Following the return of Mohammed V, a new government was formed from members of the Istiqlal and the less important Democratic Party of Independence, with an army colonel Si Bekkai as Prime Minister. It was this government which negotiated the agreement with the French to create a sovereign independent state of Morocco. On March 2, 1956, Morocco gained her independence and the nationalist struggle was won.

It is interesting, too, that in the following month Spain surrendered her protectorate, allowing a united Moroccan nation to be formed. Franco's Spanish government had been anxious throughout the struggle to avoid conflict with the Arab world. Its own protectorate was highly militarised and used as a training ground for the Spanish army, but Spanish Morocco had never recognised the deposition of Mohammed V and had thus maintained friendly relations with the Moroccans. This was in general line with Franco's pragmatic policy towards Spain in Africa. Some years later, at the end of 1963, he was to show this again by allowing the two Spanish colonies on the west coast, Fernando Po and Rio Muni, to hold a referendum on whether or not they desired autonomy.

So Morocco ended its forty-four years as a French and Spanish protectorate and entered the international community as a sovereign state. It had many dangerous problems to face. It was still largely a feudal society with virtually no experience of popular participation in government. The population was growing at a dangerous rate, over three per cent per annum, with the accompaniment of rising unemployment in the towns and cities. In the rural areas apathy might safeguard the régime, but was handicapping any attempt to modernise agriculture, in which seventy per cent of the population was engaged. Perhaps the greatest problem for the future was how to turn the people of the countryside into new ways of tilling the soil without at the same time provoking rural unrest. Morocco had not built the bridges seen in Tunisia between the largely illiterate poor and traditionally-minded masses and the advanced élite which formed the government.

Moreover, in government circles themselves, tensions had begun to rise soon after the return of the Sultan. The older guard of nationalists, people like el Fassi and. Balafrej, had been out of the country in exile during the last phase of the independence movement. Younger leaders had inevitably taken their place. Men like Mehdi ben Barka and Abderrahim Bouabid had had to carry on the national resistance in the absence of the older leaders. In the terrorist groups and in the Army of Liberation too, leaders had been thrown up who would not necessarily follow the original nationalist politicians. The seeds of future conflict within Istiqlal itself were already apparent.

On the other hand, a sound trade union movement had been established by Istiqlal in March 1955, when the Moroccan Labour Union was formed and affiliated to the ICFTU. Its membership approximated 200,000, mostly from industry amongst the coastal towns and in the mines and farms of the interior. The trade union movement provided a good training in democratic processes and it came to be consulted by Mohammed V on national policy.

What is more, there were already signs of a constructive national campaign to face the major social problems of the country by the time independence was achieved. In the very month after independence, an anti-illiteracy campaign with 300,000 pupils was opened under the Sultan's patronage. This attempt to make inroads on the mass illiteracy of adults was to be the forerunner of many other similar community projects.

Finally, the newly independent Morocco would sooner or later have to face such grave international problems as the question of the American-French military bases, a part of NATO defences; relations with France, whose economic help was still badly needed, and with the Algerians, still in the midst of nationalist war against the French; the effects of the return of about half the 300,000 French colons to France; relations with the Arab world; and, in some ways the most dangerous of all, the indeterminate frontiers dividing Morocco from Algeria, together with the Moroccan claim to the French African colony of Mauritania, now on the road towards self-government and eventual independence.

Both internally and externally, much would depend on the personality of the Sultan. He had the tremendous task of transforming a medieval Islamic society into a modern state, capable of facing the problem of economic development and taking its place in the world of the new Africa. He and the small group of nationalist leaders who had kept their eyes unblinkingly fixed on the goal of independence had now to prove false the allegation the colons made by the French administration and that Moroccans were not yet capable of self-government; but that, released from French control and the threat of white settler domination, the Moroccan people could pull themselves into the twentieth century.

Algeria, the third of the Maghreb states, presented a situation combining elements which we have already seen in South Africa, the Belgian Congo and Kenya. The European community was outnumbered in the ratio of about 8:1. It was the largest European community in Africa outside South Africa and it virtually monopolised the upper and middle classes of the country. Yet, at this time, there was very little conception of Algerian nationhood amongst the Moslem population. It was Ferhat Abbas who had written in 1936 that he was unable to discover an Algerian nation. Resentment was felt because of the economic, social and political privileges of the minority group living side by side with the majority. The original objective of Algerian nationalism was to remove discrimination and provide an opportunity for all Algerians to become equal French citizens; not because of any love for Algeria being an integral part of France, but simply because there did not seem to be any rational alternative.

It was the French and European-settler opposition to this mere demand for equality which forged the foundations for an Algerian nationalism aiming at separate statehood. After the suppression of the immediate post-war movements and the abortive attempts to secure reform through constitutional means, Algeria appeared to have settled into quiescence. Yet the French administrators seemed to be as ignorant of mounting underground resentment as were their opposite numbers in the British administrations of Kenya and the Belgian officials in the Congo.

The French administration appeared to believe that the discovery of the arms cache and the arrest of members of the Special Organisation in 1950, together with the flight of the rest of its leaders to Cairo, had destroyed any revolutionary potential. They saw Ferhat Abbas organising his Union Démocratique du Manifeste Algérien, the UDMA, amongst the Moslem intelligentsia and knew that Abbas was wedded to constitutional methods. They were not even alarmed when the former Algerian People's Party of Messali Hadj, the PPA, was reorganised into a more important movement known as the Mouvement pour le Triomphe des Libertés Démocratiques, MTLD, and developed its organisation not only amongst the younger militants but through links between the Moslem working class and the Algerians in Paris. Indeed, after the arrest of the OS leaders, the MTLD reached an agreement with UDMA and the Algerian Communist Party. This coalition of national political forces was even joined by the third section of the nationalist movement, the traditionalists of ULEMA, who sought to establish an Islamic state and preserve Arabic culture against French westernism.

As all these groups believed in peaceful, constitutional methods, there seemed no reason to fear any serious attacks on the established French position.

This complacency was shattered on the night of November 1, 1954. In the previous March a militant group, despairing of any decisive action ever emerging from the association of moderate nationalists, had formed a new committee for direct action, with the same objectives as the OS. This Comité Révolutionnaire d'Unité et d'Action, CRUA, consisted of nine representatives drawn from Cairo and the various Algerian regions. It included Ben Khedda, Mohammed Boudiaf, Ben Bella and Ait Ahmed from Cairo and Belkacem Krim from Algeria. It was this committee which planned the revolutionary outbreak for November 1, 1954.

It was on this night that the Algerian revolutionary anti-colonial war against France broke out. It was begun by simultaneous attacks at various centres; by the morning fifteen people were dead. The outbreaks were followed by over seven years of unremitting conflict in which those fifteen people were to be followed to their graves by several hundred thousand others. Algeria, unlike the neighbouring protectorates, had been conquered by force; those who were determined to establish a new and independent Algerian state, frustrated in their efforts to secure their ends by constitutional means, had now decided that the only way to reconquer it from the French must also be through force.

At first, the revolutionaries received little sympathy. The French, of course, even though Mendès-France was still Prime Minister, declared that the rebellion would be crushed. But more surprisingly, the main elements of political nationalism were also opposed to the outbreaks. Despite the fact that Ferhat Abbas had in the previous months been warning that Algerian silence was the silence of rebellion, within a few days of the outbreak he was expressing the view that violence could settle nothing. The MTLD also denounced the use of force, whilst the Algerian Communist Party, anxious no doubt to maintain the association with France which inflated French communist numbers, also condemned violent nationalism. Ben Khedda, still in his twenties, and a former secretary-general of the MTLD, was arrested immediately after the rebellion, whilst the few political nationalists who sympathised with it quickly left Algeria for Cairo to join Ben Bella and the Committee of Nine.

Despite the initial rejection of the revolution by nationalist politicians, the Revolutionary Committee realised that they needed to involve politicians in a national movement. So they formed the skeleton of a mass organisation, the Front de Libération Nationale, or FLN. The object now was to break the pressure of French military control and, at the same time, to forge the Moslem masses into a nationally-conscious society.

Gradually, despite their initial hesitance, most of the political leaders joined, or at least supported, the FLN. The principal exception was Messali Hadj, who, at the beginning of the following year, 1955, set up his own national movement, the MNA, in competition to the FLN. One of the weaknesses of the Algerian nationalist campaign over the next seven years was the internecine strife, carried out, frequently with great brutality, between these rival nationalist organisations. The most important adherent to the FLN was Ferhat Abbas himself, who, eventually, after further abortive attempts during 1955 and 1956 to secure reforms constitutionally, at the end of April 1956 declared his public support of the National Front. He spent the next few years in conducting FLN publicity all over the world from his base in Switzerland. It was he who, by April 1958, had persuaded the Moroccans and Tunisians to give open support to the Algerian war of independence. Denied any response from Paris to his attempts at negotiated reform, the constitutionalist had become a fully-fledged revolutionary.

In August 1956 the revolutionary leaders took further steps to widen their organisation. The division of command between the group in Cairo and the activists engaged in the Algerian fighting, had inevitably raised some friction. It was therefore decided to call all the leaders to a conference in the Soummam River valley in order to examine the organisation and objectives of their movement. It was here that an army of national liberation, the ALN, was formed, and a Comité de Coordination et d'Exécution, consisting of five members, including Ben Khedda and Krim. It was agreed at this conference that the interests of the revolution within Algeria must take precedence over any external considerations. The conference also set up a form of parliament, the Conseil National de la République Algérienne, or CNRA, as the body to have ultimate authority over the future of the Algerian nation. The revolution had thus put forward claims to legitimacy, based on rough representative institutions, and the FLN could now claim to be the only legitimate spokesman in any negotiations with France.

Tentative moves towards negotiation were made by the French government in the following October. They were completely destroyed, however, when FLN delegates, including Bella, Khider Boudiaf and Ahmed were all kidnapped during their flight back to Tunis after a visit to the Sultan of Morocco. It appeared that this conspiracy was organised by the French army, but there was no denunciation from the Bidault government in France.

This kidnapping left Belkacem Krim as the last of the original Cairo group and therefore as the recognised leader of the FLN. By this time any hope of negotiations had been completely destroyed and the ferocity of the war was again demonstrated at the beginning of 1957 when French paratroops under Jacques Massu, swept into the Moslem quarter of Algiers arresting thousands for a type of interrogation which descended to brutal torture.

A year later the French army decided that the support of the Tunisians and the use by the Algerian nationalist forces of Tunisian bases warranted retaliation. They bombed the village of Sakiet Sidi Youssef on the Tunisian border and thereby provoked widespread international condemnation. By now the French government had begun to show signs of instability under the unceasing pressure of guerrilla warfare and strong international criticism. It was forced into once again considering the possibility of negotiating with the Algerian nationalists. In doing so, it signed its own death warrant. The two strongest elements of French hostility to Algerian nationalism, the army and the colons, combined their forces on May 13, 1958, and overthrew the Fourth French Republic, opening the way for the return to power of General De Gaulle.

It may be asked why the French people were prepared to destroy their Fourth Republic on the altar of Algeria. Algerians cost the French taxpayer considerable sums every year. It is true that the two economies complemented each other conveniently, Algeria offering a market for French manufactures and the French taking wheat and wine from Algeria. No one could suggest, however, that this interchange would have become impossible if Algeria gained independence.

The Algerian issue had acquired a mystique in France out of all proportion to its material importance. The memory of national humiliation in 1940, the feelings of disgrace aroused over Indo-China and the sense of betrayal felt by that most important of French institutions, the army, all contributed to a psychological obsession that the very existence of France depended on retaining Algeria.

On the other hand, it was much easier to understand the point of view of the European colons. They owned two-thirds of the cultivated land, monopolised the wine industry and were in control of finance, industry and public services. They had everything to lose from a successful nationalist movement.

Meanwhile the FLN had built up a force of 20,000 guerrillas, and had developed an underground administration capable of collecting levies and punishing anyone tempted into collaboration. In 1956, with the formation of the General Union of Algerian Workers, which replaced the Messali Hadj unions and affiliated to the ICFTU, the FLN secured the organised support of the workers inside Algeria. Meanwhile, in France Algerian workers were joining the

General Association of Algerian Workers, closely attached to the FLN's French organisation.

The fact that this nationalist movement, with its interlaced avenues of support, was able to keep 500,000 French troops in Algeria, was not lost on General De Gaulle. No one would ever accuse the General of lacking interest in French power. He, however, was clear-sighted enough to recognise that if France desired the reality, rather than an illusion, of power, she would have to settle the Algerian problem.

It was not long before De Gaulle made his first move. A referendum on acceptance or rejection of the Fifth Republic in September 1958 gave Algeria, along with all other French territories, the opportunity of expressing its opinion on De Gaulle as a leader. The Algerians voted to accept the Republic, in the belief that De Gaulle was more likely than the previous régime to negotiate a settlement.

Immediately before the referendum, however, the FLN had still further strengthened its political claims when it established in Tunis a Gouvernement Provisoire de la République Algérienne, the GPRA, as a government-in-exile. Ferhat Abbas was elected as first President. Thus the man to whom the doors of constitutional action had been closed by the French government, the army and the colons, faced the General whom the army and colons had raised to power from the ashes of the Fourth Republic. Arab and African states recognised the exile government, so increasing international pressures on France.

It was twelve months later before De Gaulle felt himself strong enough to make a positive proposal for an Algerian solution. He then suggested that a referendum be held in Algeria and referred to the concept of 'self-determination'. De Gaulle's words were as ambiguous as usual; yet the underlying implication of negotiation was sufficient to arouse the colons and the reactionary sections of the army to renewed hysteria. They had destroyed the Fourth Republic and replaced it with De Gaulle in order to prevent any form of negotiation with the Algerian nationalists; they now found that the man they had turned to as their saviour was adopting exactly the same tactics as the Fourth Republic they had damned. In January 1960, another attempt was made by a combination of colons and army to destroy any policy designed to undermine their obsessive ideal of a French Algeria. De Gaulle defeated the threat of their barricades, gaining a new strength from his victory over these intransigents. He still hesitated, however, to come out into the open with a forthright plan for Algerian self-government. He continued to indulge in ambiguities, always giving the FLN an impression of deliberately hedging around every proposal with unacceptable qualifications. Nevertheless, a majority of the FLN Council believed that they had a better opportunity of negotiating a solution with De Gaulle than ever before. They therefore maintained their support of Ferhat Abbas as the leading negotiator, rejecting Ben Khedda's opposition to Abbas and his demands that the objectives of the revolution should be reinterpreted. Meanwhile, De Gaulle was putting into operation a wide programme of reform which had already given the Moslems voting rights as French citizens in the 1958 referendum, and was now adding, through the Constantine Plan, rapid increases in education, medicine, industrialisation and the introduction of Moslems into the public service.

The first direct negotiations between De Gaulle's government and the FLN took place in Melun during June 1960. They ended in deadlock. The winter of 1960–61 witnessed a growing resistance to De Gaulle's policy amongst the extreme settlers, known as the 'ultras'. A further revolt at the end of 1960 was again defeated but, in the following month, the referendum on approval of De Gaulle's policies showed that forty-three per cent of the registered voters in Algeria abstained, whilst his majority amongst the remainder had fallen down to only sixty-nine per cent. The following month saw the formation by the ultras of the Organisation de l'Armée Secrète or OAS, determined to use every method to prevent agreement between the French government and the Algerian nationalists. In April a full-scale revolt against De Gaulle's government was organised by four generals, Challe, Zeller, Jouhaud and Salan. The defeat by the loyal section of the French army of this latest revolt was followed by a campaign of OAS terrorism against the Moslems in Oran, Algiers and in other towns. The OAS was now determined to destroy every administrative arm in Algeria and undermine the authority of De Gaulle's government by sheer terrorism. The campaign mounted throughout 1961, reaching its climax during the first few months of 1962, with thousands of Moslems losing their lives and suffering injuries, but with remarkably little retaliation against the settlers from their side.

Despite this atmosphere of terrorism, negotiations between De Gaulle's government and the GPRA, which he now recognised, continued through 1961 at Evian and in the summer of 1961 some agreement on the basis of discussion was reached. In August Ben Khedda finally defeated Ferhat Abbas and replaced him as President of the GPRA. Krim became his Minister of the Interior, whilst the objectives of the revolution were defined as socialism at home and neutralism abroad. Secret negotiations continued during the winter. At the beginning of February 1962, De Gaulle admitted in a broadcast that Algeria would become independent. A week later the final negotiations began at Evian, now led for the GPRA by Belkacem Krim. The negotiations reached their climax with the signing of a cease-fire agreement on March 18, 1962, and the end of the war the following day.

The agreement provided for the French army to remain in Algeria until 1965, for the Algerian people to exercise self-determination and, assuming their choice was independence, the opportunity for French citizens to take out Algerian citizenship. The French recognised Algerian sovereignty in the Sahara and the Algerians guaranteed French petrol and gas concerns there as well as recognising French property rights. The French were also to be allowed to lease their naval base at Mers-el-Kébir and the testing ground for their atomic weapons in the Sahara. Meanwhile, economic aid from France through the Constantine Plan would continue to assist Algerian agricultural and industrial development. On July 1, 1962, 99·7 per cent of the votes cast in a referendum favoured independence.

In the interim period between the cease-fire and the general elections of September 1962, however, the Algerian scene was marked by a variety of manœuvres and conflicts. A provisional executive had been established, consisting of three French Algerians and nine Moslems, to govern the country and administer the referendum. It actually continued to function until the elections of September. In May, however, the CNRA, meeting in Tripoli, created a political bureau to govern the internal affairs of the country. This was virtually a rejection of the GPRA, which had previously been recognised as the government. When, in the following month, the GPRA tried to re-assert its authority, Ben Bella and his army supporters took complete control. It was the political bureau, led by Ben Bella, which took over effective government in

August. It was this bureau, too, which approached the tasks of re-organising the FLN as a peace-time party and constructing the new Algerian state. But it began its task with some of the most prominent leaders of the nationalist movement, Krim, Boudiaf, Ben Khedda and Ahmed, in opposition to it.

So the war came to an end which could have been reached at any time during the previous seven years. It was estimated that 250,000 Moslem lives had been lost, another 250,000 refugees had left the country and 1,500,000 peasants had been brought under military control.

After the mass exodus of Europeans which followed the independence decision, Algeria was left a largely peasant society without upper or middle classes. Agriculture still accounted for thirty-five to forty per cent of the national income, with industry accounting for about twenty-eight per cent of national production. 17·5 million acres were under cultivation out of a total of 52 million. Oil flowed in the Sahara, but means had still to be discovered to channel its revenues into the national treasury. The flight of the Europeans left the country with few people with the knowledge, training or experience for modern cultivation and yet about three-quarters of the population were still living according to traditional ways in the country. A third of the children were in elementary schools, but the influence of Islam and the teaching of Arabic was hardly preparing them to take part in the national task of modernisation. There were 2½ million unemployed and the army included 15,000 troops in Algeria, 25,000 in Tunisia and 10,000 in Morocco. This number actually increased to 130,000 in the few months after independence.

At the time of independence, Algeria was still dependent on France for her economic existence and faced enormous tasks of economic, social and administrative development. The Algerian nationalists had already identified themselves politically with the neutralist world by attending the Bandung Conference of 1955 and the Belgrade Conference in 1961. The effort of nationalism had also brought them much closer to the rest of Africa, though without any break with the Arabs. Already, in 1961, they had joined the Casablanca Bloc of militant African powers.

Algerian Moslems had won their war because they had forged unity behind a single objective. This unity of Moslem Algerians appeared in sharp relief in contrast to the divisions provoked in France by the Algerian war. The lesson of Algeria, however, was the same as that in the Congo, Central Africa and Kenya. A minority white community, however powerful economically, socially, politically or militarily, could never maintain its domination against the strong will of the majority in mid-twentieth-century Africa. The capitulation of Kenya's white political leaders in 1960 had its effect in Algeria as in the rest of multi-racial Africa; the capitulation of De Gaulle's government in 1962 marked the end of white ambitions for separate political power in the whole of the African continent north of the Zambezi.

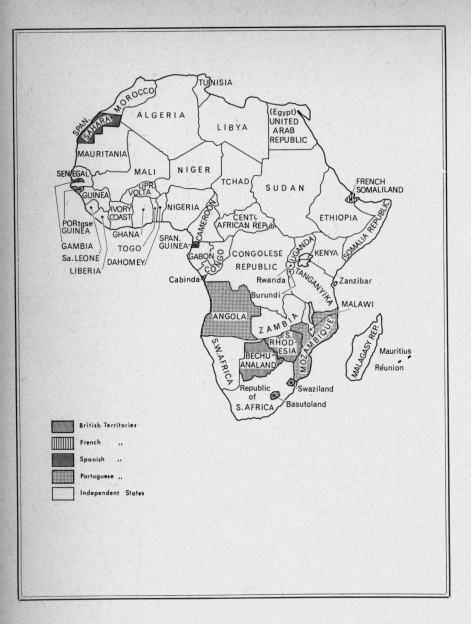

TUNISIA

MOROCCO

SPAN. SAHARA

ALGERIA

LIBYA

(Egypt)
UNITED
ARAB
REPUBLIC

MAURITANIA

MALI

NIGER

TCHAD

SUDAN

FRENCH
SOMALILAND

SENEGAL

GUINEA

UPR.
VOLTA

NIGERIA

CENTL
AFRICAN REPub.

ETHIOPIA

PORtgse
GUINEA

IVORY
COAST

CAMEROON

GAMBIA

GHANA

TOGO

SPAN.
GUINEA

SOMALIA REPUBLIC

Sa. LEONE

DAHOMEY

GABON

CONGO

CONGOLESE
REPUBLIC

UGANDA

KENYA

LIBERIA

Cabinda

Rwanda

TANGANYIKA

Zanzibar

Burundi

MALAWI

ANGOLA

ZAMBIA

MOZAMBIQUE

S.W.AFRICA

BECHU-
ANALAND

S.
RHOD-
ESIA

MALAGASY REP.

Mauritius

Réunion

Republic
of
S. AFRICA

Swaziland

Basutoland

British Territories

French   ,,

Spanish   ,,

Portuguese   ,,

Independent States

1965

13

The Independence Revolution

In 1945 four of Africa's fifty administrative units were recognised as independent sovereign states. By 1964 the number had grown to thirty-seven. At the beginning of this period some 50 million African peoples lived under indigenous governments; by the end the number had increased to about 230 million. In 1945 British, French, Belgian, Spanish and Portuguese imperial governments ruled forty-five African units and some 180 million Africans. By 1964 the figures had fallen to thirteen and less than 20 million.

These stark figures reveal the extent of Africa's twenty-year revolution. For greater accuracy they need further qualification. Of the four independent African states in 1945, Egypt was under strong British influence, Liberia remained a financial puppet of America, Ethiopia had only just been released from Italian rule, whilst the South African masses were rigidly governed by a white oligarchy. Genuine representative government existed in none of them.

The 1964 figures include Spanish Sahara, or Rio de Oro, with a population of only 13,000 and the tiny Portuguese enclave of Cabinda, inhabited by about 50,000 people. The only serious residual problems of independence were the Portuguese 'Overseas Provinces' of Angola and Mozambique – Portuguese Guinea and Cabinda would surely follow the example of these two larger territories – and Southern Rhodesia. This British colony had been domestically self-governing since 1923, but remained under minority white rule and was still ultimately subject to Britain. In the African context, the independence issue also embraced the Republic of South Africa, because of its continuing white domination, and South-west Africa, where the South Africans still resisted the trusteeship claims of the United Nations. But these two territories cannot properly be included in the figures of countries still under

387

colonial government. On the other hand, the three High Commission Territories, Basutoland, Swaziland and Bechuanaland, are included, as, although all three had forms of representative government and were on the way to independence, in 1964 they were still under the ultimate control of the British government.

During this brief, remarkable period, Africans had found the means to bring European rule almost to a conclusion throughout their continent. A combination of circumstances – the post-war weakness of the imperial powers, the growth of liberal international political principles, the impact of strong anti-imperialist groups in Europe, the anti-colonial propaganda of the communist states, increasing urbanisation, the effects of war-time and post-war experiences amongst many of their people – had given Africans their opportunity. In the absence of the usual urges towards nationhood, common history, language, culture, religion, African nationalists had relied on anti-colonial feelings. The European imperial powers had drawn their own boundaries in the continent, often dividing tribes, language groups, social communities. The nationalists knew that the frontiers were artificial, including within them communities which had no common history before the arrival of Europeans and often traditionally hostile to each other – yet they accepted them, recognising that this provided a foundation on which to build a unitary struggle against colonial rule. They set out to inspire in their people a common sense of belonging to a national community whose first purpose was to rid itself of alien rulers. They were assisted in this effort by the fact that the colonial governments had themselves instituted administrative machines for their colonial units, thus accustoming people to regard themselves as being members of a single community for some purposes. They awakened and identified a common feeling of being weak, exploited, oppressed and degraded. And they stimulated the rather vague sense of Négritude.

This latter concept had been consciously expressed by many Negro writers, particularly by Aimé Césaire and Léopold Senghor. Its cruder political expression was seen in much of the work of Marcus Garvey and his adherents. To most ordinary Africans it was a natural reaction to the colour discrimination of Europeans living temporarily or permanently amongst them and to the vast gulf fixed between African life and the observed ways of Europeans and Asians. Senghor described it as 'the whole complex of civilised values – cultural, economic, social and political – which characterise the black peoples, or, more precisely, the Negro-African world'. In short, it was a sense of community amongst people conscious of being black. Although it could be pointed out that this community embraced differences, even in skin colour, as great as those between many Negroes and whites, its existence was one of the weapons of nationalism. Of course, there was an element of racialism in the Négritude concept, especially in multi-racial societies, but, in fact, nationalist leaders were usually meticulous to denounce any overt manifestations of black racialism.

With these somewhat meagre resources, the nationalist groups mobilized sufficient hostility to alien rule to bring a century of European imperialism in Africa virtually to a close. They manœuvred, persuaded and coerced the major industrial powers of Europe to withdraw from the governance of their continent and fathered thirty new states to take their place in the international family. 'Africa for the Africans' became a continental battle cry, and white faces were replaced by black behind ministerial desks, on state occasions, in officers' messes, in professorial and editorial chairs, in business offices and Government Houses.

The significance of this revolution to African and international politics does not need emphasising. It was anti-colonialist and Africanist rather than national, social or economic. Most Africans were more conscious of local loyalties than of national affiliations. They remained in their rural and village communities, where the authority of the chief, elders or council far transcended the impact of new national leaders. Traditional observances, the sway of super-stition or mysticism, relations with neighbouring tribes or clans, were hardly affected by the new status of their nations. Moreover, most Africans continued to spend most of their lives in subsistence production, heavily dependent on weather and chance, still plagued by diseases to humans and livestock, frequent hunger and early death. For this was essentially a political revolution. In some ways it increased the burdens of the ordinary Africans, for the immediate consequence of imperial withdrawal was usually a decline in ad-ministrative efficiency. The loss of many trained technicians, agriculturalists, engineers and administrators inevitably resulted in reduced standards, which, with the leeway still to be made up in African education, would take a considerable time to restore.

Moreover, the political élites who had accomplished the revolution and inherited the positions of power were mainly townsmen. They tended therefore to concentrate first on building glossy urban façades to their new states. It was largely the rural communities, where the majority of the people still lived, who bore the brunt of neglect. Few of the new African rulers appreciated the need for an agricultural revolution to increase national food supplies and halt the wastage of natural resources. Public buildings, factories, European-imitated universities, national air lines and television stations tended to dominate their imaginations. The rural peoples remained in their slums, scratching the soil as they had always done, still regarding their cattle as currency, as remote as under imperial rule from the twentieth century.

These immediate consequences of the independence revolution were not surprising. The common political objective of those who had led the battle against colonial rule was equality. The nationalist élites all took their basic political principles from the imperialist nations and turned them against their colonial rulers. From the French they took the ideals of 'liberty, fraternity, equality', from the British the conception of equal rights of participation in representative government. But these were fundamentally political ideas. They were centred on the ambition for political equality. They roused the emotions of those who came in contact with European rulers to rebel against the discrimination which kept Africans out of the seats of power. This emotion naturally led to a desire to get rid of alien rule and could be used to inspire mass nationalist movements. But it only had a peripheral connection with the conception of social reform. Indeed, in many cases, it led merely to the satisfaction of a desire to live in the style displayed by European ministers, civil servants, professors, doctors, lawyers, engineers or trade union officials.

It is true that those African nationalists who felt some social sense aimed to secure political power in order to increase the social allocation of revenue, but they were comparatively few. In any case, they found that independence tended to decrease rather than increase their total revenues, making it virtually impossible to accelerate social development to any serious extent.

Yet the egalitarian sense which inspired African nationalism did lead some of these more far-seeing leaders into attempts to link nationalism with the ambition of social equality. Senghor wrote of developing 'co-operation, not collectivist but communal', and Nkrumah spoke of creating 'a welfare state based upon African socialist principles'. But the fact was that independence had been achieved by mobilising various forms of national unity, generally dominated from the towns by the professional, business, trade union and intellectual groups. They usually thought in terms of industrial revolutions to cement political independence by economic self-sufficiency. They were mostly uninterested in agricultural reform and often suspicious that it might be used to maintain the subordinate role of Africa in the world economy. In this objective they were frequently encouraged by European advisers, whether from the West or from communist countries. And because the mass of Africans remained rooted in rural life, they found little growth in their personal independence from the authority of traditionalism, hunger and poverty in the first few years following the revolution.

This neglect of the rural communities had little political effect during the first years of independent nationhood. Peasants rarely rebel against their accustomed poverty or inequalities unless inspired by others who provoke them to active discontent for political motives. The greater danger arose from the far fewer industrial, urbanised workers. The rapid influx into towns resulted in widespread unemployment. Moreover, it had been the custom in multi-racial societies for many urban workers to be paid as single men, on the assumption that they were really migrants retaining a stake on the land which would supplement their wages and provide their social security. This system was grossly wasteful in that it led simultaneously to neglected agriculture and inefficient industry. Inevitably it also raised grave social problems.

The difficulties of the urbanised workers were not solved by independence. Working-class organisations had been prominent in the nationalist movement, often identifying their disabilities with the presence of imperialism. Many of them expected early improvements once independence was won and they had the power of concentration in the towns together with armies of unemployed and underemployed with time on their hands. Yet in the severe economic difficulties immediately following independence, together with the need for national saving to build the foundations of long-term plans, immediate wage increases were impossible or dangerous. They would certainly have increased the already wide gap between the standards of life amongst urban and rural peoples. Similarly, the demands for extensive social services could not possibly be met. Africa was unlucky in having the example of advanced industrial nations before her people right at the start of her economic re-construction. Many younger Africans travelled and lived in these advanced countries, savoured their amenities and judged their own governments by the degree to which they matched them. This was, of course, totally unfair, but it became a serious factor in the post-independence period and lay beneath many of the political disorders which ensued.

One outcome of independence which has infrequently been observed was its effect on the social perspectives of the new nations. It cannot be described better than in the words of Dunduza K. Chisiza, one of Africa's most thoughtful leaders, tragically lost to Nyasaland in a fatal accident. Chisiza wrote in a most profound booklet, *Africa – What Lies Ahead*, 'the advent of independence curbs the influence of European social leaders almost to nil. . . . Thus, independence creates a social vacuum'. He proceeded to argue that this vacuum should be filled by the African élite to prevent a wholesale imitation of foreign customs or the danger of returning to out-dated traditionalism. He then went on to point to the threat of social conformity which 'encourages intellectual conformity so that if the tiny band of men who do the thinking, initiate change, start new styles, etc, make a mistake in one thing or another, the mistake will be imitated by the entire population. Furthermore, if the men cease to think creatively, to innovate, and to initiate social change, the consequent disaster would . . . affect the whole nation.'

This is precisely what happened in most African countries after independence. Because many African leaders ignored Chisiza's warning not to play 'the double role of political as well as social leaders', conformity became the general rule, with imitation of foreigners, particularly in ostentatious displays of wealth and status, as its commonest feature. Inevitably, as Chisiza had forecast, this led to intellectual conformity, with a minimum of critical thought and a consequent frustration amongst many of the younger generation.

Some new African governments showed a greater appreciation

of the further social problem considered by Chisiza, the position of women. In many parts of West Africa women had long played an important part in social, economic and political life and continued to do so after independence. In some parts of the continent, too, efforts had begun before independence to increase the educational opportunities of girls. These were generally continued and extended, but it still remained true that there was as much social resistance to female education in Africa as in other continents. Moreover, the subordinate position of women in many Islamic and tribal African communities, their frequent use as heavy labourers and the cruel traditional practices under which they suffered, more often than not raised the kind of emotional political issue that was avoided by the new governments. There were a few African leaders who insisted to their people that equality must apply to the whole community, not merely to the male half, but they were in a minority.

Yet by far the most important problem arising from the African revolution was the paradox between political independence and economic dependence. It was precisely during the period when independent statehood was being achieved that most African economies were seen to be too 'independent'. One of their main weaknesses was that they remained cut off from the markets and sources of a world where prosperity depended on interdependent commerce. The fact that three states, South Africa, the Central African Federation and Leopoldville Congo, still accounted for more than a half the continent's total exports demonstrates the incidence of this economic isolation. Africa contained many sources of wealth needed by the rest of the world, but those easily exploitable, like minerals, were concentrated in small pockets. The gulf fixed between these few wealthy areas and the huge rural expanses projected a reflection of the international division between developed and developing communities within Africa itself.

It may be that Africans were fortunate in facing their major economic tasks during the first age which recognised aid from wealthy to poor nations as both expedient and principled. At the same time, her peoples, in an era of easy communication, had to see most of the rest of the world living in a completely contrasting environment, with some of them living particularly luxurious lives in Africa itself. It was perhaps this circumstance which led so many African leaders in the new states to build prestige façades to their cities and to ape the ostentatious life of their white predecessors. Yet such displays were bound before long to provoke discontent amongst their own people and induce cynicism amongst the donors of aid.

It is true that the appalling poverty of some parts of Asia and Latin America has never been quite equalled in Africa during modern times. It is also true that in tropical areas the weather can often reduce the basic needs of housing and clothing essential in temperate zones. Yet the sheer size of Africa, its meagre communications, the inheritance of the slave trade, the economic distortions of imperial rule, the wide prevalence of subsistence life, the absence of any elementary infrastructure and potential savings, all left the new leaders with prodigious problems if their people were ever to glimpse the possibility of a twentieth-century life.

It was partly for this reason that many of the new leaders, including some of the most intelligent and liberal, quickly turned to single-party states. The one-party system can lead to tyranny and the obscurantist destruction of constructive criticism. It did so in some African states where a ruler and his party set out to keep power at all costs and destroy rivals. But this was not the motive of all the leaders. Bourguiba's Néo-Destour in Tunisia and Nyerere's TANU in Tanganyika certainly intended to become national movements in the truest sense of the phrase. They tried to extend the discussion of all aspects of policy down to the smallest village through the party, thus involving mass participation in policy decisions and undertaking popular education at the same time.

The main argument in favour of the single-party system was that as the new African states had such tremendous tasks of nation-building to face and so short an experience of party politics, they could not afford party conflicts and frequent changes of government. All efforts had to be mobilised for the national effort, as in war-time Europe. Moreover, the foundations of national consciousness remained to be laid at the time independence was attained. This 'nationalism' which had won independence may have had tacit support from the masses, but it was based more on anti-colonial than conscious 'nationalist' emotions. The majority of Africans still remained more closely attached to local ties and loyalties than to the new conception of the nation. Many of these local communities still felt historical antagonisms towards each other, with the consequent danger of forming communal parties fighting over the body of the newly-born state. One of the first tasks of the nationalists after independence was to inculcate the essence of national consciousness amongst the mass of their people. Both from the stand point of national security and from that of national unity, multi-party systems could be dangerous. For until a people feel a basic attachment to a national community, their political disputes can endanger the existence of the nation itself.

There was another, deeper-rooted impulse towards the single-party system. Party politics and the system of government and opposition were importations from European experience. It is historically incorrect to assume that Africans knew nothing of popular participation in politics before the arrival of Europeans. But their participation was based on different premises. They had never adopted the modern European Hegelian belief that decision comes best from the clash of opposing views. Rather had many African tribes taken the Quaker view that a 'sense of the meeting' could emerge from active discussion without division into 'pro' and 'con'.

This historical background to African politics often seemed more suited to the immediate post-independence circumstances than European parliamentary methods. Parties were needed in the modern situation of statehood, but they could be refined by tradition to avoid division and dissent.

Of course there were dangers in this trend. The whole concept of the rule of law and its protection of personal liberties was exposed to attack. It was argued that individual opinion and criticism could be expressed inside the party, and this often occurred in practice. But there were few safeguards to avoid the danger of the party becoming dominated by a group who would use their power to suppress liberties and crush their opponents. Once the party became the sole repository of power in the state, every constitutional protection was inevitably in danger.

It was partly as a result of a consciousness of national weakness, partly through an ideology closely associated with the feelings of Négritude, that modern African nationalism was always accompanied by the internationalist ideal known as 'Pan-Africanism'. Realising that even after independence was achieved, African states would have little power in world affairs, African leaders sought the security and strength of supra-national organisations. The French colonies, with the exception of Guinea, were already part of the *Communauté*, while the British became members of the Commonwealth on attaining independence. But the *Communauté* never really established itself, and there were suspicions that the Commonwealth was dominated by the white dominions and committed to the West. In any case, both these associations were centred on a highly developed world-power state. The weak, poor African countries would have gained a status little above that of a satellite if they had confined their affiliation to *Communauté* and Commonwealth. Moreover, the sense of Négritude led them towards an association of black communities, and the fact that all black states were also weak and poor added to the attraction.

Yet it was by no means solely the motives of self-interest which stimulated Pan-African ideals. The original post-war nationalist leaders, Kenyatta, Bourguiba, Nkrumah and Azikiwe, were also internationalists. They recognised that in creating new nation states they were working against the dominant trend of their age. They found support from European movements devoted to strengthening international authority against the licence of unbridled nationalism. So they had to find some synthesis between their two paradoxical ideals of nationalism and internationalism. Later leaders like Senghor, Bourguiba, Abubakar, Touré, Keita, Kaunda and Nyerere recognised the same dilemma. It was Nyerere who expressed it most succinctly in the declaration that 'the African national state is an instrument for the unification of Africa, and not for dividing Africa, that African nationalism is meaningless, is dangerous, is anachronistic if it is not at the same time Pan-Africanism'.

There was also a sense of community, of common purpose, from the earliest times between the major African leaders. This was more marked amongst the leaders of British Africa, who had worked together in the Manchester conference of 1945, but French Africans at least knew each other in Paris, even if they did not always agree on common objectives. So when Nkrumah declared on the morrow of Ghana's independence that 'Ghana's independence is meaningless unless it is linked with the total liberation of Africa', this was no empty rhetoric. His mind must have returned to the joint efforts in which he had worked alongside leaders from other African colonies, all with the common purpose of removing alien rule from the entire continent.

Thus the Pan-African movement had several roots. Its object was to link the new independent states in order to avoid the Balkanisation which had followed nationalism elsewhere and often provoked international war. It aimed, also, to strengthen the African voice on the international stage and particularly to prevent both Cold War protagonists from exploiting the weaknesses and division of the new states. Equally important, it intended to extirpate every vestige of colonialism from the continent, and for this purpose it included minority white rule within its conception of colonialism.

The independence of Ghana in 1957 marked the opening of the serious phase of Pan-African activity. In April 1958 the first Conference of Independent African States was held in Accra. It was attended by Ghana, Liberia, Egypt, Tunisia, Libya, Sudan, Morocco and Ethiopia. Only South Africa was omitted, as she was to be from each succeeding conference. From the start it was plain that Africa was to be considered as a whole, with no Saharan barrier, but that only countries where African governments ruled would be considered independent.

At the second conference, held in Addis Ababa in June 1960, five new members attended, the Algerian Provisional Government, Cameroun, Guinea, Nigeria and Somalia; Togo and Leopoldville Congo were invited, but did not arrive.

Meanwhile, the Pan-African ideal of removing all imperial rule and extending independence to the whole continent had also been stimulated by Ghana's independence. The first All-African Peoples Conference was held in Accra in December 1958. To it were invited delegations from the nationalist movements in all the territories still under colonial rule, including representatives from South Africa. From this conference the various nationalist movements were able to secure moral and material assistance in pursuing their anti-colonial activities, including such objectives as universal suffrage and the abolition of colour discrimination. It was to meet twice more, in Tunis in January 1960, and in Cairo in March 1961.

It was at this point that the Pan-African movement began to encounter friction. In May 1959 the Ghana-Guinea Union had been proclaimed. This was a quixotic gesture on the part of Nkrumah to demonstrate Ghanaian support for a newly-independent African state left almost destitute by the French. The Union never had much practical effect, but it was the first concrete example of Nkrumah's belief that the Pan-African ideal should lead to a union of all African states.

Yet the move foreshadowed an ideological division within the Pan-African movement. Both Nkrumah and Sékou Touré believed in the need to associate with communist states in order to secure a genuinely neutral position after the long association of their countries with the West. They also shared similar ideas of social reform and national economic planning. None of these beliefs were fully accepted by the rest of independent Africa. The belief that ideology had begun to divide the new African states was strengthened when Mali became the third member of the Union in July 1961.

By now two African issues, Algeria and Leopoldville Congo, had become matters of international significance. The Franco-Algerian conflict led to most of the former French colonies – Togoland, Guinea, Mali and the northern states were the exceptions – meeting together to discuss their attitude to it. From a conference held in Brazzaville in December 1960 was born the Union of African States and Malagasy, commonly known as the Brazzaville group. The one factor which they held in common was their continuing close military and economic links with Paris. The conference decided to establish a permanent association and set up an economic secretariat.

A month later, in January 1961, the Casablanca group was born, when Morocco, Ghana, Guinea, Mali, the UAR, Libya, the Algerian Provisional Government and – a strange member – Ceylon, met to discuss policy in the Congo. With the exception of Libya, the states agreed on a Charter and established permanent committees.

To complete this chain reaction, the following May saw the Brazzaville states joined by Liberia, Nigeria, Somalia, Sierra Leone, Togo, Ethiopia and Libya, meeting in Monrovia. Originally the conference was to be sponsored by Togo, Liberia, Nigeria, the Ivory Coast, Cameroun, Guinea and Mali. It was hoped to represent the full concourse of independent Africa. But after opposition from Ghana, Mali and Guinea withdrew. This left the Monrovia states organised as a separate group from the Casablanca powers. Division had become rivalry within the Pan-African movement. A strenuous effort was made to rebuild the bridges at a further conference in Lagos at the beginning of 1962, but it failed when the Algerians were excluded. This Lagos conference thus became the second meeting of the Monrovia group.

There were a number of specific issues on which most of the members of each group took different attitudes. The Moroccan claim to Mauritania was one, the Congo another, the attitude to Israel a third. But these were of minor significance compared with the contrasting approach of the two groups towards African unity and international neutrality. The Casablanca group generally supported Nkrumah's policy of a determined drive towards a Union of African states with a central legislature. The Monrovia powers, usually led by Nigeria, believed in a gradualist approach towards some form of association of African states. The dispute may be summarised as one between a unitary or federal African state and a confederation of sovereign African states.

The division between the two groups over neutrality was illustrated at the Belgrade conference of non-aligned states in 1961. All the Casablanca members attended, whereas only Somalia and Ethiopia of the Monrovia group were present. Behind these divided counsels lay the close military and economic links retained by the Monrovia powers with France and Britain, and the Casablanca insistence on withdrawal from all bilateral or multilateral military alliances, together with a complete absence of foreign military bases.

There were, of course, many lesser irritants helping to keep the two groups apart. The Casablanca states were to be found urging African trade unionists to withdraw from association with both international bodies, the International Confederation of Free Trade Unions and the World Federation of Trade Unions, believed to be participants on opposite sides of the Cold War. They hoped to see all African trade unions affiliated to an All-African Trade Union Federation first demanded by the All-African Peoples Conference in Accra in 1958 and established in Casablanca in May 1961. Although this issue divided many trade unionists in various African countries, it was the Casablanca states, and particularly Ghana and Guinea, which waged the offensive against international affiliation. In January 1962 a rival to AATUF was established at a conference in Dakar which saw the birth of an African Trade Union Confederation which allowed unions to retain their international affiliation in addition to membership of the new organisation.

There were also a number of inter-African national disputes which heightened tension within the Pan-African movement and

exacerbated division. Morocco claimed Mauritania as part of her
territory and opposed Mauritanian membership of the United
Nations. The Moroccans and Algerians also had a dispute over their
frontiers which resulted in warfare. Cameroun accused Guinea of
harbouring the Moumié rebels, Somalia, Ethiopia and Kenya
continued a running war over frontier disputes. The Tunisians
blamed Egypt for an attempt to assassinate Bourguiba. Ghana and
Togoland continually quarrelled over the Ewe problem. The issue
of the Congo disaster frequently produced conflicting policies.
Moreover, there was considerable jealousy over apparent claims to
African leadership. Many fellow African nationalists resented the
impression that Nkrumah was staking a claim to lead the whole
continent, particularly when his diplomacy seemed to be interfering
in their internal affairs and considerable groups of their younger
generation looked to him as their militant inspiration.

Nor were these tensions eased by the general insecurity experienced by the leaders of Africa's new states. The dangers arising from
popular disillusion with the immediate effects of independence, the
threat of military coups d'état or assassination, the invitation to
violence implicit in single-party and authoritarian rule, the possibility of inter-tribal conflicts and the fear of external intervention,
all caused African leaders to wonder how long they could retain
power. Many of them were displaced from one of these causes
during the first few years following independence, and more were
threatened. The atmosphere of fearful insecurity is not conducive to
tolerance and co-operation.

Yet, despite all these handicaps and the lessons of failure littering
the history of attempted international unity, Africa made remarkable progress in her international relations before the independence
revolution was even complete. Although the Ghana-Guinea-Mali
Union never achieved much in practice, and the Monrovia group
scarcely got beyond the discussion stage, the Brazzaville powers
achieved some minor, but useful, joint action, such as a Post and
Telecommunications Union and a common airline. The organisation known as the Pan-African Freedom Movement of East and
Central Africa, founded in Tanganyika in 1958, played a leading
role in co-ordinating the nationalist, anti-colonial activities of parties
throughout east and central Africa. It also laid the preliminary foundations for a federation to start with Kenya, Uganda, Tanganyika

respect the established frontiers; but to try and observe them economically made nonsense of effective development. After seeing
much of their aid wasted, by being used for party and personal
advantage, America, Britain, France and West Germany began to
examine the problem of aid more closely. They inevitably found
that the provision of aid to each separate state, varying in size from
the 40 million of Nigeria to the half-million of Gabon, was destroying any chance of economic growth. Meanwhile, the ECA had itself
been discovering the same fact and beginning to plan on regional
lines. It became clear that in the future African economic growth
depended on cutting across national frontiers and establishing
economic regions capable of co-ordinated development.

Yet this still left the dilemma unsolved. By far the greater share
of development capital still had to be sought in the West. The ex-
French colonies remained heavily dependent on France and willingly
accepted the offer of associate status with the European Economic
Community. The ex-British states regarded the Common Market
as a rich European club attempting to keep them in the subordinate
status of primary producers. They therefore rejected the invitation,
despite the fact that it left their French-speaking competitors in an
advantageous position. Meanwhile, all the new African states which
had won political independence from Britain, France and Belgium
were constantly aware that the greater part of their economic activities remained in foreign hands. They bitterly protested their
determination to remove this 'neo-colonialism' as they had its
political counter-part, but they knew that their national economies
still depended on foreign business.

In the meantime, the gap between the developed nations, including the West, Eastern Europe and the Soviet Union, and the
under-developed, of which all Africa was a part, steadily widened.
The vast majority of Africans lived no more healthy, secure or free
lives after independence than before, despite the valiant efforts of
those leaders who saw political power as an opportunity to transform the lives of their people. The political revolution of African
independence had virtually wiped out alien rule. It had given the
African élite a new dignity in the world. It was used to warn all
external forces, communist and capitalist, to cease interference with
the continent. It served notice on South Africa, the Portuguese and
white settlers that independent Africa would not rest until Africans

had gained fully representative, majority government in every part of the continent.

Yet this was but the first act. Political independence had been achieved, yet it had hardly touched the personal life of most Africans. Economic revolution had still to appear. And it was economic change which would shake the roots of African life. The climax of the African drama lay in the future, a climax heralded by the political revolution of African independence.

SELECTED BIBLIOGRAPHY

Footnotes have been deliberately avoided to prevent interruption of the text. In their place this extensive bibliography will allow readers to pursue their study of those areas which particularly interest them. The books suggested are drawn from a wide range, including journalism, fiction and scholarly works. Most of them contain their own bibliographies, inviting wider study.

GENERAL

THOMAS R. ADAM, *Government and Politics in Africa South of the Sahara*, New York, revised edition, 1962.

ALAN BURNS, *In Defence of Colonies*. New York and London, 1957.

GWENDOLEN M. CARTER (Ed.), *Five African States*. Ithaca, N.Y., and London, 1963.

GWENDOLEN M. CARTER and WILLIAM O. BROWN (Eds), *Transition in Africa*. Boston, 1958.

D. K. CHISIZA, *Africa – What Lies Ahead*. New York, 1962.

SIR ANDREW COHEN, *British Policy in Changing Africa*. London and Evanston, Ill., 1959.

Communauté. Paris, 1959.

BASIL DAVIDSON, *Old Africa Rediscovered*. London, 1959. Published under the title *The Lost Cities of Africa*, New York, 1959.

STEWART C. EASTON, *The Twilight of European Colonialism*. New York and London, 1960.

JOHN D. FAGE, *An Atlas of African History*. London and New York, 1958.

FAO, *Africa Survey*. Rome, 1962.

WALTER FITZGERALD, *Africa: A Social, Economic and Political Geography of its Major Regions*. London, 8th edition, 1955.

CYRIL D. FORDE (Ed.), *African Worlds*. London and New York, 1954.

MEYER FORTES and E. E. EVANS-PRITCHARD (Eds), *African Political Systems*. London, 1940.

WALTER GOLDSCHMIDT (Ed.), *The United States and Africa*. New York, 1963.

JOHN GUNTHER, *Inside Africa*. New York and London, 1955.

LORD HAILEY, *An African Survey*. London and New York, revised edition, 1957.

W. K. HANCOCK, *Wealth of Colonies*. London and New York, 1950.

RICHARD HARRIS, *Independence and After*. London and New York, 1962.

JOHN HATCH, *Africa Today – And Tomorrow*. London and New York, second revised edition, 1965.

ARTHUR HAZLEWOOD, *The Economy of Africa*. London and New York, 1961.

MELVILLE J. HERSKOVITS, *The Human Factor in Changing Africa*. New York and London, 1962.

THOMAS L. HODGKIN, *Nationalism in Colonial Africa*. London, 1956; New York, 1957. *African Political Parties*. London and New York, 1961.

J. F. HORRABIN, *An Atlas of Africa*. London, 1960; New York, second revised edition, 1961.

GUY HUNTER, *The New Societies of Tropical Africa*. London, 1962; New York, 1964.

SIR CHARLES J. JEFFRIES, *Transfer of Power*. London, 1960; New York, 1961.

GEORGE H. T. KIMBLE, *Tropical Africa*. 2 vols. New York, 1960.

HELEN KITCHEN (Ed.), *A Handbook of African Affairs*. New York, 1964.

COLIN LEGUM, *Pan-Africanism*. London and New York, revised edition, 1965.

W. M. MACMILLAN, *Africa Emergent* (revised). London, 1949. *The Road to Self-Rule*. London, 1959.

LUCY MAIR, *Safeguards for Democracy*. London and New York, 1961. *New Nations*. London and Chicago, 1963.

GEORGE P. MURDOCK, *Africa: Its Peoples and their Culture History*. New York, 1959.

ROLAND OLIVER and J. D. FAGE, *A Short History of Africa*. London, 1962; Now York, 1963.

NORMAN J. PADELFORD and RUPERT EMERSON (Eds), *Africa and World Order*. New York, 1963.

GEORGE PADMORE, *Pan-Africanism or Communism*. London and New York, 1956.

MARGERY PERHAM, *The Colonial Reckoning*. London, 1961; New York, 1962.

JOHN PLAMENATZ, *On Alien Rule and Self-Government.* London, 1960.

ALEX QUAISON-SACKEY, *Africa Unbound.* New York and London, 1963.

PHILIP W. QUIGG (Ed.), *Africa: A Foreign Affairs Reader.* New York, 1964.

I. SCHAPERA, *Government and Politics in Tribal Societies.* London and New York, 1956.

RONALD SEGAL, *Political Africa.* London and New York, 1961.

C. C. SELIGMAN, *Races of Africa.* London and New York, 1957.

ANTHONY SILLERY, *Africa: A Social Geography.* London, 1961.

NDABANINGI SITHOLE, *African Nationalism.* London and New York, 1959.

L. DUDLEY STAMP, *Africa: A Study in Tropical Development.* New York, 1953.

ANNE WELSH (Ed.), *Africa South of the Sahara.* London, 1951.

DIEDRICH WESTERMAN, *The African Today and Tomorrow.* London and New York, 3rd edition, 1949.

Politics in Ghana, London, 1964.

DONALD L. WIEDNER, *A History of Africa South of the Sahara.* New York, 1962.

MARTIN WIGHT, *British Colonial Constitutions.* London, 1952.

WEST AFRICA

DAVID E. APTER, *Ghana in Transition.* New York, 1963.

DENNIS AUSTIN, *West Africa and the Commonwealth.* London, 1957.

OBAFEMI AWOLOWO, *Awo; The Autobiography of Chief Obafemi Awolowo.* Cambridge and New York, 1960.

NNAMDI AZIKIWE, *Economic Reconstruction of Nigeria.* Lagos, 1948.

MICHAEL P. BANTON, *West African City.* London and New York, 1957.

F. M. BOURRET, *Ghana, the road to independence, 1919–57.* London and Stanford, Calif., revised edition, 1960.

HENRY L. BRETTON, *Power and Stability in Nigeria.* New York, 1962.

RAYMOND L. BUELL, *Liberia: A Century of Survival, 1847–1947.* Philadelphia, 1947.

ALAN C. BURNS, *History of Nigeria.* London, fifth edition, 1956; New York, sixth edition, 1963.

R. J. HARRISON CHURCH, *West Africa*. London, second edition, 1960; New York, 1961.

J. S. COLEMAN, *Nigeria; a Background to Nationalism*. Berkeley, Calif. and London, 1958.

ROBERT CORNEVIN, *Histoire de Togo*. Paris, 1959.

L. GRAY COWAN, *Local Government in West Africa*. New York, 1958.

MICHAEL CROWDER, *The Story of Nigeria*. London, 1962; published under the title *A Short History of Nigeria*, New York, 1962.

ROBERT DE LA VIGNETTE, *Service Africaine*. Paris, 1946.
Freedom and Authority in French West Africa, London and New York, 1950.

JOHN D. FAGE, *An Introduction to the History of West Africa*. Cambridge and New York, revised edition, 1962.
Ghana: A Historical Interpretation. Madison, Wis., 1959.

HARVEY GOLDBERG, *French Colonialism: Progress or Poverty?* New York, 1959.

THOMAS HODGKIN (Ed.), *Nigerian Perspectives*. London and New York, 1960.

DAVID KIMBLE, *The Machinery of Self-Government*. London, 1953.

JEAN-MARC LEGER, *Afrique française; Afrique nouvelle*. Montreal, 1958.

ROY LEWIS, *Sierra Leone*. London, 1954.

PHILIP NERES, *French-speaking West Africa*. Oxford and New York, 1962.

KWAME NKRUMAH, *Ghana;* the autobiography of Kwame Nkrumah. London and New York, 1957. *Consciencism*. London and New York, 1964.

GEORGE PADMORE, *The Gold Coast Revolution*. London and New York, 1953.

F. J. PEDLER, *Economic Geography of West Africa*. London and New York, 1955.

ARTHUR THOMAS PORTER, *Creoledom*. Oxford and New York, 1963.

J. RICHARD-MOLARD, *Afrique occidentale française*. Paris, third revised edition, 1956.

LÉOPOLD SEDAR SENGHOR, *On African Socialism*. New York and London, 1964.

BANKOLE TIMOTHY, *Kwame Nkrumah*. London, 1955; New York, second edition, 1963.

VIRGINIA THOMPSON and RICHARD ADLOFF, *French West Africa*. London and Stanford, Calif., 1957.

J. Spencer Trimingham, *Islam in West Africa*. Oxford and New York, 1959.

William E. F. Ward, *A History of Ghana*. London, second revised edition, 1958; New York, 1963.

Ronald E. Wraith, *Local Government in West Africa*. London and New York, 1964.

SOUTHERN AFRICA

Peter Abrahams, *Tell Freedom*. London and New York, 1954.
Return to Goli. London, 1953.
Mine Boy. London, 1946; New York, 1955.
Wild Conquest. London, 1951.
The Path of Thunder. London, 1952.

Edmund H. Ashton, *The Basuto*. London and New York, 1952.

G. H. Calpin (Ed.), *The South African Way of Life*. London and New York, 1953.

Gwendolen M. Carter, *The Politics of Inequality*. New York and London, 1958.

Basil Davidson, *The African Awakening*. London, 1955.

John A. Davis and James K. Baker, *Southern Africa in Transition*. New York, 1965.

James Duffy, *Portugal in Africa*, Cambridge, Mass., and London, 1962.
Portuguese Africa. Cambridge, Mass., 1959.

Eugene P. Dvorin, *Racial Separation in South Africa*. Chicago and London, 1952.

F. Clement C. Egerton, *Angola in Perspective*. London, 1957.

Ruth First, *South West Africa*. London and New York, 1963.
A Handbook of Race Relations. London, 1949.

John Hatch, *The Dilemma of South Africa*. London, 1952.

W. H. Hutt, *The Economics of the Colour Bar*. London, 1964.

Noni Jabavu, *The Ochre People*. London and New York, 1963.

Dan Jacobson, *A Dance in the Sun*. London, 1956.
et al.

Arthur Keppel-Jones, *South Africa: A Short History*. London, 1953; New York, 1961.

D. W. Kruger (Ed.), *South African Parties and Policies 1910–1960*. London, 1960.

Peter Lanham, *Blanket Boy's Moon*. London and New York, 1953.

JULIUS LEWIN, *Politics and Law in South Africa*. London and New York, 1963.

LEO MARQUARD, *The People and Policies of South Africa*. London, 1952; New York, third edition, 1962.

L. E. NEAME, *The History of Apartheid*. New York, 1963.

JORDAN K. NGUBANE, *An African Explains Apartheid*. New York and London, 1963.

ALAN PATON, *Cry, the Beloved Country*. London and New York, 1948.

Too Late the Phalarope. London and New York, 1953.

SHEILA PATTERSON, *Colour and Culture in South Africa*. London and New York, 1953.

The Last Trek: A Study of the Boer People and the Afrikaner Nation. London, 1957.

S. PIENAAR and ANTHONY SAMPSON, *South Africa: Two Views of Separate Development*. London and New York, 1960.

JOHN REDFERN, *Ruth and Seretse*. London, 1955.

PATRICK VAN RENSBURG, *Guilty Land*. London and New York, 1962.

DAPHNE ROOKE, *The Greyling*. London, 1962; New York, 1963.

EDWARD ROUX, *Time Longer than Rope*. London, 1948; New York, second revised edition, 1964.

PRUDENCE SMITH (Ed.), *Africa in Transition*. London, 1958.

WILLIAM HENRY VATCHER, Jr, *White Laager*. New York and London, 1965.

E. A. WALKER, *A History of Southern Africa*. London and New York, revised edition, 1957.

CENTRAL AFRICA

BASIL DAVIDSON, *The African Awakening*. London and New York, 1955.

FRANK DEBENHAM, *Nyasaland*. London, 1955.

CYRIL DUNN, *Central African Witness*. London, 1959.

L. H. GANN, *The Birth of a Plural Society*. London, 1958.

L. H. GANN and P. DUIGNAN, *White Settlers in Tropical Africa*. New York and London, 1962.

J. GERARD-LIBOIS and B. VERHAEGEN, *Congo 1960*. Brussels, 1961, 2 vols.

RICHARD GRAY, *The Two Nations*. London and New York, 1960.

A. J. HANNA, *The Story of the Rhodesias and Nyasaland*. London, 1960; New York, revised edition, 1961.

ARTHUR HAZLEWOOD and P. D. HENDERSON, *Nyasaland: The Economics of Federation*. London, 1960.

MAURICE N. HENNESSY, *The Congo: A Brief History and Appraisal*. London and New York, 1961.

PIERRE JOYE and ROSINE LEWIN, *Les Trusts au Congo*. Brussels, 1961.

KENNETH KAUNDA, *Zambia Shall Be Free*. London, 1962; New York, 1963.

PATRICK KEATLEY, *The Politics of Partnership*. London and New York, 1963.

JEAN LABRIQUE, *Congo Politique*. Leopoldville, 1957.

BERTRAND LAMBEZAT, *La France Equatoriale*. Paris.

DORIS LESSING. *Golden Notebook*. London and New York, 1962. et al.

COLIN LEYS, *European Politics in Southern Rhodesia*. London, 1958; New York, 1959.

COLIN LEYS and C. PRATT (Eds), *A New Deal in Central Africa*. London and New York, 1960.

TOM MARVEL, *The New Congo*. New York, 1948.

PHILIP MASON, *The Birth of a Dilemma*. London and New York, 1958.

Year of Decision: Rhodesia and Nyasaland in 1960. London and New York, 1960.

Report of the Advisory (Monckton) Commission on the review of The Constitution of the Federation of Rhodesia and Nyasaland, Cmd. 1148. London, 1960.

Rwanda Politique (1956–61). Brussels, 1961.

ANTHONY ST JOHN WOOD, *Northern Rhodesia: The Human Background*. London, 1961.

RUTH SLADE, *King Leopold's Congo*. London and New York, 1962. *The Belgian Congo*. London and New York, 1960.

DON TAYLOR, *The Rhodesian*. London, 1955.

C. H. THOMPSON and H. W. WOODRUFF, *Economic Development in Rhodesia and Nyasaland*. London, 1954.

VIRGINIA THOMPSON and RICHARD ADLOFF, *The Emerging States of French Equatorial Africa*. Stanford, Calif. and London, 1960.

EDOUARD TREZENHEM, *L'Afrique Equatoriale Française*. Paris, 1955.

HENRI ZIEGLE, *Afrique Equatoriale Française*. Paris, 1952.

EAST AFRICA

DAVID E. APTER, *The Political Kingdom in Uganda*. Princeton, N.J. and London, 1961.

GEORGE BENNETT, *Kenya: A Political History*. London and New York, 1963.

B. T. G. CHIDZERO, *Tanganyika and International Trusteeship*. London and New York, 1961.

H. DESCHAMPS, *Madagascar*. Paris, 1951.

JOHN DRYSDALE, *The Somali Dispute*. London and New York, 1964.

The East Africa Royal Commission Report 1953–55, Cmd. 9475. London, 1955.

NEGLEY FARSON, *Last Chance in Africa*. London, 1949; New York, 1950.

R. MUGO GATHERU, *Child of Two Worlds*. London and New York, 1964.

W. E. H. HOWARD, *Public Administration in Ethiopia*. London, 1947.

A. J. HUGHES, *East Africa: The Search for Unity*. London and New York, 1963.

ELSPETH HUXLEY, *White Man's Country*. New York, 1935; London, second edition, 1953.

ELSPETH HUXLEY and MARGERY PERHAM, *Race and Politics in Kenya*. London, 1956; Hollywood-by-the-Sea, Fla., 1957.

KENNETH INGHAM, *The Making of Modern Uganda*. London, 1958.

MARK KARP, *The Economics of Trusteeship in Somalia*. Boston. 1960.

JOMO KENYATTA, *Facing Mount Kenya*. London, 1938; New York, 1962.

L. S. B. LEAKEY, *Defeating Mau Mau*. London, 1954.
Mau Mau and the Kikuyu. London, 1952; New York, 1954.

NORMAN LEYS, *Kenya*. London, second edition, 1925.
The Colour Bar in East Africa. London, 1941.

J. F. LIPSCOMB, *White Africans*. London, 1955.

TOM MBOYA, *Freedom and After*. London and New York, 1963.

ROLAND A. OLIVER and GERVASE MATHEW (Eds.),
The History of East Africa, Vol. I. London, 1963.

SYLVIA PANKHURST, *Ex-Italian Somaliland*. London and New York, 1951.

SYLVIA and RICHARD PANKHURST, *Ethiopia and Eritrea*. London, 1953.

MARGERY PERHAM, *The Government of Ethiopia*. London, 1948.

G. K. N. TREVASKIS, *Eritrea, A Colony in Transition, 1914–1952.* London and New York, 1960.

E. ULLENDORFF, *The Ethiopians.* London and New York, 1960.

SUSAN WOOD, *Kenya: The Tensions of Progress.* London and New York, 1960.

NORTH AFRICA

DOUGLAS ASHFORD, *Political Change in Morocco.* Princeton, N.J., 1961.

ANWAR AS-SADAT, *Revolt on the Nile.* London and New York, 1957.

NEVILL BARBOUR, *A Survey of North-West Africa.* London, 1959; New York, second edition, 1962.

JACQUES BAULIN, *The Arab Role in Africa.* London and New York, 1962.

Face au Nationalisme Arabe. Paris.

PIERRE BOURDIEU, *The Algerians.* Boston, 1962.

JAQUES DUCHEMIN, *Histoire de FLN.* Paris, 1962.

FRANTZ FANON. *The Wretched of the Earth,* New York, 1965.

A. GAITSKELL, *Gezira.* London and New York, 1959.

MAURICE HARARI, *Government and Politics of the Middle East.* New York, 1962.

P. M. HOLT, *A Modern History of the Sudan.* London and New York, 1961.

MAJID KHADDURI, *Modern Libya.* Baltimore, 1963.

ISMAIL RAGHIB KHADIDI, *Constitutional Development in Libya.* Baltimore, 1960.

JEAN LACOUTURE, *Cinque Hommes et la France.* Paris, 1961.

ROGER LE TOURNEAU, *L'Evolution politique de l'Afrique du nord musulmane.* Paris, 1962.

TOM LITTLE, *Egypt.* London and New York, 1958.

JOHN MARLOWE, *Arab Nationalism and British Imperialism.* London and New York, 1961.

CHARLES A. MICAUD, *Tunisia: The Politics of Modernization.* New York and London, 1964.

MOHAMMED NAGIB, *Egypt's Destiny.* New York, 1955.

P. S. N. PRASAD, *The Economic Development of Libya.* Baltimore, 1960.

NADAV SAFRAN, *Egypt in Search of Political Community.* Cambridge, Mass., 1961.

P. J. VATIKIOTIS, *The Egyptian Army in Politics*. Indiana, 1961.

KEITH WHEELOCK, *Nasser's New Egypt*. New York and London, 1960.

I. WILLIAM ZARTMAN, *Government and Politics in Northern Africa*. New York, 1963; London, 1964.

Appendix

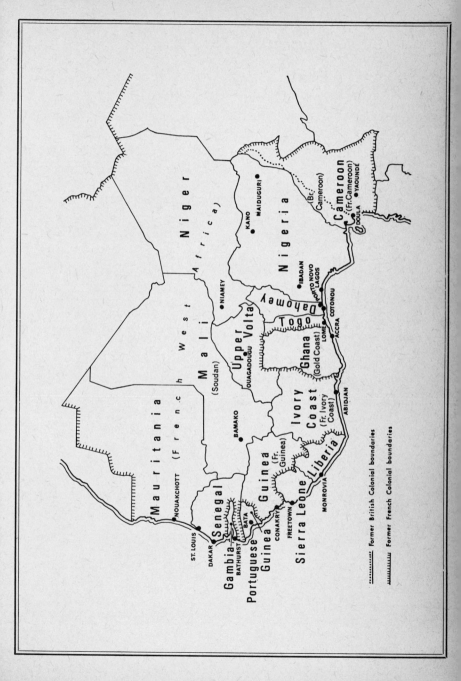

WEST AFRICA

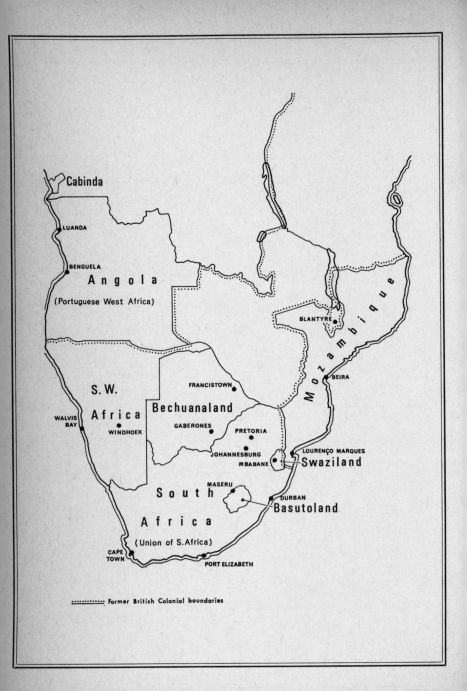

SOUTH AFRICA

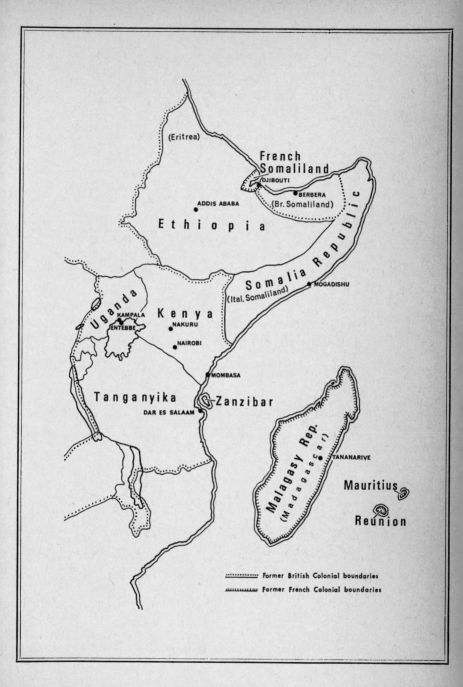

EAST AFRICA

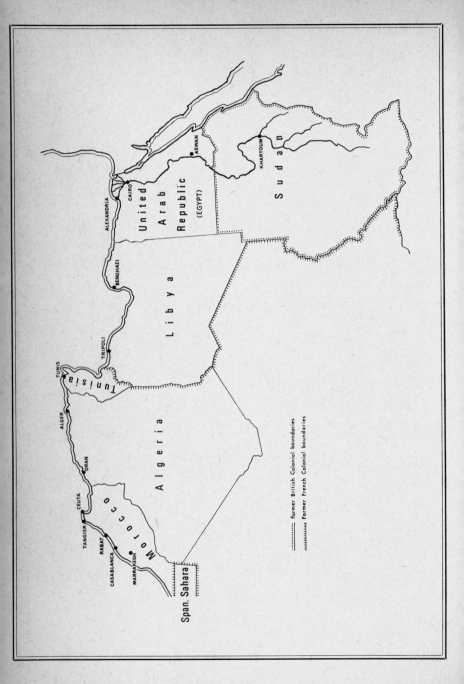

ARAB AFRICA

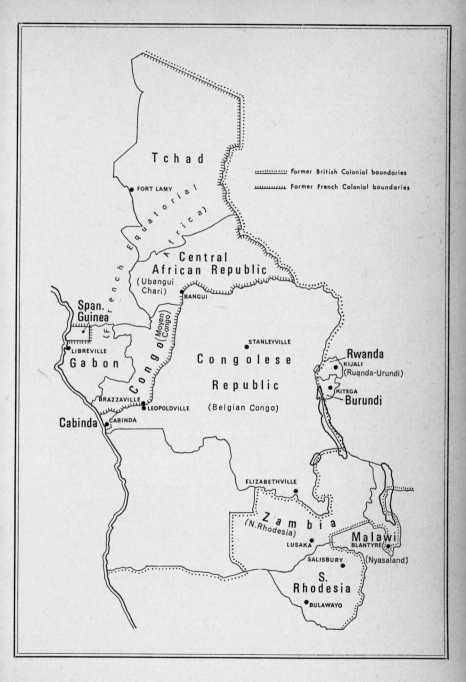

Tchad

FORT LAMY

Former British Colonial boundaries

Former French Colonial boundaries

F r e n c h   E q u a t o r i a l   A f r i c a)

Central
African Republic
(Ubangui
Chari)

BANGUI

Span.
Guinea

(Moyen
Congo)

LIBREVILLE

Gabon

STANLEYVILLE

Rwanda

KIJALI
(Ruanda-Urundi)

KITEGA

Burundi

Congolese

Republic

(Belgian Congo)

BRAZZAVILLE

LEOPOLDVILLE

Cabinda

CABINDA

ELIZABETHVILLE

Zambia

(N. Rhodesia)

LUSAKA

Malawi

BLANTYRE

(Nyasaland)

SALISBURY

S.
Rhodesia

BULAWAYO

CENTRAL AFRICA

Index

Abbas, Ferhat, 160–1, 377–9, 381–3
Abboud, General Ibrahim, 366
Abd al-rahman al-Mahdi, Sayyid, 154
Abdurahman, Dr Abdullah, 81
Abomey, kingdom of, 55
Aborigines' Rights Protection Society, 42
Abrahams, Peter, 34, 50, 140
Abubakar Tafawa Balewa, Alhaji, 191, 192, 396
Abyssinia, 19 (*and see* Ethiopia)
Accra, Gold Coast, 50, 65, 66, 68, 175, 187; All-African Conference (1958), 263, 397, 399
Addis Ababa, Ethiopia, 125, 353, 402; conferences at (1960, 1962–3), 354, 397, 401
Aden, 16
Adowa, battle of (1896), 19
African Affairs Board, 278, 338
African International Association, 15
African Mineworkers Union (Northern Rhodesia), 106, 270, 272
African Protectorate Council (Nyasaland), 108
African Representative Council (Northern Rhodesia), 106
African Trade Union Confederation, 399
Aga Khan, 123
Ahidjo, Ahmadou, 205–6
Ahmed, Ait, 377, 379, 384
Alexandria, Egypt, 149
Algeria, 28, 162, 198, 208, 296, 356, 357, 363, 369, 376; seized by France, 15; under French rule, 41, 158; impact of the war, 158–9; the Setif massacre, 159; French policy, 159–60; nationalist movement, 160–1, 376–7; its privileged minority, 376; the anti-colonial war, 377–84; formation of FLN, 378–9; the revolutionary organization widened, 379; FLN leaders kidnapped, 379; French paratroops attack Algiers, 379; mystique in France about Algeria, 380; the European colons, 380; the FLN guerrillas, 380–1; de Gaulle's referendum, 381; de Gaulle's proposed solution, 381–2; negotiations between GPRA and the French government, 382–383; agreement with France, and the end of the war, 383–4; mass exodus of Europeans, and social and economic problems, 384; the war won by Moslem Algerian unity, 384–5
Algiers, 379, 382
All-African Conference at Accra. *See* Accra
All-African Trade Union Federation (AATUF), 365, 399
ALN (Algerian army of liberation), 379
Amer, Tahar ben, 371

Andrade, Mario Pinto de, 238
Andriamanjato, Richard, 298
Angell, Norman, 31
Anglo-American Corporation (Northern Rhodesia), 270
Anglo-Nigerian Defence Agreement (1960), 193
Angola, 15, 17, 35, 70, 208, 241, 248, 255, 293, 387, 401; lack of representative institutions, 39; miscegenation in, 94–5; Portuguese policy, 235–6; emigration to, 236–7; growth of nationalism, and uprising in, 237–8
Ankole, kingdom of, 133, 319, 320
Apartheid, 87–94, 109, 215, 216, 218, 219, 224, 229, 235, 310, 335, 401
Apithy, Souron, 58, 195, 203, 204
Arabs: in Kenya, 135, 332, 335, 342; in French West Africa, 55; in Zanzibar, 322; in Sudan, 365
d'Arboussier, Gabriel, 57–9
Arden-Clarke, Sir Charles, 67–8, 170, 171, 177, 308, 328
Argwings-Kodhek, C. M. G., 337
Ashanti, 51, 68, 178; added to the Gold Coast, 19; the separation movement, 176–7
Ashanti Wars, 18–19
Asians: of East Africa, 123–4; of Northern Rhodesia, 285; of Zanzibar, 322; of Kenya, 332, 333, 339, 340, 342, 344; of Tanganyika, 304–6, 310; of Uganda, 311–314
See also Indians
Asmara, Eritrea, 144
Assimilado theory, 95, 236
Aswan High Dam, Egypt, 359, 362
Atlantic Charter, 33, 42, 158
Attlee, C. R., 173
Aubame, Jean, 119, 120, 244–6, 248
Australia, 20
Awolowo, Obafemi (of Nigeria), 64, 188, 192
Azhari, Ismail al-, 154, 364–6
Azikiwe, Nnamdi, 42, 43, 50, 52–3, 64, 182, 186, 188, 190, 192, 199, 396
Azores, 239

'Baaskap' (white masterdom), Afrikaner concept of, 79, 88
'Babu', Mohammed, 327
Bahutu people (Ruanda-Urundi), 116
Bakary, Djiko, 202
Bakongo tribe, 241, 253, 255, 257; their association (ABAKO), 260, 261, 263, 265
Balafrej, Ahmad, 164, 165, 375
Balali section of Bakongo tribe (Moyen-Congo), 253

Nigeria—*cont.*
the Cameroons, 192–3; independence attained, 193
N'Jie, Pierre, 182
Nkomo, Joshua, 280, 283, 286, 292–3
Nkrumah, Kwame, 34, 37, 42. 50, 65–8, 140, 169–73, 175, 176, 179–81, 186, 187, 199, 201, 207, 303, 308, 391, 396–400
Nkumbula, Harry, 107, 275, 276, 279, 284, 286, 288, 289, 290
Northern Cameroons, 189; decides to continue association with Nigeria, 193
Northern Frontier Region, of Kenya, 347, 349–50
Northern Nigeria, 249; protectorate in, 19
Northern Rhodesia, 17, 38, 70, 94, 97, 100, 128, 208, 220, 241, 268, 287, 295, 296, 306, 315, 316, 401; a protectorate, 18, 39, 102, 103; increase of exports, 99; racial problems, 105–7, 276; and the proposed Central African Federation, 108–12, 269–276; constitutional changes after federation, 277; a new constitution, 278–9, 284–6; disturbances in, 280; nationalist movement, 284; the Kaunda–Nkumbula coalition government, 286, 288; granted right to secede from Federation, 288; attains independence, and becomes Zambia, 289–90
Nquku, John, 231
Nyasaland, 17, 28, 100, 208, 220, 268, 285, 315, 316, 401; a protectorate, 39, 102; population density, 97; political evolution, 107–8; and the proposed Central African Federation, 108–12, 271–6; constitutional changes after federation, 277; disturbances in, 280; the Devlin Commission's report, 281; constitutional discussions, 282; prospect of African government, 283–4; granted right to secede from Federation, 287; internal self-government, 288; attains sovereignty, and becomes Malawi, 289
Nyerere, Julius, 301–6, 308–10, 324, 327, 338, 347, 355, 394, 396
Nyobe, Um, 62, 205–6

Obote, Milton, 318–21, 327, 347
Odinga, Oginga, 339, 340, 343, 347
Ogaden. *See* Haud and Ogaden Regions
Ohanga, B. A., 138, 139, 335
Okello, John, 327
Olympio, Sylvanus, 62, 205, 206
Omdurman, Sudan, 153
Opangault, Jacques, 118, 248, 253–5
Oppenheimer mining concern (S. Africa), 212
Oran, Algeria, 382
Orange Free State, 15, 19, 71, 77, 213
Organisation de l'Armée Secrète (OAS; Algeria), 382
Organisation of African Unity (OAU), 401
Ormsby-Gore Commission (Kenya; 1927), 128

Osman, Aden Abdullah, 351, 352
Ould Daddah, ruler of Mauritania, 205

Padmore, George, 34, 50, 140
PAFMECA group, 401
Pakistan, 123
Pan-African Conference of Heads of State, Addis Ababa (1963), 354
Pan-African Congress, Manchester (1945), 34, 42, 44, 50, 140, 396
Pan-Africanism, 395–403
Pandit, Mrs, 85
Paton, Alan, 215
Pemba, 17, 322
Perham, Margery, 138
Permanent Mandates Commission, 129
Peters, Karl, 16
Petillon, Leo, 262
Peulh chiefs, of Upper Guinea, 56
Pléven, René, 61
Pointe Noire, Moyen-Congo, 253, 254
Political parties and nationalist organisations
GENERAL
African Revolutionary Front for the Independence of the Portuguese Colonies, 238
Arab League, 152, 159, 162, 165, 356
Convention Africaine, 199, 246
Pan-African Freedom Movement of East and Central Africa, 354, 400
Parti du Régroupement Africain (PRA), 199, 201, 202, 246
Rassemblement du Peuple Français (RPF), 118–19, 243, 248, 250
Rassemblement Démocratique Africain (RDA), 57–62, 119–20, 146, 195, 196, 199–202, 204, 205, 243–5, 248, 250, 254
West African Youth League, 42
ALGERIA
Algerian People's Party, 377
Amis du Manifeste et de la Liberté, 160
Comité Revolutionnaire d'Unité et d'Action (CRUA), 377
Communist Party, 377, 378
Front de Libération Nationale (FLN), 378–82, 384
MNA, 378
Mouvement pour le Triomphe des Libertés Démocratiques (MTLD), 161, 377, 378
Organisation Secrète (OS), 161, 377
Parti du Peuple Algérien, 158
Parti Populaire Algérien, 161
ULEMA, 377
Union Démocratique du Manifeste Algérien (UDMA), 160, 161, 377
ANGOLA
Movimento Popular de Libertacao de Angola (MPLA), 238–9
Union of Angolan People, 238
BASUTOLAND
African Congress, 230
Congress Party, 230